W9-CXL-145

HIDE IN PLAIN SIGHT

Hollywood Q in
Mid-Late 40's
Dassin's Films

Rebecca:
Tony Franciosa (Anna
Cromman (1959)

ALSO BY
PAUL BUHLE

Marxism in the United States
C. L. R. James: The Artist as Revolutionary
Popular Culture in America
History and the New Left: Madison, Wisconsin, 1950–1970
Encyclopedia of the American Left
    (co-edited with Mari Jo Buhle and Dan Georgakas)
The Immigrant Left in the United States
    (co-edited with Dan Georgakas)
William Appleman Williams: The Tragedy of Empire
    (with Edward Rice-Maximin)
C. L. R. James's Caribbean
    (co-edited with Paget Henry)
Tender Comrades: A Backstory of the Hollywood Blacklist
    (with Patrick McGilligan)
Images of American Radicalism
    (with Edmund Sullivan)
Taking Care of Business: Samuel Gompers, George Meany,
    Lane Kirkland and the Tragedy of American Labor
Insurgent Images: The Agitprop Art of Mike Alewitz
The New Left Revisited
    (co-edited with John McMillian)

ALSO BY PAUL BUHLE
AND DAVE WAGNER

A Very Dangerous Citizen: Abraham Lincoln Polonsky
    and the Hollywood Left
Radical Hollywood
The Film Lovers' Guide to the Blacklist Movie

HIDE IN PLAIN SIGHT

*The Hollywood Blacklistees in Film
and Television, 1950–2002*

PAUL BUHLE
AND DAVE WAGNER

palgrave
macmillan

HIDE IN PLAIN SIGHT
Copyright © Paul Buhle and Dave Wagner, 2003, 2005.
All rights reserved. No part of this book may be used or reproduced in any
manner whatsoever without written permission except in the case of brief
quotations embodied in critical articles or reviews.

First published in hardcover in 2003 by Palgrave Macmillan
First paperback edition published in 2005 by PALGRAVE
MACMILLAN™
175 Fifth Avenue, New York, N.Y. 10010 and
Houndmills, Basingstoke, Hampshire, England RG21 6XS.
Companies and representatives throughout the world.

PALGRAVE MACMILLAN is the global academic imprint of the Palgrave
Macmillan division of St. Martin's Press, LLC and of Palgrave Macmillan
Ltd. Macmillan® is a registered trademark in the United States, United
Kingdom and other countries. Palgrave is a registered trademark in the
European Union and other countries.

1–4039–6684–2 paperback

Library of Congress Cataloging-in-Publication Data
Buhle, Paul, 1944-
Hide in plain sight : the Hollywood blacklistees in film and television,
1950–2002 / by
Paul Buhle and Dave Wagner./
      p.   cm.
   Includes bibliographical references and index.
   ISBN 1–4039–6144–1; ISBN 1–4039–6684–2 pb.
   1. Blacklisting of entertainers—United States.   2. Blacklisting of
authors—United States   3. Communism—United States.   I. Wagner,
Dave.   II. Title.

PN1590.B5B84   2003
331.89'4—dc21

                                                                2003043313

A catalogue record for this book is available from the British Library.

Design by Letra Libre, Inc.

First Palgrave Macmillan paperback edition: January 2005
10 9 8 7 6 5 4 3 2 1
Printed in the United States of America.

CONTENTS

POLITICAL EXILES
AND AMERICAN LIFE

LATE ON THE EVENING OF OCTOBER 29, 1947, two distinctly out of place figures abandoned their hotel in Washington, D.C. out of fear that their rooms had
been bugged and took to the "empty streets of that mausoleum city." They were
Joseph Losey and Bertolt Brecht, the latter the world's leading playwright, author
of *Das Leben Galileos*, which Losey had directed for the stage. Brecht was in the
national capital because he had been subpoenaed to appear before a congressional
committee the very next morning to give whatever assistance its members required on the question of the communist influence in Hollywood. Losey was there
to support him as a friend. During the next day's hearings, Brecht smoked cigars
and dissembled freely, aided by a translator whose English was almost as unintelligible to the committee as his own, and by the committee members' utter unfamiliarity with his work. When it was all over, Losey accompanied the playwright on
the train as it sped north to New York. It was then that Brecht turned to Losey
and likened his experience of appearing before the House Committee on Un-
American Activities (HUAC) "to a zoologist being cross-examined by apes."[1]

Twenty years later, Brecht's acid remark was dramatized in *Planet of the Apes*,
the 1968 science fiction classic in which a panel of orangutan politicians cross-
examine a human astronaut played by Charlton Heston. There was no larger connection between Brecht's observation and the scene in the movie except the fer-
tility of the historical moment, when politicians who could not have cared less
about the work of high-brow literary types nonetheless professed a deep concern
about popular artists, their ideas and their influence. Confrontations between pols

and artists peppered the news early in the Cold War, which was bound to give rise to ironies of all kinds, including the hauling up of the author of *Galileo* for questioning on his political beliefs—not to mention its recapitulation twenty years later with screenwriter Michael Wilson. He had been subpoenaed by a congressional committee four years after Brecht, refused to testify and was placed on the blacklist until the late 1960s. *Planet of the Apes* was Wilson's first major credit since he was allowed to return to work, and he made the most of it, transforming Rod Serling's action fable into an allegory on the blacklist itself.

Planet of the Apes takes on two political themes at once. The first and more obvious one concerns the social responsibility of the scientist and the reciprocal obligations of the state toward new scientific knowledge, the very themes Brecht had addressed in *Galileo*. The point of this theme was to warn against the dangers of nuclear war. The role of the gagged scientist is here taken by the astronaut Taylor (Heston) and begins with his capture, along with dozens of other feral humans, near the place where his spacecraft has crashed in the year 3978. During the dragnet in the fields, Taylor is shot in the throat by a gorilla, and the injury leaves him unable to speak. In that regard he is no different from any of the other humans in the film, who for some unexplained reason have no capacity for speech or any other kind of vocalizing. It is only when Taylor recovers his voice that his immediate captors, a pair of chimpanzee scientists, realize that they have an unusual specimen on their hands and bring him to the attention of the orangutans, the authorities who fund their research.

For reasons they cannot understand at the time, the chimpanzee-intellectuals' extraordinary discovery, which they regard as a major contribution to their culture's zoology, is not welcomed by the orangutan ruling class. Taylor and the chimp scientists who are now acting as his legal defense grow even more deeply puzzled when they find themselves facing the three-member orangutan Tribunal of the National Academy, chaired by the "President of the Assembly."

On the pretext that Taylor's rags stink, the chairman (played by James Whitmore, unmistakable even through rubber facial appliances) pointedly orders that Taylor be stripped naked. Then the chimpanzees rise to make their first challenge: the tribunal has not explained the purpose of the hearing, they point out. "At the very least, this man has a right to know whether there's a charge against him."

"This exhibit is indeed a man," interrupts Dr. Maximus, one of the three orangutans on the tribunal. "Therefore *it* has no rights under ape law."

Whitmore presses the legal point on one of the chimpanzees, Dr. Zira. "In all fairness, you must admit that the accused is a non-ape and therefore has no rights under ape law."

Dr. Zira: "Then why is he called 'the accused'? Surely, your honors must think him guilty of something!"

Dr. Zaius: "It is not being tried, it is being *disposed* of. It's scientific heresy that is being tried here."

Zaius (played by the accomplished British actor Maurice Evans), who simultaneously holds the title of Minister of Justice and Defender of the Faith, explains the charge: "Learned judges, my case is simple. It is based on our first article of faith, that God created the ape in his own image, that He gave him a soul and a mind, that He set him apart from the beasts of the jungle and made him the lord of the planet. The second truth is self-evident. The proper study of apes is apes, but certain cynics have chosen to study man, perverted scientists who advance an insidious theory called evolution."

By this time, even the casual viewer will have presumably gotten the point that this allegory is a satire on contemporary American society. Wilson seized on the opportunity created by Serling to recast the orangutans, with their rich leather vestments and carefully combed hair, as the very sort of southern politicians and their allies who had subpoenaed Brecht and Wilson; they were smooth men with ideas rubbed smooth by the ages and alert to any flicker of insurrection.[2]

The filmmakers worried that talking simians would not be taken seriously by the movie audience. Indeed, Wilson's lampooning of the southern, anti-evolutionist pols on the House Committee on Un-American Activities was apparently buried so deep that no one noticed it. Even the biographer of Pierre Boulle, the French novelist who wrote the novel on which the film is based, missed it. In the movie version, wrote the biographer, "All philosophical inquiry and all social criticism have been ignored."[3] But Wilson cut deeper into recent social events than mere mockery. The satire is finally sharpened when orangutan tribunal member Dr. Maximus growls at the chimpanzees: "Let us warn our friends that they are endangering their own careers by defending this animal."

The chimps exchange shocked glances at this first explicit reference to the fact that their jobs might be in jeopardy because of their defense of the human. But did Dr. Zira's eye have a knowing glint? If so, perhaps it was because the actress in the monkey suit was in reality Kim Hunter, who had been named in the red-baiting publication *Red Channels* and blacklisted for four years in the mid-1950s.[4]

It is at this point that *Planet of the Apes* blocks the doors, allowing no escape from the fact that it is also a film about the Hollywood blacklist, a social fantasy that relies on the tradition of "the grotesque" to speculate on the fate of a society that gags its artists and intellectuals for political reasons, forces them to confess and recant and suppresses their role in history. Beneath the dark humor are even darker allusions to anti-Semitism and the fate of friendly witnesses (artists spared the blacklist after they agreed to "name names" before the committee), issues that had never been raised before in a popular film and would have to wait until well into the following decade to be dealt with more directly (if still discreetly) in Sydney

Pollack's and Arthur Laurents's *The Way We Were* (1973) and Martin Ritt's *The Front* (1976), films that will be looked at in some detail later in this volume.

That Taylor and his two astronaut companions are regarded as dangerous intellectuals is made clear in a scene in which Taylor finds one of his comrades, Landon (Robert Gunner) with half his head shaved to reveal a lobotomy scar. The scene works fine as a plot point, but without the key to the story, its deeper meaning is lost. After spotting Landon, Taylor cries out, "They cut him!" After receiving reassurances from Dr. Zira that the chimpanzee scientists had nothing to do with the surgery, Taylor whirls around to confront his orangutan tormentor, Dr. Zaius: "You cut out his memory, you took his identity, and that's what you want to do to me!" In other words, Landon is, metaphorically, a friendly witness, a man who has had his memory removed by force. Taylor is correct: That's exactly what they want to do to him—cut out his social and political identity.[5]

It is interesting, finally, to note that the animus of Dr. Zaius against the two chimp scientists rests on the fact that each of them is on the verge of a discovery that will pose a threat to the whole orangutan system. Cornelius (Roddy McDowall) is a kind of postdoctoral student in archeology whose excavations have unearthed evidence of an ancient human civilization, thus challenging the historical claims of the ape religion. Meanwhile, Dr. Zira has determined that there is no physiological reason why the humans should be mute, meaning that suppression of human speech has been orangutan cultural and political policy for centuries and that ape culture will no longer be able to claim divine uniqueness.

And so Dr. Zira is indicted as a troublemaker, which was what Zaius was after all along. This is the political point on which the story turns. Zaius admits to Taylor, "Your case was preordained. You made it possible for me to expose" the chimpanzees. In Wilson's inner narrative, then, there was another warning accompanying the larger one against nuclear war contained in Serling's famous ending, when Taylor finds the ruins of the Statue of Liberty. The inner warning was addressed to the liberals of the Cold War: you may think they are after Communists, but in fact they are after you.

Planet of the Apes had an evolution of its own. It was so successful that it became a minor branch of the entertainment industry, an early example of multi-level marketing with no fewer than four film sequels, three full-length adaptations for TV, two TV series (one in animation), a series of comic books issued by Marvel and Gold Key, another series of graphic novels, dozens of action figures and a full-blown movie remake by director Tim Burton in 2001 that relied on Boulle's novel, which Wilson and Rod Serling had all but discarded. This success meant that science fiction would no longer be restricted to B-movie budgets and cheap special effects. Most of the themes of outsider/insider cleverly exploited in *Alien Nation* (1988), among other features, had already been explored here; even the omnipresent "alien" faces of actors in films and television, notably *Star Wars* (1977) and its innumerable knockoffs, owed much to *Planet,* which won an Oscar for makeup.

Planet was the second epic and grandly commercial film adapted from the pen of Boulle. The first was *Bridge on the River Kwai* (1957), one of the most admired films of its era, with seven Oscars, including best picture and best director and, most ironically, best screenplay for Boulle (a flat impossibility since he neither wrote nor spoke English). *Bridge* was a realistic drama set in World War II about a military martinet (Alec Guinness) who seeks to drive his mostly British fellow prisoners in a Japanese POW camp to complete an engineering project of some potential use to the enemy, while unrestrained patriots (perhaps they are also militant anti-fascists) plot to destroy it and finally succeed in the last moments of the film.

These two movies had a key figure in common: the co-writer of both screenplays was Michael Wilson (1914–1978), whose footprints will be seen leading off in all directions in the chapters that follow. An Oklahoma-born and Berkeley-educated writer for several remarkably New Dealish *Hopalong Cassidy* features of the 1940s and well known as a Hollywood Marxist, Wilson made his name as the script genius behind *A Place in the Sun* (1951), the Oscar-winning adaptation of novelist Theodore Dreiser's *An American Tragedy* and considered by Charlie Chaplin to be the best movie in Hollywood history. Wilson's career trajectory seemed to end there, however. For more than a decade afterwards he remained a blacklisted writer, and to the end of his life never recovered his professional standing. Although he was credited for *Planet of the Apes,* he received no screen acknowledgment at the time for his work on *Bridge on the River Kwai* nor for the hugely successful *Lawrence of Arabia* (1962). That would only come decades later, after his death.[6] One of the few screenwriters with three films among the hundred "American Best" chosen by the American Film Institute, Wilson's artistic contribution remains little understood, just as the category of screenwriter (or teleplay writer) is still, for the most part, the most misunderstood and underrated creative pursuit in American media culture.

We can learn more and find an otherwise invisible line connecting the dots by considering Wilson's collaborators. *A Place in the Sun* was a solo effort, but his co-writer on *Kwai* was Carl Foreman (1914–1984). Chicago-born son of Russian Jewish immigrants, novice lawyer and sometime carnival barker, Foreman broke into the business by turning out scripts for the Bowery Boys before eventually becoming the key writer for liberal producer Stanley Kramer, notably contributing all or part of *Champion* (1949), *Home of the Brave* (1949), *Young Man With a Horn* (1950), *The Men* (1950, memorable as Marlon Brando's debut film) and *Cyrano de Bergerac* (1950)—and one of the recognized all-time classics of American cinema, *High Noon* (1952). These tales of tortured manhood, of racial conflict at the heart of American dilemmas, of war's unending human damage, of individual courage and of love gave sophisticated audiences of the mid-century heightened expectations of film's dramatic possibilities just before these possibilities and Hollywood's Golden Age collapsed from McCarthyism and declining receipts.

Foreman was another of the major casualties of the cultural repression; he was literally chased off the set as *High Noon* was being completed. Removing himself abroad, he retreated from writing. After his uncredited contribution to *Bridge on the River Kwai*, his most notable film work (apart from serving as president of the British Film Institute) was as producer of *Born Free* (1966), which may rightly be called the first major cultural artifact of the "animal liberation" movement that would soon embrace the fate of dolphins, whales, great apes and all manner of persecuted and endangered species.

Wilson's other collaborator (for *Planet*) happened to be an even more influential figure in popular culture, but one who rose out of the much different milieu of mid-century American liberalism, Rod Serling (1924–1975). A local radio host in the later 1940s following his military service, Serling had moved into the creative vacuum of early video drama by the haste of his pen. After some early efforts, his teledrama *Patterns* (1955), written for the Kraft Television Theater, surprisingly was able to etch images of corporate corruption (softened by the promising possibility of internal reform) in a medium in which sponsors often demanded and usually won script changes in the very middle of production. "Patterns" won Serling the critics' admiration and an Emmy, which was followed by four more Emmys and a Peabody within a career that was shortened by a fatal heart attack.

No one fresh to television and lacking either film or theatrical credits better exemplified the contemporary critical hopes for uplifting workaday Americans' dramatic tastes. Serling admitted accepting serious compromises in the bargain.[7] But it could also be said that Serling successfully outlasted the rise and fall of television drama's Golden Age (usually dated around 1950–1960, but for our purposes better extended to 1966 or so) better than anyone else, through shrewd adaptation and by the grace of his one enduring success. That most singular television program might be rightly called the precursor to the *Planet of the Apes*, the original: *The Twilight Zone* (1959–1965).

Bringing science fiction's capacity for political and ethical themes to television as no previous effort had managed, Serling all but announced the end of McCarthyism as the dominant note of the culture. His weekly dramas pointedly asked viewers to consider alternatives in their habits of thinking, perhaps even in the ways they lived. Television has never seen anything like it again, nor, sadly, did Serling himself. By the time cable competition had forced a greater explicitness, ending with the outright abolition of the networks' standards departments, the shock effects of *Twilight Zone* were long gone and the huge network audiences with them. Serling had done his best work just in time.

Serling was better suited to the small screen even when, as in the film version of *Patterns* (1965) and his signature proletarian-pug drama, *Requiem for a Heavyweight* (1962), he successfully oversaw a teleplay's translation into Hollywood terms. His *Seven Days in May* (1964) offered a political shocker of the type that only the victims of the Hollywood blacklist were likely to have made previously, about the rise of a right-wing generals' cabal to overthrow the American presidency and generally have things their own way.[8] In the aftermath of continuing questions about the Kennedy assassination, but even more in the coming bipartisan project to win the Vietnam War no matter how many lies had to be told to the public and how many millions of lives destroyed, *Seven Days* was a few years too early but, like *Twilight Zone*, arguably helped prepare the way for the dissent to follow.

The disconnect between Wilson and Foreman on the one side and Serling on the other was not only or even primarily attributable to the fact that the older men had been Communists during their early careers. The Popular Front of the 1930s and 1940s had made its converts primarily by preaching antifascism and support for the Roosevelt administration as well as rallying the troops behind a global victory for the Allies, along with taking strong moral stands and vigorous action on such domestic issues as racism, anti-Semitism and the need for unionizing the film industry. Had he been ten years older, Serling might have moved within circles in sympathy with the patriotic wartime Communist Party or signed the kinds of petitions later considered proof of subversion. He certainly shared the blacklistees' passions for depicting themes of race, empire and the threat of nuclear war, although no evidence has turned up that he asked blacklist survivors to write the relatively few scripts that he didn't write himself for *The Twilight Zone*. He belonged to a different generation and a different crowd.

Serling nevertheless did the kind of thing in television that Hollywood blacklistees and their writing partners, including protégés and repentant friendly witnesses, likely would have done in the absence of the blacklist. Some actually managed to do the same sorts of things despite the blacklists and long odds—in a dozen or so more and less memorable TV series from the 1950s to the 1970s as writers, directors or producers—without ever being able to consolidate their successes or recuperate anything like a radical milieu either in New York or Hollywood. These series would include television's first "quality" show, *You Are There*, and the early drama series, *Danger*; the first British-originated show to be successful in the United States, *The Adventures of Robin Hood*; the foremost social drama series of the middle 1960s, *The Defenders* and *East Side/West Side*; the laconic, hip hits of Warner Brothers television, *Cheyenne*, *Maverick* and *77 Sunset Strip*; and the all-time detective favorite, *The Rockford Files*.

As a genre, the TV series stands more or less apart from the prime-time drama that the best-known Hollywood veterans would have considered themselves properly suited to write. A handful did participate in television's Golden Age dramas, and 20 years later, a few more found work writing for them as the drama anthology reemerged in another form as made-for-TV films. But prestige genres, up to the middle 1960s, would have been the most carefully scrutinized by the self-appointed guardians of political morality. The great majority of the black-listees' writing was done within the TV counterpart of the B-movie genres, in which the less fortunate or less well connected Reds had found work in the forties and in which the origins of the television sitcom (in parallel development with radio comedy series) could first be discerned.

The list of TV shows turned out by the Left is as intriguing as it is impressive. It would doubtless be more intriguing if so many promising leads—individual shows and series created or written by known talents under assumed names or fronts—did not literally become dead ends with the passing of the writers. But now, at least, the larger scene can be acknowledged and appreciated at nearly full scale for the first time, because virtually all the quietly left-wing personalities have died or retired and because world crises have left the Cold War behind. The evidence, sprinkled like iron filings on a sheet of paper with a magnet passing under them, reveals patterns hitherto invisible—especially when they are assessed in light of the favored subject matter and stylistic approaches adopted from work done decades earlier, in the palmy days of the Hollywood Left.

The hidden, often deeply personal but sometimes purely opportunistic connections between generations of liberals and radicals in Hollywood and in the television industry—the ways in which shows written from under cover of pseudonyms came to be made and produced—raise still more interesting questions about continuity and change in the Hollywood activist quarter. Potentially, the most historically interesting question of all might be this: what happened to the missing generation of radical media baby-boomers—those connected with their age cohorts in the civil rights, peace and assorted liberation movements of the 1960s?

This last question is not central to the volume at hand. But it is one in a constellation of issues, both political and artistic, about the continuing legacies of the American popular arts and entertainment of the 1930s and 1940s and how they continued to shape the models afterward for artists who took the dramatization of troubling issues, as well the urging of social reform, to be a natural part of their work. Celebrations and revivals of all kinds, of the work of Aaron Copland and Marc Blitzstein, Ben Shahn, Clifford Odets and Arthur Miller, among many others, offer public appreciations at the highest levels. In a more vernacular vein, consider the character of Katie in *The Way We Were* (1973), the most empathetic and most interesting of Barbra Streisand's roles, which continued to reverberate all the way to cable television's *Sex In the City*, in which Katie was claimed, albeit sans politics, to be a continuing role model for purposeful feminist characters. Arthur Laurents, the graylisted screenwriter of *The Way We Were* and one of the rare gay political exiles from forties Hollywood, vindicated at the film's release, was now vindicated all over again—in culture if not in politics.[9]

The examples of such cases could be multiplied almost endlessly as we cross the border from blacklistees or reluctant friendly witnesses to those whom they befriended and influenced. Television's all-time residual leader, M*A*S*H, adapted by two old friends of the blacklistees, Larry Gelbart and Gene Reynolds, from a film co-scripted by Ring Lardner, Jr., remains in some ways the most audacious television show in history. It was the first to criticize an American war (if metaphorically), to experiment with black-and-white episodes and soundless episodes and to use writers drawn in part from the cast. Or consider the assorted "social sitcom" brainchildren of the Left-connected Norman Lear—a sort of Clifford Odets of the small screen with the friends to prove it—rising against the background of larger vindications within the film world, from *Midnight Cowboy* to *Sounder*, *Norma Rae* and *The Front*, all of them written or directed by rehabilitated victims of the blacklist.

It would be too much for the moment to carry this study forward to neo-noir *Miami Vice* and *Crime Story*, neo-progressive *Homicide* and *100 Centre Street*, not to mention *Third Rock from the Sun*, among other Emmy winners. But the connections are there to be made, carrying on the story to the end of the century and beyond. The links would include the work of a long list of artists, including many of those features starring or costarring Robert Redford, Paul Newman, Joanne Woodward, Jane Fonda, Donald Sutherland, Bruce Dern, Jeff Bridges, Michael Douglas, Sally Field, Edward Asner, Martin Sheen, James Earl Jones, Ossie Davis, Ruby Dee, Richard Dreyfuss, Susan Sarandon, Tim Robbins, Sean Penn, Willem Dafoe, Mandy Patinkin, Danny Glover, Ruben Blades—a list that could go on at quite considerable length and include show business antiwar protesters right down to the present.

What connects them all is a legacy that, even in its heyday in the 1940s, was scarcely understood and since then has been at times barely discernable after its most skillful heirs went into exile abroad or remained at home to write an anonymous "under the table" literature of scripts for movies and TV. With the general loosening of American culture during the sixties and thereafter, the legacy was revived, often in unpredictable ways. A story large and strange in equal parts, it can be characterized as the artistic leap of writers and directors who had been constrained by the studio system and then suddenly (and ironically) "freed" by the anonymity of the blacklist, for this was the moment many of them seized to go for broke in a series of artistic experiments that would be as daring as the genre-transforming *Rififi*, the *Rashomon*-inspired western *The Outrage*, the remade *Medea* (retitled *Dream of Passion*), the montage-spliced *Johnny Got His Gun* or the exquisite savaging of Hollywood thirties culture, *Day of the Locust,* to name only a few.

Their work was almost always camouflaged or attributed to other artists even when their real names were used, but the tradition continued in films made in corners of studio back lots in Hollywood or in production deals created to exploit front lots built on the cheap in Spain and Yugoslavia, from the occasional fancy budget to threadbare productions that barely provided nourishment. Self-conscious art films, the genre remnant of a late 1940s drive toward a niche audience of avant-garde film lovers, could even be popular. Misbegotten spectaculars and Cinerama features like *Krakatoa, East of Java* (1969)—the title a bit garbled, since the volcanic island Krakatoa is actually *west* of Java—and oddball horror films (with *Zombies of Mora Tau* surely the worst but *Horror Express* arguably one of the best) likewise credited films rewritten beyond the original scriptwriter's imagination or desire (*Jailhouse Rock* with Elvis), flopped comeback films of all types, the occasional stunning success in a politically censored classic (*Spartacus,* which lost its key gay scene as well as some of the best moments of its victorious slave uprising), children's films of all kinds and family-hour television—all this is part of the story to be told herein and in considerable detail for the first time.

British critic Christine Gledhill has shown that the unease of critics in dealing with popular and populist themes in film has a considerable heritage, with roots in the history of the stage.[10] The rise of modern theatrical drama from the eighteenth century onward was naturally shaped by, but also in some ways ran at cross purposes with, the rise of the middle class and the creation of a modern public. To oversimplify, the emerging elites affirmed their anti-aristocratic values by embracing drama about the individual conscience and its hero or heroine. But they also looked down upon the "lower" stage entertainments in which melodrama thrived. Here lay a paradox, because the new audiences congregating in the cities were the successors to the masses of Shakespeare's own audience, not the comfortable and tasteful but the many. They craved entertainment and escape, sensationalism rather than realism. It was therefore mainly "illegitimate" theater that most prepared theatergoers, in Western Europe and pioneer America, for the appearance of "moving pictures" and later television.

Silent film offered a background of photographic naturalism that the mass theater audience had demanded in set design, foregrounded by a melodramatic storyline and acting. It could be realistic or even naturalistic, but more often it was sensationalistic, amplifying the possibilities in characterization to the point that they became shared mythologies of the twentieth century. Sound added immensely to the prospects of sensationalism, with action and violence on one side (mostly for the male audience) and romance or assorted domestic concerns on the other.

There was no particular historical reason why radical intellectuals should have found themselves in Hollywood at the birth of sound—except that the sound revolution coincided with the Depression and sound demanded for the first time the importation of large numbers of writers who could handle dialogue. They came from all walks of life. They included novelists, short-story writers, radio-script writers, journalists on daily newspapers, "screen readers" (those who examined potential stories and plays, at a low piece-work rate) and even studio clerical employees who taught themselves the tricks of the trade. Many of the most famous came from the world of the stage, including a small crop of radical directors, a few years after the bulk of the writers arrived. The New York stage was just reaching a high point of radical and progressive drama and comedy by the mid- to late 1930s, exporting some of its best and youngest talent to the Federal Theater of the New Deal's Works Progress Administration (WPA) and even a bit of it to the grassroots labor union theater, like the road shows of Clifford Odets' famous *Waiting for Lefty* and Harold Rome's hugely popular *Pins and Needles*.

Practically without exception, the dramatists of Broadway would say later that movies, or more precisely the studio management, had let them down. They certainly had a point. Southern California proved an ideal spot for entertainment entrepreneurs to build a virtually union-free environment (or so they assumed, for nearly two decades) unlike New York, to enjoy their wealth in balmy weather and to become a racial aristocracy with a liveried servant class of an almost colonial nature. All this, especially for immigrant Jewish businessmen, seemed nearly too good to be true. The entrepreneurs possessed the organizing genius to mass produce melodrama, comedy, spectacle and occasionally intelligent fare for the rising tide of filmgoers, at home and abroad. Why would they want to waste it on social criticism?

But that was never the whole truth. Charlie Chaplin had proved in the 1920s that the most popular spectacles could display the universal qualities of the popular narrative, pathos and humor, embracing and at least momentarily providing the ordinary viewer with a much larger sense of the world and his or her place within it. As scholars have observed, the bourgeoisie that patronized the theater wanted individual triumph for the good reason that it believed supremely in its own triumph. But the theater of the masses was often touched with folkish pessimism: the little guy or girl frequently met tragedy and obscurity at the end, even if a "Hollywood ending" papered it over. The Depression and then war made social themes vastly more popular—when they could be treated in just the right manner, which usually meant pulling punches by providing the hero and heroine an exceptional individual solution to what was in reality (and often clearly presented as) a social problem. Hollywood moguls appreciated this kind of film and the critical praise it elicited. They even admired the occasional high-class drama film, usually adapted from a Broadway hit, because it was most likely to win Academy Awards while making back costs.

The radicals, often considered a nuisance, had the necessary talent to make these kinds of projects into winners. So instead of being marginalized as they might have been on political grounds alone, these artists often worked at the very center of production, entrusted more and more frequently with the most important social narratives in Hollywood as the Depression continued and World War II approached. Of course, this was most often a matter of radicals being of use only as long as they helped to make the kinds of films liberals agreed with. After all, there are few explicitly and unmistakably "radical" films (in the European sense) and no "Marxist" films in any formal sense in the American commercial catalog. Instead, there were and are films of a high order of popular art. Their hallmarks are sympathies for the victim, the outsider and the excluded, whether their status is expressed in the vocabulary of gender (as in many of the most successful examples), class, race or age, or in subtle social allegories, fables or extended metaphors. In nearly every case, the political meaning refuses to surrender to casual observation, particularly to the habit of distracted consumption with which most viewers engage popular art. As writer, director and leading Hollywood Marxist Abraham Lincoln Polonsky once remarked to the authors with a smile, "I have no politics, only sympathies, and my sympathies are for the underdog."[11]

But if the "underdog" and his or her situation was the heart of the radical message, it could be enhanced by the skillful introduction of an unexpected point of view or emphasis on an incongruous character. Sometimes the effort failed, but even when it succeeded it was often expressed with such subtlety and indirection that it could lead to critical confusion, indifference or incomprehension. The more sophisticated critics may have come to understand that Abraham Polonsky's *Body and Soul* (1947) was a "fable of the streets" in the reverse Aesopian sense in that its humans took on the behavior of jungle animals, and they may have divined that his *Force of Evil* (1948) was an elaborate metaphor for the predations of Wall Street. But that was film noir, and that—well after the fact, at least—was "art." Meanwhile, the allegorical attack on the blacklist that Michael Wilson buried deep in a commercial project like *Planet of the Apes* remained evidently undetectable.[12]

The intellectuals of the Popular Front were not attracted to Hollywood work overnight. They went through an internal development that started from the position of largely self-taught avant-gardists who saw the popular arts as a living and a calling. But once they were hired and working, American radicals had such proximity with the tools of artistic reproduction in such numbers that their work had a cumulative weight independent of any single one of them, an influence magnified by similar trends elsewhere in the culture. Too often overlooked is the fact that they found their way to the production centers by writing quickly for pay and working for large organizations, such as newspapers and radio networks, in which skill at slipping a message of some authenticity past the scrutiny of editors and censors was a necessary part of the ethical writer's art. Needless to say, this was not the sort of skill that a genteel novelist, particularly a practitioner of high modernism, ever required. But for radical artists and writers, it was an acquired technique not so different from those cultivated by unionists on other shop floors in their own daily dance with authority.

These were the writers, directors, actors and technicians who would one day face the blacklist and who, with surprisingly few exceptions, would accept banishment from a bountiful Hollywood rather than the alternative, obsequiousness and hackery. Their fate was doubly bitter because just a few years earlier they had seemed so firmly grounded in their work and even in academic respectability. A grand Hollywood Writers Mobilization conference held at the University of California, Los Angeles, in 1943 had rallied leading film producers, writers of all kinds and the first American scholars of the popular media in sessions about the struggle for global democracy and the future of writing. The Hollywood Quarterly, launched by the Continuations Committee of the mobilization meeting and the first true film magazine published in the United States, proceeded from its origins in late 1945 to explore the technical issues seriously and at length. A New York Times reporter commented on the publication of a symposium volume from the conference that the participants seemed intent on taking over Hollywood.[13] It was never possible. But they had built a unique set of coalitions, from an all-star cast of Hollywood personalities and sympathetic film scholars to figures high in the Roosevelt administration eager to see a postwar program of democratic mobilization. If FDR had lived to finish out his fourth term, it might even have happened.

The hopes for a different and more democratic cinema had, of course, grown out of the undue optimism of the moment. The same year as the UCLA conference, another exile with friends in the same camp, Marxist Theodor Adorno, had warned that "cultural monopolies cannot afford to neglect their appeasement of the real holders of power, if their sphere of activity in mass society (a sphere producing a specific type of commodity which anyhow is still too closely bound up with easygoing liberalism and Jewish intellectuals) is not to undergo a series of purges." [14] Adorno, as it turned out, knew best.

Yet if the making of good movies, thoughtful movies or artistically interesting movies was ever the real intention of anyone in Hollywood, the radicals had succeeded grandly over a decade and a half or so. The authors of this volume have explored those accomplishments in detail in Radical Hollywood (2002), which traces the work of the Hollywood intellectuals from their first appearance in Southern California in the early 1930s to their banishment by the blacklist between 1947 and 1952. This volume continues their story after the blacklist, when survivors began to find toeholds as individuals in the film industry in England, France and Mexico and the television industry in New York and, under vastly different circumstances, in Spain, Italy and, covertly from time to time, even in the back lots of Hollywood itself. Like the earlier volume, *Hide in Plain Sight* is neither a political nor aesthetic history but a reconsideration of both in the light of a particular social history of Hollywood. But it differs from the earlier work in several key respects that deserve a brief explanation here.

Radical Hollywood surveyed the work of dozens of artists who were active in the Popular Front in Hollywood with a view to evaluating their contribution to the Hollywood style of filmmaking and its social message. The sources were the surviving artists themselves, mostly from oral history, their offspring and younger co-workers, their journals, novels and screenplays (in some cases unproduced), correspondence and biographies and, of course, the films—some 900 of them. The size of the undertaking required a fairly narrow focus on the milieu of the Popular Front because it provided the leadership for the culture front in Hollywood and because its shared ideology and background, from Communist to "conscience liberal," provided a unique way of comparing the work of a large group of artists to one another and to the larger creative output of the industry. Moreover, its members had in effect been written out of history by the blacklist. At least as artists, this group represented a true *terra incognita* for the historian.

The writing of the present volume encountered different problems and opportunities. For one thing, the decline of the studio system, the collapse of the Communist milieu and the scattering of former comrades to foreign winds and new entertainment media meant that comparisons of their work would of necessity be more tenuous and less reliant on an approach organized around genre. It would also have to include the films of some key friendly witnesses who continued to work in films and television. It would include as well a look at relations with and influences on younger artists and protégés who may have identified with the most liberal purposes of the Popular Front, but who had come to filmmaking or television too late for any personal identification with the vanished milieu.

If we experienced any unanticipated reaction to *Radical Hollywood*, it was not a political attack as such (although the intent of some hostile critics was clear enough) but rather the fear, often indirectly expressed, that the book's real purpose was to perturb and replace the established narrative of the history of Hollywood. According to this view, a small number of highly gifted directors had created the American style of filmmaking. This narrative retains its influence because it empowered American criticism by allowing serious observers to trace the impact of real human personalities, almost always directors, on what were perceived as otherwise homogenous studio products. If these assumptions nearly always meant identifying the more formal qualities of filmmaking at the expense of social content, they at least provided a foundation for systematic study.

But they also posed unnecessary limits. Established film theory ignored cinematographers, composers, editors, sound and visual artists, inventors of innovations in cameras, lenses and film stock and the rest of the army of technicians and staff whose role in the creation of the Hollywood style and message may have been slight as individuals, but whose participation was essential and something very new to dramatic art. In their industrial organization and urban milieu, the technicians in this vast army of film production were not so different from the like-minded audiences who came to see their work, and for the first time in history, a popular art developed in a complex (and still barely understood) relationship between its workers and their vast audience. Somewhere in this part of the story awaiting further discovery is one of the founding secrets of popular culture itself.

Above all, the narrative that came to be called auteur theory excluded from consideration the contributions of actors (the very part of filmmaking and viewing to which the audience related most intimately). Yet it was the actor, we argue—and particularly the radical, "thinking" actor after the arrival of the Group Theatre veterans in Hollywood in the late 1930s—who may have transformed Hollywood more than any other single cultural force. A theory that is forced to underestimate this contribution surely requires some reconsideration.

Still, it was not the intent of our research to gather evidence against the prevailing interpretation, but instead to recover the lost record of those who had been excluded from the actual history of filmmaking and to evaluate their political and aesthetic contributions. Those who perceive the mere act of recovery as a threat may be more farsighted than the authors. Or they may be examples of something more familiar—stragglers from ancient battles made bitter and exhausted by past victories.

One of the unexpected discoveries of this volume has been the uniform and virtually unrelieved political hostility with which the working critics in the mainstream periodicals of the United States during the Cold War confronted the work of the blacklistees, writers and directors alike. With the honorable exception of Bosley Crowther, whose roots remained planted in the theater of the 1930s and film of the 1940s, and a very few others, the best-known film reviewers of the Cold War period and after acted as self-conscious spokesmen for the defense of what they regarded as a benign American hegemony over global economics and politics and against excessive and unpatriotic intrusions of conscience on issues of race, gender or class wherever they were raised on film and regardless of the level of art involved.[15] The real differences among these critics were, then, essentially personal and idiosyncratic; otherwise, they were united against dissent (especially from well-known dissenters) in this most vigorous and dissenting of popular arts.

The Hollywood radicals, for their part, sometimes shared this low estimate of their own accomplishments. They had run out of time around 1950, only a few years after opportunities for making significant films were at their highest point, and so naturally it seemed to the more recent arrivals in particular that they had barely gotten started. The most determined among them, and the most fortunate, went underground or abroad. Those with their movies already completed or well into production at major studios remained hidden in plain sight, with the additional irony that writers and directors who were no longer allowed to set foot into Hollywood's business offices had their older films shown around the clock on local television stations. A raft of movies made between 1950 and 1954 that had been scripted by blacklist victims were finished as though nothing had happened, but of course with their credits removed. Meanwhile, television offered new vistas for them, albeit largely under assumed names.

The core of the Hollywood Left had always been semi-underground as Communists, reporting only to the party's New York headquarters. Not that such measures protected them from the intense scrutiny of FBI informers; but the strategy did successfully insulate them from public discussion of *being* Communists, and Jewish Communists to boot. Few of them ever went public politically of their own volition, and with the Cold War looming, they collectively resolved to fight for their rights on constitutional grounds of free speech alone. Therefore, they could not describe their past films or aspirations for future films in Marxist or any other cutting-edge political terms; they would claim only that their films were "democratic" or "humanist."

This description was accurate in the sense that studio and industry censorship obstructed all sorts of themes, some as simple as movie plots supporting the labor movement—the heart of the Left's own activity off the sets. But it was also an evasion or smokescreen hiding a decade of intense conversations and experimentation behind the dozens of highly awarded films and several hundred other fine films that they could claim (along with hundreds of disappointments that they preferred not to). If *The Hollywood Quarterly* had been allowed to continue in the spirit it began, it would doubtless have conducted this discussion by way of dialogue with other screenwriters, directors, technicians and academics. A marriage of the film industry and the academy, it had encompassed such apparently unlikely allies as animator Chuck Jones, who like many other liberals respected the film work and the union commitments of the Hollywood Left. But things fell apart, or, rather, were forced apart, and the fruitful exploration practically ceased.

Instead, the story of the Hollywood blacklist, a central drama of American culture, went through a headline-grabbing phase and then disappeared from sight along with most of the people who had been forced out of their jobs. Like flotsam from a wrecked vessel, it bobbed back to the surface at least a half-dozen

xxii / HIDE IN PLAIN SIGHT

times, each time bearing familiar inscriptions from the past but revealing something new. It reappeared over and over, from the HUAC entertainment industry hearings that ended in 1953 (but continued to simmer for a decade in private and corporate circles in films and television) to the famous failure of Oscar-winning screenwriter "Robert Rich" to appear at the Academy Awards three years later for the family film *The Brave One* to the controversies around the academy's Lifetime Achievement Award to Elia Kazan in 1999 and beyond, with no end in sight.

Some of the reasons for the perennial controversy have almost nothing to do with the blacklistees and their creative effort. Over the decades, conservatives and (some) liberals, including Billy Graham, Jerry Falwell, Steve Allen and Senator Joseph Lieberman, have taken out their frustrations on filmmaking and television production, the whipping-boys for the assorted problems of a celebrity-conscious, morally jaded and materialistic society. The anxieties are understandable, even if the attacks have a hoary pedigree and are invariably misdirected at effects rather than causes. Mass disillusionment with politics of all kinds actually expands and extends the importance of the artistic statement which, in a variety of unpredicted forms, holds the interest of more ordinary people than can any politician.

Artists, for their part, will be responding to the effects of poverty and violence for a long time, in unpredictable projects with familiar messages. These controversies double back to our subject because left-wing screenwriters, directors, producers and their liberal allies have had a purpose, the necessary talent and sometimes the necessary connections to offer models of what public art can be. Their films and television shows have steadily and effectively criticized racism, upheld democratic patriotism (while bashing pseudo-patriotic rationalizations for wrongdoing) enshrined strong women and admirable representatives of assorted minorities, all as much as urging viewers to take a higher path. Ironically, films and their subjects despised by conservatives (and not only conservatives) in times past have even become objects of national pride: no one would have expected the face of Malcolm X to be looking out from a postage stamp, just as the films of the 1940s attacking anti-Semitism, once the subject of conservative ire, became in retrospect welcome messages of melting-pot America.

How did it happen? We come to the question with many, many pieces of the puzzle still missing. Reexamining the blacklist narrative of how previous generations coped with war, oppression, poverty and the threats of ever wider war, we uncover, for instance, a curious inside story of theatrical experiments and artistic debates that predicted and in some ways actually shaped their later and highly influential work and the work of their protégés and sympathizers in film and television. Buried deep in Hollywood history, those traditions still spring amazingly to life, unbidden and unexpected, as in *The Majestic* (2001), a Jim Carrey vehicle explored in our final chapter.

The task of this book is to make the memories and sense of tradition evident. If everything seemed to change after 1950, much stayed subtly the same. We will see that key themes unmistakably readapted from the various motifs of Depression poverty included the physical and existential conditions of the oppressed of every kind, the stresses of the atomic age and above all, with the help of a new kind of actor, the discovery of new rebellious layers within the population, not only minorities but also outsiders of all kinds, whose refusal to accept the mere materialism of the surrounding society gave them voices to speak to power. Performed in rage or in ridicule, in narratives of many different media and in floral variety, its proponents banned but its deepest themes beyond suppression, it was the great tradition revived.

ACKNOWLEDGMENTS

Thanks go to many quarters, but some special ones to the writers who attended a panel at the Brecht Forum of New York City on a spring evening in 1994. The topic was the Left in film and television writing, with panel members Paul Buhle, Ring Lardner, Jr., and Walter Bernstein. Veteran television writer/story editors Albert Ruben and Edward Adler added their experiences, along with John Weber, the former Communist "cadre" sent to Hollywood in 1939 to create a Marxist school for film industry workers. (He promptly joined the Hollywoodites against the party leaders.) From further interviews with Weber, the one-shot producer of the stunning American-Italian neorealist *Stranger On the Prowl* (1951), and various other writers, a new understanding of television writing and its Hollywood connections has slowly emerged. Without that evening in the metaphorical company of Bertolt Brecht, this book might never have been written.

Premier television scholar David Marc, in his insights and his interviews with Frank Tarloff, Albert Ruben, Jack Klugman and many others in television history has added immensely to our understanding. Acknowledgments go also to Joan Scott, widow of Adrian Scott and herself a television writer of the 1950s through the seventies; to other television progressives including actress-director Lee Grant, writers Edward Adler, Albert Brenner, Robert Lees, Albert Ruben, Walter Bernstein, the late Millard Lampell, the late Richard Powell and the late Abraham Polonsky for conversations and correspondence; to the staffs of Special Collections at Columbia University, University of California, Los Angeles, the State Historical Society of Wisconsin, the Academy of Motion Pictures and the American Heritage Center at the University of Wyoming; and also to screenwriters Jean Rouverol Butler, Bernard Gordon and Alfred Lewis Levitt. We also wish to thank fellow researchers Larry Ceplair (who provided notes of an interview with Michael Wilson) and Robert Hethmon (who in large part created the "Hollywood Ten" archival collection at the State Historical Society of Wisconsin, and among many other kindnesses to us, supplied an interview that he did with Roy Huggins); thanks to Judith E. Smith and Steven W. Bowie, two fine cultural scholars who with great thoughtfulness read chapters one through three; to Ted Wagner, for the cannonball run into Wyoming; and to Grace Wagner, without whose research skills, patience and persistence this book would not have been possible.

Finally, we would like to thank critics of our earlier works, whether private or public, amicable or hostile, for enlarging our view of the subject. We have learned something from all of them. In a field with few previous scholars and a vast number of uncertainties, we anticipate, in the words of Samuel Johnson, that "a few wild blunders, and risible absurdities, from which no work of such multiplicity was ever free, may for a time furnish folly with laughter, and harden ignorance into contempt; but useful diligence will at last prevail, and there never can be wanting some who distinguish desert."[16]

CHAPTER ONE

LIVING ROOM MODERNISM

WOODY ALLEN FANS AND OTHER CASUAL VIEWERS OF *The Front* (1976) have often been puzzled that a film about the entertainment blacklist of the 1950s was set in television and Manhattan, rather than movies and Hollywood. Even more puzzling was why the plot had to be a comedy rather than the dark history it really was, both for those who were punished and for American culture at large. Director Martin Ritt and writer Walter Bernstein explained early on that the film could only have been made with the participation of Allen—and so was necessarily a comedy. Ritt and Bernstein's personal experiences with the blacklist, moreover, had been in their up-and-down careers in television. It was the world they knew best.[1]

Other films plotted around the blacklist have been more popular, but none (with the possible exception of *The Way We Were*) has had *The Front*'s lasting impact.[2] The cruelty and the opportunism at the heart of the blacklist as an institution, not to mention its undeniable anti-Semitic undertones, are revealed here in the sheer absurdity of anathemizing popular entertainers as "Un-American."

The Front was about more than the individual lives of the entertainers, though. It also effectively dramatized the loss of New York's role as the leading forum for the Popular Front culture of the 1930s and 1940s and the transformation of the city's role in that culture into something more discrete and more private. The steady if ultimately unsuccessful attempt to suppress the social possibilities in the new medium of television was also meant in part to show that even New York, if only under extreme duress, could be as "normal" and as "American" as Indiana—or at least New Jersey. And if New York could be forced into line, so could the rest of the country.

That *The Front*'s writer, director and actors are reenacting history is established early on, when Michael Murphy (in the role of Bernstein) drags Woody Allen, as the front, into a deli to meet two blacklisted writers. They are clearly stand-ins for Abraham Polonsky and Arnold Manoff. Bernstein, Polonsky and Manoff had all been blacklisted in Hollywood, and in New York they formed a kind of collective to help each other survive by writing under the table for television, notably for *You Are There*. One of the further ironies of the movie is that several of the actors themselves had barely returned from the blacklist. The Polonsky figure is played by blacklistee Lloyd Gough, the villain in the Polonsky-scripted *Body and Soul* (1947), starring John Garfield. (The great proletarian actor of the 1940s had died of a heart attack at 39, between HUAC subpoenas. By way of poetic justice, his daughter, Julie, was given a cameo in *The Front*.) How all of these characters came to be in this time and place is the real backstory of the movie and of the blacklist itself.

During the late 1930s, native Brooklynite Bernstein had attended Dartmouth and been recruited into the Young Communist League by Budd Schulberg, scion of a Hollywood producer's family who earned midlife fame by writing *On the Waterfront* and simultaneously fingering old friends. Bernstein had been one of the admired younger writers of *The New Yorker* during the war, and a correspondent for the armed forces paper *Yank*.

After the war, Bernstein tried his hand at theater, writing a never-produced play for his then-close friend, Elia Kazan. He also had an early shot at Hollywood, working with director Robert Rossen, whose *All The King's Men* would capture the 1949 Academy Award ceremonies and propel the ex-Communist auteur first toward resistance, then abject surrender to HUAC. Bernstein meanwhile retreated from Hollywood for personal reasons, returning to New York at the invitation of a fledgling television director and fellow future blacklistee, Martin Ritt.

In New York, Bernstein's real media career began. Sometimes as "Paul Bauman," sometimes as himself, the young man quickly became a regular writer for *Danger*, one of the most admired dramas of the new medium, many of whose episodes were directed by another rising talent, Sidney Lumet. Named and then pursued, Bernstein acquired one "front" after another. Then he found something like a calling: Bernstein, Polonsky and Manoff became the principal writers for television's multi-award-winning "docu-drama" *You Are There*, decades before the genre had been invented. Liberals in particular loved the program, although as Polonsky quipped, several of the nation's most famous liberals would have demanded the heads of those who wrote it if they had only known the truth.[3]

By the time he returned in earnest to the theme of his early days on television in *The Front*, Bernstein settled on two comic figures to tell the story. Along with Allen, the larger-than-life Zero Mostel was cast as "Hecky Brown." Mostel, too, had been blacklisted in real life, and one of the scenes in the movie was based on an incident in which Bernstein drove the beloved actor and stand-up comic to a hotel in the Catskills, where he had been promised $500 to do his stage act (his pre-blacklist fee had been $3,000). In the film, the hotel manager informs Hecky when he arrives that he will be paid $250, and Brown responds to this humiliation with drunken rage by rifling through the manager's pockets for bills. Later, after grieving for his old life while pleading to be "cleared," reminiscing about how in the old days he might woo a gorgeous comrade with "a big ass" by joining her in a May Day parade, Brown moans to the Woody Allen character, "It's all Brown-stein's fault. I wouldn't be in trouble if it wasn't for Brownstein." This was, of course, the Jewish name and identity that he was born with.

"People change their names," the front shrugs, "It's no big deal." But the au-dience comes to understand that discarding an old identity for the sake of a new one is painful and humiliating—and meant to be. Even the now-prosperous front, who loves his new uptown apartment with its grotesque mid-century wall sculp-tures and avocado chairs and carpets, is not in the end willing to pay the price, which was not so much to abjure his political views (he didn't even know what the Fifth Amendment was) but his Jewishness and his humanity.

The genius of *The Front* is that it managed to capture the absurdity in all of this, as when the self-described "practically illiterate" front, in an incident that actually happened to Bernstein, rejects a script by one of the writers, telling him it's just not up to snuff. "I can't submit just anything," Allen says indignantly, "My name's gonna be on it." In a similar but real incident, famed 1950s television writer Reginald Rose recalled, 40-some years later, that he had once proposed a television drama about race relations and, knowing it would be turned down, agreed to drop the idea if he could write a script about blacklisting. The executive in charge of program practices at CBS first demanded that the show be about something other than television because the medium had no blacklist—even though he was the very network executive personally responsible for enforcing it! The executive then decided that the cast list of the show had to be cleared in ad-vance to make sure there were no controversial figures on it. A show about the blacklist, then, could be made only by submitting names.[4]

In the short run at least, the absurdities were mainly distractions. The medium was so full of promise that writers like Bernstein, far from looking down on it, were eager to join in. "Television," the later Emmy Award–winning Bern-stein reflected in his memoirs, seemed "this wonderful electronic *tabula rasa* that everyone was rushing to write on."[5] Neither film nor theater, it was at once simul-taneously live *and* shot with a camera. Experimentation flourished in a world of fresh talent and of artistic discoveries. Something hugely important was being in-vented in practice, and talented left-wingers were definitely in on the ground floor. As would become clear in later decades, despite the relative success of the suppression of both themes and talent, Bernstein's generation and its liberal younger colleagues had a lasting influence, unfolded over time in unexpected and surprising ways.

Behind the story of the television blacklist lay the metaphorical smoking ruins of the film capital. The sentencing of the Hollywood Ten in 1951 to prison time and the continuation of the Hollywood hearings frightened many, but in the light of the Korean conflict and the growing dread of a World War III, it was only one of the terrors of the day. In Hollywood, prospects were bad for everyone. Investors and studio executives were fleeing from mature themes and from much of the best talent, attendance figures had fallen down around the industry's ankles and the rapid rise in the number of television sets and eyes glued to them was cause for serious worry for everyone in the film industry. It was not until theater receipts began to pick up again in the late 1950s that the new medium would be revealed as a major source of salvation for the movie studios.

From a longer perspective, all this turned out to be only one more turnaround in the evolution of popular media, scarcely more dramatic than the appearance of network radio and the corresponding crisis of vaudeville a generation earlier; or, for that matter, the arrival of the daily penny newspaper, the cheap novel and the popular magazine over the course of the nineteenth century.[6] There was a difference, of course. By 1950, American daily life had become scrutinized as never before by an expanding field of specialists in market research. TV had caught them largely unawares—but not for long. The realization that huge profits were to be made from the consumer prosperity of the moment led everyone connected to the new medium to search for fresh ways to exploit it, with often predictably banal results. In this context, the "militant highbrows" (in Arthur Schlesinger, Jr.,'s memorable phrase), that is, the prestigious cultural critics of the day who had earlier derided film, now elevated it to the status of "art" as they singled out television as commercialism's chief engine for dumbing-down the masses.

In the medium's ferocious demand for new product, though, one question was going unanswered. Where was the talent to come from? The most obvious answer was that they would arise from the ranks of the most celebrated entertainment-industry veterans of the 1940s, which meant substantially the Popular Front milieu. But there was a problem. In their search for work, many of these figures had to rely upon official amnesia, the kind that permitted so many former radicals to become leading liberals of the anticommunist variety, including labor functionaries, magazine columnists and so forth. Who really cared if Burl Ives, Mitch Miller, Eric Severeid, Mike Quill, James Wechsler, James Burnham or, for that matter, Eleanor Roosevelt had dabbled in left-wing ideas and associations just a few years back?

Those among the writers and directors who remained unrepentant radicals had an even deeper need for eluding vengeful memory. At a time when the conservative political mood and advertisers wielded such power over the content of television shows, producers had virtually nowhere else to turn for the experience and creative energy for the new storytelling medium except to those who had been steeped in the left-wing traditions of the New York stage and the Hollywood film. And so the content of television shows was prepared by new generations of writers and directors who owed to the 1930s–1940s their inspirations for form as much as for narrative content.

Some performers, most notoriously Lucille Ball, got a free pass from the blacklist. The committee forgave not only her family connections with the 1930s Left when she had registered in California as a Communist elector; they also overlooked her participation in assorted Left events of the recent past (among other things, she had hosted fundraisers as well as study groups for new party members at her home). This lapse suggested that the blacklisting system was somehow more porous than the blacklisters had claimed.[7] A surprising number of actors, directors and writers slipped through the net, especially if they had not been active in Hollywood or well known to informers during the forties—or if they made the right financial payoffs. On the other hand, since the "names" had been well known to the investigating committee members well before they asked the questions, perhaps the entire system of punishment was conveniently selective after all.

When the smoke of the McCarthy era started to clear and détente became a favorite term of early 1960s media for describing the relations of those telegenic fellow-reformers, John F. Kennedy and Nikita Khrushchev, the connections of left-wing artists and their work, if not the Byzantine logic of the blacklist, began to make more sense. From a distance, it now became evident that radicals had invented some key elements of presenting stage drama that were eventually synthesized as the Hollywood style of filmmaking. It was this aesthetic development that early TV was built on, and without which the new medium could not have made claims to respectability among the critics or won its audience of middle-class consumers. Along with camera and editing techniques, foremost among these was a performance tradition that came to be called "Method" acting. It was Method that provided the historical depth of vision, the degree of irony, the training and the sensibility that was to be characteristic of the new medium. Here lay the source of the richness of television's best early work, before the blush faded from the rose.

In part an exaggerated nostalgia for the trickle of creativity amid the chaos of heavy local programming (in reality as often mediocre as the days of early cable, and more than likely to reflect such dubious venues as talent contests staged at auto dealerships), the memory of a television "Golden Age" has a real basis in the boldness of its experimentation with live entertainment. Early television seemed, as many veteran theatergoers of the time excitedly observed, something like the last revival of vaudeville, with old-time vaudevillians like Ed Wynn still very much on hand. Given low expectations for profits (and production costs), it also had a looseness, a range for experimentation in other live programming aside from drama, that would vanish by the 1960s.

In part because the audience was smallish, largely urban and disproportionately Eastern in the first postwar decade, television boldly poked at the political or social conservatism of America and the security-obsessed government at the height of the Cold War—before largely if not entirely subsiding into the conformity of the age. *You Are There* mocked McCarthyism as surely as *The Beverly Hillbillies* and *Hee Haw* later showed the networks doing their best to keep the counterculture and antiwar movement out of the "entertainment" schedule and confining the latter, however distortedly, within "news."[8] But even the subtlest mockery had its limits. What might be called the Pink Scare of the middle 1950s, a second round of attacks from advertising agencies as well as the familiar red-baiting columnists and the American Legion, went after television shows and their performers. Conservatives' scalp-hunting often succeeded, with the compliance of sponsors and ad agencies eager to avoid the "controversial," whether in the talent they hired or the narrative themes they approved.[9]

All too quickly the prestigious video experiments in live theater were abandoned. They were replaced with prerecorded programming, particularly episodic series with continuing stars—mostly sitcoms and Westerns. This change was framed and accelerated by the move of most television production from New York to Los Angeles, a process that was all but complete by 1960. And yet it would be wrong to conclude that the networks, despite their huge capital investments, had complete control of all issues of social content in television. For one thing, neither the network execs nor the sponsors and their agencies could successfully predict what would be the audience-winning shows a year or two ahead. For another, deep within the entertainment production process forces were at work and artists in place that pink-baiters in the press, ad agencies and network execs seemed equally unaware of. Radical methods, themes, writers, directors, actors and technicians were already at hand in the process that produced the sitcom, the detective show, children's programs and the weekly dramatic series. Just as remarkably, these people sometimes worked with the assistance of HUAC's friendly witnesses who had grown ashamed and were themselves now eager to reinstate social themes.

The survivors, with their liberal Left friends of long-standing and a handful of protégés, replicated in some key ways the experiences of writers and directors for B-movies of the 1930s and 1940s. By now they had no illusions about the Soviet Union, but they shared the hopes of the civil rights movement and other idealistic impulses of the time, among them the efforts to slow down the nuclear arms race and to welcome the newly independent countries of the Third World into the family of nations. As the supposed threat of internal communist subversion faded toward the end of the fifties and the beginning of the sixties, some powerful liberals and many more ordinary ones seemed to want to close ranks around generic visions of social justice.

The liberal public could by now watch or read, discuss and even champion the work of unapologetic ex-Communists and those formerly close to the Popular Front, so long as the personal details were not too specific. As for the veteran radicals themselves and their circle of fellow writers, directors and such, they had no direct political role in the youthful Left that was about to emerge. But through their work, they vigorously upheld free speech and old-style liberal values, seeking to shame the right-wing craving for renewed repression. When possible, they quietly cheered on the new radical moods of protest from positions of influence near the creative centers of popular culture.

Economics, as any veteran Marxist knew, would ultimately be central to the failure or success of any efforts to restore a voice of conscience to the mainstream. The status of the screenwriter had been won through decades of struggle for unionization and negotiation over credits. The victory had always been incomplete and temporary at best. Then television suddenly changed everything by elevating a handful of writers to the status of charismatic American intellectuals, as only playwrights had been earlier—and predictably relegating the rest to hired-hand status with no union representation and without so much as staff jobs on even the most popular series.

The most successful writers, including a handful of the conscience liberals who had quietly allied themselves with the blacklistees, experienced sweet revenge. Whether prestigious or not, successful television writers, like their counterparts in the film industry, could become extremely well-paid hired hands, moving on if they chose to direct or, more usually in later years, produce shows in one medium or the other. With this prospect, the old collective élan of progressives in the entertainment industry had vague prospects for renewal. But some of the most successful figures created jobs for others who were still formally barred by their political status.

Not that it was easy; it never had been. In 1950, CBS announced to employees that a loyalty oath was mandatory. Private agencies formed by ex-FBI men circulated names of suspected Reds to advertisers and producers, and they did a booming business for years.[10] The blacklist and the nature of television had successfully reduced the Hollywood Left's aesthetic and political projects of the 1930s and 1940s to networks of personal contacts and good intentions. But their continuing work, resumed in earnest, was an impressive accomplishment. Seen in retrospect and as a whole rather than in fragments of dispersed and cryptic comments on U.S. society, it explains why, within a generation, the Left had the cumulative power to change the direction of quality television programming.

THE STAGE BACKGROUND

Hardly anyone appreciated how much the controversial issues in television programming owed to debates held decades earlier and far way. Nor were critics yet prepared to think about television within the age-old saga of dramatic performance. Television history, like that of film, has rarely been examined in the light of the history of theater, even if television scripts are still dubbed "teleplays" (as their counterparts are "screenplays") and the drama anthologies of the 1950s still hold a special place in memory as television's finest hour. Not that any such examination can be simple or direct. As critic-historians David Marc and Robert J. Thompson acidly observed, in a drama where the protagonist must be spared death in episode after episode, the crucial classical distinctions between comedy and tragedy vanish—posing, at a minimum, the need for rethinking some of TV's basic narrative categories.[11]

Hollywood before 1950 had turned out literally hundreds of films that had first been successful stage productions, including a generous handful of film classics. But by 1950, it seemed easier to get serious drama into the living room than into movie theaters. Thanks to television producers and network executives who considered it cheaper to hire a writer to adapt literary classics than to pay for the rights to existing theatrical works (or to subsidize new works), quite a number of prestigious plays successfully made the transition to the new medium. In later decades, efforts to revive the theater-of-the-air in the style of radio or early TV foundered on low ratings, making the painful reality clearer as Broadway drama itself repeatedly struggled against virtual extinction.

To appreciate the deeper issues we need to go back a few decades and a few centuries. Cinema had its beginnings in the storefront benches of immigrant neighborhoods, its techniques located squarely within popular melodrama, adding more than a dash of the circus, the carnival, the religious festival and assorted historic mass entertainments. But by the 1920s, the film industry already had begun to affirm its social aspirations to move onward and upward toward the preferred consumer.

Radical critics, who played important roles in the emergence of modern theater a generation or more before the advent of popular films and television, naturally feared that movies would reduce the artistic possibilities of the theater by making cinema its mechanically reproduced replacement, now with its political and avant-garde heart removed. The fears were real because there was something to lose: from the 1890s to the 1920s, middle-class theater had brought to its audiences new themes of class and gender, along with sometimes sweeping experiments in form, and thus new prospects for social relevance. From the feminist plays of Henrik Ibsen to the early Marxist efforts of Bertolt Brecht and American avant-gardist Eugene O'Neill, theater often seemed the carrier of the Zeitgeist, drawing to itself the most daring talents. Now, everything that had been gained might be lost—a glum sentiment reinforced as global film production came to be centered in Hollywood, where twenties' capitalism ceaselessly celebrated its triumph and, most hypocritically, its virtue.

The pessimism, like earlier optimism about the theater, turned out to be overblown, or at least misdirected. Outside of Russia and Germany, the mainstream of the theatrical tradition had never transcended the triumphant march of middle-class realism, apart from a gentle ribbing of the subjects, while the plot complications of gender and class were most often played for conservative purposes. Silent movie drama, when it came, rarely exploited its potential dramatic advantage over drawing-room satire of the Shavian kind, despite the popular artistry of Chaplin and the abundance of slapstick ridicule of the social order. Grand possibilities remained to be realized.

In revolutionary Russia from the vantage point of 1929, the didactic virtues of theater as political propaganda had become suspect on artistic grounds, and for good reasons. Vsevolod Meyerhold, who wrote with the special authority of the figure most responsible for organizing the Soviet stage after the revolution, looked back critically upon the early enthusiasms of Bolshevik-inspired drama as the "thundering broadsides of ours [that] were just so many blank charges . . . so often dull and sometimes just plain stupid."[12]

By the time Meyerhold wrote these words, he had already directed two silent films (both now lost) and was addressing media workers who after ten years of agitprop came to share his craving for artistic "authenticity." In retrospect, with the shadow of Stalin falling across the land, this proposal for a new and different art, free of the revolution's own dogmas, sounds remarkably romantic. And indeed it was. In the same speech, "The Reconstruction of the Theatre," Meyerhold called not for anything like the abandonment of political drama in the name of pure art, but appealed instead to the old reactionary Richard Wagner and his famous theory of the Gesamtkunstwerk. That is to say, he evoked the integration of all the arts into one dramatic form as the appropriate model for the true revolutionary theater.

However distant it may now seem in political time from Jazz Age America and mercenary Hollywood in particular, this apparently quixotic appeal held a special significance. The same romantic notion of authenticity was about to seize the folklorists who were sifting through the popular arts to "discover" an American culture. It was as though Walt Whitman had come back to life and gone on the radio. By no means restricted to radicals, this impulse was to develop a considerable audience and become a keystone sentiment of the Popular Front. With Woody Guthrie as bard and unemployed intellectuals conducting interviews with aged former slaves to recover lost history, the folkloric pursuit of the authentic would eventually remake large segments of American entertainment.

During the 1930s, a parallel impulse was in the process of transforming the American stage, for better and also, according to its critics, for worse. Meyerhold and his most influential student, Constantin Stanislavsky, both insisted, on a purely technical level, that stage actors be elevated from mere performers into interpretative artists, with an authority nearly equal to directors and playwrights. They too would discover the authentic—the authentic emotion, that is—for themselves. It was just the message that the emerging generation of actors, and every generation after them, badly wanted to hear.

Actors would be trained to *think* as they delivered their lines, varying the interpretation as their understanding of the character deepened or changed, and this would be the hallmark of the Stanislavskian method. It caused a revolution far beyond the avant-garde, even within an Anglo-American tradition where great actors (many of them European-trained) had always been held in high esteem and where dynasties had been launched on established talent. To fast-forward for a moment, anyone who has followed Marlon Brando's career can immediately glimpse the centrality of the impulse of modern acting as an extraordinary cultural force of the mid-twentieth century. The thinking actor has driven many a director to distraction and encouraged many a less-skilled performer to delay production by hours or days until a supposed need for "meaning" has been satisfied. But for all the alternatives, notably the classical tradition of the English stage, none has exceeded the influence of Method.

This technique of acting made a comfortable home for itself within the Hollywood star system, for all the obvious reasons. But it also helped shape the narrative style of theater and film at large. When it was successful, it transformed Hollywood melodrama into something much more immediate and compelling, in both film and television. In the hands of Stanislavsky and his famous American student, Lee Strasberg—a left-winger who trained generations of stars and character actors—the impact on the content of radical drama in particular would be decisive.[13]

As a child of modernism, Method sought to achieve its ends without any trace of didacticism even though it arose in a milieu (the radical stage) in which there was frequently an expectation that it would be put in the service of a political movement. By its very nature, however, its recollection of emotion through techniques designed to heighten the immediacy of performance, Method required a narrative close to realism. Method emphasized a specific intensification of effects in which the buildup of emotion itself became the driving force of the story as well as its resolution.[14] Whatever the specific conflict, the struggle of the individual against the odds or against his or her own nature or situation, whether successful or unsuccessful, tended to push everything else into the background.[15]

In practice, Stanislavkian theater developed toward an all-encompassing naturalism, a "realness" considered by its participants and (in time) by serious critics as well to be the mark of serious drama, whether in theater, film or television. One of the most gifted teachers of Method, Bobby Lewis, later complained (in 1957) that in practice, some of the founders themselves had ignored or downgraded the purely technical aspects of actor training in voice and body movement as cultivated in the English schools. Strasberg apparently considered these complaints irrelevant because of the overriding necessity for training the actor to respond to imaginary stimuli regardless of whether the subject matter happened to be classical or modern drama.[16]

That said, Method was also an instrument that could be exquisitely responsive to social change as the individual actor internalized the changes around him or her. The danger was that it could also reduce social reality to a series of merely personal crises, which was precisely what Elia Kazan's former collaborators and protégés concluded about the director's purpose as they ruefully watched On the Waterfront or East of Eden. Much as in other arenas of modernism, such as poetry or painting, form had thereby triumphed over content.

This was not, of course, what Meyerhold had had in mind. If the playwright-theorist had foreseen the outcome of his theories, he might have associated himself more closely with the other tradition of twentieth-century radical theater: the German "epic" model. As developed by dramatists Erwin Piscator and Bertolt Brecht, it sought to encourage audience identification not with the characters as such but rather the social circumstances in which they functioned. They sought to elicit the educational power of "astonishment" rather than empathy. Brechtian theater in particular famously introduced "interruptions" in the form of documents torn from contemporary society, pop songs and film clips that served as ironic or distancing comments upon the action. By these means, Brecht intended that the abyss separating the stage from the people would be abolished—at least symbolically—and the stage would in effect become a dais.

Brechtian epic theater thus in some sense anticipated postmodern theatricality, from camp to MTV, but with a revolutionary purpose that is alien and probably incomprehensible to the grab-bag logic of the postmodern. Even in its time, cut off from its cultural base by Hitler's triumph, the Brechtian stage demanded concentration from the ordinary theater- and filmgoer, particularly among the self-educated working class whom Brecht sought to reach. The Brechtian film

Kuhle Wampe (1932), scarcely distributed by the time Nazis hijacked German *Kultur* and unlikely to be a hit in any case, had no imitators except perhaps in the Soviet Union.

Depression-era New York, however, offered the exiled radical dramaturge (and there were dozens, if not hundreds) one other opportunity in the form of the radical Yiddish-language theater. Here the effort was to elevate characterization over plot *and* to make the stories a sweeping view of existing reality. Socialistic sentiments were for the moment common coin, and the avant-garde was admired if rarely imitated. In the extreme left of Yiddish theater, particularly under the direction of Benno Schneider, the ARTEF (Yiddish workers theater), the audience could be assumed to have been prepared by revolutionary sentiments and a working knowledge of Russian and Jewish drama. Its critics, in the Communist-connected Yiddish press, had an erudition that reached from the classics to the contemporary Broadway musical comedy. But on Broadway, few of those in the cheap seats would likely share this degree of erudition.

It was within this complex of theatrical traditions that the Group Theatre arose. Considerably more lower-middle-class than the Yiddish radical milieu, less avowedly radical and more professional, the Group adopted the dramaturgical theories of both Meyerhold and Stanislavsky and remade American drama in its own uncertain image. It managed to raise the intentionality of the thinking actor into what was, at its best, superb theater, if also often little more than melodrama expressed as proletarian uplift. The Group's stage designer, later Hollywood set designer, Mordecai Gorelik, once summarized the essential story line with gentle sarcasm by quoting the Biblical verse, "For what is a man profited if he shall gain the whole world and lose his soul?" It was a good question for materialistic America, even in the midst of the Depression, and a perfect one for Clifford Odets, whose "golden boy" from the hit play of the same title learns that the violinist's fingers can earn more as a boxer's fist.

When members and former members of the Group responded to its dissolution by abandoning New York and the theater for the sound stages of Hollywood (some had earlier moved on to the Works Progress Administration's Federal Theater, closed out by Congressional fiat in 1940), it seemed to many critics and its hard-core audience an act of desertion. But the Group contributed, directly and indirectly, more good and influential actors to Hollywood than any other single theatrical source. Generations of protégés also carried forward the Gorelickian message, now without irony, as a critique of American life. Group's iconic characters, if often promethean proletarians, just as often included figures like the Good Doctor (*Men In White*, Group's biggest success, established the popularity of the Dr. Kildare role that spawned so many film and television successors) or the detective-iconoclast Columbo, likewise rooted in a Group drama, who reveals the criminal practices of the privileged elite who are guilty of violating democratic standards yet so cocky that they think they can get away with anything.

Hollywood made good use of all of these and more, including the archetypal rebel who made appearances in one guise or another in most Group productions, and the kindly elder (often a grandfather or uncle) who pronounces the (quietly socialistic) moral lesson of the personal imperative to act decently in an indecent world. Add a femme fatale here or a good woman there, troubled teens uncertain of their future, throw in a supporting actor/sidekick for laughs or pathos, find an urgent social dilemma with a personal and romantic solution, evoke the moral dimension of it all at the final curtain (or reel), and the possibilities become almost literally unlimited—at least in the details.

Much of the original avant-garde intent of Method would be lost in this process. But the list of Group members involved in film in one way or another is considerable. The best-remembered include several Adler family members, Tallulah Bankhead, Roman Bohnen, Morris Carnovsky, Harold Clurman, Lee J. Cobb, Richard Conte, Hume Cronyn, Howard da Silva, Albert Dekker, Frances Farmer, Betty Furness, John Garfield, director Michael Gordon, producer Sidney Harmon, Van Heflin, Sam Jaffe, playwright Sidney Kingsley, Marc Lawrence, Francis Lederer, Lotte Lenya, Philip Loeb, Karl Malden, E. G. Marshall, Burgess Meredith, Harry Morgan, Jean Muir, Lloyd Nolan, Robert Ryan, Gale Sondergaard, David Opatoshu, Larry Parks, Franchot Tone and directors Nicholas Ray and Joseph Pevney. Others who advised the troupe or worked with it in some fashion included William Saroyan, Joseph Schildkraut, playwright Irwin Shaw, director Vincent Sherman, Sylvia Sidney, drama teacher Lee Strasberg, composer Kurt Weill and playwright Tennessee Williams.

This list does not by any means exhaust the former Group members who filled out the casts of 1940s films and radio, and 1950s–1970s television shows.[17] But its breadth explains the logic of the many lasting personal connections, and helps establish the talent that bore a family relation with the Left—some of it admittedly dysfunctional, that is to say the relative few who gave friendly testimony out of a desire to distance themselves from former mentors. Out of the Group came the Actors Studio, co-founded by Kazan (with Bobby Lewis and Cheryl Crawford) to intensify the teaching of Method. It continued under Kazan's tutelage even after his break with the Left; despite political disagreements, Lee Strasberg was later its leading figure. Actors Studio graduates included Rod Steiger, Paul Newman, Bruce Dern, Geraldine Page, Rip Torn, Al Pacino, Ron Leibman, Christopher Walken, Kevin McCarthy, Ellen Burstyn, Harvey Keitel, Robert De Niro, Jill Clayburgh, Michael Moriarty, Dustin Hoffman, Susan Anspach, Martin Balsam, Anne Bancroft, Robert Duvall, Anne Jackson, Cloris Leachman, Walter Matthau, Steve McQueen, Jack Nicholson, Carroll O'Connor, Sidney Poitier,

Maureen Stapleton, Eli Wallach, James Whitmore, Gene Wilder and Cindy Williams, among others.[18]

This list passes over the Actors Laboratory Theater in Hollywood, which overlapped heavily with the Hollywood Left; the Actors Studio in San Francisco; the Neighborhood Playhouse in New York, run by Group veteran Sanford Meisner; the later Stella Adler Conservatory of Acting; the Lincoln Center Repertory Theater, run by Harold Clurman and Kazan in the early 1960s; and the various private tutorial work among emerging actors that blacklisted actors like Jeff Corey in Hollywood, and Lewis and Clurman in New York, all did in the Group tradition. Most of it was not overtly political, but in none of it was the Left's tradition and sensibility absent.[19]

Minus the Group tradition, the new crop of Hollywood actors of the 1950s and sixties, including Brando, James Dean, Montgomery Clift, Paul Newman and Joanne Woodward, among many others, would not likely have been so central to American film's minimal respectability in its worst days and its revival thereafter. Because intelligent actors watch old movies as musicians listen to the classics, and because Method elevates the actor to a dignity previously undreamed of, Group influence is guaranteed show business immortality. Indeed, its inner logic may contain the crucial update of the theater of antiquity. The (Method) character's need to *make a choice*—and the actor participating somehow in the choice—has supplanted the fixed fate of Oedipus and Antigone.

The Brechtian influence could not be so direct, but has been lasting in other ways. Piscator, leaving the Soviet Union in 1941, organized the Dramatic Workshop in New York, where he taught many of Strasberg's students, including Brando, Rod Steiger and Eli Wallach, but significantly also Harry Belafonte, Elaine Strich, Martin Balsam, Walter Matthau and a handful of actors who would later have a major impact on television, including *Maude*'s Bea Arthur, Tony Randall, Tony Franciosa and even the avant-gardist future "Spock," Leonard Nimoy. Piscator's version of epic theater gave them, and those who followed them, the sense of themselves as actors in a grand social drama.

During the early 1940s, gathered in what came to be called the Writers Workshops, Hollywood's screenwriting radicals had debated the inescapable dichotomy in the social dimension of narrative and its meaning for cinema high and low. One faction—not political but aesthetic—insisted, according to the memory of screenwriter Paul Jarrico, upon the "historical method" of seeing the individuals within the sweep of social forces. The opposing faction argued just as determinedly for the "personal" approach that drew the dramatic and social possibilities out of the development of individual characters and their relationships with each other.[20]

Neither side could be accused of cheering for current Russian theories or of willingly surrendering their creative energies to studio demands for box office gold. Both had rightful claims on sincerity (as well as shared activity in the union movement, the assorted causes of antifascism, and so on). Neither side could be displaced by the other, although the "historical" was always at a disadvantage among producers and most of the popular audience as well. Unlike efforts by either red-baiting columnists or Communist officials to dictate content, this radical tension was itself a source of creativity, then and in later films and television—if artists could be free to explore its possibilities.

GOLDEN AGE DRAMA

Television drama began almost with the medium itself. In 1939, when CBS started closed-circuit programming for the few hundred New Yorkers (many of them bar owners) who owned their own rudimentary and expensive television receivers, the network chiefs called in populist critic Gilbert Seldes and, as his assistant, veteran Broadway director Worthington Miner.

These were interesting choices. Seldes, an essayist best known for his unique pioneer volume, *The Seven Lively Arts*, which actually praised elements of popular culture, continued to hold the bully pulpit as network executive and *TV Guide* contributor into the later 1950s. But he was nevertheless an avant-gardist of sorts, product of the free-spirited twenties and brother of famed radical newspaperman George Seldes, who gleefully exposed corporate and government misdeeds. Miner, well to the left of his boss, had begun directing in the Federal Theater and reached his creative apex in the fifties' television drama. He would be forced out of the industry for his liberal views and for past connections he did not care to disown. His and practically everyone else's idol, it might be remembered, had been Orson Welles, the biggest name in radio drama, with Welles' Mercury Theater of the Air among the most admired programs. Politically, Welles was a socialist; aesthetically, a genius and *sui generis* radical surrounded by creative reds.

Without a real audience, there was not yet much money to be made in television over the next decade except from live sports broadcasts, which met the needs of bars for (mostly male) clientele and sprouted ads for beer, cigarettes, shaving cream and other products. The numbers of viewers began to rise sharply from the war's end onward. Along with much local programming of the talk-show type, programming for children and syndicated cowboy films, low-cost drama persisted as a way to fill low-value airtime. The non-tavern audience, still mostly in big cities and especially east of the Hudson, was in considerable part a theater audience, well-to-do, sophisticated and demanding. As sales of television sets multiplied thousands of times over in the era to follow, tastes would change—and for a variety of reasons, sponsors would become more censorious. For the moment, however, a remarkable grace period for drama existed.

That this development should occur more or less exactly as America entered McCarthyism was the greatest of ironies. As Judith Smith has noted, the earliest major televised drama was "Abe Lincoln in Illinois" for NBC Television Theater by erstwhile FDR speechwriter (and 1930s antiwar dramatist) Robert Sherwood—just the kind of evocation of democratic advance that marked Popular Front productions, from music to film. The first three seasons of regular television drama bore the same kind of promise, with the Actors' Studio awarded one of the first Peabody awards for its innovative work in writing the teleplay. CBS's director of dramatic programming, Charles Underhill, made himself an outspoken enthusiast for getting theater people to retrain themselves in the particulars of television drama.

Meanwhile, across American society, the FBI devoted thousands of agents to the pursuit of supposedly dangerous radicals, often harassing them on a daily basis, making sure of their loss of employment but also offering them amnesty if they turned informer. The "Attorney General's List," set out in 1947 at the behest of Harry Truman—himself hounded by Republicans charging omnipresent treason—provided a messy compilation of organizations, many of them no more than defunct memories of 1930s movements or cultural and fraternal organizations that sponsored an amateur theater on the side. Membership present or past now constituted *prima facie* evidence of disloyalty, with the burden of disproof on the suspect. Civil service rolls were examined for those who had signed the wrong statements or been present at the wrong meetings, or were suspected of being homosexuals (and therefore, in the logic of the day, not only morally abhorrent but subject to blackmail by enemies of the nation). Tabloid newspapers and gossip columnists warned daily of threats posed by all of those—and not just communists—who opposed U.S. global policies or who simply urged dramatic changes in race relations.

Television's pioneer executives, looking for theatrical talent and finding it in likely places such as the descendents of the Group, quietly invited at least some of the apparent subversives into the back door. Why did they risk it? Perhaps television was a way of hiding in plain sight; it was Hollywood, after all, that got the spotlight for supposed subversion.[21] As future television and film director Arthur Penn later recalled, the early television executives in charge of recruiting talent also understood that the sudden decline in Hollywood was preventing the rising generation of talent from gaining experience.[22] In any case, there was a creative vacuum in the early years in New York that led inevitably to interest in the (experienced) writing talent of the liberal left.[23]

We come full circle now by entering the left-wing circle of the entertainment world, an intimate, modern-day version of the Yiddish-Jewish writers' ghetto, and correspondingly warm.[24] Writer Walter Bernstein had the good fortune of being close friends with Martin Ritt (1914–1990). The son of Russian and Polish Jewish immigrants (including a mother who became an agent for chorus girls), Ritt grew up in Manhattan and the Bronx at the end of 1920s prosperity and the beginning of the Depression. He was a literary sort, bright but also tough, a high school athlete who dreamed of becoming a coach. His parents divorced and his father died not long after the son's high school graduation. While the surviving family faced poverty, Ritt accepted an athletic scholarship from the one place that offered it— the "Fighting Christians" of Elon College in Burlington, North Carolina.

A more anomalous spot could hardly be imagined for a young New York Jew. But as his widow later recalled to us, this accident of fate was in many ways the making of Ritt.[25] Unlike high school classmates who scarcely ventured west (or south) of the Hudson, save perhaps to go to Jewish Hollywood, and also unlike so many of those entertainers who shared his left-wing political inclinations, Ritt plunged into middle America. He might have fled immediately, repelled or frightened by what he experienced. He did lose interest in football, but he found the semi-rural community almost idyllic, a promise of what might be possible, with the compelling need for racial equality a source of his idealism. Whatever else he gained along the way, those images of the South would prove decisive for him.

Ritt nevertheless abandoned Elon before graduating, transferring to law school at St. John's University on Long Island, but leaving that, too, as his attraction to the theater grew. In spells at the Catskills summer entertainment circuit (playing blackface in *Porgy and Bess*), at the Federal Theater, the Left's own agit-prop Theater of Action, then the Glasgow Theater (where he briefly became a dancer, like his future wife Adele), he found his real home in the Group in 1937. He decided against enrollment in the Abraham Lincoln Battalion, then suffering heavy casualties in the Spanish Civil War, and he continued to mull his own commitments. He learned from radical director Harold Clurman that theater was itself a form of politics, demanding something better than aesthetic didacticism.

Ritt's sponsor was none other than Elia Kazan, who brought him in as the boxing coach for Luther Adler in Adler's role of the boxer in *Golden Boy*. The young Ritt, often chosen for the proletarian parts because of his physical stature and bearing, costarred or played supporting roles in various Group productions. As the Group dissolved, Ritt moved on to other acting jobs until his induction into the Air Force in 1943. There he found himself "drafted" into theater and films again, tapped for a supporting role in the Hollywood version of *Winged Victory* (1944), a home front morale-booster.

By the time of his 1946 discharge, Ritt was off and running. His most notable direction before turning to television was a stage dramatization of the life of Denmark Vesey, the hero and martyr who guided a slave rebellion in 1823 that shocked the

South. Its stars, Juano Hernandez and Canada Lee, were already among the very first feature players in the few pre-blacklist Hollywood films about American racism.

Television, for Ritt as for Bernstein, was a pleasant surprise. He started with a documentary short on boxing and quickly accepted a contract with CBS, and was destined to produce more than direct.[26] An experienced director and a fanatically hard worker like many others in those early days of the new medium, he directed from 25 to 50 live shows each year, moving from dramatic anthologies to series, sometimes (as on *Danger*) mainly as a producer. In 1952, however, Ritt's political past suddenly caught up with him. His chief crimes included organizing a stage show and fundraiser for the Retail, Wholesale and Department Store Workers union, with its patently left-wing leadership, and directing a show for Russian war relief—during the war, that is, when the Russians were allies. These were enough for banishment, and unlike a writer, as an actor he could hardly keep working through a front.

Ritt's Crimes

While on the blacklist, Ritt spent serious time at the track and was later remembered by Bernstein and other intimates as the shrewdest handicapper they had ever known. He managed to get some theatrical work, mostly directing and occasionally acting. He even managed to persuade Arthur Miller to let him direct on a double bill two of the author's plays, *A Memory of Two Mondays* (arguably Miller's most "proletarian" work, about life in an auto parts warehouse) and the first production of *The View From the Bridge*, a response to the rationalization of friendly testimony in *On the Waterfront*. Thanks to the impression the show made on producer David Susskind, the path to Ritt's film career now lay open.

The television experience had been invaluable for Ritt and other left-wingers who had been caught up in the new medium. Both the quality and political shading of its dramas taught them lessons about the political narrative. *Danger*, for instance, often featured guarded references to "betrayal" (carefully personalized). But in the long run television may have been more important for the people it produced than for its narrative devices. When Ritt was purged in 1952, Yul Brynner replaced him as producer and director, then moved on to a new acting career (*The King and I*). Brynner was replaced as director by one of the ablest descendants of 1930s and 1940s left-wing theater in film and early television: Sidney Lumet.

Son of a Warsaw-trained actor and director, Lumet (1924-) had made his acting debut as a child actor in Yiddish, and regularly played in a Yiddish radio drama staged by his father, auteur turned popular entertainer. The younger Lumet appeared first on Broadway in the original production of Kingsley's *Dead End*. At puberty, he was already something of a political veteran, having begun reading Karl Marx at eight and joining the Young Communist League at the earliest age permitted. Later the same year, he was praised by critics for his role in a William

Saroyan production. But that was 1939, and an era of social drama was swiftly coming to an end.

Lumet enlisted in the Army after Pearl Harbor. He spent five years with the Signal Corps and claimed later to have gained invaluable experience with the details of lighting and camerawork. After the war and a phase of acting and studying with the Neighborhood Playhouse, he helped organize the Actors' Workshop, a cooperative troupe working backwards from modern drama to Shakespeare and the Greeks. The future director undertook his own first plays under these auspices, meanwhile making a living teaching high school drama.[27]

Still in his mid-twenties when at the helm of *Danger*, Lumet later recalled that he acquired there the skills needed to become a film director—camera, lighting, shot selection and set design—and gained as well the experience of working with some of the best actors around. In 1952, *Cue* magazine called *Danger* "the finest dramatic half-hour in television" and invited the director (along with its sympathetic producer, Charles Russell) to discuss the making of the show. Lumet declared that, in the absence of rigid guidelines, "some of us decided to try and do what we believed in," the kind of "melodrama in which someone has to be involved in some sort of perilous situation" resulting in "being human, honest and occasionally illustrative of some major point about living." If no more than twenty percent of the programs they produced were fully satisfying to them in form and content, that was still a lot: without the summer reruns of later television, the pace of 52 episodes per year could have killed their inspiration and dragged down viewership. *Danger* held steady against all comers, including ball games.[28]

Lumet, like Ritt, worked frantically. Directing plays in several of the dramatic anthology series on the networks, from *Play of the Week* and *Best of Broadway* to *Goodyear Playhouse* and *Playhouse 90*, he was considered by insiders the outstanding auteur of the most controversial program, Worthington Miner's *Studio One*. Within a decade, Lumet had directed no fewer than 500 teledramas. The most memorable, both for him and for the history of television, were his episodes of *You Are There*.

The inside story of *You Are There* is one of the most truly remarkable in the early saga of the small screen. First, it took part, with only slight effort at disguise, in the public struggle against Senator Joseph McCarthy at a moment when liberals as a group ran for cover and many former (or future) liberals embraced the idea of blacklisting, arguing only for an accurate identification of the guilty. Second, *You Are There* was the original docudrama—a fictionalized historical drama—narrated by many of television's (and radio's) distinguished real-life newscasters, including Eric Severeid, Harry Marble, Winston Burdett, Edward P. Morgan, Lou Cioffi, Charles Collingwood, Bill Leonard (later head of CBS news), Mike Wallace and lastly Walter Cronkite, the usual anchor of the show. It was as if the idea of *Sixty Minutes*, the often hard-hitting liberal news show of later decades, had to be placed into the past before being allowed to interrogate the issues of the present. Last if scarcely least, *You Are There* happened to be written, in its best years (1953–1955) by Walter Bernstein, Arnold Manoff and Abraham Polonsky.

Although originally a popular if hardly most-listened-to show in the fading years of American radio drama, the television version of *You Are There* was nonetheless an original because every show, pegged to a specific historical incident, had to be based upon known historical fact. The dialogue would naturally be fictional, but a narrator set the stage and brought the incident back into focus. The show premiered on CBS in the spring season of 1953, when Joe McCarthy and McCarthyism were at high tide and the attack on film was being replaced with an attack on television, with private agencies supplying "names" of those suspected and network officials culling them out without ever acknowledging (in case of a lawsuit) that a blacklist was in effect.[29]

Producer Charles Russell, a thoughtful network executive who considered himself a civil libertarian if by no means a left-winger, had worked with Bernstein on *Danger* and gladly met Bernstein's two friends, former poet and sometime novelist Arnold Manoff and screenwriter-director Abraham Polonsky. There was no mystery about their status. Bernstein had already arranged for a "front" for the last of his *Danger* shows, and one of the other writers for *Danger*, destined to become associate producer for the last live episodes of *You Are There*, was to offer his name for several of Polonsky's scripts. Nearly all the other live *You Are There* episodes were credited to nonexistent writers.

Together, the three delivered 56 scripts that were actually produced. They included such challenging topics for the time as the Salem witch trials, the death of Socrates, the deafness of Beethoven, the trial of John Peter Zenger, the Scopes "Monkey Trial," the execution of Joan of Arc and the trial of Susan B. Anthony—all of them by no accident legal or moral dramas with parallels in contemporary experiences of the writers themselves. Such obvious historical personalities as criminal badmen Jesse James and John Dillinger; political rogues Benedict Arnold, John Wilkes Booth, Rasputin and the Emperor Nero; Washington, Lincoln and Jefferson; the creation of documents like the Magna Carta and the Bill of Rights; and the writing of the "Star Spangled Banner" were all treated here.

Kinescopes of the show, produced with the limited technology of the day, went out post-production free of cost to schools and civic groups, where they were met with enthusiasm. Producer Russell was cagey enough to schedule the least controversial episodes on the weeks sponsored by Prudential Insurance and the most controversial on the weeks that went unsponsored—something unknown to later television and practiced here only because the network was willing to cover the low costs of its most admired and freely distributed program, which garnered awards that included a Peabody.

Within the show's bare 25 dramatic minutes, small-screen miracles were common. "Cortez Conquers Mexico" features the Spanish conqueror's dialogue with his Incan mistress, a princess who served as the "tongue" for the conquered people. They discussed not only politics, religion and war but their own interracial intimacy ("What soldier does not have a wife somewhere across the seas?" she asks). In "The Secret of Sigmund Freud," an analysand (plainly the famous "Dora" in Freud's self-training) speaks of her dreams and unconscious desires—while his colleague Wilhelm Fliess talks about bisexuality and about taking cocaine with the great doctor! The episode, "The Emergence of Jazz," featured Louis Armstrong himself with a score of other famous black musicians; it was set in 1917, as the Navy threatened to close New Orleans' Storyville and jazz spread everywhere, all the way to Paris, where intellectuals understood it as the voice of African American culture.

The complications of jazz as an artistic revolution could be played dramatically as a straightforward attack on cultural repression. *You Are There* episodes on Nathan Hale (with Paul Newman, in his second leading role on television, pronouncing his unwillingness to turn witness against the revolution), and "The Crisis of Galileo" in particular proved so startling that network exec William Dozier felt compelled to clear the script with the New York Catholic archdiocese and suppressed all hints of the historically accurate account of the torture of the scientist-philosopher. The Church was not the real point of the episode, in any case: the scientist backs down, but the facts remain.

The keynote of *You Are There*'s most intriguing moments was the complexity of culture's relation to politics and personal life. Beethoven thus tries to find himself amid growing deafness, poet John Milton faces Protestant revolutionaries worse in their desire for repression than the royalists had been, and a like-minded Savonarola, the anti-aristocratic Florentine reformer, seeks to sweep away the Medicis and their Renaissance cultural artifacts amidst a populism gone awry.

These were challenging themes. But the triumph was relatively brief; by the spring of 1955, boss Dozier, who appreciated the show's success but wanted to move it to Hollywood production studios where he could bring it under his own immediate guidance, lobbied the network for a new arrangement. Lumet, who considered Hollywood a "company town," made clear his determination to stay and work in New York. According to Russell, Dozier then revealed to the network his supposedly "recent" discovery that the three writers were blacklistees working under fronts.[30] That was the end for Russell at CBS and the preparation for what turned out to be a final season marked by flag-waving and mediocrity. The show lost its audience and died. Lumet, for whom this marked a high point in Golden

Age televised drama, was by no means the only television director who was well connected to the Hollywood Left and destined to make a name in social films.

Robert Aldrich, scion of one of the true patrician Yankee families—his uncle Nelson Aldrich had been the political boss of a staggeringly corrupt Rhode Island and the manipulative "magician" of the Senate during the early years of the century—had started out as a production clerk in Hollywood in 1940. Always leaning leftward, he got his key production experience as associate producer on Polonsky's *Force of Evil*. He worked in a like capacity with Edward Dmytryk, Lewis Milestone, Jean Renoir, William A. Wellman, Joseph Losey and Charles Chaplin before moving to television. Joining his blacklisted friends in Mexico for a spell, he made the Western *Vera Cruz* while guiding the exotic television series, *China Smith* (1952–1955), directing and occasionally also fronting scripts for blacklistees Hugo Butler and Adrian Scott.[31]

Another socially minded director was John Frankenheimer (1930–2002), assistant director of *You Are There* who was promoted to director after Lumet left to take other work. A Korean War pilot with no previous television experience, Frankenheimer somehow managed to get into the creative cockpit right away. Afterwards he directed more than a hundred teleplays and many films, including *Birdman of Alcatraz* (1962), *The Manchurian Candidate* (1962) and *Seven Days in May* (1964).

Another such figure was Arthur Penn (1922-), a son of immigrant Russian Jews who formed a dramatic company during his war service and joined NBC in 1951 as floor manager of the *Colgate Comedy Hour*. He graduated into directing for *Philco Television Playhouse* and *Playhouse 90*, then moved on to Broadway and finally to Hollywood for the anti-western *The Left Handed Gun* (1958), *The Miracle Worker* (1962, about socialist Helen Keller), the noirish *Mickey One* (1965), *Bonnie and Clyde* (1967), Arlo Guthrie's *Alice's Restaurant* (1969) and the staunchly revisionist, pro-Indian *Little Big Man* (1970). Frankenheimer and Penn were personally removed from the 1930s experience, but only by a step. Television connected them until Hollywood was revived. In many respects, these were the artists who fulfilled some of the promise that had been denied to the blacklistees.

It would not be difficult to compile a dossier of the actors who went on from *You Are There* to the films of Aldrich, Frankenheimer and other director/producers on the cutting edge of Hollywood and independent production during the late 1950s to the middle 1960s. Paul Newman, Rod Steiger, Kim Stanley, E.G. Marshall, John Cassavetes, Leslie Nielson and Richard Kiley would figure in this troupe. An expanded list of those actors, editors and writers known to share the program's values would cross generations and genres, including many of the most talented and nearly all the socially concerned—an "underground" that was really overground but barely visible to those unfamiliar with the deeper connections.[32]

TV: PURSUIT OF THE "NORMAL"

What did the writers, directors, actors and others gain in this television interlude, apart from experience and exposure? Arthur Penn once called this period the "nouvelle vague in television" that "flirt[ed] with a new way of using the visual medium."[33] That meant, in part, new methods of editing live and on the run, with the director using the many lenses available on the television camera. It also meant a redefinition of melodrama itself for the largest simultaneous mass audience that any form of entertainment had ever enjoyed. Given the themes of television's Golden Age, it demanded a displacement of the Left's popular narrative—but definitely not an erasure. What became possible, or even mandatory, was a deeply personal way of depicting how characters dealt with social shocks and unpleasant consequences.

Again and again, television drama exploited the melodramatic narrative that begins with an innocent but misunderstood victim pursued by an evildoer, gathers social context through the other characters' gradual awareness of the victim's plight and is resolved by the intervention of someone who rights the wrong and restores social calm. It was a coherent, humane and popular frame.

As scholar Judith E. Smith has suggested, the disrupted family of wartime, most especially the married or marriageable woman who lacks the necessary male, had inevitably been a major source of 1940s drama. So was the ethnic drama of generational Americanization: the older generation craving the comforts of familiar values, while the younger tries to fit itself into the emerging patterns of consumer culture. And so were the assorted confrontations (usually but not always comic) of the "sex war" of women seeking self-definition. All of these subgenres had flavored the domestic radio drama of the forties, and to a lesser extent films as well. It was in this context that television developed a "normalizing" strain, something that evolved during the first years of massive sales of TV sets and followed the logic that the set itself was a prime consumer item of the young family. The newest consumer durable good in the vast privatization of life after the trauma of Depression and war, television entertainment (amid the rather more abstract but still harrowing arms race and Korean conflict) nudged its audience back from social crisis and dislocation toward what President Harding, in a similar moment of American life, had dubbed "normalcy."[34]

What was "normal"? In this view, the habits of the middle class, naturally; the suburbs, increasingly; and, for men, employment in some kind of service sector or corporate structure rather than the blue-collar production of goods. As television producers and directors soon learned, this meant few treatments of racial minorities except in some servile roles, and very few inner-city or slum dramas, or for that matter rural shows (except as locations for one-shot dramas).

There were exceptions to these rules, and in any case there was also still plenty of room in contemporary America for angst and its depiction. In the middle of what W. H. Auden called the "Age of Anxiety," television viewers found escape or solace or a measure of both in dramas about those who could not attain their role expectations or who found their own success ultimately frustrating, even meaningless. The omnipresence of talented Method actors of the Actors Studio provided a pool of virtuoso hand-wringers, and dramatists like David Shaw (close to the Left and brother of 1930s antiwar playwright Irwin Shaw), former longshoreman Robert Alan Aurthur, Reginald Rose and a young Gore Vidal (already famous, but only in some quarters, for his gay fiction) played to these strengths.

Paddy Chayefsky was at all odds the big name, the writer whose career for many observers traced the rise and fall of television drama at large. Like so many others, he was the son of Russian Jewish parents (in this case, a father who had been involved in revolutionary activities of the lower middle class before immigration, then amateur acting). Chayefsky grew up in a mostly Catholic section of the Bronx, which may explain his decision to rename himself from Sidney to the distinctively Irish "Paddy." Like Martin Ritt, he was an athlete, a semi-professional football player, a tough guy who met his show business connections in the Army. These included Garson Kanin, whose brother Michael had co-scripted *Woman of the Year* with Ring Lardner, Jr. Michael Kanin, who had his big theatrical hit in *Born Yesterday*, with Judy Holliday (who had been politically active but managed to play dumb before HUAC, making no personal admissions and giving no names), also produced *A Double Life*, hiring Chayefsky on the spot as an extra to help him along as he struggled to make a writer's living.

Chayefsky circulated through Hollywood's left-wing circles, married a modern dancer and looked on in horror as crowds assaulted Paul Robeson's followers at the famed Peekskill, New York, concert of 1949.[35] Dissatisfied like his soon-to-be friend Walter Bernstein, he returned to New York and the new medium. Chayefsky made his television debut co-scripting a *Danger* episode with exactly the kind of drama that Hollywoodites had for decades been forbidden to make: a sympathetic union drama about an assassinated proletarian leader, co-starring a very "proletarian" Martin Ritt and directed by Lumet.

Chayefsky found himself—or, rather, found his métier—in the ethnic drama and love story. "Holiday Song," broadcast in the *Philco Television Playhouse* series in 1952, won plaudits for its gentle treatment of a rabbi who loses his faith and finds it again. His first solo writing credit, "The Reluctant Citizen," already fit squarely into the "normalization" pattern through the story of a concentration camp survivor who needs to move past the memory of horrors and into the mainstream of American life. These general themes of normalization, so popular in the conformist 1950s, continued to mark his most popular work.

Marty, whose appearance on television in 1955 and remake as a film two years later offered the condensed version of the author's social views, lifted Chayefsky several notches above other talented television dramatists. The story of a Bronx butcher (played by Rod Steiger on TV, and Ernest Borgnine in the film version) and a spinster schoolteacher (played by Nancy Marchand on TV and on film by Betsy Blair, the blacklistee wife of Gene Kelly, escaping her fate only for this one project) offered skeptical critics the supposed proof that television could deliver serious drama.[36] It also demonstrated that the modern-day melodrama of ordinary people seeking personal happiness had captured a moment in cultural history. Indeed, the film version, much softened and sentimentalized, won Academy Awards for the author and veteran television director Delbert Mann. It also won best picture—a first and nearly a last for a television production adapted to film. This success gave Chayefsky a bully pulpit: he was the first television writer to have a collection of teleplays published and, virtually overnight, became a prestigious and much sought-after voice on the state of popular culture. As a visiting scholar from India put it, by virtue of *Marty* and the fame it gave him, Chayefsky was "the most discerning critic and expositor" of the unpopular view that television was already or might become an art rather than entertainment.[37]

Seen from a distance of almost half a century and in the context of the television drama of the time, *Marty* offered a sort of closure on the social drama, which was replaced by romance—but not entirely. While Chayefsky had translated the Jewishness of his earlier work into Italianness, making the character more understandably lower-class as well as more acceptable to some gentile viewers, he had retained the Bronx location and emphasized or actually exaggerated his naturalism, depicting people who at first glance seem less than handsome or interesting.[38]

Ring Lardner, Jr., with his own career hitting bottom, rather harshly described *Marty* and similar quaint exercises in realism as "truth without consequences," the carefully calculated observation of certain kinds of lives (not minorities, notably, but interchangeable white ethnics with the same yearnings), and people who escape their dilemmas altogether too easily by shedding their personal loneliness along with their working-class skins.[39] Other writers close to the pulverized Hollywood Left similarly accused Chayefsky of simple social myopia. At their most favorable, they granted that he had effectively captured alienation as the modern condition in the venue where it counted most.[40]

It is tempting to speculate about what television might have added to the idea of social drama in the United States if the mass audience had come to it even half a dozen years earlier, when many political and social topics were almost as safe to explore as they would become during the 1970s and 1980s. Dramatists and their collaborators had to be cautious about going too far, with the result that self-censorship became something of an art. Walter Bernstein recalls that he was sometimes asked, in all seriousness, if he were the "real" Paddy Chayefsky—using the famous writer as a front but employing greater caution on social issues than he might otherwise.[41]

Casual criticism of self-censorship was a bit unfair because everyone who wrote for television had to contend with advertisers' quest for homogeneity. Indeed, social critics eventually came to suspect that the real narrative of television, the heavy push for normalization, was expressed not in the resolution of anxiety through romance or in upward mobility but in the acts of consumption dramatized in the commercials.

Drama was inevitably the television form that came under the most careful scrutiny from sponsors and blacklist investigators, and nothing illuminated that point quite so well as the career of the writer and network exec whose successes and disappointment spanned the period from the best television drama of the early 1960s to the eventual return of blacklisted writers and actors. Reginald Rose (1920–2002) was a New Yorker who attended the City College of New York so familiar to 1930s radicals and was drafted after he dropped out. He emerged from the Army and took a position as a film studio publicist and advertising executive. He began writing for television successfully in 1951, when he sold a half-hour teleplay, "The Bus To Nowhere," about aliens who come to Earth on a research project to understand why humans are irrational enough to make war against each other. Sidney Lumet agreed to read it, Charles Russell bought it and Rose had a foot in the door.[42]

More than anyone else, Rose owed his subsequent rise after that to producer Felix Jackson (1902–1992; born Felix Joachimson in Hamburg, Germany). A Nazi-era refugee from the Berlin film industry to Hollywood, Jackson had been a quiet part of the antifascist crowd there. He was perhaps best remembered for his co-scripting of *Destry Rides Again* (1939)—along with a future blacklistee (Henry Myers) and a future friendly witness (Gertrude Purcell), as it turned out—and for being quick to abandon declining Hollywood for the new medium. Jackson's feelings ran deeper than the courage of his political convictions, and as he sought to avoid the personal consequences of artistic controversy, he also spent his last productive years attempting to write a biography of his left-wing Berlin friend, lyricist and composer Kurt Weill. But Jackson had enough influence in CBS productions to support Rose's efforts. He encouraged Rose at *Studio One* and ardently defended the most controversial scripts that the young writer offered up.

"Thunder on Sycamore Street," broadcast on *Studio One* in 1954, dealt with white violence against attempts to desegregate Cicero, Illinois. Thanks to sponsor pressure, the African American was transformed into a convict. (Rose remembered angry phone calls coming into the network: "You *Studio One* Commies . . . If you don't like [America], why don't you get out."[43]) "Tragedy in a Temporary Town" was more effectively hard-edged in its actual presentation, broadcast on the *Alcoa Aluminum Hour* in 1956. In a trailer camp of migrant aircraft workers, the employed but restless bunch craves some form of excitement and (falsely) pinpoints the resident Puerto Rican family as unwanted and perhaps dangerous outsiders. The "committee" of whites is plainly a lynch mob. By contrast, the Puerto Ricans are depicted as human, even humane. A false charge of sexual assault is trumped up against one of the Puerto Ricans (it was actually committed by one of the white teens), which leads to a kangaroo court, a savage beating, very nearly a collective murder, and finally a successful counterattack for decency by the morally awakened father of the real culprit.[44]

The potential social crisis was resolved too easily, no doubt. But compared to most television drama, this was hard-hitting stuff. For the director, Sidney Lumet, and the star (as the conscience-ridden father), former Communist actor and reluctant friendly witness Lloyd Bridges, it must have also been terribly familiar, a revisiting of standard left-wing 1930s and 1940s drama. In writing an afterword to a volume of teleplays intended to encourage potential dramatists, Rose commented that he recognized the sharp limitations of the form but insisted that the "compression of time" in the live drama allowed for a kind of "immediacy of . . . construction" that created an excitement unavailable in any other medium.[45]

Twelve Angry Men, Rose's counterpart to *Marty* in the sense that it was remade as a film three years after its 1954 television appearance, was directed (like the teleplay) by Lumet, starred Henry Fonda and was the highest point the writer reached in the 1950s. It was also one of tele-liberalism's grand moments in any era.[46] A wise critic suggested that "by facing up to the facts of modern life, Rose belongs to a pathetically slim minority."[47] But not an entirely unappreciated one; Rose later remembered sitting in the subway sometime in the mid-fifties and hearing someone say, "Hey, I heard there's a Reginald Rose play on tonight." For that writer, for that moment, the experience was almost like legitimate theater. The teleplay would be duly reviewed and the writers would wait up for the morning papers.

Twelve Angry Men, as a courtroom drama, was a perfect vehicle for Henry Fonda's earnest morality, as it was likewise a perfect vehicle for Jack Lemmon in a 1997 remake and for the same reason: one type of actor represents the idealized American type, miseducated by corporate culture but soon deprived of his illusions and eager to do the right thing. One jury member knows that the defendant, a boy on trial for his life, is innocent, but he must convince the vindictive eleven, arguing his case for the heart above the law book.

Rose's still more didactic teleplay, *An American Liberty Almanac* (taken from the title of a book by Chief Justice Oliver Wendell Holmes and narrated through a step-by-step rendition of the Bill of Rights), was too contrived to have the power of *Twelve Angry Men*. But Rose had hit his mark. He wrote an episode of *Studio One* called "The Defender." It was the basis for one of the best liberal dramas ever shown on TV and had the same name, pluralized as *The Defenders* (1961–1965).

The promise of Rose and those around him had been scarcely announced and celebrated when it was cut short by the new economics of television and the old politics of mass entertainment. Television's commercial success, once millions of sets had been sold, rapidly exceeded all expectations. By 1952, its revenues exceeded radio advertising sales, and by 1955 had outstripped the advertising sales of all magazines and newspapers put together (in other words, practically the combined revenues of the printed word). With greater success came new marketing decisions. As the network affiliates expanded rapidly in 1952, the networks assumed a commanding control over local programming. But they also faced the rising strength of major advertisers. At this point networks internalized the censorship that advertising agencies historically had exercised over radio shows.

The anecdotal information on the character of repression is the stuff of legend, especially in the world of the writer. Beginning in 1955, Philco representatives complained that stories of the *Philco Playhouse* were too downbeat and depressed to encourage sales. To remedy the situation, they demanded to see the scripts before production. The company mainly wanted two things: big stars and happy endings. A few years later, in an incident recorded in *The Front*, the American Gas Association insisted that all references to poison gas be dropped in a *Playhouse 90* drama about the Nuremberg Trials. General Electric, with Ronald Reagan as its corporate spokesman, similarly vetoed programs bearing downbeat messages incompatible with the corporation's cheerful motto, "Progress is Our Most Important Product." Miles Laboratories banned all references to headaches and upset stomachs on their shows. In these days, even generic terms that inadvertently suggested the names of rival products were forbidden. Meanwhile, cigarette smoking was both romanticized and normalized as the relaxed and presumably healthful practice of glamorous and wholesome stars.[48] These were only the most egregious examples of a pervasive phenomenon.

To a growing list of sponsors, any psychodrama of the *Marty* type, or controversial themes involving race or war, or for that matter experimental drama of any kind, smelled of abnormality or at least an unnecessary unpleasantness. Anthology series began to be replaced piecemeal, within the same time slots, by spectacles and big-star melodramas (especially Westerns). Both forms were compatible with the new TV production facilities in Hollywood and to filmmaking in general during the later 1950s. Conservative television critics, especially those of the Catholic press, added to the pressure against what one called "Chayefsky . . . misfits who inhabit the lower depths of the Bronx," by pointing out that "Mr. Serling's twisted introverts [and] Mr. Rose's rebellious outcasts" were unwelcome interlopers.[49] Producer David Susskind, who would play such a large role in 1960s teledrama, dolefully told a Federal Communiations Commission panel that 1954 was "the last year of freedom and the last year of intelligent, unfettered expression" in the medium.[50]

Worthington Miner, the creative genius of early dramatic television now on the verge of being fired, complained more precisely that the formulas had become so rigid as to exclude any real creativity on the part of the writer. Story sessions, slicing out one unwanted line of dialogue or image after another, left less and less behind. Soon, ironically, even sponsors began to complain about "sameness"—the sameness that they had compelled with their increasing reliance on program ratings and their own representatives smoothing out any possible source of discomfort. Rod Serling rationalized to investigators from the Fund for the Republic that sponsors ultimately reserved all rights to demand changes and that he, as writer, never challenged those decisions. "I write those things that can be shown," he explained without apparent irony.[51] By 1959, nearly all the drama shows had been cancelled—in effect replaced by Westerns of the most predictable quality.[52] Directors who actually wanted to remain on television but felt they had been forced out included Lumet, Penn and Frankenheimer, all of them soon to be successful in film. Outstanding writers like Reggie Rose, J. P. Miller and Bob Aurthur enjoyed only sporadic success, if any, in Hollywood.[53]

Melancholy light is cast on the entire history of dramatic television by the fate, and the expression of bitter disappointment, of Felix Jackson. In a memo to CBS chiefs in 1956, this thoughtful producer revealed his dismay at the rejection of ambitious teledramas, one "property" after another, by studio executives making the decisions at *Studio One*. Pleading for a serious response to scripts rejected either by the networks or advertising agencies, he claimed that he could compile an entire season of "outstanding shows" which were, "yes, controversial!" but important in themselves and would avoid "the easy way to mediocrity."[54] The answer was not unpredictable. "Extremely limited appeal," came down the judgment of the network execs. "We should," Jackson's boss explained, "do stories that concern the people the American audience can understand . . . we should not choose properties whose sole recommendation is that of character development."[55] That fairly summarized the case and seemingly closed it, one way or another.[56]

There was still another undercurrent that contributed to the decline. The Screen Actors Guild had traditionally used its leverage to fight against the practice of talent agencies also acting as producers on the logical basis that such a conflict of interest would be sure to create a monster that would devour the dream that someday creative control would repose in the hands of the artists, a dream nourished by the Group and its successors. But in 1952, the Screen Actors Guild under Ronald Reagan's presidency made a galaxy-sized exception for MCA. The very next year, MCA's production company hired Reagan to host GE *Theater*, its flagship program, giving him the exposure and the corporate financial backing he needed to launch a major political career.

Whether or not these connections amounted to a bribe of history-changing proportions remains to be seen.[57] But the result of the deal in centralizing production companies was decisive. Within a decade, MCA produced 60 percent of all prime-time television shows in the United States. A Justice Department hearing in 1962 into this extraordinary development, if it had bothered to ask Reagan the right questions, might possibly have truncated his political career. But lawmakers instead lobbed their largely harmless questions at MCA, which by this time was happy enough to abandon the talent agency business for the richer rewards of production. For decades, actors struggled to get out from under the costly agreements that Reagan had made for them. Potential strikes over a variety of issues continued to be threatened by the flat refusal of leaders of the International Alliance of Theatrical Stage Employees (IATSE) to honor picket lines—just as in the early Cold War years IATSE, supported by the police and professional goons, had broken the back of aggressive Hollywood unionism.

The truth is, the Cold War in Hollywood never ended; the final collapse of communism hardly registered a blip there. The familiar, continuing tensions and outbursts between business, art and labor solidarity continued as they always had, as though the repression of McCarthyism had really been little more than a political dumbshow, regardless of whether its result—the ruination for a time of the most popular of popular arts—had been intended or not.[58]

BEYOND DISAPPOINTMENT

The ubiquitous predictions of television's downfall into total, irredeemable mediocrity were nevertheless premature. The blacklist on the small screen had subsided sufficiently by the end of the 1950s that at least a few of the most talented writers (although not, to be sure, members of the Hollywood Ten) had begun to sneak back in with their credits properly listed. In 1958, a special production of *Wonderful Town* (the original 1940s stage version of *My Sister Eileen*, which had seen two film versions by this time) based on *The New Yorker* short stories of then-Communist Ruth McKenney, appeared on television with the proper identification of playwrights Edward Chodorov (a blacklistee) and his collaborator of decades, Joseph Fields.[59] The next year, a special educational television production with limited outlets saw *The World of Sholem Aleichem* accurately credited to

Arnold Perl. It was no left-wing theatrical renaissance, but it was a promising rip in the cultural Iron Curtain.

One reason for the change could be found in a few of the most influential producers. David Susskind (1920–1987) offers the outstanding example. A Harvard-educated press agent for Warner Brothers and MCA with no particular political connections but a personal background in the progressive mood of the later 1930s and 1940s, Susskind broke off from MCA to found Talent Associates in 1948, then moved his operation from Broadway to television and emerged as a producer for an assortment of dramatic anthologies.[60] Abrasive, domineering and often treating the writing or acting talent as a mere extension of his own personality, Susskind nevertheless had the connections and charisma to become a force in the industry. He quietly made himself known early within the cloistered blacklist circles as a man eager to rehabilitate victims, albeit mainly in order to get good work at low prices and never without assuring himself a degree of security against the possibility for backlash.

It was Susskind who produced the landmark series *Justice* (1954–1956), which can be described as the fullest prototype for *The Defenders*. The pilot, broadcast in April of 1953, was actually produced by *The Defenders'* later producer Herb Brodkin. The story was about a wife seeking help for her husband when he is blackmailed. The wife was played by actress Lee Grant, already on the Hollywood blacklist herself for refusing to name her husband and about to join the television list, too.

Justice's liberal story lines, purportedly drawn from the files of the National Legal Aid Society and almost certainly adapted in part by blacklistees who were never credited, were nonetheless also often properly credited to a Marxist and former Communist who had slipped under the radar, Alfred Brenner (1920-). A war veteran and former *New Masses* contributor, he had close personal contacts with the *You Are There* writers, Arnold Manoff in particular, and through Manoff, he found his way to Susskind. Brenner's television career quickly took off and included episodes of the best contemporary (and mostly live) television: *Danger*, *Suspense*, *Armstrong Circle Theater*, *Philco Playhouse*, *Studio One*, *US Steel Hour*, *Matinee Theater*, *Kraft Theater* and the *Alcoa/Goodyear Theater*, for which he wrote an Emmy-winning script in 1959, with Mickey Rooney as a handicapped figure striving for dignity.

Justice was an almost perfect series for the novice television writer. The 28-minute slot discouraged complexity, but the live performances had the spontaneity and more limited censorship of shows of that period, with social themes of criminals as victims that were a far cry from the law-and-order melodramas of *Dragnet*. It predicted, in some important ways, the ambience of *Naked City* (1958–1963) and *East Side/West Side* (1963–1964). Like these later shows, it opened up a Manhattan in which tragedy, including the self-inflicted tragedy of the casual lawbreaker destined for a life of punishment, was an everyday counterpoint to poverty. It also served as a natural outlet for Method and its descendants.

Justice was also a veritable godsend for many young avant-garde actors. Rod Steiger later recalled making his living on the show, changing roles from week to week. Virtual repertory casting in the opening season, in the spring of 1954, allowed plenty of room for youngsters. Beginning in the fall of the same year, Gary Merrill became the Legal Aid attorney and thus a series regular, succeeded in the final season by William Prince. Around them ranged the guest stars. No better formula was ever devised to show the faces of deprivation, and perhaps no series so nearly approached the prestige of the teledramas of the day in exploring these themes.[61]

Aesthetically, Susskind was already close to peaking with A Man Is Ten Feet Tall (aka Edge of the City, 1957), a 90-minute drama co-starring Sidney Poitier as a respectable longshoreman and family man who is drawn into comradeship with a white Army deserter, both of them pushed to the edge by the mob until they unite to save themselves (and thereby, Poitier's striving family as well). By turning the blue-collar framework of On the Waterfront and its sub-theme of the rat into a saga of racial trust—and making the young actor Poitier the most admirable figure— playwright Robert Alan Aurthur had opened a set of questions most Americans were not yet prepared to tackle, but that liberal New Yorkers were proud to raise as public issues. Filmed much like a documentary in black and white, A Man was intense but subtle. Pleased at its success, Susskind hired Martin Ritt to direct the retitled film version, and it was there that an important cinematic career began.[62]

A few years later, Susskind followed up this interracial story with another, still more remarkable play, A Raisin in the Sun, by the Communist (and lesbian) African American playwright Lorraine Hansberry. It was the first black-written drama and also the first with a leading black (nonmusical) cast to be a big hit on Broadway. Indeed, it was the 1959–1960 season's biggest hit, one strong clue to the distance remaining from Broadway to middle America. In 1961, Susskind produced the film version, directed by Daniel Petrie (a future Directors Guild officer close to several blacklistees), precisely as if shot for a television camera in a single set. Performances by Poitier as the frustrated blue-collar worker, Ruby Dee (his wife), Diana Sands (her sister) and Claudia McNeill as her mother offered a more truthful view of ordinary black life than had ever been seen by an American mass audience.

Susskind also produced several more television series, the most successful of them Alice (from the feminist film that he also produced, Alice Doesn't Live Here Anymore), one of the very few shows, to that late point in television history, about the workplace life of a single mother. Arguably the new medium's most famous liberal until Norman Lear, and one of the "beautiful people" who made a mark on television as they likely would have on theater or film in an earlier part of the century, Susskind lived his milieu and in a sense outlived it, still working up to the moment when Ronald Reagan took office, when the liberal dreams of the 1950s were more or less permanently exhausted. But he had helped make the rehabilitation of the Left possible.

This was no small thing. An astute commentator of the middle1960s took a far more positive view of television drama than the critics, writers, directors and producers who lamented the censorship and loss of serious programming a few years earlier. If legitimate theater had been so reduced financially (in part thanks to the advance of television) that it offered mainly entertainment without a message, television had proven itself an "electronic classroom." If viewed as a universal medium with overtones of social uplift (in contrast to the movies, whose early decades had been most disrespectable), loaded with highly paid but also guilt-ridden professionals eager to rationalize their commercial success with dollops of "meaning," it had also abandoned most of the serious purpose it had inherited from theater and replaced it with the deeply didactic tradition of the sentimental novel.[63]

The most compelling evidence was not the theater of the air, however, but the social drama series that were shortly to follow. Theater, if prestigious, had never been the locus of most dramatic television. The series, an outgrowth of network radio with its crime and comedy shows (usually dominated by a single personality), had the necessary numbers of shows and viewers. If the single most important element of plot was what television writers later called "character maintenance," or, the need to keep the stars in character, the breadth of programming and the durability of stars also allowed a degree of latitude.

A few stars and their handlers widened that narrow degree by a means familiar to a Hollywood generation that aspired to independent production, free of the moguls' commanding presence. Following months of frustration at not being able to engage a production company for their new show, Desi Arnaz and Lucille Ball established their own, Desilu, and enforced the demand that their show be produced close to their home in Los Angeles. Others followed hesitantly, uncertain about the new medium, the complex relations with the networks (and advertisers) and the difficulty, until well into the sixties, of persuading local stations to show network offerings.

Several of the most important production companies bore the liberal stamp of 1940s Hollywood veterans, enabling left-wingers to return (under the cover of fronts or assumed names) to paying work. Four Star Productions came down to Dick Powell and Ida Lupino, who even more than her progressive husband

Howard Duff had worked often and amiably with left-wingers throughout her career.[64] Teaming up with Dick Powell, Charles Boyer and David Niven, Lupino successfully produced several shows, including the anthology *Four Star Playhouse*. Danny Thomas formed T&L Productions in 1961 with Sheldon Leonard, packaging several of the hottest and most sentimental shows. Within this latter entity, a handful of blacklistees found themselves working again, if not usually with any overt political-social effect. Tandem Productions, founded by Norman Lear and Bud Yorkin in 1959, did a decade of mildly escapist films before becoming for a few years the most successful unit in the history of television bearing social themes at the forefront. Bing Crosby Productions launched *Ben Casey, Breaking Point* and *Hogan's Heroes* in the sixties, all of them employing leftist and/or black-listed talent. And so on.

In effect, these were mini-studios with unique (or at least differing) tastes and demographic expectations. Joined early on by former studio giant Warner Brothers (now practically an ABC subsidiary, unless the ABC of the later 1950s could be called a Warner subsidiary) with its own package of detectives and Westerns, the independents and semi-independents opened up some new space. To survive, independent productions required continuing access to large amounts of capital and almost uninterrupted success. But they also offered hope for the future as well as reminiscences for old-timers of what Hollywood's banished artists strove to achieve so long before.

CHAPTER TWO

ART OF THE TELEVISION SERIES

WHEN THE NEW SCREEN ACTORS GUILD PRESIDENT (and volunteer FBI agent "T-10") was asked in 1949 whether his organization would seek to represent actors in the new medium, the future president of a considerably larger and different entity recalled answering simply, "The plain truth was and is that television is . . . simply a new kind of theater."[1] It was a disarming thought, articulated mainly to fend off challenges to his leadership from a suspiciously radical effort to bring actors of the large and small screens together into one big union. But Ronald Reagan's observation also suggested what actors in television series of every type often came to suspect from their own perspective from within the creative process. Like their fellow actors on the one-hour dramatic anthologies, they stood on the proscenium stage facing lights (and cameras) and sometimes even a live audience. For a variety of reasons it was for them, as well as for writers, particularly in those first years of the television craze, very unlike Hollywood film work. Sometimes it was more like radio.

One of the most important developments could be found in the TV family drama. Nothing so epitomized 1950s culture and the special role that television seemed destined to play in American life, literally entering the living room. The concept of family TV viewing, which cut dramatically into the audience for the family film, made perfect marketing sense for the accompanying advertising of consumer products and the ethos that the agencies assiduously developed. Not only would the sexuality hinted at ever more strongly in films be ruled out here (aside from titillating jests on late-night television about the breast size of certain celebrities), but the social anxiety so visible on the dramatic anthologies would be virtually banned from the rest of the entertainment schedule.

This was neither the result of conspiracy nor a natural development, but the consequence of a process illustrated most perfectly by the expunging of a certain crucial question mark. *Father Knows Best* had begun in planning as *Father Knows Best?*, originally a sort of updated *Life With Father* (a Broadway hit coincidentally adapted with great success for film in 1945 by future blacklist victim Donald Ogden Stewart), with subtle subversion gently undercutting the patriarchal authority and creating the fun of the show. Casting was perfect for this kind of gentle satire. Popular film actor Robert Young had been one of the ardent supporters of the anti-blacklist Committee for the First Amendment, and back in the days before the U.S. entry into World War II he had courageously supported the isolationist position. He had also effectively played dark and beaten-down characters in his more recent films. Playing opposite him in the new series was Hollywood veteran Jane Wyatt. She had flown to Washington in 1947 to support the subpoenaed writers, flatly refused to testify against fellow unionists and made the transition to television largely because she had been in effect banned from films. Not that she was part of the Left but, like Young, she considered herself a determined civil libertarian. The two were ideally suited to play the strong mother and the limpid father.

The question mark was stripped off and the irony or ambiguity eradicated, as the two of them ruefully recalled to interviewers decades later, because the all-powerful ad agencies had demanded it. Here, at least, father *did* always know best; mother had no thought of a career or even talents outside mothering; and son and daughters were raised to appreciate these rigidly distinct gender roles, with real life (such as the presence and poverty of minority races) scarcely ever troubling mythical Springfield.[2] The show was one of the first ever to end at the stars' insistence while still near the top of the charts. Two of the three young actors developed real-life psychological problems, and only Young opted to go on playing similar roles in future series.

The Donna Reed Show (1958–1966), often regarded as ABC's knock-off of *Father Knows Best*, was just slightly more tilted in the direction of "Mother Knows Best." Her husband (played by the distinguished stage actor, Carl Betz) was the busy pediatrician in their similarly small and homogenous town, while she raised the kids. The structure of the plots so narrowed the focus of drama that no dissonant note (even something so obvious and current as rock music, or teen wall photos of rock stars) could be introduced from the society outside for fear of damaging the symmetries of domestic life.[3] Did it matter that left-wingers Alfred Lewis Levitt and his wife Helen Slote Levitt were writing for the show under the names of Tom and Helen August? Probably not much, if at all: formula refused to yield.[4]

By this time, the combination of psychoanalytic themes and the relaxing of censorship in popular films prompted an abasement of mothers (as in *Rebel With-*

out a Cause), making "inadequate" women the real cause of much emotional turmoil. But films were not television. Not only did censorship prohibit issues like teen pregnancy, alcohol abuse and family violence, but the dramatic structure of the 24-minute drama—interrupted several times for commercials—demanded a drastic simplification of plot and characterization.[5] Father *had* to know best or chaos loomed.

Toward the end of the 1950s, as the depiction of teenage troubles in films continued to grow more intense and elaborate, it was no surprise to insiders that *Hatful of Rain* (1957), about youthful heroin addiction, and *Blue Denim* (1959), about teenage pregnancy, brought back some blacklistees and their allies. The first was directed by Fred Zinnemann, coscripted by Carl Foreman and Alfred Hayes, while the second co-starred Marsha Hunt and was co-scripted and directed by longtime anti-blacklist Hollywood liberal, Philip Dunne.[6] Golden Age television drama about intergenerational conflict did not usually go this far.

By the 1960s, television entertainments with no pretensions to dramatic seriousness could afford to go a good bit further and for a good market reason: the audience of new consumers, the largest generation in history, voted with their channel-changers. Hints at last emerged that the established narrative of a happy, suburban, middle-class America, based in turn on a handful of obligatory historical myths (such as the heroic version of the "Winning of the West"), was far from the whole story and might even be the wrong story. When Warner Brothers' shows offered the teenage public the cynical cowboy and the swinging detective, tales of the fractious post-nuclear family could not be far behind. The Hollywood transition into television production may have closed the door on the television of live theater, always dominated by New Yorkers in any case, but it opened others, like those to M*A*S*H, *Quincy, M.E.*, *Good Times* and *One Day At a Time*.

In warm-and-fuzzy liberal TV views of changing American life, as scholar David Marc has observed, the past is often acknowledged to have been harsh, if the rough remnants of racial and ethnic exclusion (in later decades, also sexism and homophobia) are explained as being sloughed off by a gradual democratization.[7] Tolerance is taught through gags (in M*A*S*H, singularly, mixed with images of death), a more effective or at least less uncomfortable technique than the older method of instruction through melodrama.

It comes as no surprise that the left-wing writers capable of transforming the sitcom into something socially critical found a natural home here; it would be too much to say, of course, that they had any decisive influence. But without doubt, the generation of producers and writers who were just a few years younger—successors to the conscience liberals of 1950s and 1960s television drama—learned crucial lessons from the old-timers, shifting gears as needed to remarket liberal values associated with the Popular Front and sometimes improving upon them.

If any gains for humane television are inevitably temporary, regression to plots of macho heroes (or the laugh-tracked witless) and bizarro villains, which form a large part of the never-ending succession of mediocre shows, audiences could still often be impressed, when given the chance, by interesting plots and complex and convincing characters. As "New York" would always suggest the possible location of interesting oddballs and sophisticates as well as the worthy poor and somewhat existential cops, the contemplation of life's ironies and injustices between jokes and gunplay proved that Method acting could survive even the demands of the sponsors.

ACTION DRAMA

For years, Hollywood painted the new medium as an enemy, but could hardly ignore the economics of the growing demand for narrative product to fill the airwaves—nor stand by idly as syndicators and small production companies rushed in to do the job. The film studios grudgingly saw the error of their ways, thanks in part to an overwhelming public response to the broadcasting of film classics (notably The Wizard of Oz) and a corresponding decline of foot traffic to the theaters. Television sales, along with foreign sales, were keeping major studios out of the red by the end of the 1950s.[8] Warner Brothers, known best within the industry during the heroic 1930s and 1940s for the social-action film that combined liberal and occasionally downright socialistic sentiments with melodrama and action, proved the most nimble studio. The presiding genius of this outcome happened to be a friendly witness, Roy Huggins.

Huggins (1914–2002) was the scion of an Irish-American Oregon family that had fallen on hard times during the Depression and moved to southern California. He barely graduated from high school. But after a start at a community college he managed to transfer to UCLA. There, at the end of the 1930s, Huggins found himself, to his great surprise, spokesman for the causes of the (mostly Jewish) Young Communist League. Joining and then abandoning the party shortly after the Hitler–Stalin Pact, he took a wartime job in the administration of a government personnel office. Huggins suddenly had a lot of time on his hands, and he spent much of it writing mystery stories with an anti-capitalist twist, managing even to place several of them with the Saturday Evening Post. Meanwhile, he briefly rejoined the Communist Party for what he later described as intellectual reasons: then and for the rest of his life, he accepted a Marxist economic analysis of society, whatever his political views.[9]

Personally indifferent to screenwriting but attracted by the prospect of making real money, Huggins was named as a Communist and became a friendly witness just as he'd snared his first assignments. He rationalized his testimony, over the years, with the insistence that world communism had grown dangerous, and besides, having a wife and mother to support, he had had no other choice. Signed as a writer, he quickly stepped up to directing and producing. Warners' new television unit, formed with a historic agreement to boost the fortunes of the badly slumping ABC network, made him a producer with considerable freedom of action.[10]

Cheyenne (1955–1963), originating from a rotating series, including several of the studio's films made in the previous decade (*Kings Row* and *Casablanca*) under the umbrella title *Warner Brothers Presents,* was the only one to survive the first season. Thereafter alternating with various other shows, *Cheyenne* went over like gangbusters. It was only the fourth ABC series ever to reach the top twenty in the Nielsens. The half-Indian, half-Anglo protagonist played by Clint Walker, a frontier scout, was transformed into a James Dean (or better, Marlon Brando) figure who could not bring himself to settle down. Drifting from town to town, gunfight to gunfight, woman to woman, he helped those in need and collected just enough payment (when he got any) to move on again. In contrast to the cop-like figures of most television westerns, *Cheyenne* was already close to the "anti-western" that brought left-wing writers and directors back into mainstream film production a few years later. Although mostly downplaying the racial implications, the show hinted at the mood of America's real underdogs. It was, Huggins later insisted, aimed at the young and alienated viewer.

A near-instant cult favorite on college campuses of the silent (or silenced) generation, *Cheyenne* established the Huggins brand. Building on his success and pushing the same elements of characterization a bit harder, Huggins created *Maverick* (1957–1962) largely on the basis of a dramatic premise matched to a young actor he had met in an L.A. bar: James Garner. Huggins sized up the politically cynical Korean War vet (and swimsuit model) as the perfect antihero and trained him in the dramatic anthology *Conflict* (1956–1957) before establishing him as the unforgettable Bret Maverick. This character would do anything to avoid a gun- or fist-fight, dressed like a dandy among otherwise badly tailored cowpokes, cheated at cards and generally acted the confidence man regarded in the usual lore of the Old West as a sneak and a coward.

"In the traditional western story," Huggins directed his writers, "the situation is always serious but never hopeless," while in a *Maverick* plot, "the situation is always hopeless but never serious."[11] Late in life, he insisted that this twist was a projection of his Marxist view that the social system needed to be replaced, not merely fixed. Stuck in a flawed world, Garner played the ironic "disorganization man" (a play upon William Whyte's *The Organization Man,* about the corporate personality) in a morally ambiguous world in which even the bad guys were not necessarily all that bad. There had certainly been anti-westerns before in Hollywood, some of

the best of them written from the Left. But no one working the television series options had borrowed so playfully or so intelligently from literary sources, even breaking the narrative rules of the western by introducing satire and parody—sometimes
pointedly directed at competitors like *Gunsmoke*—in a TV genre heretofore immune to humor.[12] The sixth-highest rated show—quite an accomplishment for
ABC, with far fewer station affiliates than its rivals—*Maverick* was also an Emmy
winner in 1959.

The hottest producer in television by this time, Huggins may actually have
preserved ABC from the fate of the defunct Dumont network by aiming again and
again at the younger viewer. *77 Sunset Strip* (1958–1964), its pilot based upon
 Huggins' 1949 novel, *Lovely Lady, Pity Me*, could be described as the original
"hip" show about a detective agency that was also the lifestyle headquarters of
those who solve crimes while surrounding themselves with beautiful dames, never
losing their cool or spilling their martinis. *Strip*'s resident hipster, a parking lot attendant whose prototype was based on a real-life Sunset Strip pimp Huggins had
observed, attracted attention from women viewers just by running his comb
through his hair (thus the 1959 top ten hit song, with vocal by non-singer and almost non-actor Edd Byrnes, "Kookie, Kookie, Lend Me Your Comb"). Even the
show's jazzy theme song, with finger-snapping in the background, had the lilt of
life on the fringe. Huggins left the show and Warners when the production company refused to cut him in on the profits, but *Sunset Strip* was always his creation.

 Huggins, as David Marc and Robert J. Thompson observe, thus proved himself repeatedly able "to adapt and synthesize ideas across medium, genre and time,
and yet somehow invest these recombinations with a fresh inventiveness" that depended more on his ideas than on formula or stars.[13] He had another side as unknown to the public as his tenacious socialist sentiment. Feeling guilty for his
friendly testimony, he made a small point of arranging jobs for a handful of blacklist victims and those on the graylist, most often for lesser shows like *Surfside Six*
(1960–1962), a *77 Sunset Strip* clone at water's edge in Miami Beach. With a great
deal more sex, violence and brooding, *Surfside Six* could be described as the prototype for *Miami Vice*, although these private detectives working out of their house-
boat had no official status or snazzy outfits. Nor did the series episodes written by
Hollywood Ten writer-producer Adrian Scott and his wife Joan Scott (whose
pseudonym was "Joan Court") offer anything more unusual than a "girl detective"
solving Miami crimes while entangling herself in trouble.[14]

But the writing pair got work on several of Huggins' projects. So did Leo
Penn, a suspect director remembered best as actor Sean Penn's father, and likewise
the talented veteran director Vincent Sherman, unnamed but unwilling to sell
out old friends. So did Millard Lampell, one of the original Almanac folksingers of
the 1940s. A handful of independent producers (in film more than television),

were happy to exploit the talent of blacklistees at bargain rates; Huggins had no compelling reason to do so, but good reason to make up, in small ways, for what he considered his participation in a great wrong.

Easily the strangest of Huggins' projects, in several ways, was *The Fugitive* (1963–1967), usually assumed to be based on the well-known case of physician Sam Sheppard, who had been accused of murdering his wife. Huggins is acknowledged as the initial creative force, though he declined to continue with the series after it was launched. His account of how he came up with the idea has some interesting inconsistencies. After breaking with Warners and moving briefly to Twentieth Century-Fox, Huggins recalled, he sold ABC on a dramatic concept that he claimed to have adapted from *Les Misérables*. Looking back at the story of a hunted man on the run week after week, Huggins admitted that the germ of the plot might not have been either a real-life murder case or nineteenth-century novel but rather the fate of his former comrades a decade earlier, the blacklistees dodging the authorities in general and the FBI in particular while former comrade Huggins consolidated his career.[15] It was an odd thought, but the idea of the moral figure relentlessly pursued made for a good TV hook, repeated with some success (and detectable leftish content) in *The Incredible Hulk* (1978–1982), *Beauty and the Beast* (1987–1990) and well beyond. Meanwhile, Huggins went to work at Universal and lasted 17 years, producing several unusual series, notably *Alias Smith and Jones* (1971–1973), his last comic western.

The very best and most lastingly popular of Huggins' work happened to be his most political (or antipolitical) and his last serious effort: *The Rockford Files* (1974–1980). It was a modern and urban version of *Maverick*, with the James Garner character virtually intact. Huggins, who lasted through the first season this time, proposed the series when Garner asked him for an opportunity to get back into television. A mostly light-hearted take on the life and hard times of a habitually broke private eye, Jim Rockford—Korean vet, bachelor and wary social observer—lives in a rundown trailer on a Malibu beach. While solving cases, or sometimes not solving them, he spends serious time with his intimates: an aging father, delightfully played by character actor Noah Beery as a retired truck driver and ardent union man; a call girl played by the sexy and politically progressive veteran of *West Side Story* (as well as the medium's most prominent Latina), Rita Moreno, who was always in trouble; a neurotic and habitually disloyal street hustler played zestfully by Stuart Margolin. The only insider among these outsiders, the Los Angeles Police Department sergeant played by Joe Santos, often found himself in trouble with the higher-ups for supplying information to Garner on cases that had been written off as hopeless. Like *77 Sunset Strip*, *Rockford* offered viewers images of deepest and funkiest L.A. and the hills beyond, car chases and all.[16]

Stephen J. Cannell, a protégé of Huggins destined for his own auteur status in television, took over the show after the first season. Still, Huggins' stamp remained, above all in the quality of the characterizations and the satirical bent of most of the plots, which were regularly directed at police heavy-handedness and occasionally at CIA misadventures. According to many critics and millions of viewers, *The Rockford Files* remains the best private-detective show in the history of the medium.[17]

Decades before *Rockford Files*, television had already seen a certain degree of noir and considerable irony. *China Smith* (1952–1955) was the brainchild of the Left's intimate ally, Robert Aldrich. It starred Dan Duryea as a sleazy but sentimental con man and occasional private eye working out of a bar in Singapore, struggling to defeat but also to protect the scheming "Empress," a ruthless dame in the Dragon Lady mold played by Myrna Dell. The first 26 shows (of 52) were actually shot in Mexico, where the director was making low-budget films, and written in substantial part by Hollywood exile Hugo Butler. Aldrich was also directing noirish episodes of *Four Star Playhouse*, starring Dick Powell, with the graylisted Howard Duff as a moody gambler.[18] If television soon finished off B-film noir, as some critics have claimed, the likely culprit was *Peter Gunn* (1958–1961).The most stylish of the TV detective dramas, featuring a jazz score, it co-starred blacklistee Herschel Bernardi.

Meanwhile, Four Star Productions had also hired one of the Hollywood Left's self-conscious successors, Albert Ruben, to begin to capitalize on the gap in programming that Huggins had exposed with his unconventional characters. After working as script editor with several of the most talented of the blacklisted writers on *The Adventures of Robin Hood*, Ruben headed back to California, and there he connected with Adrian Scott, who mentored him personally and politically. Ruben got on as story editor with *Richard Diamond, Private Detective* (1957–1960).[19]

It was no great drama. But *Richard Diamond* became a crucial stepping-stone for Ruben to *Have Gun Will Travel* (1957–1963), an entirely different story. The continuing tale of "Paladin," the man in black with a mission, earned billing as the first "mature" western, depending less on shootouts than on ethical and psychological conflicts. It became, Ruben later observed, "the closest that westerns got to meeting the requirements of the Sixties," meaning it stretched the genre to its limits, although a good case could be made for *Maverick* having reached the same edge of the envelope a year or two earlier. Paladin, played by veteran character actor Richard Boone, was a conscious anachronism, a knight errant with a taste for fine clothes and fine literature; but he also relished quests into the dusty towns and lonely homesteads of the West to rescue some endangered or only slightly tarnished innocent who was about to be framed, trampled or murdered by local bullies. Often, pointedly, the villains were power-brokers like the local banker, merchant or lawyer. Paladin bested them with as little bloodshed as possible, preferring to shame them into recognizing and acknowledging the evil of their deeds. Hired on in the show's third season, Ruben had no chance to make changes in this underlying narrative. But he could manage plots that confounded the usual sense of television. An especially bold episode of Have Gun Will Travel written by Ruben found Alfred Nobel, the Swedish inventor of dynamite, traveling in the West and, at the end of the episode, witnessing an explosion that takes the unmistakable shape of a mushroom cloud. Only Twilight Zone could have done better.

Another remarkable episode of Have Gun Will Travel, written by Joan Scott, keys on the character of a bold lady bandit whom Paladin captures to protect her from bounty-hunters. At one point, as they lie side by side, her pants off under the covers so that she will not escape, she explains that she was miserably exploited as a child and refused to become an exploited wife, choosing instead the pistol as gender equalizer. She must go to jail for her crime, the story acknowledges, but smitten as much by her spunk as her good looks, Paladin is tempted to cross the border with her into a life different from the one he had lived or had ever intended to. No contemporary television western was going to go this far in unleashing spirited women.[20]

Have Gun Will Travel gave opportunities not only to radicals but to promising new writers like Gene Roddenberry as well.[21] Destined for fame as the creator of Star Trek, the former airline pilot moved on to write for Naked City (1958–1963), a show that captured lasting attention from scholars for one chief reason: location. In many ways a standard policier not so different from others of the time, it was still the child of 1950s grand teledrama. It kept Manhattan as its vast set after a majority of other shows had left and went the survivors one better. Each episode opened with the proud declaration that the drama had been shot in the naked city itself, and the sweep of the music—Billy May's theme of the metropolis awakening at dawn—along with the narrator's voice evoked the sense of a 1930s or 1940s dramatic style otherwise vanishing along with the manufacturing base of the city.[22]

Naked City really was its buildings and bridges as much as its inhabitants, and in that sense very much the offspring of the 1948 film of the same title directed by Jules Dassin. Here, cops lacked not only the poise of their counterparts on the Untouchables but also their sense of being the avengers of civic justice. "Gentle creatures," these police seemed "almost disabled by pity" and possessed an "infinite capacity for being pained" as witnesses to humanity's "folly and anguish." The crimes, ordered by bosses, were likely to be performed by desperate men and women in the city's darkest corners; sinning, they mainly brought destruction upon themselves.[23] Contrary to the new serial standard of radio and television drama that the star must live on, here life itself could also be fleeting, even for the empowered. The show's first police commander, played by John McIntire, was killed off in a car crash, precursor to the better-remembered exit of actor McLean Stevenson (but off camera) on M*A*S*H in 1975, often mistakenly considered a daring first on television.

To play those marginal characters and bystanders, all victims whether cops or petty crooks, the show grabbed the talent at hand. As casting director Marion Dougherty recalled, Naked City was "the big window on New York talent that people from the West Coast watched."[24] The program was a showcase for emerging talent, including Robert Alda, Martin Sheen, Robert Duvall, Dustin Hoffman, Geraldine Brooks, Dennis Hopper, Carroll O'Connor, Gene Hackman, William Shatner, Ed Asner and Geraldine Fitzgerald, and among the older Hollywood actors Mary Astor, Sylvia Sidney and Jack Gilford, among the first television or film work for several of these returning blacklistees.

Fifties drama veteran and ardent liberal Stirling Silliphant (1918–1996) wrote most of the early Naked City shows. He left to work on Route 66 but kept a hand in as an executive story editor. Blacklistees Arnold Manoff and Ben Maddow, joined by unblacklisted Marxist Albert Brenner, filled the gap. No television drama, however celebrated, could or perhaps ever would exceed this wealth of talent. Indeed, for actors like Jack Klugman, a veteran of Lee Strasberg's personal tutoring, Naked City was a logical stop in a career that spanned the earliest television programming (from the lowly Captain Video to the prestigious Studio One) to the later era of teledrama series such as Quincy, his own unique melodramatic vehicle.[25]

Naked City proved revolutionary in yet one more way that was inspired by the original Dassin film. High-quality cinematography was virtually unknown in 1950s television network productions, but editing in the style of the quasi-documentary film had been practiced within the news divisions (where, not surprisingly, CBS had placed You Are There) in such prestige venues as the original BBC-style Omnibus (1953–1957) on Sunday afternoons. The camera crews would shoot hours of some scene, whether public event or nature setting, and then throw the mess at the editor, who was responsible for turning it into a watchable narrative. Much the same process happened in contemporary filmmaking, of course, but without the luxury of long hours of broadcasting to fill or the sense of discovery at working in a new medium. Early television was thus as much a rediscovery of the film art as it was of theater.

The underpaid and nearly thankless art of editing moving images went back to the dawn of cinema and film. As in theater, if to a lesser degree, the Russians had a lasting influence, because most of the creative American documentarians of the 1930s, including Joris Ivens, Paul Strand, Irving Lerner and future blacklistees

Leo Hurwitz and Ben Maddow, were heavily influenced from the Left. By the very nature of the enterprise—its art, politics and budget—to document was to edit. None of these men, with the partial exception of Maddow, enjoyed any notable success in Hollywood, although Lerner and Maddow worked in television.

The documentarian giants and their protégés, along with many left-wing (and non-left-wing) Hollywoodites, had patriotically rushed into war work, where they received considerable government backing, public approval and almost compulsory viewing from members of the armed services and even paying audiences, who were presented with government propaganda between features. A portion of left-wingers, audience as much as filmmakers, dreamed of an independent documentary cinema coming out of the war, and a few specialty theaters in big cities had a certain success with this kind of programming. Then came the postwar downturn in audience and politics.

But early television, the noted film and TV editor Ralph Rosenblum (1925–1995) has recalled, offered a place to use talent acquired directly and indirectly from the masters of the 1930s and 1940s. Growing up in Bensonhurst with left-wing relatives close at hand, trained in editing by Ivens assistant Helen Dongen, Rosenblum worked in 1950s television across the board, from *Omnibus* to *Guy Lombardo*. In 1959, he met Sidney Lumet and cut his first art film, *The Pawnbroker* (1964), with the comradely collaboration of the director, which he considered a rare experience. Lumet himself had by that time become the most important television director to make the leap not merely to film but to the circle of serious filmmakers. Others, including some of the most important liberal film directors of the 1960s through the 1980s, followed him out of the ranks of television workers. A sizeable list of blacklisted actors also found their way into jobs behind the camera as directors in TV during this period, including George Tyne, Joshua Shelley, Jeff Corey, Leo Penn and Sam Wanamaker.

Rosenblum's own successive editing projects included *A Thousand Clowns*, *The Producers*, *Goodbye Columbus*, *Bananas*, *Sleeper* and *Annie Hall* (for the last of which Rosenblum got a British Academy Award). These films epitomized the sixties cinematic "new look" of recombining the visual document and the film narrative, utilizing familiar themes with a more or less unmistakable leaning toward rebellion in both cinema art and politics.

Rosenblum didn't do any cutting for *Naked City*. But a counterpart unheralded television technician and highly skilled editor actually provided key action scenes for that show. The stage-trained son of a concert mandolin player, an assistant cutter at Warners in the 1930s who organized the studio's montage department (and designed the famous montage that opens *Casablanca*), this Hollywood veteran found himself working as a director in television 20 years later. With the reputation of driving actors to distraction with his insistence on including passersby (and on occasion himself) in nearly every scene, he contributed a documentary ambience to the video drama. That ex-cutter was Don Siegel.

SOCIAL-PROBLEM DRAMA

One of the most disconcerting and, for network and advertising executives, most discomfiting developments in television history was the declaration in 1961 by Federal Communications Commission chair Newton Minow that broadcast television had become a "vast wasteland." Minow was ignored as much as possible in network practice and, within a few years, eased out entirely. Such a shocking pronouncement from such regulatory heights would never happen again. In future, top television execs would often double as heavy hitters within the Democratic Party, at once burnishing their liberal reputations and protecting their product line. But Minow's remark rankled for a long time.

Minow didn't have to work too hard to convince critics. His pronouncement came, after all, just two years after Charles Van Doren testified to the House Committee on Interstate and Foreign Commerce in November 1959 that television's current hot number, the quiz show *Twenty One* (1956–1958), had been systematically rigged. Despite persistent rumors that contestants were coached, the real shock was for execs themselves, who could not believe that what they always considered "entertainment" akin to pro wrestling had been taken so seriously or so politically.[26]

The same year as Van Doren's testimony, Senator Thomas Dodd of Connecticut opened hearings to investigate violence on television and its influence on youngsters. The Kennedy administration, appropriately grateful for the effect of the televised debates pitting the glamorous young senator against jowly and undershaved Richard Nixon, set in motion a committee to study the social role of the medium, and Minow, a young Chicago lawyer with a public service background, was to be its star witness. Minow did succeed in persuading Congress to pass an "all-channel" bill requiring that every new set sold in the United States have the capacity for both VHF and UHF reception. It was considered a major victory, albeit mainly for the consumer, with little ultimate effect on show quality. He also urged the creation of public television stations in the two leading markets, New York and Los Angeles, and guided the Ford Foundation in assisting the public acquisition of a VHF station in New Jersey, the soon-to-be-famous Channel 13. But Minow flatly failed in his hopes of resetting television's basic direction. The networks, even before they were owned by still larger corporations than their originators, had too much power.

Minow had one more victory, however inadvertent. Stung by his charges, CBS brought back one of the best of the anthology-drama producers, Herbert Brodkin, to create two of the three "quality" hour-length shows of the period, *The Nurses* (1962–1965), *East Side/West Side* (1963–1964) and *The Defenders* (1961–1965). These three, especially the last two, along with several other medical series (most successfully, *Dr. Kildare* and *Ben Casey*), were distinguished entries within what came to be called the "problem show" genre. All received significant contributions from victims of the blacklist.[27]

The dissatisfactions of contemporary American life had hardly been absent from the theatrical teledramas of the 1950s. But race, forever a central problem, had been conspicuously absent, with rare exceptions. Black actors were rarely seen on television at all except as happy servants, and the closest thing to an implied racial drama at the heart of American life happened ironically to be CBS's *The Gray Ghost* (1957), which romanticized the brave and handsome Johnny Rebs of a Confederate guerilla band. This series was abandoned by the network amid real-life controversies over school integration, just as in 1963 ABC dropped plans for showing the Academy Award–winner, *The Defiant Ones*, for fear of alienating Southern white viewers.

Black entertainers enjoyed a larger presence in television of the late 1940s than they would again for three decades, as variety acts yielded to series based on conservative themes.[28] From Birmingham on, news documentaries about civil rights rather than narrative drama, comedy or variety shows were making the real breakthrough in subject matter, but in many ways it remained a symbolic one. The news shows were far less popular than entertainment and the ones most often denied air time by local affiliates. The network response was dubbed "relevancy programming," a concept stemming from a decision at the highest levels of the network, mostly at CBS and NBC. Audiences were deemed ready for controversial issues, if always within limits. The most important was the inclusion of black faces; the paucity of nonwhite actors with realistic social roles could be brushed aside no longer.

By the 1963–1964 season, "racial" stories suddenly appeared in a dozen series, with actors like well-known progressives Ossie Davis and Ruby Dee, but also Diahann Carroll, James Edwards, Cicely Tyson and Diana Sands. Assorted jazz and folk musicians, singers and dancers, visible on the small screen earlier but erratically and in small numbers, now also made their delayed entry into television stardom.

Political and media liberals, now fully aware of the push for civil rights, sometimes liked to attribute the new interracialism to benign influences from the top, what might be called the "Kennedy Effect." Television scheduling is so often a matter of uncertainty and audience restlessness, of new trends that rise, prove commercially viable but also ultimately worse in only a few years, that such conclusions are uncertain at best. In this case, as in the stories of occasional hits that got off to a bad beginning but were not cancelled, there may be a particular truth to the suggestion that power among the executive moguls counted. Perhaps they wanted to help society accommodate people of color, a mission regarded from the White House as practically mandatory in a world of nonwhites emerging from colonialism, with communists competing for ideological loyalty in the Third World.

The Kennedy image itself mattered greatly. By way of contrast, for example, one would hesitate to ascribe a Trumanesque quality to television's earlier era. Since the days of Roosevelt's fireside chats, when certain radio soap-opera heroes were also suspiciously older men confined to wheel chairs but capable of great vision, American mass entertainment and the presidency had seemed to move along on different tracks. The Kennedy years would be different and would have been different, even without the appointment of Minow and the launching of the National Endowment for the Arts.

The world-class charismatic couple Jack and Jackie, ignoring threats of American Legion protests, boldly turned out to the Washington premiere in 1960 of *Spartacus*, the first blockbuster acknowledged to be written by a former Hollywood blacklist victim, Dalton Trumbo. To make matters worse, the novel had been written by another Popular Front favorite, Howard Fast, while in jail for refusing to testify.[29] The Kennedyesque gesture was presumably a way of bowing politely to the wishes of powerful figures in Hollywood to recuperate some of the writing and acting talent lost for a decade. The Kennedys' own tastes also doubtless reflected the sophistication and the quest for "relevant" culture in the mass media, something that liberal intellectuals around the president considered another vital break from the Eisenhower era. Recovery of a few ex-Communists may have seemed part of the package.

Just a few years earlier, at the height of the Cold War, there had been a quiet but remarkable turnaround from the collaboration of some noted liberals with red-hunting conservatives. Arthur Schlesinger, Jr., personal liaison with the CIA in the creation and funding of the Congress for Cultural Freedom and the American Committee for Cultural Freedom (ACCF), surprisingly shifted his political ground. Where he once treated Hollywood as a hotbed of red propaganda and congratulated the studios for turning non-cooperators out into the cold, he continued to hail Elia Kazan as an exemplary patriot for testifying against former friends but, unlike some of his closest associates in the CIA-funded world of intellectuals, Schlesinger lost his taste for a further possible round of purges in the entertainment world and urged a measured separation of politics and art.[30] In 1957, the ACCF itself, riven by internal disputes between hardliners and center-leaning liberals, went out of business. Intelligence operations among intellectuals and artists continued undaunted, and dependable American intellectuals were generously funded to take part in them until the dawn of the 1980s and consolidation of a new network of avowedly conservative foundations. But within the United

States, the end of the intellectual and cultural "hot" Cold War had arrived.[31] In television, it was almost détente.

The Nurses (retitled in its last season The Doctors and the Nurses), a Herbert Brodkin baby starring teenager Zina Bethune, might be regarded as little more than a counterpart to the contemporary "doctors shows" and precursor of the 1970s through the 1990s medical series that drew some of the highest ratings and best acting as well as a handful of the most progressive actors, scores of Emmys and the most elaborate budgets (and salaries) in television history. But The Nurses might alternatively be considered closer to an improved version of the old Men in White because it was primarily women in white, the view of hospital life not precisely from the bottom up (that would have been the orderlies' perspective) but from the lower-middle caregivers who did the work between doctors' visits in an always-strained healthcare system. The usual collection of poor, minority, young or otherwise troubled patients offered fodder for comment from a few of the self-described left-wing writers who had never been named to HUAC along with relative youngsters who were consciously following the blacklistees' familiar strategies for dealing with social themes.[32]

East Side/West Side (1963–1964), produced by David Susskind, was a much more tough-minded dramatic series, so much so that it had few rivals before the changes in television drama of the 1980s and later. It lasted only 26 episodes but has remained memorable in the chronicles of media history. Its title was appropriated from the 1949 soap of nearly the same name—East Side, West Side—written by sometime Communist (soon to be a reluctant friendly witness) Isobel Lennart and starring one of the Left's favorite actors, Van Heflin. The television show shared the two contrasting Manhattan worlds of haves and have-nots.[33]

Set in a poor section of Manhattan, the television counterpart has social-service providers struggling with the many problems of the contemporary poor. Thanks to location shooting—now rarer still than in the first days of Naked City—and a very special set of personal connections, it shared the earlier show's most important asset, the best younger stage actors and some of the most visible blacklistees just coming up for air.[34]

East Side/West Side's regular cast of George C. Scott, Elizabeth Wilson and a young Cicely Tyson was notable for its arch moral tone and repartee. The supporting cast and guest stars included Martin Sheen, Maureen Stapleton, Coleen Dewhurst, Ruby Dee and blacklistees Howard da Silva, Will Geer, Lloyd Gough, Joshua Shelley and Lee Grant, and among its directors was returnee John Berry.[35] The editor of the pilot was none other than Ralph Rosenblum, who dropped out afterward to move into films. But its most distinct qualities may be traced to its sometime executive producer Arnold Perl, story editor Edward Adler and writers Millard Lampell and guilt-ridden friendly witness Allan Sloane.

Perl (1914–1971) had been in the same Communist writers branch in early 1950s Manhattan with *You Are There* trio Walter Bernstein, Arnold Manoff and Abraham Polonsky—all Jews on their way out of the party but with their dreams of a cooperative society intact. Perl had mainly been a radio writer up to that time, and for that reason managed to work a bit in television under his own name until and occasionally even after the blacklist caught up with him. He was already laboring on one of the grand small successes of the 1950s Jewish stage, *The World of Sholom Aleichem*. Produced first in New York in 1953 by Perl and Howard da Silva, with da Silva directing, it starred the blacklisted Jack Gilford, Morris Carnovsky and Phoebe Brand, and also featured Ruby Dee and da Silva himself.

A folkish rendition of three Sholom Aleichem short stories, *The World* climaxed with an invocation: "This is the dawn of a new day. No more pogroms, no ghettos, no quotas . . . In this fine new world, there will be no Jews, no gentiles, no rich, no poor, no underdogs, no undercats . . . You don't have enough to eat, strike! The draft is taking your sons, strike! You don't like the ghetto, strike!" The stage direction underlined the point: "If we have succeeded in moving from fantasy to mild criticism to statement in the three pieces, the audience will move with us."[36] This was liberal-progressive dramatic didacticism in the extreme, framed by the work of Jewry's most beloved folk author. The educational station broadcast in 1959 of *The World of Sholom Aleichem* marked a kind of return for Perl, establishing his reputation for future episodes of *East Side/West Side*.[37]

As executive producer of the show, Perl joined Edward Adler (1920-), a former Young Communist League member and industrial union activist, later a New York cabby and highly regarded novelist who managed to make his earliest connections in television with *The Nurses*. When his first *East Side* script reached production, treating a cab driver's struggle against a compulsion to gamble, *TV Guide* posed him on top of a Checker Cab with a typewriter. It was perhaps a curiosity, a throwback to the worker-writer of the 1930s and 1940s; or perhaps the moment for this kind of homage had arrived, once again, within the mainstream of mass culture. Whatever the cause, television commentators from both coasts leaped into print to praise the series.[38]

That *East Side/West Side* veered toward the didactic was never in doubt. A single, remarkable episode could crowd into the 50-minute frame racial discrimination, slum housing, joblessness, children's endangerment, gender issues, troubled teenagers, fearful teachers and students and the force of the civil rights movement, with the good white liberals (and one black one) of the Community Welfare Service validating the grievances of the poor and desperate and striving to mitigate the worst of them.[39] Perl, Adler and their colleagues (who included *New York Post* liberal columnist Pete Hamill as a creative consultant) were also skillful enough to achieve a theatrical balance within the drama.

East Side/West Side reflected what was still a New York style of TV storytelling that would differ in interesting ways from the no less effective approach to narrative that had already emerged in Los Angeles. In this series and in the dwindling few other New York productions of the time, including *The Nurses, The Reporter, Mr. Broadway, For the People* and *NYPD*, stories would be marked by strong realist aesthetics, liberal social views and an emphasis on the political implications of the resolution. The Los Angeles productions, by contrast, nearly always emphasized the personal and traditional Hollywood narrative strategies: among these were *The Lieutenant, Ben Casey, Dr. Kildare, Breaking Point, Saints and Sinners, Mr. Novack* and *Judd for the Defense*. In dealing with themes involving racism, for example, the L.A. production *The Lieutenant* (1963–1964) would focus on an individual bigot, while *East Side/West Side* would use a much larger canvas.[40]

Winner of a Writers Guild award and nominated for eight Emmys, the much-discussed *East Side/West Side* episode "Who Do You Kill?" reflected the social rage of the day as no other show ever dared. In this episode, a guest cast with rising black star James Earl Jones as the unemployed husband and Diana Sands as his tavern-waitress wife (and the comic Godfrey Cambridge in a cameo as a bar patron) delivered the message. Harlem parents with an 18-month-old baby living in a miserable tenement, Jones and Sands seem immune to the movement arising around them, convinced that it will do no good. But when their child is bitten by a rat, suffers blood loss and infection, they need the help of the Welfare Service to meet the immediate crisis and to investigate the husband's factory (where African Americans are mere maintenance men, never allowed entry into the apprenticeships necessary for better jobs). The death of the child underlines the tragedy and pointedly forbids a happy ending. Along the way, a Harlem minister evokes the memory of Harriet Tubman, as the main characters meet in the church for the funeral, looking silently at each other as the episode closes. "Who Do You Kill?" was written by Perl, with an uncredited assist by Millard Lampell.[41]

Lampell (1919–1997), who left his native Paterson, New Jersey, as a teenager to go on the road, fell into singing topical music, touring one political rally after another with Pete Seeger and Woody Guthrie of the famed Almanac Singers. At the end of the war (and of his own military service), Lampell wrote the then-famous cantata "Lonesome Train" in 1945 about Abraham Lincoln's death—metaphorically about Franklin Roosevelt's death—broadcast on network radio. He moved on to films in his last years before the blacklist. During the difficult fifties, Lampell staged his own drama, *The Wall*, about the 1943 Warsaw Jewish Ghetto uprising. It attracted the attention of David Susskind, who recruited him to *East Side/West Side*. In 1966, awarded an Emmy for his teleplay "Eagle in a Cage" (about Napoleon exiled on St. Helena), Lampell began his acceptance speech with the phrase, "I think I ought to mention that I was blacklisted." His comments were recruited as an op-ed piece for a *New York Times* apparently eager to end the blacklist era—another breakthrough, and not only for Lampell.[42] That said, he had precious few other triumphs in the life of a writer of such promise.

Lampell's controversial script, "No Hiding Place," was unique for that era in setting *East Side/West Side* into the world of unscrupulous realtors who successfully stir up panic among white home-owners when a black family moves into the neighborhood. The normal television (and film) treatment of the issue would have been to find the good people and the bad people, with perhaps a little character development on both sides. Instead, "No Hiding Place" watches calm liberals turn into quivering racists, an uncertain wife become committed to ending housing discrimination and a new black neighbor announce that he is not the white Negro that his liberal neighbors wanted but rather an angry black man whom they have never seen before. A savaging of liberalism as much as of bigotry, the story went further than any network executive would consider comfortable for a very long time. The episode reminded viewers that no easy solutions were likely to be found in general expressions of kindness or abstract humanism. America's race troubles were, in short, not going to go away easily, if at all.[43]

A noble and notable experiment, in its way rivaling the best dramatic television ever offered, *East Side/West Side* was troubled from its beginning by internal divisions of authority and temperament. Susskind, never far from his background in talent agency work, alternatively encouraged and discouraged writers and actors on his whims, creating uncertainty and demoralization. Lead George C. Scott, whose reputation had made the series possible, proved difficult the whole way through, every bit the theatrical (and future film) star determined to make himself the center of attention.[44]

But the factor that really killed the series was not the production company. A number of Southern network affiliates and some outside the South simply refused to air a dramatic show with a black co-lead, and the network received a record bundle of hate mail, threatening a boycott of sponsors. Even that might not have been decisive, but the show seemed to network executives "depressing," thus predicting early failure. An attempt in what turned out to be the final five episodes to lighten up on the themes and recast Scott as a liberal congressman's aide in a white-collar setting was worse than no use. No matter that the real senator, Jacob Javits, had praised the show from the floor of Congress. In later years, Susskind was said to have kept two telegrams framed above his desk, one from the network congratulating him on a National Critics Award for the year's best filmed series, the other giving him notice that it had been cancelled.[45]

Critics and discerning viewers would nevertheless remember *East Side/West Side* as an unrecoverable high point of television social drama, one that set the measure of all later shows. By contrast, the other most hard-hitting of the contemporary dramas as well as the most successful of the bunch, *The Defenders*, offered broad hints of where television might be allowed to go politically, under the proper conditions.

This show's roots, after *Justice*, can be traced back to a two-part *Studio One* drama in 1957. Herbert Brodkin had produced the double episode called "The Defender," with Ralph Bellamy playing the fatherly E. G. Marshall role and William Shatner the son, defending the poor and miserable against the power of the prosecutors. Years went by and the memory of that two-hour piece eventually served as a kind of pilot. Brodkin brought it back as a civil liberties show par excellence. Looking for fresh blood after the first season, Brodkin put Albert Ruben on staff—then a bit of a revolution, because practically all writing for dramatic series, including *The Defenders*, had been done more or less on a freelance basis up to that time.

Ruben got a guarantee of credit for either a teleplay or payment for a revision of some other writer's work; hardly creative control of the show but something close to it. That the single most successful progressive writer on television would be guiding the most liberal show on television, and one of the most admired, marked a quiet return of the Left. Brodkin, always vigorous in monitoring production expenses, insisted on tight story lines and talented writers and directors. Among the other writers was Reginald Rose (1920–2002), who wrote many of the first year's shows. Behind the camera was Franklin Schaffner (1920–1987), director of the original *Studio One* drama who was also responsible for many *Defenders* episodes, including an Emmy-winner, and would go on to direct *Planet of the Apes*. Together with the actors and editors, they created a kind of Actors' Studio ambience.

The public-interest law firm, a low-budget and uncompromised version of the later *L.A. Law*'s corporate-style staff and setting, week after week assisted the star-crossed, the oppressed and assorted victims of other wrongs, sometimes demonstrating that police and prosecutors had stepped over the line. In contrast to the phenomenally popular *Perry Mason* (1957–1966), the identity of the guilty party was not all that important. Instead, *The Defenders* treated the contentious issues of the day like capital punishment, abortion, the denial of passports to the politically suspect, the right of police to break into homes of suspects without notice (then known as the "no-knock" procedure) and so on. The riskiest political topic of them all was tackled in the episode "Blacklist," written by Ernest Kinoy and aired in January, 1964. Never before had television taken up this political cause in this precise way or with sympathy for this precise victim. Unlike the vast majority of other media treatments well into the 'nineties, it dramatized the case of someone who was tagged not altogether wrongly with the red label, that is, if one considered as proof of wrongdoing having once joined in a crowd of demonstrators or raised money for a relief group or an antifascist committee.

Kinoy (1925-) was a particularly interesting choice. Brother to the famed left-wing civil liberties lawyer Arthur Kinoy, Ernest was a veteran radio writer in the last decade of that medium's network programming. He also wrote widely during television's Golden Age and after, including the drama programs *Studio One* and *Playhouse 90* and comedies *Imogene Coca*, *Dr. Kildare* and *The Nurses*. In future years he would specialize in telefilms, often on Jewish or Israeli themes. His most famous work after his Emmy-winning dramatic shows of the 1960s was for the original *Roots* (1977), the most watched miniseries to that time; and for its successor *Roots: The Next Generations* (1979), for which he served as principal scriptwriter.

"Blacklist" was the story of an actor, played by Klugman, accused of suspicious affiliations dating to the 1930s (he reflects laconically: "I don't like to say who is or who isn't a Communist. I guess there were . . . there must have been. I knew one man who said he was a member of the party. He was a cellist"). He sees the prospect of a revival of his career after years of denial, and just then, the blacklist looms again.[46] "Blacklist" portrayed many and various true-to-life characters, including the professional red-baiters, their colleagues who perform the dirtier work of soliciting financial payoffs, the wavering film producer who reluctantly sells out Klugman for the success of the project and the politicians and civil liberties lawyers disputing among themselves whether to fight "on principle" or just to get the guy his career back.

If there was a damaging compromise in the show, it was in E. G. Marshall's warning to his son and junior legal partner, played by Robert Reed, that the blacklisting system could not be successfully challenged legally and that it would end only "when people have faith in . . . well . . . the Constitution. In . . . freedom!"[47] Perhaps this kind of statement was the best that could be done on such a controversial matter—at least on television. Within a melodramatic story line intended to "argue on behalf of a generalized middle class ethic which will enable us to get through the tense, troubled, and crowded sixties," as one critic put it, the general idea seemed to be to urge audience members to be good people without demanding anything in particular from them.[48]

The perceived need to offer a clearcut conclusion without complicating (or darkening) the depiction of American life also drove the writers into taking narrative shortcuts. They often wanted to develop ethical and social ambiguities, if only for dramatic reasons, but network executives insisted upon the contrary principle expressed in the network office slogan, "Confuse 'em and lose 'em." Any troubling uncertainty, however momentary, would presumably prompt viewers to change channels.[49]

Considered for a moment strictly as drama, *The Nurses*, *East Side/West Side* and *The Defenders* had been in part an attempt to retain and reinforce the traditions of

Method acting. Most of their principal cast members had gone through the same theatrical training and shared the élan that came with the self-conscious distinction of doing something other than routine "Hollywood" work. Uniquely for their time, the shows, at their best, actually moved *through* Method (so far as continuing weekly series could allow the intense emotions required) back toward the epic model.

In *East Side/West Side* in particular, the stories invariably treated the circumstances of slum life and the struggle for survival and dignity. This framing owed everything to the contemporary civil rights movement, so much so that the African American guest stars often seemed to stand in for the unseen community. Resolutions, as in real life, remained open-ended and elusive. Television was not likely to go much further—or even this far—for some time to come. On another level, if it was in the epic sense a return to some of the earliest live dramatic television shows, it was also a way of moving on.

It might also be said that a certain liberal melancholy regarding the human condition, so obviously the overwhelming affect of later shows like *Hill Street Blues,* had already established its presence as an acceptable alternative to feel-good sitcoms and too-easily-resolved cop dramas. When Kennedy's New Frontier and Lyndon Johnson's Great Society waned, with the redirection of the social budget to war and with rising conservative rage at "black power," what one critic calls the "New Frontier character dramas" swiftly drew to a close.[50] *The Defenders, The Nurses* and an interracial cop show, *NYPD* (1967–1969, not to be confused with the later *NYPD Blue*), all of them written in part by Albert Ruben, might rightly be seen as the end of a tradition in which the melancholy did not paralyze the urgency in the need to press for social change.[51]

These new dramatic series also came up against other kinds of limits not so different from those built into Paddy Chayefsky's work. To go further would require of the networks assorted things they were not prepared to accept, for example the jump-cut editing, musical experimentation, explicit violence and implied sexuality of *Miami Vice*. Even as social disturbances and the sexual revolution unfolded in real life, the old rules held. Still ahead was the relaxation of attitudes, language and partial nudity, the unapologetic noir quality of a series like *Crime Story,* the hand-held camera of *Homicide* and the various assorted experiments of "indie" films that would become familiar on the cable networks by the first years of the new century.

The question of television drama's rise and fall could also be posed in yet another, more tactical way. Given the repression on every level in the contemporary United States, the "playhouse" features of the 1950s, with all their limitations, had offered a memorable contribution to American drama and American culture. But what if, as the Cold War eased, a more lively alternative to Kennedyesque social and moral drama had already made its way into the network lineup? Blacklistees, who had offered up series that never flew, might possibly have changed the nature of television's offerings, making them more in tune with the real rebelliousness of the new era and an audience eager for representations, however vicarious and metaphorical, of themselves and their anti-establishment feelings.

Daniel Mainwaring, personally close to left-wing screenwriter-unionists, took the considerable risk of collaborating with and fronting for Adrian Scott and Joan Scott in a quietly organized atelier of sorts, including both films and television. In 1959, the same year that the teen pregnancy drama *Blue Denim* reached movie screens, they sought to put across "The Stormy Age," a tough (for television) pilot that was to be devoted to contemporary teenage life, with an average adolescent standing up for herself, and her parents arguing realistically (in distinctly non-*Father Knows Best* fashion) about how and whether to hold her in line. Another pilot by the same three was to feature a Latino detective in San Diego with close personal ties in Tijuana, crossing the border literally and culturally through the unfolding police drama, with more substantial reflections on race in one episode than producer Aaron Spelling's *Mod Squad* would manage in an entire season. It, too, didn't fly. Meanwhile, William Attaway, a former Communist and a novelist of some note, became one of the first African American writers in television. His apex came with *One Hundred Years of Laughter* (1966), a special on the history of African American humor, with the first appearances of Redd Fox, Moms Mabley and Flip Wilson on television. Most of his other work was bitterly disappointing to Attaway, including a film script (eventually turned over to Rod Serling) about the first black man to become president of the United States. These were normal disappointments.

The most direct path to the audience for social commentary seemed, then, to come from an unexpected quarter: the made-for-television movie. Movies themselves had come to network broadcasting surprisingly late. NBC did not take the bold step of showing more "recent" movies made by major studios (defined as films made after 1948), apart from the B westerns offered by movie syndicates, until 1961. (ABC had, in 1957, quickly abandoned a half-hearted effort at something similar.) Universal Studios had begun to edge toward the TV movie as a form in 1964 with *See How They Run* (1964), written by friendly witness Michael Blankfort, and in a remake of *The Killers* (1964), directed by Don Siegel. The popularity of *Saturday Night at the Movies* might have prompted the next logical step, the "original" television film, but it did not arrive until 1969, when ABC launched the *Movie of the Week*.

Introduced too late for anything but the tail end of the blacklistees' careers, the TV movie lent itself to extended melodramatic treatments of assorted innocents (usually women and children) endangered by mentally unbalanced men, or to the recounting of diseases or the community effects of natural disasters. But it also offered openings to writers like Edward Adler and Albert Ruben, actors like Lee Grant and Mike Farrell among others. The made-for-TV-movie more than occasionally offered, in the next decade or so, themes as resonant to left-liberal memory as the Triangle Fire and as current as the chemical poisoning of Love Canal (with heroine Lois Gibbs drawn from real life, a characteristic fighting housewife). When they were topical, these socially relevant films were most often attuned to the changing issues of ordinary women's lives, by no coincidence mirroring the experiences and sentiments of television's largest demographic viewership.

Remnants of 1930s and 1940s social sentiment also survived in the rare outstanding series drama. At the liberal apex was *Quincy, M.E.* (1976–1983), veteran actor Jack Klugman's personalized vehicle for social criticism. Klugman, who candidly described himself as the professional "Walther Matthau Replacement" (if the affable progressive Matthau wasn't available, Klugman would be called) and made his mark as a public celebrity on the sitcom *The Odd Couple* (1970–1975), happened to be a forties-style avowed socialist and veteran stage actor whose favorite earlier television roles were, as we've seen, support work on *The Defenders*. *Quincy* was packaged as a vehicle for this now-major television personality, and Klugman made the most of it. When producers tried to cast him into a cops-and-robbers role with him pursuing the guilty, he insisted instead on a strong emphasis on social themes.

Playing a former private physician who has made a social choice to become Coroner of L.A. County, Klugman/Quincy was a pathologist solving crimes, getting in the hair of police who invariably resisted his suggestions and often blunderingly victimized again those who had already been made victims. Whether directly or glancingly, Quincy regularly struck blows against repression. The grand jury system, with its rules that prevented a subpoenaed witness from refusing to answer any questions if he or she had answered a single one, was seen to be especially dangerous to democracy when Klugman had the camera turned toward him and spelled out the episode's implications. Klugman's personal politics, his contempt for the behavior of Elia Kazan and others (and downright puzzlement that the petitions he'd signed hadn't gotten him into serious trouble), could hardly have been more obvious to insiders and careful viewers.[52]

Quincy, M.E. was originally one of the four segments of the NBC *Sunday Mystery Movie*. Of the others, *McCloud* (1970–1977) and *McMillan* (earlier *McMillan and Wife*, shortened with staff changes, 1971–1977), both hired blacklisted or left-wing writers. The fourth, *Columbo* (1971–1979), was broadcast intermittently as a shorter series and then as a series of full-length television films featuring rumpled detective Peter Falk (a sometime avant-garde actor) on the trail of mostly rich and arrogant evildoers, a role with firm origins in a Group Theatre production of the 1930s.[53] In the social-problem drama, the impact of the 1960s and memories of earlier progressive-liberal themes had arrived at last. *The*

Rockford Files was the most garish in its funky iconoclasm; most others, especially, *Quincy*, preferred to cast protagonists as idealistic public servants, or balanced the two styles.[54] Limits to acceptable criticism would return under Reagan, and avidly right-wing series had never been absent. But suspicion of society's rulers and the personal crises of supposed law-enforcers (likewise lawbreakers) would now be certain to reappear within the quality drama. Without that edge, it was just a lot of dull posturing.[55]

THE SITCOM

The television writers of New York in the 1950s took pride in themselves as dramatists. They endured constraints no worse in most respects than those facing screenwriters, and in some ways their burden of censorship was lighter. They considered sitcom projects to be hack work, a warmed-over version of radio-comedy writing just a step above game shows and, by the later 1950s, typical Hollywood TV banality.[56] Left-wing writers for sitcoms hardly took themselves more seriously. But for complicated reasons, it was comedy that was destined to become the vehicle for social criticism too hot for drama, or at least for the sustained popularity that success demanded of the television series as a form.

The roots of this development had been there all along. But through the rise of topical comedy-variety shows and the parallel success of socially critical film comedies during the later 1960s, the sitcom became a venue for words never before spoken on television, ideas rarely voiced and even occasionally a radical critique of liberal rhetoric that had been the pride of the industry's best efforts.

One of the curiosities of television writing, from its beginning, could readily be traced back to the 1940s and network radio. Advertising agencies, acting on behalf of the sponsors, kept a tight rein on content, but during the war and shortly after, patriotic themes found airtime, including treatments of U.S. history, opening the way for more troubling topics like the difficult adjustments of returning GIs. A relatively small community of several hundred writers, predominantly Jewish, were organized in the Radio Writers Union (RWU), with Sam Moore (a quiet Communist destined for the blacklist) their organization's founder and admired leader. Moore himself, like a number of other leftwingers, worked in family comedy shows like *The Great Gildersleeve*, *Fibber McGee and Molly* and *My Date With Judy* or comedy-variety programs like *Archie's Place* and *The Maxwell House Coffee Hour*. While a nation listened, dad's authority was regularly kidded and social snobs put in their place.[57]

To get ahead of the story a bit, members of the Radio Writers Union naturally evolved with the popularity of the new medium to form the heart of the Television Writers of America (TWA) in 1950. They had no collective position on the content of television shows, although obviously they would have preferred socially critical material if it had been possible. What they demanded was the kind of closed-shop authority over fellow writers that they had achieved in radio. But it was already too late; the era of solidarity was drawing to a close, and the masters of the new medium had no wish to make such concessions. The TWA's first and only president, Dick Powell (not to be confused with the actor), no Communist but a close ally, was a radio-union activist who had been toiling on family sitcoms like *The Life of Riley*, the original blue-collar radio comedy that crossed over easily into the new medium.[58] There Powell joined fellow TWA enthusiasts like Frank Tarloff, a Communist who had several false starts in a film career before moving on to the likes of radio's *Henry Aldrich* and *My Date With Judy*. Among the progressive crowd in and around radio work could also be found such younger liberal, non-communist good friends as Carl Reiner, Norman Lear and Larry Gelbart.

The networks quickly found the issue with which they could beat the new union to death: the loyalty oath. By this time, the Screen Actors Guild and the Screen Writers Guild had rolled over, resolving to expel any member (including some of the founders and the hardest-working members of these unions) who refused to sign such an oath. The TWA, with a smaller and more homogenous constituency, decided to live or die on the issue. When the TWA refused to enforce the loyalty oath and the networks refused to bargain, the union collapsed.[59]

Frank Tarloff was the major exception in keeping his work immediately afterward. Danny Thomas quickly recognized him as the single finest talent for *Make Room for Daddy* (1953–1971, aka *The Danny Thomas Show*), the warm-hearted continuing tale of the entertainer who also strives to be the perfect (single) father despite his necessarily frequent absences from home.[60] What special talent did Tarloff have? The modest writer commented that "You could go pretty far with Danny's character . . . before you had to pull back,"[61] and referred for inspiration to the Restoration comedy of manners in which the wife, children and servants together conspire against the patriarch. Tarloff might have given himself more credit. A major breakthrough in the history of television just ahead may have owed its survival to his work.

Sheldon Leonard (1907–1997) was one of the most successful 1950s–1970s television producers and one of the most interesting. A theater graduate of Syracuse University in the 1930s, familiar to audiences from numerous films as a Runyonesque gangster with a nasal sneer, Leonard in real life nurtured extensive contacts in the SAG and the social networks of the Left. He had branched out into radio writing during the later 1940s and moved easily into television work with scripts for assorted shows. But his aspirations lay in the executive suite. In 1953, he joined Danny Thomas in a partnership to create *Make Room for Daddy*, and they won several Emmys along the way. It was Leonard, with an eye for talent, who quietly decided that Tarloff was welcome—if not yet under his own name. Toward the end of the fifties, when Tarloff abandoned Hollywood for London, Leonard offered him his own network show. The writer concentrated on films instead, writing television on the side until he was offered the position of lead writer on Leonard's new project, *The Dick Van Dyke Show* (1961–1966).

To understand the success and influence of this unique program—and why its originator, Carl Reiner (1922-), would turn to Tarloff in desperation after writing the first thirteen shows and seeing the ratings collapse—it helps to go back a few years. The impetus for the show came from two directions more or less simultaneously. Reiner, one of the most talented comic writers in the history of television, had made his reputation on *Your Show of Shows*, *Caesar's Hour* and *Sid Caesar Invites You*. When the comedy-variety format died toward the end of the 1950s and even Milton Berle found himself under contract hosting the plebian *Celebrity Bowling*, Reiner turned first to the game show format (unsuccessfully) and then to the sitcom. But he never forgot where he came from: he even gave one of his comic memoirs the unmistakable title, *Paul Robeson Saved My Life*.[62] Like Alan Arkin's passing references to Robeson records and the Peekskill Riot in the later television series *100 Centre Street*, it was a dead giveaway. (In "Fifteen Things I Know about God," listed on the final page of the memoir, Reiner attributes this view to deity: "He is upset about the unfair distribution of wealth."[63])

That the Kennedy revolution reached as far as a sitcom pilot is one of the oddities of the age, thanks perhaps to the president's fondness for starlets or to swinging parties with Frank Sinatra's celebrity circles, or both. Reiner had just written a play, *Enter Laughing*, about the life and loves of an aspiring comedy writer. This thinly disguised self-portrait would become a Broadway show in 1963 and a rather modest feature film in 1967. Meanwhile, he recast the material as a sitcom about a writer in New Rochelle, his work and his family. For the first time, a television show was to treat the life of a television writer, and a Jewish writer to boot. As television historian David Marc describes the sequence of events, Reiner's agent took the story to Peter Lawford, a Kennedy inlaw struggling to establish himself as a television producer. Presidential father Joseph P. Kennedy insisted upon reading the script before Kennedy money would be used, and the patriarch approved, offering his own personal cash for the project.[64]

"Head of the Family," debuting amid the summer rerun season of 1960, was not a hit. *The Times* liked its New Yorkishness because it recalled those early days when the small audience for network television was Eastern and ethnic. But the wider and presumably blander audiences of 1960 proved indifferent. At that point Leonard changed the show's affect. As he squired Reiner through T&L Productions studios, showing him the fine points of the successful sitcom, he offered to direct a markedly different pilot with Tarloff, his favorite writer, handling the script.

It was not, one imagines, an offer that could be refused (as fictional mobster, Leonard had made many of that kind, but behind this one was cash and a reputation, not just a "heater"). Leonard also selected the star, specifically a gentile with no New York qualities, the virtually unknown Dick Van Dyke. The "Jewish" character was not to be abolished entirely but displaced from first to second or third banana, becoming the funny-man fellow writer played by Borsht Belt veteran Morey Amsterdam. Leonard also formed Calvada Productions (a combination of the names of Reiner, Leonard, Van Dyke and Thomas) specifically to produce *The Dick Van Dyke Show*. It quite simply remade the genre of the television sitcom.

It may have been, Marc suggests, partly a way of inveigling Neil Simon's style of Jewish *arriviste* comedy-dramas into television (something Simon himself, working in theater and films, would never do successfully). The status anxiety of the upwardly mobile combined with the residual funky ambience of the city with its "characters" was a volatile mix that worked, in part because of the glitter of perky Mary Tyler Moore, who could appear endearingly embarrassed week after week. As *Naked City* and, to a lesser degree, *The Defenders* had advanced television with grainy naturalism and the "montage of Manhattan," so *Dick Van Dyke* surged forward technically with the use of a third camera, successfully synthesizing theater, film and video so that a monitor-watching live audience could share certain important aspects of the filmmaking experience.

The net consequence was something more than the sitcom had ever been, a decisive reworking of social comedy in forms immediately recognizable to insider observers of Old Left talent. *The Dick Van Dyke Show* had, at least in potential, become a sort of demographic shorthand for a multiculturalism as yet only glimpsed, one that included not only family members but co-workers of every variety, including an independent and single career woman (with no aspirations of marrying the boss) working side by side with a middle-aged expert at *shtick*. To add to the complexity, the nominal hero not only has a college diploma, which marks him off from his fellow writers, but sports a haircut carefully styled after Jack Kennedy's, as Mary Tyler Moore's is (more evidently to most viewers) after Jackie's. These two were thus Kennedy liberals, a small step upward in a medium where real-life progressives could heretofore be no more than actors playing "nice" men and women.

Whether because of Tarloff's writing or Leonard's liberal inclinations, the cast was fleshed out with scatterings of minorities, seen mostly in crowd settings but never in menial or comic-relief roles. Likewise, for the first time ever in television, jokes about racial ambiguities were permitted in contexts starkly different from the *Amos and Andy* lampoon of black culture: the stars accepting an award for interracial unity accidentally dye their hands black just before the ceremony, and so on.[65] Audiences were ready for this kind of complexity. Perhaps it all might have been accomplished without the presence of blacklistees and their friends, but experience suggests otherwise. Tarloff, the past master at kidding daddy, was taking on the WASP social rules that most Americans now found increasingly absurd.

Some of the fun was also deeply rooted in jokes that might have been cracked in the Bensonhurst of the 1940s. Even before a notorious *Dick Van Dyke* episode featuring bar mitzvah lessons, a Jewishness that had hardly spoken its name since Milton Berle's *shpritzing* was now sophisticated pop irony. A few years later, the spinoff *Mary Tyler Moore Show* would propose a gendered postmodernism of the single woman struggling to make her own rules. She did so with the inadvertent help of her boss and journalistic muckraker Lou Grant, played by Ed Asner. Just a few years later, as president of the Screen Actors Guild, real-life Asner would be the anti-imperialist member of the notoriously hawkish AFL-CIO executive board and the star of his own courageously political (also fatally controversial) spinoff series about news shows, *Lou Grant* (1977–1982).

All in all, television wasn't what it had been, and it was not likely to go back. As David Marc quipped, amending Theodor Adorno's famous maxim, "If there could be no poetry after Auschwitz, there could at least be New Rochelle."[66] This was an imagined New Rochelle, no doubt, with an active Solidarity Committee supporting George McGovern for president or rooting for populist victory against the CIA-led human rights abusers in Central America or against the U.S.-allied Apartheid government in South Africa.[67]

Aside from the success of *The Dick Van Dyke Show* and the introduction of a literal Jewishness that included more than the stand-up comic, other heretofore forbidden subjects could also be reinterpreted through humor. The most unexpected was certainly the horror and stupidity of armed conflict, with nation-states throwing up false hierarchies of the heartless figures who know only how to give and take orders, to kill or be killed.

Before M*A*S*H and arguably paving the way for it was *Hogan's Heroes* (1965–1971). Nearly all of the stupidity was imputed to the German side, set in a prisoner-of-war camp with the captors weekly outwitted but allowed to retain the illusions of power. One of the industry's inside jokes was the antiwar, liberal and left-wing character of the series' writing staff and most of its actors, except for conservative star Bob Crane. Several of the actors actually had been POWs in the "good war." Dick Powell, none other than the former president of the banished Television Writers of America, was the lead writer who enjoyed the semi-sweet revenge of lambasting authority. Did the German officers thereby seem so laughable as to be incapable of endless sadism and mass extermination? Perhaps. But the obverse of these laughable figures would surely not have made for a watchable series.[68]

Newer developments did not depend solely upon veterans of the Old Left. Things began to open up further politically on television with *The Smothers Brothers Show* (1967–1969 at CBS, then in 1970 at ABC and 1975 on NBC), which introduced topicality into television humor through stand-up political satire and music lyrics. *Smothers Brothers* was, in its generational affect, a descendant of *Cheyenne* and *Maverick* and the first openly "anti-establishment" show aimed at the younger generation. *Smothers Brothers* inevitably faced more continual threats of censorship than any show before it, and the experience of those battles was useful to the writers and producer of M*A*S*H a few years later. The militantly anti-war Smothers (one of whom was reputed to be a warm supporter of the Socialist Workers Party, the political descendants of Leon Trotsky) actually won decent ratings but could not survive the hostile atmosphere when CBS higher-ups (including William Paley, reputedly seeking an ambassadorial appointment from incoming president Nixon) concluded that the series was not worth the fight against conservative critics and censors. Network executives lost a lawsuit for three-quarters of a million dollars to the Smothers by violating their contract, canceling before the end of the 1968–1969 season.[69] Next time, at least some of the TV brass would know better.

Rowan and Martin's Laugh-In (1968–1973) marked the kind of turning point that might have been reached by blacklisted writers a decade earlier. *Laugh-In* also introduced, by no coincidence, more comedic talent than any television show until the equally irreverent *Saturday Night Live*, and did so in prime time with feminist Lily Tomlin on display. Even PBS got into the act, briefly, for two seasons (1970–1972) of the Boston-produced *Great American Dream Machine*, a high-toned and commercial-free variety combination of skits and music, with blacklistee Lou Solomon occupying the executive producer chair and veteran progressive actors like Eli Wallach on hand to cheerfully (or artfully) denounce not only the Vietnam War but the American penchant for violence generally.[70] It was a moment of overt political iconoclasm mixed with idealism that couldn't, and didn't, last. The next and more decisive turning point came from another quarter entirely.

By 1970, New Frontier social dramas were spent, young people seemed hell-bent on turning real-life campuses upside down and African Americans threatened to burn down their own ghettos. In that atmosphere, M*A*S*H and the assorted Norman Lear sitcoms redefined social criticism on TV and attracted audiences whose size would have been scarcely imaginable for *The Defenders*, let alone *East Side/West Side*. M*A*S*H (1972–1983) owed its origins to a somewhat wry novel (published under a pseudonym) about a Korean War medical unit as seen by a real-life doctor. By the merest coincidence, Ring Lardner, Jr., had been sent the galleys by the publishers for favorable comment, and he urged upon his renewed studio contacts a film to coincide with the rising public resistance against the escalating U.S. war in Vietnam. A former protégé of Roy Huggins at *Maverick*, Robert Altman, was recruited as director.[71]

That Lardner's political persecutors of the early 1950s had raised the specter of "American boys dying in Korea" as a reason for him and other blacklistees to be banished from Hollywood—and sent to prison for refusing to cooperate—made the film's success deliciously ironic.[72] But could it be made into a television show? Lardner did not think so, and he backed out early from a proposal that came first from an executive at Twentieth Century-Fox's television unit and then from a strangely familiar source: Gene Reynolds. A former child star who had worked in and around films written by the Hollywood Left, Reynolds (1925-) had moved on from acting to the production side of films, then television. As the plans for the series gathered steam, he flew to London to hook up with Larry Gelbart.

Gelbart (1928-), born to Yiddish-speaking immigrants in Chicago who moved to Los Angeles in 1942, by the 1960s could claim one of the most varied writing resumes in radio and television. His father, a loquacious barber, happened to cut Danny Thomas' hair and described his high school kid as a genius for writing comic skits. Thomas asked the father to get him some of the son's material for *Maxwell House Coffee Time*, which Thomas hosted, and showed it to the show's head writer, Mac Benoff (a Communist who would become a friendly witness).Young Gelbart made a sale to Benoff and was off and running.[73] On the basis of Thomas' recommendation, Gelbart next got a regular job writing for *Duffy's Tavern*. His first day at work just happened to be the last for departing Red and future friendly witness Abe Burrows.

Gelbart went on, through radio and early television, to write for Eddie Cantor, Bob Hope, Red Buttons and *Caesar's Hour*, and to collaborate with Carl Reiner, Neil Simon and Mel Brooks. He also joined the Television Writers of America, where he met left-wing writers under duress and developed a lasting hatred for McCarthyism. Gelbart continued to accumulate minor television credits until he developed the idea for a comedy that would put some old vaudevillians and recent blacklistees back to work and strike a glancing, humorous blow against the evil-doers. It was called *A Funny Thing Happened On the Way to the Forum*. Scored by Stephen Sondheim, starring Zero Mostel and Phil Silvers, with a supporting cast of Jack Gilford and Buster Keaton among others, the project was originally titled "Roman Comedy," the dream child of a fellow TV comedy writer, Burt Shevelove.

Recovering plots and characters from the surviving plays of third-century comic playwright Titus Maccium Plautus, Gelbart and Shevelove reveled in jokes about class status that affect (and afflict) every stable society, especially empires that must, to ensure relative tranquility, provide respectable citizens a cerebral version of bread and circuses. It was Plautus' original that supplied the henpecked husband, the doddering fools and of course the whores, too. Jerome Robbins, who had initially agreed to direct the stage production, suddenly backed out, but after the play briefly floundered, he re-entered to stage a second opening, this time in New York. Robbins's return involved a moment famous among blacklistees: Mostel and Gilford (whose former wife, Madeline Lee Gilford, had been named and considerably damaged by Robbins's testimony against her) agreed among themselves to boycott no one and go on with the show.[74] In the movie version, the Roman Legions, cruel conquerors who are mocked even when threatening anyone close at hand with sudden death, become laughable, and if sex is a constant, political themes are never far away.

Gelbart took the show to London in 1963 and stayed, partly because British television charmed him with the kind of sophistication unknown back home. Then Gene Reynolds came to visit, urging him to see MASH, the film. After much negotiation, the televised version went on the air in 1970. Gelbart, Reynolds and co-producer Burt Metcalfe spent more staff time over the next several seasons struggling with network censorship than anyone in the history of television, fighting off efforts to suppress sexual (and other) language and the omnipresence of blood in the operating room, among other things. Reynolds himself directed many early episodes; so did another noted Hollywood liberal, Jackie Cooper. Like the film, it was the irreverence of the politics and the reverence for the war experiences in Korea that meant most to audiences.

M*A*S*H would not have aired if not for the success of another TWA veteran (also an old friend of Tarloff and the Hollywood liberals), Norman Lear, and his grand vehicle, All in the Family (1971–1992). Lear (1922-) was raised in a middle-class family in New Haven, majored in communications at Emerson College and, after serving in the Army Air Corps, went to work in early television for the kind of comedy-variety shows whose popularity peaked in the early 1950s. In a few years he tired of the game and, with fellow comic writer Bud Yorkin, formed Tandem Productions, intending to produce commercially successful film comedies.[75]

All in the Family was a revolution in television comedy and indeed in American television as a whole. It was an adaptation of a blue-collar sitcom inspired neither by the loveable Life of Riley or The Honeymooners but rather a British TV comedy about an unlovable racist, sexist and misogynist who was condemned to live in a world changing in ways he hated. For former stage actor Carroll O'Connor's Archie Bunker, African Americans were "jungle bunnies," the Chinese (a category which he often merged with other Asians) were "chinks" and liberals were "eggheads," including the cryptically Jewish (though nominally Polish) son-in-law who lived rent-free under his roof and was played by Carl Reiner's son, Rob Reiner. As a dock foreman at home in Queens, Archie was the (surprisingly) Protestant Irishman and American jingo who had lost any sense of his own special ethnic identity and bitterly resented the self-conscious identities of others.

The show wobbled in its first season. According to some versions, only the staying power of Lear and his network contacts prevented cancellation—although adding Frank Tarloff as story editor no doubt showed network execs that talent with a track record was in charge. Rather suddenly, disregarding or perhaps adapting to the curse words of "your spics and spades," the audience greedily adopted Archie and company. For the next ten years, All in the Family remained near the top of the ratings despite multiple changes in cast (some involving spinoffs), the death of the Jean Stapleton character, Archie's abandoning the working class for tavern ownership and so on. The show never approached the toughness of the British original, 'Til Death Do Us Part, but it opened up American television.[76]

All in the Family was even in some ways a kind of update of Clifford Odets's 1930s dramas.[77] Not that the moral weight of a civilization or even a moment of class struggle were at stake; but the narrative frame of a family trapped with each other around the kitchen table, shouting, was unmistakable: this is where meaning would be conveyed. That the older radicalism had become liberalism, and that the patriarchal male figure (the socialistic grandfather now absent) was now a reactionary rather than a humane left-liberal was less important than the shouting itself. Truths emerged from somewhere around the city, where the issues are hottest and most obviously unsettled.

Lear-land would seem to be an ideal spot for the now aging Hollywood left-wingers. But Lear was no easy boss; indeed, the newly minted tradition of having a half-dozen or even more writers working simultaneously, none with any creative control, took off here. Those veteran Marxists in his corner found the work easier in some of the spinoffs, especially Maude (1972–1978). The first of the several sequels to All in the Family, Maude began with Bea Arthur playing a fast-talking, ultra-liberal (socialist and feminist) cousin to Jean Stapleton's browbeaten but characterful Edith, wife of Archie. Maude said the things that the somewhat slow Edith Bunker did not think to say or was too shy to say. Maude was a suburban wife, living in Tuckahoe (in real life a blue-collar, ethnic service community for the suburbanites of Westchester County) with a husband, divorced daughter and a grandson. The real Bea Arthur had studied with Irwin Piscator at the New School in the 1940s, scored her first stage triumph as the star of Lysistrata (under the famed teacher's direction) and rightly regarded herself as an avant-gardist for decades after, with leading parts in Sartre's No Exit and Pirandello's Six Characters in Search of an Author. No one doubted that Maude represented Arthur herself.

Maude was the perfect home for Old Left television writers mainly because Lear decided to let Arthur ventilate with unparalleled stridency the social views that Archie despised in All in the Family. Maude hated Nixon and Republicans in general but regarded as a living saint Congresswoman Bella Abzug, defeated in a 1976 primary race by Daniel Patrick Moynihan in what was then considered a landmark victory of neo-liberalism (and its neo-conservative allies) over 1940s leftish liberalism. It was made known that Maude herself had had an abortion, and when she went through menopause the older, female audience was informed of every hot flash. Maude's husband, played by Bill Macy, watched his business go bankrupt and had alcohol-abuse problems. And so on, through several seasons that made *Maude* one of the most popular shows on television.[78]

The same went for African American–centered spinoffs. *The Jeffersons* (1975–1985), with Tarloff as story editor, displaced economic frustrations; here, the black middle class family living in an Upper East Side apartment complex is discomfited mainly by the confusion of changing race roles, to no small degree the Archie-like blustering of Sherman Hemsley as the nouveau riche African American (shortly before, he had been Archie's next-door neighbor in Queens).[79] *Good Times* (1974–1979), initially a vehicle for the dignified Esther Rolle (who had appeared as a maid on *Maude*), retold the story of *Raisin In the Sun* as lower-middle class African Americans facing economic and personal crises from within a high-rise ghetto building in the South Side of Chicago. By this time, a half-dozen African Americans appeared in new shows as stars or co-stars (none of them lasted long, save for comedy-variety host Flip Wilson). Instead, the "funny" sides of self-mocking black life and the enabling of bigots to voice their sentiments seemed the real legacy of controversy's royal entrance into network television. The radical alternative, Richard Pryor, was considered too controversial for television (his show lasted two months in 1979) even though he was widely regarded as the funniest man in America.

By the later 1970s, the Lear revolution was over and, with the decline of M*A*S*H, the practical end had come to the role of the Hollywood Left in television, aside from the lingering influence of their films and personal contacts. But true to the cryptic legacy of the blacklisted generation, the subtle articulation of politics as ethical sentiment continued to work its influence. It had become part of the very oxygen of liberal television.

CHAPTER THREE

CRITIQUE FROM THE MARGIN

THE FORMER NETWORK OFFICIALS, DIRECTORS AND WRITERS who had created the drama series of the 1950s Golden Age and were most responsible for its success could be pardoned for hanging crepe over the network doors and for seeing in the series' demise an end to television's promise as a new medium for public enlightenment and uplift. They could hardly be expected to notice equally promising developments emerging elsewhere in the medium that had been buried deep in the narrative structure of television "entertainment" right from the start. The same discouraging Arbitron surveys that helped kill off the drama anthologies also recorded the enormous popularity of *Twilight Zone* and *Have Gun Will Travel*. They rewarded small but not insignificant clusters of genres that the more sophisticated fans of serious drama, some of whom were television's early critics, mostly disdained. It was here, in these lesser TV genres, the sitcoms and children's shows, where the blacklistees and their younger allies (often protégés) found their berths.

Similar developments were discernable in the parallel world of B movies. In the 20-year period from the early 1950s to the early 1970s, it was in the B genre that left-wing science fiction writers expressed the kinds of messages that Rod Serling and more obscure fantasy auteurs were sending out through the younger mass medium. In both media, human beings were seen as not alone in a universe very likely populated by various (and usually more intelligent) species, and whether they were alone or not, humans evidently had little insight into their own dilemmas. At odds with these messages was another, perpetually renewed vision of a starship called *Enterprise* set on a Columbus-like pursuit of new fascinations and future commercial privileges in some fresh El Dorado that promised both gold and adventure. Even here the themes of strangeness, of unanticipated destiny and the fragility of everyday life remained deeply rooted. So did the horrors close to home, with assorted conscience-stricken vampires, zombies fighting in defense of some vaguely defined public interest, creatures too dangerous to keep alive but too valuable to die without depriving humanity of a better grasp of the world, and so on.

The literary genre of fantasy, with horror and science fiction as its two most modern expressions, had always occupied strange quarters in U.S. politics. Edward Bellamy's novel *Looking Backward* (1889) was the second best-selling American novel of the nineteenth century, just after *Uncle Tom's Cabin*. Socialists and popular literary utopians of the 1910s shared an optimism about the future, based in part on a utopian excitement over the newly discovered technology of radio—a faith that was shattered by the devastations of the First World War. But if science fiction had nearly always represented the sunnier impulse that looked to the future for the resolution of human problems, horror insisted on the recovery of the memory of ancient crimes against the oppressed and excluded (hence its preoccupation with faux philology and lost texts), and radicalism was if anything more common in the darker subgenre. Among the pulps of the 1920s and 1930s, *Weird Tales* had the most frequent, however oblique, anti-capitalist writing, including that of late-life socialist convert H. P. Lovecraft, from whose short stories scores of films and television dramas would eventually be adapted, with or without credit.

In Hollywood, horror was likewise a province of the avant-garde, with an occasional large dose of radicalism. *Frankenstein*'s adaptor/script writer, Francis Faragoh, a 1920s theatrical avant-gardist of the first order, would go on to become chairman of the Hollywood Writers Mobilization, the most prestigious of the Popular Front organizations in the film capital. It was not entirely by coincidence that the Frankenstein's monster, Boris Karloff, was himself a founder of the Screen Actors Guild and a frequent collaborator on Left projects; or that his colleague Bela Lugosi stood proudly (along with modernist composer Bela Bartok) as the most famous public figure of the Hungarian Democratic Federation, one of the ethnic Left's strongest antifascist constituency groups.

In television, some of the same threads were showing up in the otherworldly *Topper* (1953–1956) and *The Ghost and Mrs. Muir* (1968–1970) both heavy in (hidden) left-wing writing talent. The sight gags of ghostly manipulations of everyday objects may have had no particular political affect, even if the fantasy element owed greatly to the iconoclastic and antiwar novelist Thorne Smith's racy 1920s and 1930s literary adventures of spirits upsetting bourgeois respectability.[1] Later, critical possibilities still clung to fantasy, as for instance the critique of the pursuit of normality exposed in *The Munsters* (1964–1966). Starring Method actor Fred Gwynne and co-starring Al Lewis—a forties-style Jewish left-winger who later ran repeatedly for office on the Green Party ticket—the creatures of the title were cheerful beings embroiled weekly in situations that revealed the misunderstandings of conformist Americans.[2] Still later, the literally postmodern Boulder of *Mork and Mindy* (1978–1982) allowed a recollection of the vanished sixties innocence of a supposed alien played brilliantly by counter-cultural icon Robin Williams.[3]

The Hollywood Left had helped to create a postmodernist culture in various other ways, albeit few of them markedly visible. Scarcely anything could be less prestigious than the lowly profession of animator, with the skills of the cartoon-style artist joined to those of the script and virtual-set specialists, most of whose names were hardly noticed in the credits. Apart from Disney's features, cartoons had been viewed almost exclusively between feature film presentations. But animation was the only place, as one observer famously put it in the 1930s, where Charlie Chaplin could be put into a milk bottle: anything was possible, within the limits of censorship. Even censorship yielded somewhat during wartime, and the radicals had by then won their spurs in some of the best studios, including that of Disney himself, a political tyrant but also an admired technical perfectionist. When the outstanding technicians discovered the spirit of Picasso (the aging artist happened to be a notorious opponent of U.S. foreign policy), the modern animated feature was born.

More broadly, the children's or family feature, renewed with a vengeance on television, invited imaginative leaps little appreciated outside, from the days of *Howdy Doody* to *Pee Wee's Playhouse*. Who knew, as long as investigating commit-tees did not look closely enough, that the rebellious sentiment of *Cinderella* owed its origin to a certain Red under Disney's creative bed?[4] Who cared if a small leftish crew spawned *Gerald McBoing Boing* or that one of its most prominent members took over *The Mighty Mouse Playhouse* (1955–1967) for a few years while another co-created *Rocky and His Friends*? Likewise, it may have been unimportant that it was blacklistee Melvin Levy who invented the Jingles character for a 300-pound Andy Devine in *Adventures of Wild Bill Hickok* (1951–1958), because the brain-storming was just anonymous hack work. Or was it? In an era when comic books became the center of a congressional investigation seeking out the corruption of youth—and Elvis Presley was just around the corner—the influences of fluid intel-lects on the coming generation could be greater than anyone imagined.

Radicals had also been preparing for an alternative to modernism since 1920s Broadway showed sophisticated audiences how to celebrate life and its sweetness, the antidote to pathos. The largely unblacklisted Broadway of the 1940s through the 1960s contributed this same quality to Hollywood, with or without credits for the writers of the lyrics, the composers of the music and the authors of the "book." Most of those involved in left-wing theater were not able to replicate this influ-ence, particularly not the literate theater both on and off Broadway in which left-wing intellectuals took justifiable pride. Still, the popular stage, like so much other work in this interim, amounted to more than just another way of making a living. The extended memory of a Jewish and ethnic past grew more attractive to theater- and filmgoers as it receded into the distance; the vanguard role of theater introducing black (and later Latino) faces and voices grew more intense; and the sense of being different from Hollywood diminished as the musical lost its freshness and originality as a form (except as revival or camp). But for the 1950s and 1960s, its strength remained in outright fantasy.

COMMIES FROM OUTER SPACE

The first communication between beings from different planets is one of the received themes of the science fiction genre, renewed and reimagined in each generation and each time around with a heightened degree of realism and, in the case of film and TV, with ever-more elaborate special effects. The tantalizing notion that dialogue with an advanced race could give humans the knowledge to propel themselves at a single stroke out of their current dysfunctional social relations, skipping over generations of gradual change, is the central idea of what we might call critical science fiction. The future, in this vision, is the antidote to history.

When an amateur astronomer happens on the crash of an extraterrestrial spacecraft in the 1953 film *It Came From Outer Space*, he realizes that "It's the biggest thing that ever happened." He speaks the line dreamily, as though awakening to the idea of a future that only moments before had been unimaginable. As news of the crash spreads and the locals become aware that aliens may be abroad in the Mojave desert, the astronomer/intellectual comes to realize that, as the sole witness to the event and one of the few people on earth then capable of grasping its meaning, he must play the prophet in a society so hostile to change that it is determined to kill anything it doesn't understand.

That *It Came From Outer Space* was a parable of the Cold War is undeniable. But what was its meaning? We look back on the movie from a time so distant that we represent its characters' own science-fictional future.[5] Meanwhile, the sci-fi of this era has been encrusted with so many interpretations from intervening generations of filmmakers, critics and viewers that we can hardly view the films as their creators intended. They have come to be associated with the manipulation of audiences through cheap and exaggerated special effects, requiring the contemporary viewer to see them as though through two sets of eyes, one pair 50 years younger than the other.[6]

The same ambiguity of meaning, but hotter debates, have been waged over the meaning of director Don Siegel's *Invasion of the Body Snatchers* (1956), a film marked from its appearance as a classic of Cold War paranoia. Even though Siegel regularly told interviewers he considered himself a political liberal, his own *Dirty Harry* (1971) raised so much protest on the Left that even his own characterization of his Clint Eastwood protagonist as a "bitter bigot" did not calm things down.[7] The story line of *Body Snatchers* encouraged a similar interpretation: an isolated town is taken over by pods, with aliens emerging from them to take the place of lookalike humans (who need only fall asleep to be lost), and in the end a grim protagonist faces an alien conquest and a humanity helpless to resist. It was natural to interpret this as a warning of a commie invasion.

The backstory of *Invasion of the Body Snatchers* points in another direction. Its principal screenwriter was Daniel Mainwaring, working from a novel by the libertarian Jack Finney. Mainwaring was for starters a collaborator on one of the most important and daring of the very last left-wing movies made before the blacklist, *The Lawless* (1950), directed by Joseph Losey, and at the time of *Body Snatchers* was also the "front" for Hollywood Ten victim Adrian Scott in television work.[8] An additional and uncredited screenwriter for *Invasion* was Sam Peckinpah who, as we shall see, went on as a director to become one of the more gifted and misunderstood social critics in Hollywood. The final uncredited screenwriter happened to be none other than Richard Collins, a former Communist who turned friendly witness for congressional investigators, himself possibly an earlier "invader" of the Left from the FBI and definitely no science fiction writer.[9]

It seems more than possible, then, extrapolating from the other work of this unlikely combination of screenwriters and of the always ambiguous Siegel, that the alien "pods" taking over the bodies of the townspeople were metaphorically the globules of burgeoning suburban conformism that offered quiet complicity with McCarthyism. Contrasted to some other invasion classics such as *The Thing*—shot under Howard Hughes' arch-conservative guidance, with an alien who has only the worst intentions (and looks)—*Invasion of the Body Snatchers* is at the very least uncertain in its implications.[10] In any case, the director's (as well as the writers') connections with the Left were deeper than critics or devotees have ever recognized.

Before he became a director, Siegel had, as we've seen, helped invent montage, worked on any number of left-leaning films and by the 1950s worked mostly in television. His B films, considered by critics among the best low-budget features ever made, were noted for his use of non-actors in impromptu scenes, as if to bring the documentary to life, *Naked City*–style.

Siegel also directed *Flaming Star* (1960), in which Elvis stands in for an emotionally wounded Indian; *Madigan* (1968), the comeback film of blacklisted noir master screenwriter Abraham Polonsky, in which the rebellious "Dirty Harry" cop first sees the light, and definitely not as a right-winger; and a pair of dramas, the classic *Two Mules for Sister Sara* (1970) and *Beguiled* (1971), both written by Albert Maltz. At a reasonable guess, Siegel shared many of the black-listees' predilections, aesthetically as well as politically.[11]

It Came From Outer Space (1953) was more obviously about the Cold War than Invasion of the Body Snatchers, even if the evidence seems to have been over-looked at the time. Its writer-producer, William Alland, had been a member of the Communist Party intermittently from the late 1930s to the late 1940s. In 1953, at the end of the Los Angeles hearings, he had nearly escaped testifying, then made a career move by giving the committee the names of his former friends and comrades.[12]

Jack Arnold, a frequent collaborator with Alland and the director of It Came From Outer Space, had no such specific links with the Hollywood Left, but he did have an equally interesting political past. Breaking into films as a documentary maker in the thirties, first for the Jewish Consumptive Relief Society and then for the International Ladies Garment Workers Union (ILGWU), Arnold attained his pre-Hollywood high point in 1950, in With These Hands. It was a hagiographic history of the ILGWU, made in expectation of State Department (or CIA-funded) showings to trade unionists around the world. Arnold's film mixed stills, historic film clips and highly colored fictional recreations and meanwhile ignored the union's well-known pockets of corruption, its bossism and its growing ethnic discomforts (by the late 1940s, it had a substantially Puerto Rican membership ruled with an iron hand by Jewish functionaries). With These Hands focused in-stead, after the union's heroic formative years, on the successful expulsion of elected Communist officials and the global pursuit of a "free" (noncommunist) unionism in the Cold War era. In what must have been a memorable role for an incipient science-fiction director of the fifties, Arnold himself played an evil com-munist organizer.[13]

For all of these reasons—albeit without reading too much into them—it is not hard to detect in Outer Space a certain social democratic tinge, the remnant perhaps of the old idea that European socialists had arranged for a better social compact than had the politicians and industrialists of the younger and still root-less United States. The film comes unambiguously to the defense of what it de-scribes as "better ideas" from the aliens, who (like Europeans) are shown as possessed of a more enlightened society than the earthlings but whose ideas the Americans in the film are too "frightened" to accept.

The idea for Outer Space was first dreamed up by Alland (1916–1997), a quirky and highly emotional man with some of the oddest if also unimpeachably left-wing bona fides. Son of two immigrant Jews, an abusive proletarian father and an emo-tionally dependent mother who, he later insisted, had once agreed to run away with him, young Alland gravitated toward the theater, first in Baltimore, then New York. Joining Orson Welles' Mercury troupe as a gofer for the impresario-star, he quickly became a stage manager and assistant director. Alland later recalled with pride that he had personally chauffeured Welles all the way to Hollywood.

Welles had rewarded him by making the young amateur actor the voice (and shadow profile) of the inquiring reporter in *Citizen Kane* as well as the narrator of the famous newsreel and the dialogue director. In any case, Alland's first tour in Hollywood was quickly interrupted by war. Returning from service as a fighter pilot, he afterward snagged bit parts in Welles' *Lady from Shanghai* and *Macbeth* but worked mainly in radio, writing and directing the first children's program about psychological problems and their resolution—a subject close to his own troubled heart. When that show died, he drifted into the production end of films, making his way up to producer for B science-fiction pictures, often those with an oblique social or psychological twist.[14]

Alland commissioned a 32-year-old writer for science-fiction pulp magazines to write the story basis for *It Came From Outer Space*. Ray Bradbury, destined to be hailed as one of the great figures of sci-fi and one of only a few genre writers ever to have a television series named after him (*Ray Bradbury's Science Fiction Theater*), had recently written *The Martian Chronicles*, a sometimes severe criticism of the future colonization of the Red Planet by often boorishly insensitive earth folk. During the shooting of *Outer Space*, Bradbury's civil libertarian classic *Fahrenheit 451* appeared. In this future world, its story named for the temperature at which paper burns, all literary classics have been destroyed by official decree. They persist only in the minds of the resisters who live communally in secret, memorizing the great books for future cultural revivals.[15] This was antifascism, Bradbury-style. Meanwhile, in 1952 he determinedly published in the pages of *The California Quarterly*—the literary organ of what remained of the Hollywood Left, a publication spotlighted by red-baiters as a center of continuing cultural subversion. He also took a frontline position defending the blacklistees, then backed off as pressure on him increased.[16]

Bradbury's frame for the story had the protagonist (oddly, Richard Carlson, the counter-spy in the anticommunist TV show, *I Led Three Lives*) telling everyone within earshot in his small southwestern town about the arrival of the aliens. His fellow citizens react first with incredulity, then determine to wipe out the presumed menace. As the sheriff organizes a posse-cum-lynch mob, Carlson learns from the aliens that they are only making a pit-stop for repairs. Now he sets himself to protect his new intergalactic friends from the rampaging McCarthyites until the visitors can blast back up through the atmosphere.

The story premise did not lack for contemporary context. By the year the film was released, a few real-life, laid-off Sunbelt aerospace workers had announced their own contact with aliens in the desert, and fresh speculation arose about presumably covered-up government examination of aliens from an unidentified flying object near Roswell, New Mexico in 1947. These early currents in the rising flow of UFO-logy also coincided with the rise of MK-ULTRA, a Central Intelligence Agency project of mind control, and observers across the political spectrum have often wondered about the possible connections. As it turned out, B-movie Hollywood was one of the few venues in the culture in which this sensitive subject could be discussed, however obliquely.[17]

Over the next decade, while the threat of nuclear war between the United States and the Soviet Union dragged on, the aliens were often seen as poised to subvert human values—pretty much as the Communists sought to subvert American values—but just as often seen as saviors; these superior beings would order a halt to nuclear testing and place the planet's governments into receivership if they refused to give up their erring ways. Somehow, the "good" aliens would force humans into a new age of good will, while offering tourist-style space trips as well as cures for ailments ranging from arthritis and cancer to old age.

The spinoffs of this mini-obsession had also begun to resonate in the narrowing world of the Hollywood Left and its diaspora. Destination Moon (1950), directed by Irving Pichel from a short story by (and co-adapted by) the markedly conservative novelist Robert Heinlein, offered the hag-ridden ex-communist director the chance to backpedal politically to a corporate saga of space-travel triumph. It was mainly memorable, though, for its special effects, winning an Oscar for animator George Pal, thanks in part to Woody Woodpecker making a remarkable guest appearance.[18]

Meanwhile, one of the best among the sci-fi pictures was the unlikely Superman and the Mole Men (1951). The first of the Superman films, it was the predecessor (with the same lead and same director) of the popular 1950s television series. Even more strikingly than in Outer Space, the political message was equally bold and literal. As Clark Kent and Lois Lane go to the site of the world's deepest oil well for a Daily Planet story, they learn to their horror that a race of harmless little beings (played by midgets with rubber bald wigs) has responded to the mechanical invasion of their subterranean culture by coming to the surface for the first time. The townsfolk immediately begin to terrorize them, shooting, burning and trying to lynch the creatures until the Man of Steel steps in to take away their weapons and warns them that they are acting not as true Americans but "like Nazi storm troopers." Happily—notwithstanding Lois's sneer that Clark seems to be "leading a double life" and disappears whenever trouble shows—things work out for everyone, and the mole men make their way back down inside the earth.

The potentially eco-catastrophic petroleum exploration is wiped out in the process, and, as Lois says, the mole men have their world again, just as "we have ours." Peaceful coexistence has been achieved—if not, lamentably, she seems poised to add, between real-life rivals on the surface of the planet. The film's di-

what Hook (handwritten)

rector, Lee Sholem, had old Popular Front ties, and the major supporting actor playing the wicked sheriff who collaborates with the rednecks was none other than left-winger Jeff Corey, recently reduced from the status of major actor in daring liberal films like *Home of the Brave* and en route to the blacklist. Further in the backstory, one of the two Cleveland Jewish adolescents of the 1930s who invented the comic book character Superman had also, like so many Jewish youngsters of the time, been in the social orbit of the Young People's Socialist League.[19]

As *Superman and the Mole Men* offered a cosmic intervention of superhuman muscularity, *The Day the Earth Stood Still* (1951), directed by the Hollywood Left's sturdy ally, Robert Wise (1914-), came close to being the best of the intergalactic liberal messages. Wise, who dropped out of college in the 1930s and entered Hollywood at the production end, actually edited *Citizen Kane* and several other of Welles' masterpieces; he was fond of telling interviewers that, since he had the same friends and political leanings as the Communists and other Popular Fronters (though without any formal affiliations), he could never quite understand why he'd slipped through the blacklisters' nets.[20] He had already made a mark, though only among insiders, with his first full directorial assignment, the neglected antifascist *Mademoiselle Fifi* (1944), written by Austrian exile and future blacklistee Josef Mischel.[21] *The Day the Earth Stood Still* has a Washington, D.C. bystander meet the aliens and hear their intergalactic warning against nuclear war. He suffers through a McCarthy-like "exposure" of their contact by a greedy informer and watches the dying alien chief as he nobly seeks to help the deluded earthlings escape their fate.

By contrast, in *It Came From Outer Space*, the protagonist is almost existential in his uncertainty. Carlson, as John Putnam, repeatedly crosses the line between alien and human society, metaphorically perhaps the line separating what had attracted the producer and director toward socialism and what they feared and rejected in communism. What is most attractive about the aliens is also the most repellent, as the sheriff in the story understands. When the sheriff learns of the aliens' ability to protect themselves against ambush by disguising themselves as humans, he turns his suspicion on the intellectual. Carlson-Putnam, in what is surely the strangest moment in a strange narrative, admits "That's right! Wouldn't it be a fine trick if I weren't John Putnam at all, but something from another world come here to give you a lot of false leads!" The possibility that he has evolved from bewildered observer to alien sympathizer is confirmed near the film's conclusion, when he confronts the leader of the extra-terrestrials, only to discover that the face he is gazing into is his own, borrowed by the alien's leader. The gaze, closely resembling that of so many former radicals from the 1930s and 1940s as they reconsidered their own pasts, seems to be one of regret and barely disguised nostalgia for something lost and never to be regained.

There is also a playfulness in *Outer Space* that anticipates developments in some of the wilder episodes of *X Files* during the closing years of the century.[22] Barbara Rush, as the endangered heroine, opens the door to her home and gives one of the movie's rare screams at the sight of an alien. The monster turns out to be a boy in a plastic space cadet's helmet of the sort made popular by 1950s salesmanship ("As Seen on TV!"). When Putnam searches for Rush later on in the film—by now she has been captured by the aliens—he suddenly spots her standing on a rocky embankment just a few yards away in an incongruous strapless black gown, her chiffon neck scarf rolling out on the desert breeze. In succeeding jump cuts she mysteriously recedes into the distance in a series of images that, taken together, are an explicit use of surrealist editing techniques in a genre that was incongruously otherwise too prosaic to exploit them. In this moment the weirdness scale in Hollywood hit some of its highest notes, as throughout the outrageously avant-garde *Pandora and the Flying Dutchman* (1951) by ex-Marxist writer-director Albert Lewin, featuring James Mason as the eternal melancholiac finding his long-awaited death in the embrace of vampish/masochistic Ava Gardner.[23]

It Came From Outer Space was, Alland finally allowed, "the most political I ever got." The movie carried the Rooseveltian message that all the human race has to fear "is fear itself." And "If you fear the Communists, we destroy ourselves—though you would have to read between the lines [of the film] to figure it out."[24] At another point, Arnold once said that "if there were important things to be said about our society and its mores, they certainly weren't said" in the mainstream film fare of the time, whereas "we could do it and get away with it, because it was fantasy."[25]

Alland avoided using Arnold for his next and most didactic feature, *This Island Earth* (1955), a bigger-budget successor of sorts that rewarded the producer for his box office (in fifties B terms, normally drive-in box office) success. As a skillful director, Arnold might actually have improved upon the thin acting and the overly complex plotting, avoiding the ridicule that was bound to follow the introduction into alienology of beings with large, prosthetic foreheads.[26] By the same token, Arnold probably did not possess the sophistication necessary to explicate the full weight of Alland's political allegory about a group of atomic scientists from around the world recruited by aliens, who have been organized into a secret society destined to "put an end to war." Dedicated classicists, the recruits play Mozart at every meal. That they are organized on the model of the Communist Party becomes evident when the leaders receive secret messages over the phone ordering them to perform certain alchemical experiments transforming lead into uranium (rather than gold, the more ancient dream). No dissent is permitted in this highly disciplined camp; a human who tries to leave the group is killed with a laser beam on the orders of the alien commissar.

Perhaps by this time Alland's attitudes about his former comrades and friends of the CP had hardened—but not entirely, for there is still plenty of opportunity to cross and recross the line. The viewer soon learns that much of the ruthlessness of these particular alien intellectuals has been reluctant, spurred only by the desperate reality that their home planet is currently under attack and their own civilization in imminent danger of extermination from the equivalent of fascist invaders. When the leader takes two human scientists back to his planet for compulsory education, in any case, the scenes of war's devastation are rather too close to the spirit and intensity of Anatole Litvak's 1943 documentary, *The Battle of Stalingrad,* to be entirely accidental. By the end of the trip, the planet has become a burned-out dystopia.

Despite the clunky special effects of *This Island Earth,* a real sense of pathos manages to emerge, particularly in the personality of the alien leader. He is so overcome with despair at what is happening to his home, its now-complete social totalitarianism as well as the environmental disaster of warfare, that he defies *his* leader and returns the humans safely to Earth. He then refuses the proffered sanctuary of humankind and resolves to wander the universe like a lonely intergalactic Trotsky, spreading the word of a revolution that "exploded" but continues to shed its light in distant places.

This particular vein of what might be called Cold War liberal or U.S.-style social-democratic science fiction never really established itself. *Outer Space* was pretty much the end of the road for Jack Arnold's political contribution. He would be remembered as a producer of another island, *Gilligan's Island,* in one episode of which—some conspiracy-minded sources have claimed in good sci-fi fashion—certain details about CIA experiments in mind control were casually leaked.[27] Arnold and Alland also would collaborate again, but never so efficiently.

Thus *Creature from the Black Lagoon* (1954), an early 3-D commercial success and monster standard that producer Alland claimed to have plotted himself (but had Arnold direct), was an unmistakable allegory as well as an exploitation feature with a silly web-appendaged monster pursuing the bikini-wearing Julie Adams through miles of swampy footage. Survivor of some ancient era, the creature means no harm, despite the moments when its libido overwhelms its otherwise good sense to remain out of sight. The thoughtful scientist, among his pursuers, wonders aloud if all things in the land of the Amazon might not be better left alone.[28]

The Revenge of the Creature (1955), again directed by Arnold but notably written by Martin Berkeley—a B-movie screenwriter who a few years earlier set the HUAC record by naming 155 Hollywood Communists—was still more literal. This time, the poor gill-man is captured and imprisoned in a Florida aquatic park, chained to the side of a converted swimming pool and gawked at by cruel consumers as a Third World oddity. He escapes for a time, wandering in canals through new suburbs en route to his doom, evoking still more pity in thoughtful bystanders. Alland himself claimed it was an eco-feature like Hitchcock's *The Birds*, by intent if not in production values.[29]

Alland soon ran out of things to say. In *Space Children* (1958), brainwashed kids set out to sabotage a Pacific nuclear test site in the Jack Arnold style of combined left-and-right paranoia. In *The Deadly Mantis* (1957), a giant spider created by a radioactive experiment heads toward Manhattan, perhaps taking revenge for that snobbery New Yorkers had continually practiced against Hollywoodites. It was hackwork, or worse.

It was also, by any standard, politically inert. The increasing odds of making a good film for a thrill-crazed or indifferent audience (many of them parked at the drive-ins, craving thrills not on the screen), wore down the genre. By the later 1950s, sci-fi productions would explode in dozens of films that were written and acted with such tinny indifference that *The Robot vs. The Aztec Mummy*, *Monster a Go-Go*, *Cat Women of the Moon* and *Santa Claus Conquers the Martians* mocked the genre even while exploiting it. In the years of what might be called the High Cold War, western and science fiction movies escaped the close political scrutiny that HUAC had brought to bear on liberal "conscience" films about anti-Semitism, race, peace and other weighty issues. Given Alland's ability to turn out films on schedule and under budget, his abundant *oeuvre* came to be seen as exemplifying what later critics, with a nudge and wink, would describe as the "mystique of failure," the practice by which the audience celebrates its superiority to the artifact it contemplates. In the end, however, it is open to question whether some of these dated sci-fi movies or their knowing critics contained the sharper political sensibility.[30]

Any further elaboration of a sympathetic argument for the creators of the B horror and sci-fi film rests partly on personal tales of where and how blacklist victims along with their friends managed to get work in difficult times. But the evidence is real. Take the case of Eugène Lourié (1903–1991), a Russian-born art director for Jean Renoir's films of the French Popular Front. Following Renoir to the United States in 1940, he stayed on to direct, among other films, *The Beast from 20,000 Fathoms* (1953), based on a Ray Bradbury short story about a monster thawed by atomic weapons. Lourié and a little-remembered blacklistee, Daniel James, rewrote the same story with a more explicit warning about environmental destruction, and Lourié himself directed this new version in England as *The Giant Behemoth* (1959).

Two years later, James and fellow blacklistee writer Robert Richards scripted a sequel, *Gorgo* (1961), also directed by Lourié (who fronted for their writing credits), about a mama sea monster who destroys great swaths of London as she rescues her baby from uncomprehending humans. The Britishers are all the more baffled (if also awed) at the close of the film when the two creatures return to the sea, displaying the grandeur of nature over paltry human civilization. The almost constant use of special effects leaves little room for plot or dialogue (screams tend to dominate), but the intent is registered clearly enough at crucial moments of this film, as in its predecessor.[31]

The creature feature, its full commercial potential realized only later on television, relied on bottom-drawer talent; its products were generally more laughable than scary. Some of its most successful producers and marketers were figures like the legendary Samuel Z. Arkoff, whose 453 low-budget features ranged from *How to Stuff a Wild Bikini* and *I Was a Teenage Werewolf* to *The Brain Eaters* and numerous misappropriations of Poe and H. P. Lovecraft.[32]

Cinematic horror also offered a last resort for sections of a vanishing *Mittel-Europa* avant-garde. Edgar G. Ulmer (1904–1972), a former Viennese film set designer who directed the classic antiwar horror film *The Black Cat* (1934) as well as several Yiddish-language classics and the famed noir *Detour* (1945), spent a lifetime on the fringes of the Left, moving ever further away from Hollywood to independent productions—most of them shot in a week or so, on almost unimaginably small budgets. Ulmer made a half-dozen cheapo sci-fi films in the decade or so after 1950. His oddest was surely *Beyond the Time Barrier* (1960), where a flyer crashes into a future world poisoned by radioactivity and barely escapes the embrace of a deaf-and-dumb princess (the only fertile female left) who is the last hope of yet another court of Viennese-accented liberals. Our flyer manages to return to the sixties. We find him in a hospital bed, revealing that he has the same poisoning from radioactivity, and offers in his last breath his warning to scientists and the military. All this Ulmer accomplished in sets that made the usual drive-in features seem expensive but that foreshadowed television sci-fi like the British *Doctor Who*, bringing back cautionary themes together with the budget-driven narrative of the endless chase in the corridor.[33]

In much the same spirit—at least in regard to production values—Bernard Gordon remembered writing *Zombies of Mora Tau* (1957) for the notoriously cheap producer Sam Katzman. Happy to get blacklisted talent at low fees, Katzman was unwilling to invest in a set that would allow the actor-zombies (protecting a sort of historic ghost ship) not to stumble around on camera without laboriously clambering in and out of their chintzy coffins.[34] Two of the most politically interesting films in this genre were born of Gordon's quick pen. In the early days of the Cold War, with nuclear confrontation seemingly on the agenda, he delivered *Earth vs. the Flying Saucers* (1956) to Katzman, who, for reasons known only to himself, enjoyed seeing "vs." in the title of his more preposterous films. Here, the invaders turn out to be nothing less than flying fascists.[35] Technologically advanced, they are the soldiers from a "disintegrated star system" sent on a mission to conquer earth and subject earthlings to their command. Most memorable are the images of alien spacecraft slicing through the Washington Monument or crashing into the Supreme Court or, in the film's climax, into the capitol dome of Congress. For many viewers, Ray Harryhausen's stop-motion animation of the attack on the U.S. government must surely have been the film's high point. So terrible is the external threat that the Soviet Union and the USA, at each others' throats since 1945, now declare human peace and return to their alliance, as in the good old days of the antifascist crusade against the common enemy. Securing planetary safety for what may be presumed to be a more cooperative future through the guidance of a functioning United Nations, they spare humanity twice over. No congressman would dare make such a proposal.[36]

The Man Who Turned to Stone (1957) is a horror/sci-fi picture of a superior kind, derived from Gordon's better narrative impulses. Credited to "Raymond Marcus," it was filmed in black and white on a trifling budget, with special effects confined to tricks of makeup and lighting. But much as the French critics found treasures of narrative among the low-budget westerns of the American fifties, this is a film whose covert criticism of the nobility is, in its best moments, not entirely unworthy of comparison with Jean Renoir's own attacks, when he mocked "the dissolution and decay of an effete aristocracy gradually sinking beneath the weight of its own artificial and lifeless conventions. . . ."[37]

At the "LaSalle Detention Center for Girls" somewhere in Middle America, the inmates are rightly terrified of the administration. A missing patient, heard shrieking in the middle of the night, turns up dead of a supposed heart attack in the infirmary. The inmates' fears of murder are listened to sympathetically by a pair of New Dealish figures, one a newcomer close to the governor's daughter and the other an investigator sent in by the state—so far, a plot greatly resembling Popular Front films about women's prisons. Together, the mutually smitten pair unearth records showing that nearly a dozen inmates have died under similarly mysterious circumstances. Suspicion finally falls upon the administrators, a collection of six refugee weirdos played by skilled character actors and led by the tuba-voiced Victor Jory. The others include a severe headmistress and three scientists—respectively English, French and German—who dress in scarves fitted with stick pins and other emblems of over-refined taste (while the administration offices are suspiciously outfitted with fine draperies and an original Rembrandt!). The sixth, the executioner, is a hulking figure deliciously played by the anvil-headed Austrian character actor, Frederick Ledebur, in real life the scion of the ancient Hohenzollern family.

The investigators discover, to their amazement, that these curious figures were all born around 1733 in various parts of Europe and found each other in Paris, where they had all gone to study the science of immortality with the same

French aristocrat. Their research revealed that humans can live for centuries with the transfer of "bio-electric energy." When a donor (ideally a nubile female) is lowered into a bath of "copper sulfate solution," her life energy is drained away and transferred to a recipient. The transferences must occur more frequently over time, for if they do not, the aging ghoul's skin gradually curdles into a petrified sheath harder than the stone of the title and the beating of the heart of the aging predator grows louder, a deafening thing, as death approaches.

The details of the happy outcome to *The Man Who Turned to Stone* are merely conventional. But it's worth noting a few more of its European qualities, including echoes (during the final rebellion of the young inmates) of avant-garde director Jean Vigo's *Zéro de conduite* (1933), regarded as one of the most successful surrealist films. More explicitly than any U.S. genre film, *Stone* uses the physical transfer of the life force from one class to another as a metaphor for economic expropriation. This metaphor has been more commonly deployed in vampire narratives, not least by Karl Marx, who wrote that "Capital is dead labor that, vampire-like, only lives by sucking living labor, and lives the more, the more labor it sucks."[38] In *The Man Who Turned to Stone*, however, we find Marx's more ominous metaphor for the cumulative price that has been paid for "progress," the weight of the combined deprivation of plain people forced to support someone else's luxurious life.[39] The horror can be expunged only with the redemption of all the countless generations of the forgotten dead in class societies from all of time.

The Curse of the Werewolf (1961), a moodily superior but otherwise stock British feature in most production respects, was nominally based upon the artistic lycanthropy novel of another day, *Werewolf of Paris*, written by future blacklistee (and horror film writer) Guy Endore in 1933, which deployed the background of the Paris Commune for the return of the werewolf. The film might have been a classic of the genre if only the novelist, driven from his screenwriting career, had been invited to write the adaptation. Enough survived in *The Curse* to have a proletarian lad, denied the right to marry his beloved, lose control of the wolf within him and be pursued (shades of the poor, misunderstood creation of Dr. Frankenstein) by hateful villagers as he makes his escape in the familiar manner by leaping across mansard roofs to disappear into the night.[40]

Gordon's final horror film, which he produced with a script by Julian Zimet and another blacklistee (former Broadway award-winner Arnaud D'Usseau), was a medium-budget feature with campy British stars Christopher Lee and Peter Cushing: *Horror Express* (1972).[41] An archeologist unearths a creature from outer space who has literally been on ice in Siberia since before the rise of homo sapiens. As the creature is boxed up for shipment on the Trans-Siberian Express, it comes to life and covertly begins to absorb information, including everything that has come to pass since the creature was frozen. The melancholy creature acquires a growing store of knowledge by aiming its eyes at various humans, whose brains, once emptied, promptly turn to pulp. This ominous process, together with the footage of the train trip and a romantic subplot of a Russian count and his inamorata, effectively uses up most of the picture. Within the attenuated plot, two egotistical anthropologists conspire against each other as the creature—who could surely destroy humankind but also represents its only prospect for truly knowing itself—grows ever stronger. Unfortunately, *Horror Express* was not itself strong enough to outgrow its action narrative to arrive at something larger. But the larger destination was hinted at. In nearly all of Gordon's films and others in the lower echelons of this subgenre, when written by leftists, there lurked the lesson Marx had written down as a curiously gothic parable: the worker observes to his own capitalist, "The thing you represent to me, face-to-face, has no heart in its breast. That which seems to throb there is my own heart beating."[42]

Not that Gordon or his handful of left-wing collaborators had this observation firmly or consistently in mind; but as so often happens, the notions that they put into the heads of monsters conveyed the wisdom of their own lifetimes. The Outsider, representative of the proletariat that does not know itself, is handed the script, figuratively speaking. It speaks (often enough, croaks) the lines prepared in the 1930s, now revised by defeat and disillusionment, but still full of insight. These lines suggest, however inarticulately, that capitalism remains determined to act as its own gravedigger, whether ecologically or psychologically, even in the prosperity of cholesterol-rich America. Who would have thought that the inscription on the gravedigger's shovel would be most legible in the horror films that were turned out strictly for money?

KID STUFF

The swashbuckler, one of those family-film genres suitable for adaptations of all kinds, was a natural for the adventurer of a certain kind: the social outlaw. The "primitive rebel" was far from imaginary. British Marxist historian Eric Hobsbawm used the term to describe the type who resisted the invasion of capitalism while appealing for a return to the social institutions of some earlier, happier age; he exemplified the counterattack of the impoverished peasant against the rapacious royalty and emerging bourgeoisie for centuries across Europe.[43] In the New World, this rebel often represented the race that was trod underfoot, especially the displaced Hispanic celebrated in real-life *corridos* (popular ballads of revenge against the land-stealing Anglos) and in Hollywood's biopic of the leading social bandit, Jaoquin Murrieta, in *Robin Hood of El Dorado* (1936), the real story of California as seen by left-wing screenwriter Melvin Levy.[44]

Burt Lancaster added another swashbuckling chapter with *The Flame and the Arrow* (1950), scripted by Waldo Salt and set in pre-modern Italy, where a rebellious and militantly populistic noble leads an uprising against the oppressive Hessian usurpers and for princess Virginia Mayo. After some doubts (but none in the moviegoers' minds, it is safe to say), Mayo will defect to handsome Burt and to the cause of the masses. The *Flame*'s opening narrative fatefully recalled antifascist partisans: "Generations of mountaineers have passed down the legends of those dark years and brave deeds of their forefathers who fought for freedom," and organized secretly in cells. From there the story moved further backward—or forward, perhaps to the contemporary anticolonial revolts across Asia and Africa—as the forest people rose against the corrupt city-state.[45] Even in the darkest days of McCarthyism, the masses could love a rebel wronged.

A British-American team crossed over from films to television by returning to the singular classic of the lore, Robin Hood. The production story really begins with the peace crusade of former vice president Henry Wallace and his badly failed presidential bid of 1948. A Broadway lawyer and Wallace campaign impresario, Hannah Weinstein, saw the political end in sight and sagely beat a path to Europe. First, she set up a television crew in Paris, making a one-season series, *Colonel March of Scotland Yard,* for syndicated release. Its star was, not so surprisingly, the aged progressive Boris Karloff. Amid the lowest production values imaginable, a certain Columbo-style plot allowed the inspector to reveal foul misdeeds, mainly of the rich. It gave Weinstein's production company a place to start.[46]

Weinstein shrewdly switched her operations to the United Kingdom, where she bought property for a set and sold her ideas to an agency successfully marketing syndicated shows. She meanwhile gathered funds and a team of pioneer video technicians who invented crucial low-cost production tricks, like interchangeable sets on wheels used as interiors of entrances, fireplaces and even mini-groves of trees. Built and disassembled at a moment's notice, these were vastly cheaper than the permanent sets of film studios. Weinstein's real secret, though, was her new show's plot, its lead and its writers.

Robin Hood had been a perennial film favorite since silent days, with Douglas Fairbanks and Errol Flynn in notable starring roles—but made in Hollywood, far from the hero's historic home in Sherwood Forest. It was a natural for handsome swashbuckler type Richard Greene, who had co-starred in *Captain Scarlett* (1953)—the courageous rebel leader in Restoration France who will not allow the nobility to have its vengeful way with the common folk—and had been groomed to rival Robert Taylor before turning to television.[47] Above all, it was a natural for the best writers that Weinstein could get cheaply: the cream of the blacklistees.

Weinstein had no difficulty rounding up former Oscar winner Ring Lardner, Jr., and his frequent writing partner, Ian McLellan Hunter, who were supplemented in later seasons by former Abbott and Costello writer Robert Lees, Waldo Salt and Hollywood Ten writer-producer Adrian Scott, among others. Under normal circumstances, none of them (with the possible exception of Lees) would have been writing for television, especially at low rates. Under *these* circumstances, it offered an extraordinary opportunity to reach millions of viewers with some extraordinary writing talent.

The writing of *The Adventures of Robin Hood* (1956–1958) was a covert operation, successful enough that it raised even fewer suspicions than *You Are There*, which had recently purged its writers. Weinstein hired young journalist Albert Ruben to serve as an intermediary with the writers. He worked from a story basis that was sent in lengthy letters to the writers in New York and Los Angeles, and they in turn sent him their scripts. Everything was conducted with great care so as not to reveal the writers' identities to anyone.[48] *Robin Hood* was an immediate trans-Atlantic hit, at once British ITV's earliest successful costume drama, the first British series to sell successfully to the United States (it was broadcast almost simultaneously by CBS), and even the source of the British network's first hit tune. It was also one of the more enduring dramatic programs of television's early years, with 143 episodes.

To look at the Robin Hood series today is to understand immediately why the show took Golden Age television by storm. Set in Nottingham, it has Robin return from the Crusades to find the hated Normans in charge. These fascistic invaders have gained the loyalty of collaborators who don't care about the fate of "free Englishmen" and who are so eager to feather their own nests that they will do anything the occupiers desire—not so different from the real-life upper-class collaborators with the Nazis across most of Europe. Evil Prince John has replaced in all but name the Good King Richard, who is still off in the Holy Land—never mind that the Crusaders happened to be on a dubious mission of mostly commercial intent, dispatching infidels by the thousands. It was a series convention.

Discovering on his return that his father has been killed and the family lands seized, Robin of Locksley joins the outlaws in the forest, becoming "Robin of the Hood," their natural leader.[49] Villagers are sorely oppressed, but not on that account free of their own sins. The nasty henchmen of the Sheriff of Nottingham are so block-headed as to be laughable when not dangerous. Maid Marion, an inside operator against the usurpers once she comes to understand Robin's true identity (and falls for him), gets to be the more-than-hinted paramour: She is a well-developed character and frequently jolly near-feminist, as well as a tactician of note in palace intrigue.

Denied other avenues of expression for their talents, the blacklistees delivered wit, pathos, masterstrokes of complication and historical insight that were entirely absent from the Douglas Fairbanks/Errol Flynn versions (and from the postmodern Kevin Costner and Mel Brooks versions). From the earliest episodes, Robin faces the real contradictions of peasant thieves as proto-revolutionaries afraid of everything, including literacy, but willing to learn. Here even the worst of enemies can join together now and then in the face of natural threats (a forest fire) or unnatural ones (invasion by the Norsemen).

Topical episodes occasionally stretched credulity paper-thin to make a point. Thus, for instance, Robin saves a York Jewish merchant (and reputed "old friend" of the outlaw king) loyally devoting his energy and treasure to saving his beleaguered community.[50] Robin also protects women accused of witchcraft from burning at the stake (a more than obvious metaphor of the contemporary witch hunt), rescues "people's priest" Friar Tuck from the oppressive hierarchy of a pre-Cromwellian church in league with the forces of the state and so on.

Robin's espousal of "freedom" and dignity presumably would have driven the high-culture cold warriors of Encounter or Partisan Review to distraction if they had guessed the identity of the writers. The series would presumably have played no better in contemporary Russia, and it is a notable fact of Robin Hood that its authors were in the process of finalizing a break with the Communist Party as the series took flight. Indeed, without reading too much into what is after all TV fiction, every work-in-progress dealing with freedom contained some degree of the writers' own rethinking. The basics of what they had fought for in the antifascist years remained but took on new emphases of individual rights, the status of women and defense of existing common law—much as the Hollywood writers had originally redefined their interventions around the New Deal and the new possibilities it provided for film plots back in the mid-1930s.

A different insight into these complications can be found in Robin Hood's principal (if unsuccessful) companion series, The Adventures of Sir Lancelot (1956–1957). Producer Weinstein relied heavily upon Adrian Scott's sagacity and imagination for this creation, but the Arthurian legend came heavily freighted with all sorts of less-than-useful mysticism. Weinstein even recruited an Oxford University Marxist group to provide detailed exposition of eighth-century England for the series, but to little avail.

In an exchange of notes, Scott proposed the depiction of a civilization going backward, all knowledge lost and civil society reduced to warring bands. Perhaps it was a natural suggestion in a moment of fear over nuclear war. King Arthur's benevolent efforts would seek to effect a sort of mini-United Nations—a reduced version of what left-wingers had earnestly expected the United Nations would be at its establishment. Arthur's favorite knight, Lancelot, assists in the task of keeping things from getting still worse, meeting all the inevitable villainy, intrigue and persecution that come with the territory—but almost never with the sense of humor that gave *The Adventures of Robin Hood* its piquancy.

Scott urgently sought to recuperate the narrative around a lesser hero—and no rebel—by strengthening the other players. In one episode, a supposed giant terrorizing the vicinity turns out to be a shadow figure created by village women estranged by the infighting and time-wasting of the (male) nobility. Or, the fearless Lancelot finds himself surrounded by women who would very much like to have him to themselves, and with good reason: they have recently, *Lysistrata*-like, denied sex to their boyfriends and husbands. For the most part, though, Lancelot (played by William Russell, sadly lacking both Richard Greene's charisma and talent for irony) engaged in a repetitive knight-errantry, rescuing various kidnapped dignitaries.[51]

The success of *The Adventures of Robin Hood* also spurred imitators, including *The Buccaneers* (1956–1957), highlighting a reformed seventh-century pirate; *Sword of Freedom* (1957–1958), about a reformed Italian pirate of similar medieval vintage; and *The Adventures of William Tell* (1958), sometimes described as the "Robin Hood of the Alps." Lardner once estimated that he and collaborator Ian McClellan Hunter had written between 100 and 150 series episodes, all told, for Weinstein. But there never could be another show like *The Adventures of Robin Hood*, with Oscar winners doing the writing for the perfect historical rebel.[52]

The children's genre offered another way out if not such an obvious allegorical way forward. After all, some of the blacklistees had been working with family films and kid stars for decades. Marguerite Roberts had written the original sound version of *Peck's Bad Boy* for Jackie Cooper way back in 1934; Hugo Butler had scripted the first sound *The Adventures of Huckleberry Finn* (1939) and delivered famously with kids' material from *Young Tom Edison* (1940) to *Lassie Come Home* (1943). Children had often been depicted as the most vulnerable victims of capitalism, whether in detention centers or the slums, and sometimes (increasingly so in the forties) as witnesses to racial injustice and minorities' accomplishments, whether as sterling athletes or plainly brave human beings.[53]

How all of this translated into the television mainstream of the 1950s to the 1970s in what Robert Lees, Adrian and Joan Scott and others on the Left contributed to *Lassie*, *Flipper* and *Daktari* may never have been obvious, but comes clear enough to the close reader of the archived scripts whose writers are identified. To take a specific episode: Lassie's owner, Timmy, is shown a half-wolf, an apparently hopelessly vicious dog who is, however, softened up for human contact by Lassie's presence. Then the dog is falsely accused of marauding sheep in neighboring farms and, like Huck Finn, takes off for the wild. It bravely and loyally returns to save Lassie from a rampaging bull but suffers a loss of blood and a serious wound. Brilliant dog that she is (making her *seem* intelligent was one of the most difficult jobs for the scripting Marxists), Lassie brings food to her new companion and commands him to be quiet as a friendly little girl tends his wounds. And so on, after more adventures and dangers, down to the final recognition by a friendly farmer that the half-wolf can indeed be socialized properly. The episode title was "The Wild One." The plot was not exactly original, of course, but it could be described in more than one interesting way as part of the continuous borrowing from comrades.[54]

For at least a few of the blacklisted writers, notably Lees, the essential Lassie theme could survive the television dog and be reincarnated into *Flipper* (1964–1968) and *Daktari* (1966–1969), veritable jewels of the residual lineup for future after-school or weekend "quality" (i.e., nonviolent) children's television viewing. In *Flipper*, a park ranger of Coral Keys Park, Florida, lives with his two cute kids while protecting sea life and skin divers. The same kind of bad guys and outright predators who threatened Lassie pester their pet dolphin. Flipper helps the kids and their dad nab the villains and return the park life to an eco-normality—with a moral lesson or two in the process.

Daktari had an American vet living with his daughter in an unspecified but apparently former British section of Africa with a pet lion and chimpanzee, curing ill animals, stopping the white poachers in their tracks and assisting the natives both to continue their lives and to improve themselves in practices consistent with sustainable development. Lees liked the work without taking it too seriously. Like the forgotten family film *Maya* (1966), directed by rehabilitated blacklistee John Berry (about an English boy and his Indian pal beating a path across rural India upon the back of a beloved elephant), *Daktari* sought to be more than it appeared. As Lees explained in a more serious note about his 1950s and 1960s work, "Love conquers all" across species lines. This was years before the environmental movement surfaced.[55]

In fact, a nascent animal liberation sensibility—if not yet a movement—drew strength from the same growing impulses. One of Carl Foreman's last brainstorms in his British exile was the selection and adaptation of author Joy Adamson's memoir of herself and a lioness for the precedent-breaking *Born Free* (1966). Foreman chose one of the most irascible and uncompromising blacklistees, Lester Cole (using the pseudonym Gerald L. C. Copley), who had penned the original Left-center film of the Roosevelt Era, *The President's Mystery* (1936). Once again, this time with a lioness, Cole had found a winner, not in a crisis-ridden little industrial town carrying the potential for cooperative production, as in the 1930s film, but rather in distant Kenya, where the yearning for freedom had not died, at least among the animals. Both the score and the film's theme song won Oscars.

The post-Lassie model of the animal film story actually had already been a great success in 1956, with affable veteran director Irving Rapper's *The Brave One*.

A deceptively simple children's drama, it won an Oscar (for best original story) for someone named "Robert Rich," aka Dalton Trumbo, who was conspicuously missing from the 1957 Oscar ceremony. It was an ingenious twist on the kid-and-pet film. Shortly after the film opens in a Mexican home with the funeral for a child, the surviving brother (played winningly by Michel Ray) watches the birth of a bull (his father congratulates the newborn for a voice like the "trumpets of Zapata") and, despite threats of its owners to reclaim the beast, he raises the animal as a pet. As the boy grows, learning about social conditions from his family and his teacher, he also learns to his dismay that the now former pet will likely be sacrificed in a blood ritual in the bull ring. Miraculously—it does happen very occasionally in a bullfight—but as a matter of necessity for this kind of film, he has raised an animal so brave and intelligent that the bull will win the fight and the crowd will successfully call for the animal to be spared.

The brilliance of the drama, especially for younger viewers, lay in Trumbo's use of Mexican personalities and themes, woven so smoothly that it did not require for its plot either adopted Americans (although a visiting blonde from north of the border does offer a little romantic interest) or the waving of the stars and stripes.[56] To the contrary, an early high point of the film—perhaps hardly noticed by most viewers—takes place in a schoolroom where the boy learns about the history of his Mexican people and how illiterate Indians won a nation's freedom from the armies of European aristocrats. So appealing are the boy and the story that no one, at least according to Hollywood legend, saw through the plot to the didactic crypto-Marxist center.

This—and not the ubiquitous money-saving location shoots in Spain, Yugoslavia and elsewhere in the 1960s and 1970s—was a true internationalization of film. It followed logically from the left-wing screenwriters' own growing interest in Mexican-American themes during the forties derived from their observations as they went into exile in Mexico or visited comrades there during the fifties. A family or children's film like this offered a way, and perhaps the only way, for American audiences to see other inhabitants of the globe no longer as exotics (common even in American films about romantically backward France or Italy) but as humans like themselves.[57]

ANIMATION

The possibilities for weightier themes in the juvenile genres had seemed far greater for a moment just before the blacklist. In this golden age of comic books, talented lyricists and former Disney animators hooked up with Lou Bunin (then famous for his "puppettoons," or half-animated creatures) for an audacious *Alice in*

Wonderland (1950). Fleeing repression, and hearing on the grapevine that Disney had postponed a similar project, a talented handful undertook the project in Paris. Among the most prominent was John Hubley (1914–1977), who had shown genius as a senior artist (more precisely an animation "set designer") in *Snow White and the Seven Dwarfs, Dumbo, Fantasia* and *Bambi*.[58] This *Alice* played against the Disney version in New York theaters the very same week, a considerable source of amusement for critics. The puppettoon version was buried by the competition. Despite being truer to the spirit of the original, it lacked the Disney pizzazz of famous stars' voices, high-priced animation and a massive advertising budget.

In this failure, the Left version of *Alice* resembled other interesting but doomed efforts at independent production in the McCarthy era, including an earnest, live-action version of *Hiawatha* (1952), written by blacklistee Arthur Strawn and directed by Kurt Neumann (as so often, collaborating with left-wing talent). The antiracist, nature-loving Indian tale tried but could not succeed commercially in its effort to explore for kids the same contradictions of colonialism that Disney's animated *Pocahontas* (1995), with catchy songs and a not-to-be-believed heroine's physique, brilliantly exploited decades later.[59]

But Hubley (joined by his wife, Faith Hubley, whose work continued until her death in 2001) had only begun independent animation. Their artistic path had been set by the veritable king of animation, Chuck Jones (1912–2002). Jones' activity in the film Left of the 1940s included joining antidiscrimination committees, which led to his identification by FBI informers, and writing for the *Hollywood Quarterly*. All of this might have got him purged except that he had developed a host of the most original cartoon characters on film, notably Bugs Bunny (and later the Road Runner). Born in Spokane, Jones grew up mostly in southern California, dropped out of high school and almost immediately entered animation at MGM, where he worked with and for some of the field's greats, including Tex Avery. Evolving as a sort of director, Jones did key drawings and managed the process for some of the most audacious, edgy and artistic cartoons.[60] But he was keenly aware that without a conceptual leap by the creators themselves, cartoons would remain the cinematic dustbin of low expectations and easy laughs.[61]

Fired by the boss personally after the unsuccessful 1941 Disney Studio animators' strike, Hubley and other ex-Disneyites meanwhile began to forge creative alternatives. They established the Industrial Films and Poster Service, making animated propaganda for the re-election of Franklin Roosevelt in 1944 and later for racial integration—notably *The Brotherhood of Man* (1945), produced with money from the United Auto Workers, which for the moment was still under heavy left-wing influence. Very much in sync with the work of their friend Chuck Jones at MGM, early Industrial Films productions were artistically bold and far more influenced by surrealism than the realism trumpeted by leading American Communist aestheticians. As John Hubley himself put it in the *Hollywood Quarterly*, "we have found that line, shape, color and symbols in movement can represent the essence of an idea, can express it humorously, with force and clarity. The method is only dependent upon the idea to be expressed."[62]

A year or two following the war, before the optimism of the Left faded, Industrial Films reorganized as United Productions of America, an artists' cooperative of sorts. Shares were held by Disney veterans like Hubley and Dave Hilberman, who had been singled out by Walt Disney for the sin of having "spent considerable time at the Moscow Art Theater."[63] UPA nabbed a distributor in Columbia Pictures and went on to transform stock studio characters like the Fox and Crow dramatically in *Magic Fluke* (1949), a takeoff on *The Magic Flute,* and *Robin Hoodlum* (1948); in the latter, the Fox plays Robin and Crow plays the Sheriff of Nottingham, something like Bugs Bunny playing Elmer Fudd. Both films got Oscar nominations. At the end of the forties, Hubley developed Mr. Magoo, destined to be UPA's biggest and most enduring commercial success.[64]

UPA also borrowed from the final strokes of radicalism in the art of the abstract expressionists, painters who were about to jettison their 1930s leftism. The war, as Hubley suggested, turned Hollywood toward the educational film, but with a difference. Abstraction had been put to work for the Allies so as to simplify and dramatize the message, usually without the distraction of familiar cartoon characters. In the period just after the war, as abstract expressionism captured the attention of *Life* magazine and of the advertising agencies, animators borrowed second-hand from popular culture, effecting an early, instinctive postmodernism. Turning the old visual narrative on its head, cartoonists rendered the space around the characters the main site of experimentation, with color their foremost tool.[65]

 The most inventive of UPA's characters, Gerald McBoing-Boing, offered a wildly imaginative visual narrative of a youngster who could not speak and whose own sense of dislocation allowed a dramatically different use of music, colors and designs. Poor Gerald McCoy, who looks to be about 10, speaks entirely in sound effects, some very loud and all disconcerting to the various authorities around him. He is a world unto himself and has a cognomen affixed to him because of his first (and most frequent) phrase, the non-vocalized sound of metal springs coiling and uncoiling, "boing boing."

This was hardly the first time, in the vast experimentation of short features, that the narrative and dialogue of a cartoon had been delivered in sound effects. But that element, along with the visuals, immediately suggested the larger experiment underway. It was also, in a sense, the world as seen through the eyes of a very human cartoon character. Unhappy and misunderstood by loving but confused parents, by teachers, doctors and supposed specialists, Gerald runs away from home and lands in a freight yard. Happily, he is rescued by a radio station mogul who appoints him the station's source of special effects. A child's story of loneliness and apparent infirmity redeemed when weakness becomes perceived as strength, it also reflected the "age of anxiety" motif. According to insiders, even Mr. Magoo hinted at the psychological myopia used by ordinary folk to distance themselves from the horrors at hand.[66]

Gerald McBoing Boing happened, by no great coincidence, to be an adaptation from a "Dr. Seuss" story by creator Ted Geisel, at the time best known for his militantly antifascist cartoons during the war and still years before his iconic status as doyen of children's books.[67] Geisel's first media triumph (albeit heavily adapted), *Gerald* won an Oscar in 1951 for best animated short subject.

UPA's continuing innovations included the first animation written around jazz pieces; a rendering of James Thurber's drawings; Edgar Allan Poe's "The Tell-Tale Heart" in 1953 (with creepy narration by James Mason); and bread-and-butter work on television ads. In 1955, the Museum of Modern Art honored the studio with an exhibit and a salute to a field not previously considered capable of producing real art. By an odd coincidence, the show was mounted during MOMA's ongoing celebration of abstract expressionism, cheered as the ultimate avant-garde (but simultaneously "free enterprise art," in Henry Luce's phrase) escape from middle-brow and popular culture.

The next year, CBS drew up plans for a "Gerald McBoing Boing Show," a project that, sufficiently sustained, might not only have brought some animated high art to a mass audience but given some dignity to animation and cartoons generally. Such an elevation was about to begin elsewhere in the world, from Japan to Eastern Europe, but in the United States it had to wait for decades. Meantime, the ax fell again and again on America's creative animators, as if the playing-card people threatened by the Red Queen in the Puppettoon version of *Alice in Wonderland* really would have their heads cut off not once but endlessly.

HUAC hammered at Hollywood animation all through the early and middle 1950s. When investigators demanded to see UPA payroll records, it was a trap: suspicious names were passed on to the distributor, Columbia, whose officials promptly demanded that the animation studio carry out its own purge. Among those leaving in order to spare UPA was (inevitably) Hubley, who threw himself into what would have been the most socially ambitious and adult-oriented animation to that day, a rendering of E. Y. Harburg's Broadway hit, *Finian's Rainbow*. The play's themes, of Irish identity, American racism and the feckless pursuit of the pot of gold (materialism in general, but most especially the American variety) were matched by Harburg lyrics that blended ethnic nostalgia with an appeal for tolerance. Librettist Peter Stone was to call it a "socialist tract that made its point at a time when the entire country was in fear" of anything approaching egalitarianism.[68] In its daring mixture of lyrics and staging, the Broadway version was, along with *South Pacific*, said to have revolutionized the musical.

At first, the animation project moved ahead smoothly. Frank Sinatra, Ella Fitzgerald and Louis Armstrong actually recorded for the production in Hubley's own little Hollywood studio in 1955. Then Roy Brewer, champion of the blacklist as power-broker president of the Hollywood branch of the International Alliance of Theatrical Stage Employees, whistled it to a halt. Neither Hubley nor Harburg had ever been Communist Party members, but they were "suspicious." (Harburg, by his own account, had been called into an investigator's office at one point and asked whether the lyric for "Happiness Is a Thing Called Joe" in the black musical film *Cabin in the Sky* had actually been dedicated to Joe Stalin![69]) Under pressure, the film's financial backers, Chemical Bank, withdrew their funding, and that was the end of the project as well as of Hubley's studio.[70]

Blow number two shortly awaited UPA—by no means entirely cleansed of quiet left-wingers. Somehow, *The Gerald McBoing Boing Show* reached television screens at the end of 1956. It received extravagant praise from critics for its inventive themes and treatments but had insufficient ratings. Other animated shows, some of the most successful by the Hanna-Barbera team, would quickly find an appreciative television audience. But not until *The Simpsons* decades later would made-for-television animation again display this level of week-to-week, prime-time artistry. CBS broadcast *Gerald McBoing Boing* for 22 months in varying time slots, then dropped it without the prospect of taking another show from UPA. The studio staggered and fell, merging its remaining resources with a competitor, in 1960.

There was another distinct irony here. UPA's style and contents effectively interpreted the ironies of the emerging middle-American society of consumerism in the way that Bugs Bunny and the other 1940s cartoons had represented the wartime situation, but with an extra splash of abstract modernism. Given few opportunities elsewhere, UPA made its point via commercials that not only revolutionized the look of animation but in the process arguably changed the look of television in general in some important ways. A critic may be right when he suggests that UPA had prepared the way for the "theme park on a surface of electronic memory" that is the newest venue for the rapid creation and consumption of animation, that is, the Internet.[71] The influences had been exerted cryptically, the surviving remnant of larger and more noble aspirations.

Another, slightly less cryptic case can be found in one of UPA's most talented younger artists, bohemian left-winger Gene Deitch. When in 1956 CBS bought up Terrytoons (17 years earlier, the site of a failed union drive by future blacklistee and television writer Al Levitt), Deitch was placed in charge of the unit to give it a new look. Deitch hired a young Jules Feiffer, among others, to revamp the operations, and took the drastic move of replacing those money-making Terrytoon favorites, Mighty Mouse and Heckle and Jeckle, with hip UPA creations like Dinky Duck, a semi-satire on the famous Donald.[72]

Carrying through such a task proved impossible given the bottom-line cynicism of the network and of Terrytoon veterans toward product. They sought footage, not quality, and certainly not risky innovation. Deitch lasted only two years in the job. On the side, he invented a superman-satire feature, "Tom Terrific," with wild and funny changes of shape for the little boy and his self-imagined heroism. The first full-fledged animation series made for television after *Gerald McBoing Boing*, its segments played on *Captain Kangaroo* for two years until CBS execs ruled Deitch's brain-child too "different" and dropped it. A decade and a divorce later, Deitch left the country to run an animation studio in Czechoslovakia, a leading wedge of the Eastern Europe animation outburst, inspired both by UPA and by the need to make art while evading political censors. Unnoticed at the time, it may have been the most important artistic defection from the West since Brecht set up his own theater in East Berlin.[73] Meanwhile, another UPA veteran, Bill Scott, co-created with promoter Jay Ward (1920–1989) the wildly funny and pungently satirical *Rocky and His Friends* (1959–1961), renamed *The Bullwinkle Show* (1961–1962), memorable for its off-beat humor, including satires of official histories and current Cold War intrigue, and for telling kids to twist the television knobs off the set.[74]

Scratching out a living, UPA veteran John Hubley meanwhile invented the "Maypo" commercial (little boy howling: "I Want My Maypo!"), among the work improvised to finance more artistic ventures by himself and his collaborator, Faith Hubley.[75] Many of the animated works the pair created are extraordinary in any terms, like the cryptically socialistic *Of Stars and Men* (1961), touching on the need for humanity to abandon nuclear weapons and meet the "marriage of science and art" in space exploration as a major evolutionary step. *Moonbird* (1959) won the pair their first Oscar as they pursued the path that Faith Hubley regarded as her specialty, the perception of the world by children. *The Hole* (1962), which won the pair another Oscar, had two hard-hat workers debating nuclear war. *Herb Alpert and the Tijuana Brass Double Feature* (1966), which the master animationists considered a mere commercial project, won their third and last Academy Award. Only in 1971 did the Academy actually change the category of the award from "Cartoons" to "Animated Films," and it was widely believed that the Hubleys' work had made a decisive contribution to the change. *Everybody Rides the* *Carousel* (1976), based on Erik Erikson's *Childhood and Society*, was equally remarkable and warmly reviewed.

After John Hubley's death, Faith Hubley dealt increasingly in myth and the artistic views of neolithic peoples. Her solo films, with evocations of surrealist and modernist painters like Miro and Klee, combined her own watercolor paintings with innovative cel animation, often treating women and pre-Christian myths. She died in December, 2001, days before the release of her final film, about the Inuit view of the earth, and only a month before a scheduled celebration of her life and work at the Museum of Modern Art.[76] One of those who was blacklisted solely because of her choice in a spouse (later Oscar winner Lee Grant was another), Faith Hubley brought out, in the days before her death, the very last of the blacklistees' fresh work. That it described a threatened environment but also delivered a message of beauty was consistent with the oldest impulses of Hollywood's reds 70 years earlier—or back ever further, to the Little Tramp of FBI-hated Charlie Chaplin's delicate sensibilities.

Most of the Hubleys' work never reached serious commercial distribution, thanks perhaps to their uncompromising artistic standards. Much of their successful commissioned work was strictly educational, and essentially propaganda for kids' literacy through The Electric Company and Sesame Street. Very occasionally, their projects were grandly commercial, like A Doonesbury Special (1977), with cartoonist Garry Trudeau pushing hard and for the most part successfully to fend off network censors' demands.

In Watership Down (1978), John Hubley (Faith Hubley chose not to associate herself with the project) might have had his artistic and commercial triumph joined. The big-budget British production even featured blacklist survivor Zero Mostel's voice. But in the end it was just the old Hollywood story, albeit in London: at post-production, with John Hubley's work finished, the animation was turned over to neophytes for reworking into visual blandness. Hubley lacked even a credit on the finished product.[77] Over two lifetimes of sometimes astonishingly inventive features and shorts, the Hubleys had nevertheless helped reconstruct a radical avant-garde from a position of exile.

CHAPTER FOUR

THE NEOREALIST AESTHETIC

IN THE LONG AND OFTEN CRUEL HISTORY OF THE BLACKLIST, of storytellers cast in the role of victims in someone else's narrative, one of the brightest notes of resistance was struck from a most surprising quarter—the lead film star and beauty of the day, Ingrid Bergman. Perhaps no event illuminated the historical moment quite so well as Bergman's flight in 1948 from her conventional marriage, her increasingly conventional roles in studio films and the stifling political atmosphere in Hollywood. The object of her passion was Roberto Rossellini, a married Italian film director whose movies were made on micro-budgets and the cheapest film stock available, often with unprofessional actors playing themselves with the support of threadbare scripts (he liked to prompt his amateur actors to speech by pulling on strings he had tied to their toes). The spectacle of the world's most glamorous film star abandoning MGM, her husband and daughter for the sake of eros and art ("Deep down I was in love with Robert from the moment I saw *Open City*," she wrote in her autobiography years later) was a scandal not only to middle-class propriety but to the idea of cinema itself, at least as it was then practiced in Hollywood. It's not clear which scandal, the erotic or artistic, perturbed the Breen Office more.[1]

Expressing his "profound shock," Joseph L. Breen wrote to Bergman on hearing the news of her escape to Italy. As the "first lady of the screen," he warned her, the elopement "may very well destroy your career as a motion picture artist."[2] Coming from this man at that moment, the threat was not to be taken lightly, and in fact it was seven years before Bergman was permitted to make another movie in the United States. (She returned to Hollywood in 1956 for *Anastasia*, where Fox put her in the reassuring hands of Anatole Litvak, who directed, and the graylisted Arthur Laurents, who wrote the screenplay.)

There is little question that Bergman was blacklisted, though it is not the usual term to describe her official disgrace. But if Ingrid Bergman was just about the remotest thing one could imagine from the world of HUAC hearings and FBI investigations of left-wing Jewish filmmakers from Brooklyn, perhaps in other ways Bergman's passion was not so unfamiliar. At the time she fell under Rossellini's spell, she was no different from filmgoers and cineastes all over the world for whom Rossellini's startlingly simple and direct images, rooted in the precise historical moment of their production, were pointing the way toward a cinema that was drawing closer than ever before to the real lives of its audiences—relaying around the world information about how things really stood in places one had only read about in the newspapers. To distinguish it from the various evolving styles of realism that had taken on national flavors during the Depression, the rawness epitomized by *Open City* came to be known as "neo"-realism, and it was the rare filmmaker who did not share Bergman's recognition of its transforming possibilities.

What started with Rossellini was broadened into a movement by other hands, notably Vittorio de Sica in *The Bicycle Thief*, released in the same year that Bergman fell under Rossellini's influence. For another decade, black-and-white film was a virtue again. It couldn't have come at a better time for Italian film and national sensibilities. Rossellini, already celebrated for ripping up a contract offered to him by Sam Goldwyn because it gave him too little directorial control, was boosted to the shoulders of the editors of *Cahiers du Cinema* and declared their guiding spirit. He was interviewed again and again until some of his interlocutors were inspired to become directors themselves. More than any other filmmaker of the immediate postwar era, Rossellini captured the mood of the time: He was an ardent Christian incapable of faith and a bohemian Marxist bored with the orthodoxies of class. His films, particularly those with Bergman, captured precisely this mood of restless disenchantment.

In the way of igniting a renewed passion for cinema, there had been nothing like neo-realism since *Citizen Kane*, which Popular Front critic Cedric Belfrage had welcomed just a few years earlier as "profoundly moving an experience as only this extraordinary and hitherto unexplored media of sound-cinema can afford."[3] *Cahiers* critic Jacques Rivette, one of those who would go on to direct films, said of *Journey to Italy* (released in 1953, with Bergman in the lead), "all other films suddenly aged ten years."[4]

If there were any lingering doubts that there was a political dimension to the Rossellini–Bergman scandal, they were erased in 1950 with the attempt by the notorious conservative (pal of both Joe McCarthy and J. Edgar Hoover) Cardinal Francis Spellman to ban Rossellini's *The Miracle* after it opened at the Paris Theater in New York (under the title, *L'Amore*). The film concerns a young woman in postwar Italy (where, despite grumblings from the Vatican, it had *not* been banned) who is seduced by a stranger claiming to be St. Joseph. When she finds herself pregnant and alone, she tells her fellow villagers that she is carrying "a special child" and is promptly shunned as a blasphemer and forced to give birth to the child alone in an abandoned church. Despite its circumstances, the film makes clear, the birth of the baby (as of all babies) is indeed an act of grace, a *miracolo*. Spellman denounced the film as "subversive to the very inspired Word of God" and, in an aside obviously directed at the Bergman scandal, suggested that the film be retitled *Woman Further Defamed*. During the film's run, pickets marched in front of the Paris Theater with signs that claimed, among other things, "This is a Communist picture!"[5]

Even before Spellman's outburst, American liberals moving rightward looked with disdain and more than a little anxiety at neorealism in general and Rossellini in particular. Reaganesque neoconservative Gertrude Himmelfarb, looking back to the 1940s and *Commentary* magazine, recalled its famous critic, Robert Warshow, bursting with rage at Rossellini and his supposed art films, which Warshow described as "garbage." By the late 1940s arguing that the fall of the Russian czars had been the major tragedy of the twentieth century, Warshow's real case against neorealism ran something like this: the abandonment of the Hollywood narrative for neorealism was an artistic apology for neutralism in the Cold War and part and parcel of the European yearning for independence from both Russian and American foreign policies. The most famous expression of neorealism in the United States to that point, *High Noon*, was little more than the counterpart to European unwillingness to accept America's destiny to rule the world.[6]

As usual, Warshow had a point. What was lost on him, however, was the larger truth that neorealism was the radical artists' response to the old dogmatic Marxist jibe that cinema outside Russia was little more than a mishmash of mindless distraction and bad art. Neorealism, in reducing cinema to the barest essentials of a camera and a group of human beings, was at once a repudiation of Hollywood's studio absolutism (the notorious "front office") and the beginning of an aesthetic revolution that threatened to remove the cinematic center of gravity from Hollywood to Europe. For a time, it did. The studios felt the aesthetic pressure acutely enough, not only in the Cold War claims made for *On the Waterfront*, but also in experiments like MGM's Fred Zinnemann films, *The Search* (1948) and *Teresa* (1951), which covered much the same ground as the Rossellini films in the rubble of postwar Europe. For well over a decade, the front office would be uncertain enough of its own judgment in these matters to accept grudgingly the notion that audiences had changed enough that a sanitized version of social realism would be worth the financial gamble—this even as fearful Hollywood moved sharply away from "controversial" themes. Left-wingers and their familiar allies would sometimes be employed openly or covertly for these projects. *The Search*, for example, had been scripted in part by Paul Jarrico; *Teresa* by Alfred Hayes, a former left-wing folksinger and novelist who had never been a part of the Hollywood Left and, perhaps for that reason, was never named to HUAC.

Entirely apart from ideological aesthetics, there was a practical side to the left-wing survivors' own enthusiasm for neorealism. While U.S. blacklistees who chose exile in Europe sometimes had access to crews, sound stages and equipment somewhat comparable to Hollywood's, those who remained in internal exile at home eked out films under conditions not so far removed from Rossellini's in postwar Italy, at least compared to what they had been used to. If shoestring budgets were suddenly acceptable and amateur actors really could be prompted to play themselves without artifice (and without strings on their toes), then movies could be made almost anywhere, under any conditions.

The radical Catholic critic Andre Bazin, an early champion of neorealism, described the movement as "a description of reality conceived as a whole by a consciousness disposed to see things as a whole." It stood in contrast, he reflected, to realistic aesthetics "in that its realism is not so much concerned with the choice of subjects as with a particular way of regarding things."[7] The methods of social realism that first arose at the turn of the century on the middle-class stage, migrated to the revolutionary stage in the 1920s and came to a dead end in 1930s agitprop, had been rediscovered and reinvented in postwar film.

The new realist sensibility would be fed from many tributaries: the poetic realism of the French Popular Front, its radical forebears in surrealism, the U.S. gangster movies and early Hollywood film noir, even the determinedly realistic war movies made by Italian filmmakers early in World War Two under Mussolini (including several made by Rossellini himself). All would share one thing: the hard, unblinking stare of the camera at the human being in all of its dispossession and the corresponding refusal of the human subject to confine itself to the expectations of mere realism, to insist rather on giving full display to all of its fears and desires. The neorealist narrative began when the knife-hard edge of the lens opened on the free play of its subject's interior life. In a sense, here was true dialectical cinema, with the lens emphasizing the material conditions of what it was filming and the subject responding by displacing the narrative toward objects of longing that lay well beyond camera range.

That was in Europe. Meanwhile, the left-wingers who remained in Hollywood, even as they resisted the blacklist, continued to push against the limitations of studio production and the limits of melodrama; some of the work they did while waiting for the axe to fall was the best they ever did. But after the HUAC hearings in Los Angeles, the once-powerful Hollywood Left, wounded by years of unemployment and FBI pursuit (and by the mid-1950s disillusioned by the revelations about Stalin), was on the ropes. Yet the inner core, most of them in early middle age and at the height of their creative energies, did not consider themselves licked. On the contrary, they traveled to Europe and surveyed the scene there carefully, watching and waiting for a shift in the wind and hoping in the long run to be able to make a triumphant trip home.

THE EXILE PROJECT

There may be no better single example of the lost cinema of the blacklist than Joseph Losey's *Stranger on the Prowl* (1951), the first film the director made in exile and in an unexpected way among the most interesting of his career. It was helped in great part by the performance of an unlikely star, Paul Muni.

Muni had always been the soul of ambivalence, torn between the Yiddish stage (where he began) and the "legitimate" theater; between theater and Hollywood; and in his film career between Warners-style social realism and much lighter fare. Most of all, he was ambivalent about political commitments. An admired actor in films admired by liberals, he joined no controversial committees and had made few features with filmmakers who would be blacklisted. Then came *Stranger on the Prowl*, co-written by fellow exile and blacklistee Ben Barzman, and based on a story by the elusive left-wing French crime novelist, Noël Calef.

Muni's political skittishness and correspondingly fidgety dignity as an actor on the way down—he had a serious heart condition and Hollywood was looking for younger leading men—made him an apt choice for the role of a fugitive on the run in a large Italian port city with nothing to survive on but a rusty old revolver, which the audience is led to believe he might have used in the closing days of World War II. Which side Muni's character might have served on is a question that remains unresolved: he could be a fugitive fascist or a resistance fighter who committed crimes to survive in the closing days of the war. In any case, the authorities are after him. In the end his political identity doesn't seem to matter, because his poverty turns him into an involuntary murderer, and all of his attempts either to elude other people (a small boy who is equally desperate) or to associate with them (a pretty young woman torn between him and the price on his head) are doomed to failure. Echoes of Marcel Carné's *Le jour se lève* (1939) are everywhere, including desperate gun battles and chases along mansard rooftops, with a conclusion eerily similar to the French film. If Jean Gabin at the end of Carné's movie is the apotheosis of the French worker abandoned to his fate by a cynical French middle class that actually welcomed the German invasion, Muni is a man without an identity, homeless and stateless, for whom postwar Italy offers nothing better than Vichy France.

There were high hopes for *Stranger on the Prowl* in Italy. When Losey arrived, the national Communist Party newspaper, *L'Unita*, ran a two-page spread on the visiting American director—an instance, like his later discovery by the French left-wing press, of his political associations raising expectations rather than the more familiar Cold War fears.[8] In the decade or so to follow, the Italian and French Left dailies and cultural publications would prove valuable in providing a sense of support at a time when the American embassies were pressuring Christian Democratic governments to crack down on the exiles.

The production was fraught with financial and technical problems, made worse (according to associates) by Losey's outsized ego.[9] But in this first European effort, he did not disappoint. As one of his better critics once noted, Losey had the "ability to blend in with his surroundings, so that his films, whether made in America, Italy, France or England, don't look like the work of an alien."[10] The truth of the matter is that Losey adapted to local styles because his political reputation preceded him wherever he went and predisposed the always left-wing European film community to cooperate with him, particularly after it became clear from one film to the next that Losey was the least abashed American Marxist director then working.

Stranger arrived at the precise intersection where poetic realism, neorealism and film noir cross paths after the war, each in its own way (as national styles) depicting the lost hopes for a postwar society. Losey's background in Hollywood film noir allowed him to move the narrative along with all the familiar force of commercial pacing but with considerably more open-ended development. The film was also helped by its international crew, in particular the great cinematographer Henri Alekan, who had worked with Jean Renoir during the French Popular Front (and later rejoined Losey for *The Trout*, 1982). Alekan's work alone is enough to recommend to posterity the survival of this film, which has been lost to all but the most avid video collectors.

For the rest of his career Losey never again did anything quite like *Stranger on the Prowl*, whose Italian title was *Imbarco a Mezzanotte* (literally, Departure at Midnight), and for all of its occasional elusiveness and rather dreadful dubbing in English it would remain his most important work until *King and Country* in 1964. By that time, Losey had regained his footing in the film industry by making a string of commercial films in London. But the artistic (if not box-office) success of *Stranger* is testimony to the reigning influence of neorealism in Europe when Losey arrived there and its compatibility with his noirish background. The film's artistic accomplishment inspires wonder about what he might have done had he remained in Italy rather than moving on to England.

 Five Branded Women (1959), shot in Italy and written by Hollywood Left veterans Paul Jarrico and Michael Wilson, followed where Losey and Barzman had blazed the trail. As tardy exiles, the two writers (along with the director, fellow blacklistee Martin Ritt) were trying desperately to get a commercial footing while making a serious film. Like *Salt of the Earth*, for which Jarrico had served as producer while Wilson wrote the script, *5 Branded Women* explores with great passion the question of how a dissenting minority within a larger political movement can assert its legitimate interests without compromising the success of the common struggle. In both films, the dissenters are women who know their concerns have been overlooked but manage to force them into the foreground and, in some sense, prevail. In both cases, they arrive at a sense of their own authority and the knowledge that there is "no going back."

Wilson was consistently more interested in and more adept at women's themes than most Hollywood screenwriters. He had written a version of *Friendly Persuasion* from Jessamyn West's short stories as early as 1945, a screenplay in which many of these same points had been touched on in the context of the Civil War. In the film that would eventually be made from Wilson's script (and for which he was denied credit), another minority, this time Quakers led by Dorothy McGuire as a "daughter of the light" (a female preacher) assert their pacifist beliefs within the context of their pro-Union and abolitionist sympathies. The film, by William Wyler, was charming and intelligent enough to win over the French (it took a *Palme d'Or* at Cannes in 1957), but the compromises it made in the handling of the story's political concerns about war and violence were made mostly at the Quakers' expense.

By the time he wrote *5 Branded Women*, Wilson's concern with this theme had narrowed considerably to a political question of immediate concern to the United States blacklistees, namely the position of those in the Popular Front during the Cold War who were dissenters but still clung to some kind of critical allegiance to it. This time, the story was told solidly within the tradition of social realism, that is, a more conventional style of realism than neorealism but hardly uninfluenced by it. In Italy the film bore the title of the original novel, *Jovanka e le altre* (Jovanka and the Others), one of a series of war novels composed in the 1950s by left-wing journalist Ugo Pirro, who would later become known for writing some of the best films of director Elio Petri, including *Investigation of a Man above Suspicion* (1970) and *The Working Class Goes to Heaven* (1971).[11]

Just about everyone else involved in the production of *5 Branded Women* was associated with the international Popular Front, the subject of the movie. Ritt had just begun to get work in Hollywood, while Wilson and Jarrico would remain "abroad" in one sense or another and mostly uncredited until very late in their lives. Both had been named so often by friendly witnesses before the congressional investigating committee that they could not have written birthday cards for Hallmark without strict anonymity. So the moment of the creation of this film was extraordinary: here were Wilson and Jarrico collaborating under the table on a war film about communist partisans isolated in the remotest Balkans, a story about demoralized and outnumbered stragglers fighting off fascists while trying to resolve complex moral disputes within their own ranks. The writers were working for an international operation (the film was produced by Dino De Laurentiis, whom Wilson had once praised in the pages of *Hollywood Review*) and from a politically sympathetic novel, with an equally sympathetic director; in the cast were Group Theatre veteran Van Heflin and the visage of French existentialism par excellence, Jeanne Moreau. It was also an immense frustration to director Ritt, shooting in the Yugoslavia of the 1950s under production conditions not all that far removed from those in New Mexico for *Salt of the Earth*.[12]

Ugo Pirro's original story traced the fate of a group of Slovenian women in World War II who discover they have all been seduced by the same Italian soldier. After he is castrated by partisans, who then turn around and disgrace the women as well by shaving their heads, the women thus "branded" take to the hills and become scavengers for food and weapons. Soon they evolve into a guerrilla squad fighting against the Italian occupiers. This unlikely band of disciplined killers eventually links back up with the very partisans who had shaved their heads, and together they form a united front against their common fascist enemies. Between the firefights that follow, the women learn the hard lessons of military discipline (partisans are executed for dereliction) even as they insist on the right to express their love physically to whomever they please, including in exceptional cases even enemy prisoners.

The movie, true to the Popular Front tradition in these matters, manages to turn the Italians of the novel into Germans. It then strengthens the dramatic confrontations between the partisan leadership and the women in order to sharpen the contemporary question, What are the limits of revolutionary discipline in this moment, the late Popular Front, after the Hungarian rebellion of 1956? How could one conduct an effective antifascist struggle without taking on the attitudes and practices of the fascists themselves? To what extent is the military organization of a worker's party possible, even in wartime, when it reflects a patriarchal absolutism that is an enemy of the revolution? In short, How can one retain an allegiance to the Popular Front when Stalinism is undermining it?

Pirro's novel concludes with this speech from Jovanka, the organizer of the women's guerilla squad:

> "I've fought and I shall continue fighting because I want the same voice in matters that men have. If any of you prefer submissive women, then you are fighting on the wrong side. This war has destroyed your privileges along with a lot of other things, and it destroys them a little more each day. You'll never again keep

us shut up waiting for a husband. Each of us will be free to love whomever she wishes. Threats about treachery won't make any difference, so don't bother. I could justify myself by showing that what you think happened never happened, but I'd rather defend my right to do what you think I did. Trousers don't fly a flag any more. . . ."[13]

The production frustrations and commercial failure of *Stranger on the Prowl* and *5 Branded Women* found an antidote in a single, instantly emblematic feature of the Cold War years, *Rififi* (1955). Jules Dassin had come out of blacklisted Hollywood with a considerably larger reputation than any other left-wing director, notwithstanding Losey's own artistic contributions, thanks to noirish thrillers *Naked City* (1948) and *Night and the City* (1950). Dassin's arrival in Paris was greeted with newspaper cries of *"L'affair Dassin,"* the circumstance of a great artist driven from his homeland. Unlike Losey, Dassin did not keep his high reputation in Paris over the following decades, but for the moment, he stood morally and artistically triumphant.

Rififi chez les hommes, Dassin's first exile feature, was the neorealist-influenced classic that did not fail. In fact, it was such a huge hit in France and the rest of Europe that industry hostility in the United States could not keep it from a 20-week run in one Manhattan theater (where it was helped considerably by a rave review from veteran *New York Times* critic Bosley Crowther).[14] It all proved that money was the single social force stronger than the blacklist, and helps to explain why the exiled filmmakers, once they actually got to the point of making movies again (for Dassin, it had been five years), began to dream of box-office hits so large that they could not be ignored. After *Rififi* won the prize for best direction (in a tie with a Bulgarian entry) at the Cannes Film Festival in 1955, it could find a place in New York. If it was circulated very sparsely elsewhere in the country because of the hostility of U.S. distributors, the fuss made over it by the European critics was enough to make it virtually certain that some money could be made. Dassin was right to point to the 20-week New York run in 1956 as the first crack in the blacklist, even if the next cracks were long in coming.[15]

Most people who have seen *Rififi* remember the extraordinary half-hour sequence in the middle of the film, which is otherwise a simply constructed story of a group of jewel thieves who (a) prepare for a robbery, (b) execute it flawlessly, and (c) suffer "punishment, vengeance, death," as critic-director François Truffaut neatly summarized it.[16] The half-hour centerpiece depicts the quartet of robbers, led by the doleful Jean Servais, cutting their way into a jewelry store through the ceiling and making off with the boodle, all in virtual silence. For French critics, to whom the silent era of filmmaking represented a kind of lost golden age, the scene was considered a compelling piece of realism.[17] A *Cahiers du cinema* critic also praised the rest of the film's lyricism, particularly the final scene, when the last surviving thief, mortally wounded, drives across Paris to deliver a kidnapped five-year-old boy to his mother (along with more than 200 million francs in cash), capturing the fragmented point of view of this dying gangster as he goes in and out of consciousness in a series of counterpointed camera angles.[18] Truffaut praised it as a "lyrical documentary."[19]

Technically, these two scenes were indeed *tours de force* of great energy and originality. Despite claims to the contrary and certain plot similarities, they were not inspired by John Huston's *The Asphalt Jungle* (1950), at least according to Dassin, who said he came up with the idea when he figured out that in a movie full of thieves who work in the dead of night the antagonist had to be—noise.[20] For nearly 25 minutes, before dawn begins to fall over the city, the technical details of the burglary become a precise description of work itself, virtually a labor documentary about a team of professionals probing the weak spots in their opponent—not merely noise but accumulated wealth.

The famed central scene was shot with the single-source lighting invented or perfected by cinematographer John Seitz for *This Gun for Hire* (1942). Dassin's cinematographer was Phillipe Agostini, who had shot the first and greatest French film noir, Marcel Carné's *Le jour se lève*. It is as day breaks that any lingering doubts over the technical genius of the film are resolved. In ever-widening circles, the camera probes the streets around the ongoing burglary, breaking out of the claustrophobia of nighttime thievery and the danger of noise to the even greater danger of all-revealing light. As the sun cracks over the tops of the buildings, a delivery van pulls to the curb and a man steps out of it and mysteriously hands a bouquet of flowers to a beautiful young woman—but why flowers at daybreak? It hardly matters. The camera is now omniscient and capable of taking the audience anywhere. "Dassin . . . reveals Paris to us Frenchmen as he revealed London to the English (*Night and the City*) and New York to the Americans (*The Naked City*)," wrote Truffaut.[21]

The astonishing thing is that Dassin accomplished all of this on the fly, rejecting everything in the novel whose rights the producers had purchased for him. He rewrote the story from the bottom up, using all of the considerable skills he had accumulated from his time in Hollywood to transform what is essentially a U.S.-style film noir (it even has a nightclub with a "thrush") with a conventional story line into a root film for a new sub-genre, the suspense techno-thriller. He pulled together all of the elements of what were then the scattered remnants of the national styles of left-wing filmmakers and recreated them as a highly successful commercial movie—something for which not everyone forgave him.[22]

As if all that were not enough, Dassin himself took a vital supporting role in the film. He plays the fastidious Italian safecracker, Perlo Vita, whose carelessness leads to the gang's undoing and adds what may be an inside joke for the old gang back in Los Angeles. The boss leans into Vita's face and growls, "You fingered him. We got along well, Macaroni, but you know the rule." Dassin as Vita the informer is then dispatched, off-camera.

Dassin's snappy little caper movie had such an impact that he managed to get financing for a film that is now virtually lost, *Celui qui doit mourir* (He Who Must Die, 1957), this time with Ben Barzman adapting a novel by Nikos Kazantzakis, and once again with Jean Servais in the lead. Of all the movies made by U.S. exiles, this one may have come closest to the spirit of Rossellini's earliest films with Bergman. The story is set in a Greek village ruled by Turks around 1921. The Greeks are preparing their annual reenactment of the Passion mystery, with the priest assigning the various roles to the local townsfolk (the local hooker is Mary Magdalene—Melina Mercouri's first of many assays of that kind of role—while the stutterer is Jesus, and so forth) when suddenly the members of a neighboring village, burned out by the Turks, arrive and ask for help. When some of the locals—played by themselves, amateur actors all—chase the newcomers into the mountains out of fear that they have been infected with cholera, the cast members of the Passion begin to act out their assigned dramatic roles and help their neighbors. Eventually, they all wind up on the barricades against their common persecutors, the military representatives of the dying Ottoman Empire.

Reviews were on the whole quite positive. Marxist critic Georges Sadoul admired the effort, observing that it was by turns filled with "lovely scenes that partake of the epic, but others of the fable," and pronounced it Dassin's "most ambitious and sincere European film."[23] An attack by François Truffaut, enraged at what he saw as clumsy religious imagery but even more by the presumption of an American to make such a film, cursed it as "slow-moving, solemn and heavy."[24] This difference likely reflected the older Marxist view of the American exiles as political artists, as against the newer cinema *engagés* who saw 1940s Hollywood, even left-wing Hollywood, as the enemy. Exhibitors in the United States offered no help and the film died. It is still not available.

Dassin was not down long. But his days of making art films were basically over. He confined his artistic projects to the stage and was driven back toward commercial film projects with big stars, most of all Mercouri herself, and toward his international mega-hit, *Never On Sunday* (1960). Meanwhile, *Rififi* had been so successful that it led to a string of burglary films from other filmmakers who thought the sequence of hi-tech silence tempting enough to steal without credit.[25] At least nine remakes were made in various international settings, including even a *Rififi in Tokyo*. A disgusted Dassin finally remade it himself as a suspense comedy set in Istanbul called *Topkapi* (1964).

Dassin was not the only exile from Hollywood taking advantage of the French interest in American noir, and the director was generous to his exiled friends in the shadow of his achievement. In the second part of a two-part interview with François Truffaut and Claude Chabrol in *Cahiers du cinema* in 1954, Dassin lavished praise on Losey and John Berry—both of whom, like Dassin, had theatrical backgrounds in Depression-era New York—clearly trying to steer whatever work he could in their direction.[26] Although he never had Dassin's skill as a director, John Berry found a corner of French filmmaking compatible with his more limited Hollywood experience. While Dassin had turned out nearly a dozen features in the United States, Berry had only begun. He had started as an actor with a good reputation, and more than most directors continued to work at every available level, from transparent commercial projects (even *Bad News Bears Go to Japan*) to difficult stage pieces (such as *Boesman and Lena,* his last film). [27] In France, Berry's first assignment had been to finish up *Atoll K* (1950), the last Laurel and Hardy—a sadly creaky if remarkably crypto-radical film about an island with uranium—after the director of the Franco–Italian crew fell ill.[28] Like Dassin, Berry had to wait years before he got another offer.

In 1954, Berry got the nod to make *Ça va barder* (roughly, "It's gonna hit the fan"), a B-noir with a connection to *Rififi* through the curious strain of American popular culture that had such an impact on French literary (and cinematic) life after World War II. The connection was made through a series of hard-boiled crime novels in the American style launched by the publisher Gallimard in1945 specifically to challenge and supplant the English style of crime-writing that had been popular before the war.[29] The continuing series, called *Série noire,* was given this name by none other than Jacques Prévert, the left-wing poet and screenwriter for the first film ever to be called a "noir," *Le jour se lève* (1939). No fewer than 600 films and TV dramas have been spun out of the series for the French-speaking world, some of them written by other American blacklistees, notably the husband-and-wife writing team Lee and Tammy Gold. Among the earliest film adaptations from the series were *Rififi,* written by August Le Breton, and the Lemmy Caution stories, written by the English novelist Peter Cheyney.[30] *Ça va barder* itself was less of a film than an occasion for melodramatic adventure.[31] But it was commercially successful, leading Berry to a string of entertaining B-efforts and one magnificently serious film: *Tamango (1959).*

By the later 1950s, the rise of the civil rights movement had begun to shake up American politics and culture. Essentially liberal films (most of all *The Defiant Ones,* described in chapter 6) now sometimes made money and reputations. Two groups of radicals worked separately on projects with similar themes. *Slaves,* made at the same time as *Tamango* by Herbert Biberman of *Salt of the Earth,* had a distinguished cast of Ossie Davis, Dionne Warwick and Biberman's wife, the Oscar-winning but blacklisted Gale Sondergaard, together in an awkward antebellum Kentucky drama about a slave attempting to assert himself. An item of journalistic interest during production for its topical oddity, *Slaves* disappeared almost before it opened.

Not so *Tamango*. Drawn from a novella by French writer Prosper Mérimée (author of "Carmen"), it was the second of a two-movie deal made with the French production company Cyclops, following the disappointing comedy guided by Berry, *El Amor de Don Juan/Pantaloons* starring Fernandel. Co-produced by Sig Shore, who would shortly make a fortune on the Superfly pictures, *Tamango* was expensive to make, partly because of the color cinematography and partly because of the stars: Curt Jurgens, Jean Servais, and the African American actress with the greatest promise (and also a long involvement with the Left), Dorothy Dandridge.[32] Berry himself wrote the script with Tammy and Lee Gold. The film was made almost simultaneously in both languages, with dubbing where the actors' unfamiliarity with another language made the dialogue unintelligible.

The result should have been an instant classic and indeed, over the next few years, it packed theaters in U.S. ghetto neighborhoods and art cinemas, setting producer Shore up for charges of blaxploitation. Seen in that light, it was the blacklistees' minimal payoff (along with the popularity of graylisted William Marshall in *Blackula*) in the rising influence of the African American box office, estimated at 30 percent of the first-run urban market by 1970.[33]

On *Tamango*'s slave ship bound from Africa to America, things are rather more unsparing than in Spielberg's Disneyfied/liberal *Amistad* and vastly more sexually charged. Dandridge is treated as a beloved concubine by skipper Jurgens, who like other slavers considers the inevitable torture and murder involved in the Middle Passage as just part of the business. Alex Cressan in the title role, as a slave and potential leader of a shipboard rebellion, appeals to Dandridge's self-respect as a human being and as an African. In the home stretch, it becomes obvious that any rebellion is going to be futile; the choices for the rest of them are probably slavery or death and for Dandridge, the prospect of being a plantation owner's mistress. When she chooses rebellion and death, it is the "revolutionary suicide" that will become almost a slogan of black uprising in the real world of Watts, Oakland, Detroit and Harlem. French critics hated it as yet another presumptuous piece (treating a beloved French novelist as well) by a presumptuous American. That was effectively the end of Berry's career as art-filmmaker until near the close of his life. [34]

And yet, if ever there was a glimpse of the kinds of filmmaking that could have been a part of U.S. cinema in the postwar era without a blacklist, it was here, in the France of the 1950s, where filmmakers integrated American noir with Italian neorealism. Both traditions were products of the Popular Front Depression era, and after they were recovered by the best film critics in France, the critics became filmmakers themselves. It was on this political and aesthetic rock that the short-lived church of the French New Wave was built, even when its prestigious savants occasionally took pains to distance themselves from the Hollywood Left's seemingly old-fashioned narrative styles.

In the oddest way, the story came full circle in 1963 in what might be called the false spring of U.S. filmmaking, when it appeared the blacklist was on the sick list and the Cold War itself might be fading away. What is remarkable is that the film adaptation of Jean Genet's play *The Balcony* was made at all. It pointed to the possibilities for a more complex kind of filmmaking that many hoped might lie just ahead under, or at least after, the Kennedy administration. Those hopes would be dashed by a presidential assassination and the Cold War spasm of war in Southeast Asia.

The Balcony was produced and directed by Joseph Strick, a friend of the Left (and scion of a trucking fortune) who hired Ben Maddow to adapt the play. Maddow, a former documentary screenwriter with a distinguished series of credits from the late 1940s until the blacklist, had afterward joined Philip Yordan's projects without credit—and given in to HUAC, providing private testimony in 1959 after holding out for a half-dozen years.[35]

For better or worse, Maddow and Strick framed the story written by the man whom Sartre had canonized as "Saint Genet"[36] with street scenes from an unidentified documentary and an uprising of uncertain location (perhaps Europe, perhaps Latin America), giving the social allegory a neorealist cast that may have been inappropriate for Genet's purposes but helpful for some viewers to grasp that what was to follow was not necessarily intended to be a comedy. The story itself is an elaborate fantasy about a trio of working-class men (a gas-meter reader and so forth) who are habitués of a bordello in which they get their kicks by play-acting the roles of a bishop, a judge and a general. Then comes the revolution, led by "Roger" (played by young Method actor Leonard Nimoy). The chief of police (Peter Falk), himself a customer, comes to the whorehouse and enlists the help of the madam (Shelley Winters) to assume the role of queen and of the three workers to play out their fantasy roles in real life to reassure the masses about the stability of bourgeois institutions. The madam's assistant and possible lover is played by blacklistee Lee Grant, a successful supporting actress on television by this time but still banished from film.

The Balcony was shot entirely on a sound stage, often against projected backgrounds, and the third act was rewritten because, as Grant recalled decades later, the production was running out of both money and time.[37] It's doubtful, in any case, that the production could have done more than capture the flavor of Genet's play, a long and complex work that he explicitly warned against *playing* as satire (in an introduction to its third and final printed edition) despite the clearly satiri-cal content. Even if the film does not entirely obey that admonition, veering in tone toward Kubrick's *Dr. Strangelove*, which appeared just a year later, it remains effective from the strength of the dialogue alone. Genet's warning on style was vindicated in a speech Falk delivers as the chief of police. In one of the finest mo-ments of his career, Falk leans into the camera and allows the words themselves to do the work. He invokes "this nation of saints and generals . . . this nation of folk-loric heroes and gigantic agronomists, this national nation, this nation composed equally of minerals and miracles . . . this national shrine, this national soil, fertil-ized daily by our heroic national cattle. . . ." As a spoof of fascism, there is little on film to match it.

A few years earlier, there had been at least one other noteworthy bit of neo-realism made by Americans on this side of the Atlantic. Long-admired 1930s screenwriter John Wexley (*Angels with Dirty Faces*), blacklisted and never again active in films, had a big hit before Hollywood in *The Last Mile* (1929), a prison drama that wowed Broadway audiences in 1929 but was made into what Wexley considered a compromised and dreadful film in 1932. All these years later, Mickey Rooney, looking for a serious dramatic lead, lent his considerable reputation to a small and very low-priced production, with a racially mixed cast of mostly Broad-way actors also earning next to nothing. As in so many prison films of yore, the men on death row dream hopelessly of the life they lost on the outside while fac-ing brutal jailers and demeaning psychological conditions.

This time, unlike the average New Deal drama, no kindly prison reformer ap-pears. The plan for a break-out has no real chance to succeed. But the men make the break, fully knowing the consequences. In that moment, as Sartre had argued for the partisans in the underground during World War II, they were freer than they had been their whole lives. They also predicted the "revolutionary suicide" that was as much artistic gesture as political defiance in ghettos and prisons over the next decade or so. And they would pay the price. This real if updated version of *The Last Mile* (1959) was a fine little film, made with the neorealist essence if not the technical specifics—and it, too, virtually disappeared.[38]

MELANCHOLY COWBOYS . . .

It's no accident that westerns succeeded film noir as the most concentrated popular expression of political ideas in the United States in the 1950s. They were to the public discourse of that decade what the gat and icy urban woman smoking a ciga-rette in half-light had been to the immediate postwar period: the vessel of forbid-den ideas. Not all westerns, of course. The grand narratives of the conservatives and the Cold War liberals were largely attempts to broaden the landscapes of the old New Deal westerns into democratic pastorals, in which an evolving republic successfully came to terms with its legacy of racism (as in John Ford's *The Searchers*) and other moral dilemmas of empire—in the process legitimizing the era's emerging sprawl of branch banks and strip malls and subdivisions. By contrast, the westerns made by the surviving remnant of the Hollywood Left—blacklistees and liberals who still supported the ideas of the Popular Front—preserved the darker themes of the 1940s. In these alternative landscapes the Indians were more or less organized politically, the women wore trousers and the outlaws were dissidents who often made pointed speeches before they drew their pistols.

Both kinds of films were shot in the high, frozen mountains of the Cold War. But the darker westerns, at first a snowmelt of resistance, slowly gathered into rivulets that, by the late 1960s, swelled into tributaries of outright narrative opposition. The western rose and fell with the Cold War because it was the one genre that provided an acceptable way of talking about the ideological "consensus" that sustained the war (and the blacklist that was its formal cultural expression). Little wonder that the western was not so much a movie genre as a national obsession, the one place in the culture where conservatives, liberals and even radicals (so long as they remained radicals *sotto voce*) could argue, indirectly and metaphorically, about the nature of "consensus" itself.

Production figures tell some of the story. The number of big-budget westerns made in Hollywood rose from 14 titles in 1947 to 38 in 1950, to 40 in 1952 (not to mention the hundreds of titles each year in B to Z cowpoke categories). After some fluctuations, by 1956 the annual production had risen to 46—nearly one new western movie every week. By the later 1950s, western TV series made up an ever-larger portion of all the prime-time programming on the three national networks, displacing (as we've seen) the high-prestige theatrical series and pushing against the crime shows that had been the westerns' action counterparts all along.[39] Perhaps it was no accident, either, that some of the best westerns were written by leftists who were actually born in the West, notably the Coloradan Dalton Trumbo and Oklahoman Michael Wilson.

In two of Wilson's best screenplays, *Salt of the Earth* (1954) and *Friendly Persuasion* (1956), he redirected the conservative narrative by showing it from the point of view of the female characters; the women, like the Indians, were now acknowledged as subjects of history and no longer merely the objects of scrutiny. Wilson's virtually unknown contribution to *Shane* (1953) is intriguing in this context. *Shane*, some film scholars argue, stands at the precise mid-point of a great cycle of westerns that began with director John Ford's and screenwriter Dudley Nichols' *Stagecoach* (1939) and concluded with Clint Eastwood's *The Outlaw Josey Wales* (1976).[40] If the names and dates of the final westerns in the Cold War cycle remain

somewhat arbitrary, nearly all critics and historians agree on the central importance of *Shane*, not least for the worldwide attention it received. It embraced a new
level of realism for this genre, though it shared nothing with neorealism.

Wilson wrote a "step outline" of the story based on Jack Schaefer's spare but
effective novella about the earliest white settlers in Wyoming.[41] Wilson's 17 pages
were delivered in March 1950 to director George Stevens while the two men were
working together on *A Place in the Sun* (1951). Paramount had bought the rights
to the novel in 1949 and offered it to Stevens the next year as an Alan Ladd vehicle, and because of their ongoing collaboration on the Dreiser novel (*An American Tragedy*, which became *A Place in the Sun*), Wilson was apparently the first
writer to have a crack at the property.

The issue of timing is crucial here. *A Place in the Sun* won an Academy Award
for Wilson, but he was called to testify before the House Committee on Un-
American Activities just six months after he wrote the *Shane* treatment (he appeared on September 29, 1951), and he refused to name names. He wasn't quite
finished in Hollywood; he would write *Friendly Persuasion* and lose a lawsuit to
keep his name in its credits. But his refusal to testify meant he was a serious liabil-
ity to any film, at least publicly. Most likely for that reason, he was finished on
Shane, and few of his specific ideas for the plot development survived the production process. But he did pull into the foreground of the story the historical theme
of the struggle over public lands between big cattle ranchers and refugee small-
holders. Schaefer, himself an historian, had touched on this, but Wilson's explicit
restatement of the theme in class terms (against a background of Indian dispossession) survived the many permutations of the narrative that were to follow, nearly
all of them apparently attributable to Stevens' own genius.[42]

As English critic Raymond Durgnat has observed, McCarthyism's "impact
forced film noir themes to retreat to the Western."[43] The noir "retreat" was truly
undertaken by Trumbo and continued in the western films of Robert Aldrich, a
director who had always been close to the Left but managed to avoid the blacklist.
Between these two talents, the genre that had always contained little more than a
handful of gestures and themes would overrun its banks and spill out into something much larger. As we will see, Aldrich succeeded not only in adapting old
Popular Front themes and methods to the contemporary western but also in revitalizing the genre for the use of filmmakers around the world.

There had been little in the way of such revisionism in the Golden Age of
Hollywood, when films with Mexican or Indian protagonists were few and the
heroism of "Injun Killers" had been an established cliché since the first flickerings
of the silents. This outright racism had been balanced slightly by images of the
"noble Red Man" and the "Good Indians" who helped the explorers. Pro-Indian
or at least honestly ambivalent films sputtered throughout the period, sometimes

showing advances but often reverses, including the undisguised condescension in John Ford's trilogy of dashing cavalrymen. The same was true for a project written by David Lang, on his way to a cheerful denunciation of his former mentors and comrades. He delivered the most typical of the newer conservative films, *Last Outpost* (1951), in which brothers (one of them aptly played by Ronald Reagan) who are divided between the Union and Confederate armies during the Civil War come together against the common red menace—the Indians.

The 1950s even had its own domestic versions of the Eurowestern, given a permanent stamp in Hollywood by *Destry Rides Again* (1939), the great satire of the genre made in a creative collaboration between German refugees and resident Hollywood leftists. In *Rancho Notorious* (1952), scripted by friendly witness Sylvia Richards, the outlaw-gang version of the Berlin demi-monde is still dominated by Marlene Dietrich, now ruling the roost in a middle-aged reprise of her role in *The Blue Angel*. Another, *Johnny Guitar* (1954), has Joan Crawford playing an unidentifiable middle European exile named "Vienna" with a bust of Beethoven on her piano. This oddity became an auteur favorite when the French critics mistakenly interpreted it as an allegory about McCarthyism and the blacklist. According to Ben Maddow, rumored for years to have written *Johnny Guitar* under a front (he may have penned an early draft), Crawford herself made a key decision by insisting that the shooter's role be rewritten *for her* on the spot. The result was an oddball B-western remembered chiefly for its camp-lesbian undertones—Crawford faces Mercedes McCambridge, pistol to pistol—and for a few classical accents, mainly Johnny Guitar as a possible Orpheus.

A few promising signs of actual rather than imagined resistance could be found, with some effort. The cinematic season dominated by *High Noon* (1952) and its cryptic populist politics also saw the release of *Hangman's Knot* (1952), the first and last film to be directed by friendly witness and soon-to-be TV maven Roy Huggins. In quality and style, the movie has the feel of Budd Boetticher's 1950s westerns that featured the same star, Randolph Scott. *Hangman's Knot* opens with a scene that was to become a standard part of the Eurowestern repertoire as a group of Confederate cavalry hijack a Union Army gold shipment. They discover moments afterward that the war between the states has been over for weeks. Because the Confederates are traveling under cover, out of uniform, the surprising impression is created in that scene of an armed insurrection by U.S. civilians. Asked not long before his death whether that imagery was intended to be subversive, Huggins responded, "it may be," in the sense that the Civil War (Huggins added, "this is a Marxist interpretation") was a war of "an imperialist, capitalist country against a colony trying to get away." Huggins evidently had the avidly pro-North Karl Marx confused with someone else, probably the 1920s and 1930s Progressive historians who cast considerable doubt upon the sincerity of erstwhile railroad corporation lawyer Abe Lincoln. But Huggins had apparently effected through his own creative efforts a demi-Marxist interpretation with a twist.[44]

A better Marxist case could be made for an utterly forgotten film, *Terror in a Texas Town* (1958), written by blacklistee Nedrick Young under a pseudonym and directed by the always eccentric Joseph Lewis. It has guilt-ridden friendly witness Sterling Hayden of *Johnny Guitar* fame playing a Scandinavian seaman who lands in his father's Texas town and learns that the whole shebang is owned by another evil land-grabber. Hayden concludes the walk-down by impaling his persecutor on a whaler's harpoon!

One of the best and most authentically neorealist westerns of this period, director Edgar Ulmer's *The Naked Dawn* (1955), is a surprisingly subtle film given its bottom-dollar budget, with unexpected turns of tenderness and dramatic intensity and one of the best performances ever given by Arthur Kennedy. Never again would Ulmer, a longtime friend of the Left and self-made exile from Hollywood, get so close to Loseyan sophistication in a story about sexuality played out across class lines. Much of the subtlety belongs to the screenplay by Julian Zimet, who has said that he adapted the narrative from Maxim Gorky's short story "Chelkash," a character whom Gorky had described as "an old hunted wolf, well known . . . as a hardened drunkard and a bold and dexterous thief."[45] Zimet's version of Chelkash is Santiago (played by Kennedy), a grizzled, whiskey-guzzling Mexican bohemian who had joined the revolution after being cheated out of his farmland.

In the film, the story opens on the moment when the revolution has failed and Santiago and his partner have turned to banditry to survive. They steal a strongbox from an Anglo railroad station, but the partner dies after taking a bullet in the escape. Santiago then finds his way to the home of a peasant and his young wife to hide out. He tries to befriend the peasant, who is envious of his stolen money and the way Santiago throws it around. The peasant's wife, embittered by her virtual domestic slavery, asks the bandit to take her with him when he leaves, but Santiago talks her out of it. When he discovers that the peasant is actually planning to kill him and steal his money, he turns the tables. In the end, however, Santiago teaches the two of them the art of revolutionary self-sacrifice.[46]

If *Naked Dawn* remains obscure in the United States, it was regarded highly enough in France that François Truffaut claimed to have found in it the dramatic solution to a screenplay he had been trying to write about two lifelong friends and their common female companion, the "first film to make me feel that a cinematic *Jules et Jim* is possible."[47] The inspiration Truffaut found here was apparently in the way Zimet depicted the ambivalence of the young peasant wife (played by Tarzan-series veteran Betta St. John). There is no woman in Gorky's story, which is the record of a single encounter between an old thief and a young and naïve boatman one evening in Odessa. Because the Mexican revolution is the political landscape for *Naked Dawn*, it's also tempting to see in it an augur of the Euro-westerns that were to follow in the next decade. But it is too *sui generis* for that, and in truth may be closer to *Shane* than to any spaghetti western, particularly in the handling of the love triangle.

These films were, however, mere preliminaries. The dark heart of the West was finally revealed in the screenplays of Dalton Trumbo. Practically raised on the range in Colorado and the grandson of a sheriff, Trumbo knew better than most Hollywood writers how to ride a horse and to assess the dangers of a sudden thunderstorm. But he knew better than perhaps anyone the meaning of the close of the frontier, pinpointed by Wisconsin historian Frederick Jackson Turner at 1890. The cowboy, in real life always more the hard-bitten and ill-treated cuss than the romantic hero, had already become a living anachronism. The cowboy's long afterlife, with dude ranches as a primary source of income and photo-ops for Eastern and European consumers as a sideline, only underlined the contradictions in the global regard for this figure. Some of that was reflected in Trumbo's pseudonymous script for *Cowboy* (1958), using Frank Harris' *Bildungsroman* to show the romantic enthusiasm of Chicago tenderfoot Jack Lemmon in joining a real cattle roundup—only to discover the greed and cynicism that drive trail boss Glenn Ford, and that learning how to be a real cowboy means standing up to the owners. The scarcely political *Cowboy* looked and felt like a slightly superior version of other genre films of the time.[48]

With *The Last Sunset* (1961), directed by Robert Aldrich and starring the ever-troubled and troubling Kirk Douglas, Hollywood might have found the heart of western noir and rediscovered Trumbo's bitter genius. The movie is well known for the protagonist's discovery that he is in love with his own daughter and his bizarre suicide by walking into a gunfight with an empty pistol. Nearly always overlooked, however, are the uses to which Trumbo puts the mildly shocking theme (particularly for a western) of incest, which he subordinates to something far more subversive. The cowboy Douglas plays is a poet and a seducer who uses his talent for verse to charm women and then snare and ultimately discard them. For this radical egoist, everyone he meets is an object put there for his personal use. He is so cut off from the rest of humanity that a shock is needed to awaken him, a shock provided when for the first time he meets a woman who provokes some authentic feeling in him, then discovers that she is his own child by a woman he had abandoned. At last he begins to understand the depth of his own corruption. Never far from this theme is the implication that some art, including much Hollywood screenwriting, is itself little more than an act of seduction. *The Last Sunset* made up for its lack of success among American filmgoers in its lasting resonance in critical circles, particularly in Italy, where the film magazine *Bianco e*

Nero championed it so fiercely that it became a cult film in that country, with un-expected consequences for the genre, as we shall shortly see.[49]

Soon afterward, in *Lonely Are the Brave* (1962), Kirk Douglas' personal fa-
vorite of his many films, Trumbo wrote the definitive "closing of the West" pic-ture. Like *Cowboy* and *The Last Sunset,* it was a commercial flop, but a more expensive one and more ambitious as well. It offered Douglas the role as the Quixote who embodies novelist and anarcho-ecologist Edward Abbey's idea of the true hero. The resister against modern order, the individualist who cannot be characterized as "Right" or "Left," sets the moral example because he has deter-mined to live as he alone understands is proper. In retreat from the Soviet Union's failures but still keenly aware of capitalism's effects on the human spirit, Trumbo interpreted Abbey sympathetically.

The real cowboy anachronism refuses to compromise with the reality of a dead frontier ripe only for corporate agriculture and subdivisions. He cuts their barbed wire just to ride his horse across heretofore open range and rides to his doom. He is pointedly struck down by a tractor-trailer driver (the young character actor Carroll O'Connor) carrying a load of commodes. It was fatal. "The horse," reflected Doug-las later, "represented his kind of life. When that horse died, he died, too."[50] This was not in any way a happy Hollywood ending—and just what writer and star had in mind. Douglas insisted that the exhibitors could not understand what had been accomplished and, if they had been given the chance, audiences would have come around. *Lonely Are the Brave* was a greater accomplishment than could be apparent at the time, namely the complete realization of the noir western, a form that would soon be overtaken by its own influences.[51]

. . . And Laughing Mexicans

The Eurowestern was made possible by director Robert Aldrich, if not exclu-sively then more than any other filmmaker. His films not only transformed the received genre but contributed a great deal to the creation of a new subgenre that challenged the Cold War consensus from a position well outside of Holly-wood. Personally close to Trumbo and Butler, his deathbed wish was for Abra-ham Polonsky to deliver his funeral eulogy, and the older director did so in 1983.[52] On his own or with Polonsky's encouragement (and very possibly some ghostwriting that neither man ever acknowledged), Aldrich developed a reputa-tion for a "baroque" style. It was actually a kind of naturalistic exaggeration that rivaled Joseph Losey's, with the difference that while Losey was slowly abandon-ing the notion of genre, Aldrich, like Polonsky before him, was intent on re-defining and reinventing it.

In Europe, where he was regarded as an authentic auteur, Aldrich had his own brief period of exile during the blacklist, writing for the cinema journals and cobbling together a series of low-budget films for German and Italian production companies. The exile was largely voluntary, caused by a contract dispute with Harry Cohn at Columbia, but it did provide the opportunity for him to see what was going on in Italy and to rub shoulders with old friends among the blacklistees. In Italy he directed the sword-and-cleavage Biblical epic *Sodom and Gomorrah* (1963), with Hugo Butler as a screenwriter and Sergio Leone, godfather of the modern Eurowestern, as his assistant director. Aldrich and Leone had a complex and often troubled relationship, but the influence of the American director on Italian filmmaking would be felt through his former assistant, who clearly studied Aldrich's films carefully.[53]

Before *The Last Sunset*, an Aldrich western had already changed the genre: *Vera Cruz* (1954), which was co-written by friendly witness Roland Kibbee and was up to that point one of the top-grossing films in history.[54] *Vera Cruz* discovered a new historical setting and exploited it to the hilt.[55] It also introduced the theme of the complex double-cross and, according to François Truffaut, a sense of irony as well, in a genre heretofore know for its deadpan literalism.[56] Now that the Indians had begun to be granted the right to their own subjectivity in the post–New Deal western, *Vera Cruz* established an acceptable new terrain for cinematic bloodshed in the Mexico of 1866, during the rule of the Emperor Maximillian. Later, the historical locus of the political western would be firmly repositioned in the border regions of northern Mexico and the U.S. Southwest. For the moment, however, in this location Mexicans who supported the hated Maximillian could die by the score to satisfy the demands of action-adventure narratives. Soon enough, the soldiers would be depicted as supporters of President (actually dictator) Porfirio Diaz and the opponents of Pancho Villa and Emiliano Zapata. But in one stroke and in the nick of time, in *Vera Cruz* an acceptable new enemy had been secured. A precedent for this new development was a film made early in the blacklist that has puzzled filmgoers for generations with its ambivalent, not to say confused, politics. The story of how *Viva Zapata!* (1950), a project begun by the Left and finished by its enemies, has been told before, but it has particular meaning here.[57]

In 1941, American novelist Edgecumb Pinchon published a fictionalized history of the Zapata wing of the Mexican revolution, *Zapata the Unconquerable*.[58] Six years later, in 1947, the front office at MGM handed the book to screenwriter Lester Cole to adapt for the screen. According to Cole's account of the incident years later, he spent about three months on the project and submitted the result to MGM. When general manager Eddie Mannix read it, he was "horrified. 'Get rid of this fuckin' script,' he said, 'this bastard Zapata's a goddam commie revolutionary!'"[59] But the producer refused to give up. He took Cole along on a trip south of the border and inquired of officials in the Mexican government whether they would be interested in helping fund the project. Indeed they were. The Mexicans offered to put up half the cost of the entire film on the condition that Cole's screenplay be shot as written. When the producer and Cole returned to Hollywood and told Mannix about the Mexican government's offer, Mannix softened. "'A million and a half [dollars]! How can we lose?'"

"So it was all ready to go," Cole wrote, "when the Un-American Activities Committee handed me a subpoena." At that point MGM unloaded the script to Twentieth Century Fox, which passed it down to Elia Kazan to direct. Mexican officials were so enraged that they refused to let Kazan into the country to make the picture.[60] As it turned out, their suspicions were vindicated.

Kazan and John Steinbeck went to work on the screenplay and quickly transformed it from a story about a revolutionary leader into one that caricatured a primitive rebel with only a remote grasp of his own motives. Zapata, in historical fact a literate man and tenant farmer, was turned into an illiterate surrounded by an alcoholic brother, a fictional intellectual of the suspicious variety and an admirable but merely liberal politician. The leader of the peasants is handed the reassuring line, "[U]p there [in the U.S.] they are a democracy." Marlon Brando as Zapata is the only saving grace in a film that is full of resentments, but in which politics are sacrificed to atmospheric anecdote and the chief dramatic moment is not the revolutionary victory but Zapata's decision to abandon the revolution and go home.

When the film was released, the Mexican film industry expressed its collective displeasure. Kazan later reported Steinbeck's remark on that point. "John said, 'I smell the party line.' I smelled it, too."[61] But of course, this was not about the party of the old kind but rather the Mexicans' nose for the American State Department's own party line. The film reflected the view held by contemporary liberal cold warriors that the idea of revolution was hopeless and unwanted in reality but had propaganda value in art. Zapata was thus the kind of film analyzed by Abraham Polonsky, a few years earlier, as the cinema that resolves itself into a "radical verbalism which accepts the status quo."[62] Not surprisingly, the film had no influence on the Mexican narrative that would soon sweep the world.[63]

It was Aldrich's influence, not Kazan's, that would be felt as the Marxist western emerged under the hands of Italian filmmakers, with the additional influence of a former Communist, Akira Kurosawa, a Japanese director also greatly interested in the western as a form. By the early 1960s, the Italians had embraced Kurosawa's success with samurai films and combined it with Aldrich's dark western to create a new subgenre, the "spaghetti western." The Italians reworked the cinematic grammar of the western that had been perfected by Ford and reinvented by Aldrich into a new kind of filmmaking that became the generational equivalent of the cinematic Popular

Front, now as part of the international movement against the Vietnam War and the global peasant struggle against neo-colonialism. It was a case of neorealism boomeranging home—the internationalization of a once strictly U.S. national genre that was virtually unprecedented in movie history. This movement would be felt in turn in Hollywood in the best of the westerns that emerged in the late 1960s, not least in the films of Richard Brooks, Sam Peckinpah and the redoubtable Abraham Polonsky. The western would never be the same.

One of the most important strands in the reweaving of the Marxist Eurowestern had been used first by Kurosawa, namely Dashiell Hammett's *Red Harvest*, a 1928 novella by the Marxist writer who had arguably reinvented the western as a detective story.[64] Hammett's protagonist was a dour, violent and amoral man, the "Continental Op" who lacked a name but shared some of the supernatural traits of the western hero invented by Owen Wister. But Hammett subordinated the usual skill with firearms to something very new: a finesse in crime detection that derived from the hero's Marxist understanding of class relations.[65]

Kurosawa, the first Asian filmmaker to appropriate and translate Hammett's device, had already made his political views clear in a series of searing antifascist films produced shortly after World War II, notably *No Regrets for My Youth* (1946), which actually called for revolutionary students to join with the peasants in building a political movement in the countryside. Kurosawa would never again make anything quite so politically explicit, and yet something crucial from that period remained in his work. One of his greatest films, *Red Beard* (1965), was a barely disguised demand for universal medical care, which revealed a soul at equipoise somewhere between socialism and social Buddhism. Along with *Red Harvest*, Kurosawa acknowledged *Shane* as an influence on his hugely influential *Yojimbo* (1961), in which a rootless samurai wanders into a village dominated by competing groups of gangsters and resolves the conflict. The samurai is not a hired gun but a man like Shane, a reluctant fighter who can summon the compassion to save a peasant family from injustice.

In Hammett's *Red Harvest*, the detective enters a crime-ridden American village that is divided into two factions; he then plays one off against the other until both gangs have consumed themselves in acts of revenge. Like the Op, the samurai takes little delight in swordplay, preferring to use his keen understanding of class relations to stage-manage the behavior of others to bring them to ruin.

How all of these distantly connected strands of the international culture of the Popular Front were brought together by the neorealist Marxists of Italy in the 1960s is surely one of the most unusual stories in the history of cinema, and predictably misunderstood within the United States. But perhaps the story should not be so surprising, after all. The New Deal western had been received with great enthusiasm in every corner of the globe, leading Andre Bazin to observe, "the Western does not age. Its worldwide appeal is even more astonishing than its historical survival."[66] Why should not a more radical version of it take root in a later era, when intellectuals, artists, students and peasants were on the march in those same corners of the globe that had welcomed the first stories of justice on horseback?

Millions of moviegoers casually associate the Eurowestern with Sergio Leone, whose A Fistful of Dollars (1964) made a star of an obscure TV actor named Clint Eastwood in a movie that was virtually a shot-for-shot remake of Kurosawa's Yojimbo (and with whom Leone had to share the profits for that very reason, under threat of a lawsuit). Leone had so much success with this particular scene that, as far as most U.S. movie-lovers are concerned, they represent the sum total of the output of the "spaghetti Western" as a subgenre.[67] In fact, more than 500 Eurowesterns were made, mostly by Italian, German and Spanish production companies, during the 1960s and 1970s.[68] Few of them were given theatrical distribution in the United States, but a fan following has for years supported a number of specialized video import companies. Among these many titles there is to be found a smaller cycle of films called "political spaghetti," whose greatest practitioner was Franco Solinas.

In the United States, Solinas is known as the best writer of the political films that arose out of neorealism in the 1960s and imitated the terse and objective style of the documentary. He wrote two of the best of these political films, The Battle of Algiers (1965), directed by Gillo Pontecorvo with music by Ennio Morricone, and State of Siege (1973), directed by Costa-Gavras, among the most beloved foreign films exhibited by the campus film societies of the era. Less well known in the United States are Solinas' actual contributions to neorealism, including The Wide Blue Road (1957), based on his own novel, and the screenplay for Roberto Rossellini's Vanina Vanini (1961). Almost entirely unknown except among devotees of the Eurowestern are the films Solinas wrote in a three-year burst of energy, namely The Big Gundown (1966), A Bullet for the General (1967), Long Live the Revolution (1968) and The Mercenary (1968). Some of these titles boasted scores by Morricone and were directed by the most "political" of Eurowestern filmmakers, men who never won much of a reputation outside of Europe but were highly regarded in the same European left-wing circles in which U.S. blacklistees were working at the time.[69] In fact, one of Solinas' last and strongest screenplays was Monsieur Klein (1976), written for Joseph Losey.[70]

In the United States, the Eurowestern may have been misunderstood as mere adventure, but in Europe its meaning was evident to nearly everyone. The leading scholar of the subgenre recalls that the United States had been viewed from the United Kingdom in the 1950s as a wonderful place filled with cars and music and the rising excitement of a universal popular culture. Then came Vietnam, and a "kind of sourness set in." Most westerns had celebrated the American dream, but "here was a movie saying to us [that] most men south of the border worked solely for cash. 'Why are you doing this for us? For 500 dollars?'"[71] In these films, Yankees could not get off the hook for their debauch, and they did not look so invincible after all.

The rest of the world's filmgoers had much the same reaction. In the universal laughter of the Mexican banditos and revolutionaries depicted in many of these films, they saw the lingering bad conscience of the U.S. *gabacho* who had crushed so many native cultures underfoot in the search for loot. Even Hammett's Op has a dream about "a small brown man who wore an immense sombrero. He was standing on the steps of a tall building on the far side of a wide plaza, laughing at me."[72] The actual historical source of the laughter that so maddened the austere, Calvinist gringo leaders probably derived from the national embarrassment over the failure of U.S. General "Black Jack" Pershing's so-called punitive expedition against Pancho Villa in 1916, ordered by the ostensibly liberal, morally pinched president, Woodrow Wilson. The expedition resulted in nothing more than a brief skirmish and a great deal of fruitless pursuit.[73]

The Eurowestern evolved into a highly stylized set of variations in music, gunplay and plot outcomes, but almost always depicted a relation between a taciturn American (or sometimes a blond European) intent on profit and a band of passionate Mexicans bent on revolution. In the hands of liberal writers and directors, the gringo businessman with the handgun is sometimes converted to the revolutionary cause. But in the Solinas classic *A Bullet for the General* (1967), directed by Damiano Damiani in a sure-handed style reminiscent of the Left's old ally Richard Brooks, the gringo, after fighting in many battles alongside the revolutionaries, is revealed in the end to be an assassin in the pay of the Diaz government—the kind of intelligence operative whose type would become much more familiar in later years. Meanwhile the Mexican revolutionary, about to be lured across the U.S. border by the promise of an easy life, finally refuses the temptation, kills the *gabacho* and, as he runs away from the *federales*, throws his money to a shoeshine boy, yelling, "Use it to buy dynamite!"[74]

Meanwhile, back at the subgenre, Leone's *Fistful*, itself a remake, was remade again as *Django* (1966) in an even more operatic stylization, and it was just as successful at the box office as the first two filmed versions of *Red Harvest*. The story went through more than 30 sequels from many different hands, which were seen by audiences from Indonesia to Argentina, an extraordinary example of how a Popular Front narrative that began in the pages of *Black Mask* could be carried to the ends of the earth as a kind of replicated cultural DNA molecule, now no longer in the service of the struggle against fascism but of the international movement against imperial war and neo-colonialism. It was, altogether, a very long way from the stoic images of *Shane*, the Protestant masterpiece that had swept the world in the darkest days of the Cold War.

All of this success at the box office for the Eurowestern could be ignored neither by Hollywood money men nor what remained of the Hollywood Left. The lasting impact of the Italian experiment on Hollywood may be understood best by looking briefly at a group of the last great westerns made in the late sixties: Richard Brooks' *The Professionals* (1966), Sam Peckinpah's *The Wild Bunch* (1969) and Don Siegel's *Two Mules for Sister Sara* (1969).

By changing the name of Frank O'Rourke's novel *A Mule for the Marquesa* to *The Professionals*, Richard Brooks got straight to the central theme of the Eurowestern.[75] Four gringos, disillusioned veterans of the campaign in the Philippines who later fought for Pancho Villa for half a decade, have now turned freelance mercenaries. They accept a commission to rescue the wife of a railroad magnate kidnapped by a Mexican revolutionary and a former comrade in the Villa campaign (Jack Palance as "Raza," literally "the race"). Each of the gringos is an expert in some martial skill, including automatic weapons (Lee Marvin), explosives (Burt Lancaster), the long bow (Woody Strode) and managing horses (Robert Ryan). Using the usual supernatural skills of the Yankee abroad, they move south by night, find Palance's camp and locate the magnate's wife, who has quite a story to tell.

Played by Claudia Cardinale with all the strapping bosomy fervor of Marianne, the spirit of 1789 France, the wife turns out to be Raza's lifelong companion, lover and fellow revolutionary, who as a young woman was sold as chattel to the railroad magnate when he bought her father's ranch. Betrayed by the facts, the gringos nonetheless determine to fulfill the contract and take her back to the United States and the arms of her much older husband. Like virtually all of the cinematic Mexicans and other representatives of Latino and Indian cultures, Raza lacks any specialized skill except the skill of the heart, particularly for love and revolution, and so it is no surprise when he pursues the gringos north with such determination that he cannot be stopped by three or four gunfights and two serious bullet wounds. After the second wound, he delivers the famous aria, "The revolution is like a great love affair," which chides the gringo revolutionary for abandoning the cause because he demanded "perfection or nothing."

This is a very long way from Hopalong Cassidy, but it is equally far from *Shane*, a measure of the impact of the Italian western on Hollywood. *The Professionals*, nominated for an Academy Award, was a huge hit at the box office, where it prepared the way for the great westerns of the next few years that for all practical purposes closed the book both on the genre and subgenre.

The influence of the Eurowestern on Don Siegel's *Two Mules for Sister Sarah* (1969), written by an Albert Maltz newly restored from the blacklist but mostly too late for his failing energies, is still more evident than in the Brooks film. Clint

Eastwood is now at last given a name (Hogan) but remains the misplaced gringo in a land of revolution and business opportunity.

The central gesture in *Two Mules* is the familiar and persistent doubt over motives and suspicions of betrayal over the question of who is working for gold and who is working for revolution (in this case, against the French occupation). A happy ending has been provided at the moment when the nun and the mercenary, who have been misleading each other all along, reveal themselves as an honest hooker and a revolutionary on the same side of history. Thus Hollywood at once embraced the Italian attitude and legitimized it in the context of an advanced Yankee filmmaking technique and a large budget (confirming the point of many a Eurowestern) and giving it major star treatment as well. By turning a Budd Boetticher story over to Maltz to make into a screenplay, the producers were in essence evoking the spirit of World War II all over again, when it was the lefties who were given the choice anti-fascist assignments.

That radical *annus mirabalus*, 1969, saw the release of Sam Peckinpah's *The Wild Bunch*, of all U.S. westerns after John Ford perhaps the only undisputed masterpiece. Although its credits reveal no direct ties to the blacklist, Peckinpah's movie must be noted in this context because of the director's own experience at the hands of critics who often misunderstood his westerns—or understood them all too well. More than any other independent liberal filmmaker, Peckinpah came under attack from critics who operated under the rules of Cold War liberalism, which is to say, rules governing just about every critic working in the mainstream media in the late 1960s—and in many cases right down to the present. In these quarters, deviations into positions that opposed U.S. wars or the domestic order simply would not be tolerated. And so Peckinpah—a veteran of southern civil rights marches—came under attack for his penchant for depicting war and gunplay in slow motion, not so subtly rubbing the fiction in the faces of those who supported the fact.

The canard among these critics was Peckinpah's supposed political conservatism, overlooking a series of inconveniences: the dedication of one film to the memory of Pancho Villa; Peckinpah's screenplay for *Villa Rides* (1968); and, finally, the extraordinary narrative of *The Ballad of Cable Hogue* (1970), nothing less than a delving into the nature of primitive accumulation in a western setting.[76] Even the best of the forties westerns do not prepare the viewer for *The Wild Bunch*, simultaneously the darkest western made after *The Last Sunset* and a thoughtful exploration of the politics of the Mexican revolution from the gringo perspective.

The story of *The Wild Bunch* is simple enough. A group of gringo bandits led by William Holden make one last big score in a southwestern town but have to hightail it into Mexico after they discover that a reformed member of the gang

(Robert Ryan) is on their trail. Trapped in Mexico, they agree to hijack a train to provide arms for a counter-revolutionary Mexican general. But in the end they turn on the general and, in one of the bloodiest gunfights ever filmed, they kill and are killed in a ballet of bloodletting that still astonishes. The point is made at the very end when Ryan, sitting amidst the carnage while holding the reins of his horse, awaits the arrival of Villa's troops as he dreams that a revolution will put an end to the bloodshed. As occasionally happened, Cold War–minded critics were right to hate this film. It was, after all, a demonstration of the emptiness of their supposed humanism. In its lasting brilliance, it stands as the tombstone to many a critical reputation in the U.S. culture war that ricochets down to the present day.

This part of our story would hardly be complete without a mention of *Tell Them Willie Boy Is Here* (also 1969), attacked by Pauline Kael in the *New Yorker* as "New Left guerilla Existentialism"—a point on which, despite the hyperventilating rhetoric, she was largely correct.[77] *Willie Boy* is no Eurowestern, but it certainly belongs to the strain of the dark western, now come under the influence of Polonsky's own exercises in film noir in the 1940s. Here a John Garfield character, Robert Blake, is crushed equally by impossible hopes and social corruption. On a variation of the old theme of the closing of the frontier but based on a real historical incident, Blake plays the last Indian in California to revolt against white authority. Observing an old custom, Blake as a Chemehuevi laborer attempts in 1910 a "marriage by capture" of a maiden from her unwilling father, but accidentally kills the father. The law steps in, in the person of an unwilling sheriff played by Robert Redford and satirically named "Coop" after the Gary Cooper type. The press gets involved, hyping the danger to a presidential party about to arrive on a campaign swing. As the noose tightens, it is up to the remnant warrior to decide how the chase will end. It ends with an echo of *The Last Sunset* in a suicide-by-surrender. *Tell Them Willie Boy Is Here* captured the mood that *The Professionals* had only begun to anticipate three or four years earlier of an empire devouring its own.

If there was one element that Polonsky's single western might have owed directly to the Eurowesterns, it was the idea of the music. Whereas Ennio Morricone used an often strange and slap-happy assortment of percussion instruments to emphasize a very European sense of irony in the Italian westerns, Polonsky carefully elicited from composer Dave Grusin a score that would emphasize the distance from European experience of the tribal customs and desert life forms, and match the desaturation of color in the cinematography of Conrad Hall—a kind of noir in reverse, but just as bleached out, morally speaking, as the single-source lighting in Polonsky's own early films.

With the rise of Ronald Reagan and the scary side of Hollywood and its predatory relation with global culture, the promise of the 1960s was soon to disappear. Franco Solinas, the inventor of the Marxist western, died prematurely in

1982 at the age of 55. He had written other screenplays, now widely lamented for the fact they were never produced. One was for Sam Peckinpah under the title *La vie c'est comme un train* (Life is Like a Train), and the other an aborted epic with Joseph Losey in 1978 that was to be called *Ibn Saud*, the loss of which is perhaps now felt even more keenly. It was to be a kind of response to *Lawrence of Arabia* (1962), and according to film scholarship the "Shakespearean rendering of a single critical year, 1929, when a major battle occurred between 'progressive' and 'fundamentalist' forces in Saudi Arabia."[78]

When Solinas died, he had long since turned away from the Marxist Euro-western, the form he had mastered above all others. By this time, Leone and Peckinpah had abandoned it as well. For whatever reason, both the subgenre and its mother had become orphans of cinematic history, and who could say why? The best critic of these matters observed that "by extending the western genre in all sorts of outlandish directions, [Peckinpah and the others] may well have succeeded in killing it off altogether," not only as a movie type but as style of discourse. In any case, the "rhetoric could be taken no further."[79]

Perhaps in a larger sense, with the grinding to a close of the Cold War, there was no longer a perceived need for the genre. It was not so much that the rhetoric had reached its limit but that the debate was over, for the moment. Not that the Marxists had won, by a long shot. But looking back, it had been one hell of a ride.

CHAPTER FIVE

WORKING UNDER COVER

THE PREMIERE FOR THE RELIGIOUS EPIC *The Robe* (1953) caused a stir of the kind the film industry had not seen in years. The BBC and the Voice of America followed the event with live, worldwide coverage as 12,000 people jammed New York's Roxy Theater. In the audience on that balmy mid-September evening were stars Loretta Young, Milton Berle, Charles Boyer, Joseph Cotton, Sophie Tucker, the current Mrs. Vanderbilt and assorted film moguls. Even the admired First Amendment liberal whose name was on the writing credit for the film, Philip Dunne, was there. Just one relevant person happened to be missing: the one who had years earlier written the original screenplay, Albert Maltz.[1]

Opening night excitement had little to do with the film's story line, even in this era of orchestrated fervor against "godless Communism." The real star was CinemaScope. As one of London's film critics gushed, the film process promised to "bring the missing millions back to the movies."[2] *The Robe*, Bosley Crowther observed, was "a sweeping display of colorful settings and costuming on a unique pictorial scale," romanticizing Christians "amid sumptuous and scenic surroundings." It was, in brief, the Greatest Story Ever Told "on the largest movie screen ever used."[3]

Thus was a heavy burden of expectations laid on a weak and melodramatic narrative, one neither especially entertaining nor educational. Richard Burton, as one of Caesar's proconsuls, is sent out to conquer the Jews—and that he does, even as inner doubts grow with his attraction to a brave and pretty Christian played by Jean Simmons. The proconsul's manservant, overplayed by Victor Mature in his usual fashion, is sincere to the point of eagerness to die for his adopted faith. The film's overall identification of Christianity with the slave class more than with the Christians of the commercial classes (such as Simmons) may reflect the original emphasis on certain elements in the Lloyd Douglas novel that Maltz first adapted. It also may owe something to *Sign of the Cross* (1932), the first biblical sound spectacular, written by another future blacklist victim, Sidney Buchman. In both films but more pointedly in *The Robe*, cinematic early Christians are the Jews who choose to rebel against empire and bravely hang on to their faith through ridicule, torture and violent death, themes stuffed into a casing of melodrama and larded with romantic subplots and plenty of undraped flesh.

At 135 minutes (again, following precedent: *Sign of the Cross* was 125 minutes even with the goriest scenes cut), *The Robe* might have been unendurably tedious if not for the dazzling technology. Yet it has its moments, such as Burton careening through the streets on a chariot looking for followers of the Savior, only to come across a devotee who urges the despairing to keep the faith. The devotee, we quickly learn, is none other than a repentant Judas—one more reference that Dunne as well as Maltz could have been making to liberal Hollywood and its own contemporary, conscience-stricken Judases.

By contrast, former Communist director Irving Pichel's *Day of Triumph* (1954), a low-budget epic about the rise and suppression of a utopian sect of early Christians, never surfaced.[4] *Day of Triumph* drew closer, both in its narrative and its fate, to the real experience of most of the blacklisted writers and directors from early exile to the middle 1960s. Surviving utopian visions of a different cinema in the United States were thoroughly quashed. Personal success here and there was overshadowed by the more frequent disappointment when one lead after another petered out. The once-influential lefties weren't licked yet, but the opportunities, at least in the short run, were drying up. Each year spent out of the Hollywood dealmaking merry-go-round made return more difficult.

The eschatological themes and blacklistee blues might also be taken as a subscript for the whole industry seeking a different kind of savior. In the decade or so after 1955, RKO crashed, leaving MGM, Paramount, Warner Brothers and Twentieth Century-Fox in a race for dwindling receipts. The later obsession with blockbusters had been a principal strategy all along, but more and more frequently it proved an abysmal strategic failure, finishing off the smaller films that might have reached niche audiences and putting all the chips on the table for big stars and budget overruns.

Meanwhile, a lot of valuable time went by. Hollywood survived, but at a cost that could hardly be measured. Later efforts by critics like Andrew Sarris and Pauline Kael to magnify the artistic (or entertainment) value of 1950s–1960s American films relative to the Golden Age of the 1920s–1940s had more to do with Cold War politics than either audience interest or critical estimations from within the industry itself. Camera technology, to take a case in point, really did improve the cinematic possibilities—but the payoff only came at the end of the 1960s and into the 1970s, when the pioneering work done by Haskell Wexler, among others, using a host of innovations (most noticeably, the zoom lens) came to be seen as the visual grammar of the New Hollywood. Further innovation, such as improvements in lighting and color film stock, arrived with the challenges of location shooting and the use of portable Steadicams. The era of accomplished special effects and Dolby Sound lay still further ahead. For now, the doldrums ruled.

It was hardly surprising, then, that so many victims of the blacklist also found themselves amazed at Hollywood's myopia and wondering whether there might be a film industry to go back to.

BARELY HANGING ON

From the first, the hardcore activists set their face to the wind, determined to triumph through a combination of talent and grit. Hanging on in Hollywood, they had a different kind of revival in mind for the industry, and one they believed could pack the theaters again. The publication of the *Hollywood Review* (1953–1956), a newsletter-size, four- to six-page newspaper with an irregular bimonthly schedule, was their organ of expression—just as they were succumbing to collective silence and more comprehensive exile. They knew the film business well enough to grasp that a comeback is always against the odds but rarely impossible. More important to our story, they understood as keenly as anyone that the movie studios had not resolved their problems by purging the radicals and turning to mega-spectaculars. Far from it.

The Hollywood Left's best and most successful films, whether the cinema of dripping liberal conscience or buoyant antibourgeois comedy, exemplified and, at least in fantasy, sometimes realized the dreams of the Popular Front. They viewed themselves as a vast movement seizing the chance, during the Roosevelt years, to criticize and sometimes correct social wrongs—but also to make their own way upward personally. Their favorite actors provided great images on celluloid. Female viewers could taste the self-determination denied in society at large, and men, emphatically including boys, vicariously experienced the courage and the rock-hard conscience required to meet the tasks of the day, including combat. Practically everyone could enjoy a good slapstick jest at the expense of the foolish rich or the pompous, as well as the genre satires, like *Abbott and Costello Meet Frankenstein* (1948), which became more common toward the end of the 1940s. Hollywood radicals, because of their talent and energy but also because of their placement in an industry full of Jewish contacts and relatives, thus became the artists who developed the formulas and techniques for urging the liberal purpose continually forward.

Had these Hollywoodites actually relied upon the guidance of the American Communist Party (or worse, the Soviet Union) for artistic sensibilities, or even upon the mainstream of American liberalism as it wavered and wobbled, they would have been lost before they began. It was the Popular Front that turned them loose to tackle local issues, in a large if never absolute sense. Hollywood's sharp Right/Left division, which divided unions between the mob-influenced and industry-friendly on the one hand and the democratic left-influenced unions on the other, had helped harden their resolve even when their faith in Russia waned. By the early 1950s, defeated across the board and already a half-step out of the Communist Party (the twin 1956 disillusionments of Khrushchev's revelations and the Russian invasion of Hungary finished off the loyalties of nearly all black-listees), they clung to a few surviving institutions. The nominal sponsor of the *Hollywood Review,* the Southern California Council of Arts, Science and Professions, was the merest remnant of a once-powerful group. In Hollywood of all places—continually spotlighted by red-baiting newspaper columnists and pursued by congressional investigating committees—the Popular Front held on for dear life, showing wit as well as making some shrewd observations in the bargain.[5]

The *Hollywood Review* had, according to the later recollections of participants, about a thousand subscribers, mostly intellectuals of one kind or another around the movie colony. It was put together in the living room of the former personal secretary to John Garfield, Helen Sloate Levitt. Together with her blacklisted husband, Al Levitt, she was just breaking into television writing for the *Donna Reed Show* and other programs pseudonymously, as we've seen. The *Review's* two most prolific (if also pseudonymous) writers were local journalists, reputedly hard-drinking, left-wing women, each of whom later committed suicide.[6] Its other most active organizer, Sylvia Jarrico, had been managing editor of the *Hollywood Quarterly* before the purge, trained in the sociology of film at UCLA but now with her comrades scrambling to keep the Left alive.[7]

Nowhere could the word "Communist" be found in the nine published issues. Most of the writers had stopped thinking of themselves in such specific terms. The group nevertheless continued their own tradition, updating a viewpoint that badly needed to be aired within a film colony driven back into timidity on any possibly controversial social issue, but especially on the festering American sore of race.[8]

The *Hollywood Review* therefore pointed with particular care to the plight of the African American actor and the "race problem" film that surfaced in a handful of later 1940s productions, only to be stalled and almost abandoned (along with the Screen Actors Guild's own "Minority Committee," eliminated on the command of SAG President Ronald Reagan) as too "controversial" in the emerging era.⁹ The kinds of films that left-wingers most wanted to make would clearly have elevated the status of African Americans (as well as Native Americans, Asians and others) from victim to protagonist and from simplistic story lines to characters sufficiently complex for serious drama as well as uncondescending comedy. Popular Fronters had made real progress with such films as *Intruder in the Dust*, *Home of the Brave* and *Broken Arrow*, not to mention providing direction or lyrics for the then-unprecedented race musicals, *Cabin In the Sky*, *Stormy Weather* and *New Orleans*. The reality of 1950s Hollywood not only blocked progress of this sort for a decade, but its defining films, when they included race at all, actually grew worse in certain key respects.

The social drama, even one with a cause as respectable as the anti-anti-Semitism of *Gentleman's Agreement*, had likewise all but disappeared. As we shall see, 1950s filmic southern drama was drenched in pathos but scarcely any of it was racial—surely an amazing fact in the era of latter-day lynchings and the Montgomery bus boycott. The wide-screen spectacular saw instead the proliferation of swashbuckler heroes winning fortunes by besting troublesome natives across the planet. It was an old story in films, right back to the silents, but one renewed perversely in the era of anticolonial rebellion with familiar champions like Gary Cooper, John Wayne, Jeff Chandler, Alan Ladd, Robert Mitchum and even the noted Hollywood liberal Burt Lancaster portrayed dramatically and with much rippling muscle saving the ignorant from themselves and (usually) dallying with alluring native women before returning to their own kind.

Likewise, the reemergence of the "weak woman" or the misguided woman in films, after the relatively strong women of what might be called the Katharine Hepburn era amply demonstrated the drifting melancholy mood in Hollywood. As Sylvia Jarrico observed in the *Review*, now the "woman who thrives on submission is juxtaposed against the woman of will," the force-of-evil vamp. Women who resisted male control were bound to be neurotic if not actually murderous.¹⁰

For that matter, the artful presentation of working-class conservatism, particularly in the heroic priest and erstwhile proletarian militants eager to give testimony to the authorities in *On the Waterfront*, could most accurately be described as the gendered equivalent of the submissive women.¹¹ No longer rebelling against authority, McCarthy-era moralists actually craved the obedience that church and state demanded of them. Of course, neither the church nor police had ever been greatly out of favor in Hollywood, and pro-union films simply had never been permitted. The protest ambience of the great "conscience" drama of the 1930s–1940s, *Mr. Smith Goes to Washington* or *Grapes of Wrath*, was now definitely out of fashion.

If Hollywood had indeed lost its métier, it was likely not attributable to the competing medium of television, which studio spokesmen derided before leaping into television production themselves. Hollywood changed because the audiences were changing. Surveys of the mid-1950s suggested that Americans of all kinds watched television, much as their earlier counterparts had gone to local movie theaters; in both cases, viewers were fascinated by the medium itself and craved the entertainment without bothering to choose a show carefully. Latter-day moviegoers were, however, far more likely to be middle class and white, a detail that did not (in a development disappointing to some political trend-watchers) make them so much conservative as selective. They had to have a reason to turn out, thereby demanding of producers and studios something like the niche marketing for youth that had already been glimpsed by the makers of exploitation films for drive-in audiences and would be so well cultivated by later Hollywood producers.[12]

Contrary to the 1950s Hollywood elite's hopes for the blockbuster picture, it was not the answer. By the middle of the decade, as dj/producer Alan Freed crashed the music establishment with a multiracial rock 'n roll and crypto-sexual suggestiveness in the lyrics, rebellion again emerged as the candidate for rejuvenating the movie industry. But rebellion against what? As film scholar Lary May observes, "to young people and others who wished to rebel but did not wish to 'sound like a communist,'" in the telling defensive phrase of icon James Dean, "the turn toward Method [acting] and depth psychology provided a way to critique the core elements of the postwar consensus, particularly the family."[13]

This judgment is not quite right, because *The Wild One* (1954) and *Rebel Without a Cause* (1955), not to mention the dozens of knockoff B-versions of youthful hot-rodders and hoods made especially for drive-in audiences, did hint at the problems of alienation and dispossession that society had not found a way to resolve. Occasionally (as in *The Girl Can't Help It*, 1956), the soundtrack successfully carried the message of rebellious music over a banal plot. But May correctly suggests that Hollywood, in turning fearfully away from social themes, had largely missed the boat.

The survivors of the Hollywood Left, wedded as they still were to the liberal narrative of the 1940s and its clearcut motivations, probably would have preferred the kind of antifascist hero that Bogey had been in *Casablanca,* or the working-class hero of the sort played so effectively by John Garfield, not to mention the strong women and so on. But they had definitely grown more interested in psychological themes, as their participation in noir showed. That Hugo Butler and his wife Jean Rouverol had bought the rights to the story that became *The Wild One,* arguably the most avant-garde of the day, as the true "rebel without a cause" is most revealing. No one who has seen it has ever forgotten the answer of motorcycle-pack leader Marlon Brando when asked by a respectable citizen of the small town his group has invaded what they are rebelling against: "Whaddaya got?"[14]

The story behind the story of the adaptation from print to screen began with an option purchased on a story that appeared in the *Atlantic*; an option regretfully abandoned because the Butlers were going underground. Their friend and comrade Carl Foreman bought it from them shortly before his own exile. Ultimately, it fell into the hands of fellow blacklistee Ben Maddow, who wrote an early script without credit. Afterward, Clifford Odets served as mentor for director Nicholas Ray on the set of *Rebel Without a Cause*, where the rebel really does have a cause (even if it is opposition to a domineering mother, symbol of a society that does not understand him). Hollywood producers would soon be looking desperately for writers who could handle the themes of rebellious outsiders, and it was probably only the lack of availability of the blacklistees that kept them from monopolizing the field. They were the past masters in writing rebellious protagonists, after all.

The search for the apt rebel led back to women (even if the studios remained cold to strong women), charismatic male outsiders and the mentally disturbed, as well as (later) homosexual men and of course racial minorities—and the disadvantaged but culturally alert whites that Elvis Presley was to embody.[15] By the early 1960s, Hollywood liberalism, so badly disoriented for a decade, had begun to find its footing again.

Of course, by this time only a fraction of the Hollywood Left was still around to make use of an artistic and box-office vindication. Nevertheless, the little milieu around the *Hollywood Review* had anticipated the softening of war rhetoric during the middle 1950s. Michael Wilson thus wryly observed "New Trends Visible—If You Squint," and from the viewpoint of 1956 he could foresee that the social film had returned for a share (and a most prestigious share at that) of the niche market with the prospective film production of Broadway hits like *The Diary of Anne Frank* (1959) and *Inherit the Wind* (1960). The glorification of war generally and the swashbuckler conquering the Third World began to fade. Meanwhile, curious dramas, often enough adaptations from television, suggested that the contemporary hero was at home and troubled. Paddy Chayefsky's *Marty*, like Martin Ritt's *Edge of the City*, earned a public status that the Left could not claim as its own without giving away the secret behind the screen credits—that they contained crucial fronts.[16]

Unfortunately, Wilson's optimistic observations were published in what turned out to be the final issue of *Hollywood Review*. Loyalty to Russia had almost always held back the Hollywood Left, severely punished it back in 1939–1941 and allowed its supporters to be all but crushed after 1945. The shocks of 1956 proved immeasurably difficult to withstand. But sections of Popular Front veterans who were detaching themselves from Soviet illusions struggled to hold together a vision of a global cooperative society drawing back from the specter of nuclear war. The civil rights movement, mirroring anticolonialism across much of the Third

World, and the newer "Ban the Bomb" movement (led in part by old Southern California ally Linus Pauling), were promising along these very lines. But with their own careers at a standstill, brothers-in-law Paul Jarrico and Michael Wilson headed for Europe, as much as giving up on Hollywood.[17] Losing this talented pair, the Hollywood Review group decided not to continue.[18]

In retrospect, the assiduous liberal-radical commentary in the columns of the Review would have proved more valuable than ever, in the decade or so to follow, if they had been available to the younger writers, actors and directors as they tried to make their own way within a slowly reviving industry. Many of these, especially the ones with theatrical backgrounds, sought out the wise men and wise women of the Left who were still around and sometimes still working—but only as individuals, and often behind closed doors.[19]

In a historical moment when so many film veterans struggled to make a decent living by any means available, the idea of creating the great social film or art film receded into memory. A fortunate handful staying in Los Angeles or returning early, along with a smaller handful elsewhere, managed to get steady work in television or uncredited script rewriting. Musical comedy on stage was another outlet, this one almost exclusively for New Yorkers (and far more for actors than for writers). Even some of the formerly most prestigious and highly paid writers found themselves angling for screenwriting jobs under pseudonyms, which now more and more were likely to be found abroad. By the early 1960s they were earning their salaries in cheesy spectaculars, separated from the kind of opportunities they had envisioned for themselves before the curtain fell, which was a disappointment even if this work was no worse than the usual range of mediocre material available before 1950.

Those who had not abandoned movies altogether did their best with the opportunities at hand. A dozen or so writers and a few less-than-famous directors managed to create a handful of dramatic features and comedies in which some remarkable moments could usually be found. They also became involved, not so differently than in the years before the blacklist, in star-driven, over-budgeted or badly rewritten films that made them wince or entirely avoid the sorry celluloid outcome.

Here and there, with good luck and unusual contacts, quality showed. If one of the bankable missions of the blacklistees was the recollection of heroic antifascism in the "Greatest Generation" films that were popular among vets and others during the 1950s–1960s, the other and usually less bankable mission was the familiar saga of the outsider, whether Jew (especially in historical epics, as often written by gentile blacklistees as by Jews), black, woman, lower-class American or just plain nonconformist. If they'd had their choices, the blacklistees' projects would no doubt have included more satires of the ugly sides of American life, from

war profiteers and corporate (or top government) conspirators to the more familiar racists rarely attacked on the screen up to that time. But even perfect choices
would not have protected blacklistees against the counterattack launched from
some of the most prestigious quarters of film criticism, where the return of the repressed was met by a degree of rage that was almost inexplicable, if altogether
consistent with the limits of contemporary liberalism.

The blacklistees did have one grand film project all their own. When a young
Pauline Kael charged that *Salt of the Earth* (1953) was made by men and women
who had given up hope of succeeding in Hollywood or reaching American audiences, intending instead to propagandize Europeans and citizens of the developing
countries into hating America, she could not have been more wrong. The makers
of *Salt*, the inner crowd of the *Hollywood Review* plus Hollywood Ten director Herbert Biberman, still believed that they could break through the cultural iron curtain, find an audience large enough to make back costs and even make a living
creating the kinds of films that they had been forbidden to make in Hollywood.
Bosley Crowther cheered them on in the pages of the *New York Times*. But Roy
Brewer refused to permit his IATSE members even to show the film, and the theater chains caved. A last-gasp alternative of union screening collapsed when ostensibly liberal United Auto Workers leader Walter Reuther banned auto locals from
becoming, in effect, blue-collar film societies. The film did get foreign raves, and
not only from Communists. But without a domestic market, it just wasn't enough.

Salt is the tale of Mexican-Americans in Silver City, New Mexico striking for
improved safety conditions and wage parity (in the film, "equality") with Anglo
miners after a series of accidents caused by speed-ups and job cutbacks. Meanwhile, the miners' wives have concerns they complain are being ignored in the
strike demands—principally a lack of the same sanitation and running water provided to the white miners' homes. As the women say, "Maybe we need to have
equality in plumbing, too." The women's demands are largely ignored by the men
until the union's picket line is slapped with a federal injunction and the women
step forward to take their places. The result, naturally, is that the women's concerns are integrated into the strike demands as they join the strike leadership.
(When the men are forced to take up domestic chores at home while their wives
picket, one miner says, "I'll never go back to that job unless they install running
water for us." He then makes his son, against all custom, help wash the dishes.[20])

Salt's opening sequences, with composer Sol Kaplan's bright march music and
Biberman's frequently repeated visual motif of miners and their families backlit
against the horizon (as though to suggest the larger historical implications of this
remote struggle), seem straight out of Pare Lorentz's environmental documentaries of the 1930s, or perhaps the Russian films of Alexander Dovzhenko. These
are not neorealist gestures; a younger European director more likely would have

pushed the strike into the background and focused on the subjective life of one of the lesser characters. And yet, it shares vividly the production techniques and the same intended audience as neorealist projects. It may well be that the neorealist movement actually prepared audiences for *Salt*, especially in Europe, where the film, much to the horror of the U.S. State Department, was met with enthusiasm and prizes.

In the Hollywood context, *Salt* was clearly an unusual kind of art film. At the same time, whatever techniques of neorealism it deployed could better be said to serve as a kind of relegitimation of the left-wing drama and occasional outright agitprop Biberman had excelled at as a stage director in the 1920s–1930s. By shooting the story of a strike from the point of view of the picket line, employing only a handful of professional actors for the leads and amateurs in the supporting roles, the *Salt* filmmakers were in effect adopting neorealism to recover the practice of radical Depression street theater, like the Theater of Action—in short, a different path to the art film.

Most comparable to Losey's *The Lawless* (1950), employing small-town California locals in a tale about racism directed at Latino teens, *Salt of the Earth* showed Latinos on their own turf (New Mexico), in a standoff against mine owners and the local WASP establishment. Until the Taft-Hartley bill, HUAC hearings, expulsion from the CIO and membership raiding by other unions drove it from the field, the real-life Mine, Mill and Smelters union was indeed winning these very struggles. But free enterprise for filmmakers did not extend far enough for a dose of this realism.

The high point of *Salt of the Earth* is the community-based resistance, but most memorably the struggles of Latinas against their miner husbands as well as against the employers for dignity and a change of social status. The luminous photography of the women, with Mexican actress Rosaura Revueltas at their head, remains the most vivid of images. American film had simply never seen anything like her or it. *Salt of the Earth* did indeed achieve cult status on college campuses, thanks in no small part to feminist enthusiasts; younger labor historians gave the film another vindication, as a key document of American film's crushed potentiality to depict class and gender. But all this came too late for the filmmakers.

CRIME, CLASS AND GENDER

One can only guess, of course, what might have been possible for the themes of film noir, psychological conflict and of race and class rebellion in an alternative Hollywood where the blacklist had been successfully beaten back. As it was, the familiar class themes of the later 1940s, when they were not recuperating memories of the poverty and the longing of the 1930s, had already begun to be displaced into westerns and other genres, a displacement that accelerated in 1950s–1960s Hollywood as the news media and magazines created the impression that practically all white people had entered an age of consumer abundance. Veterans of the Left knew better than anyone that class hadn't gone away—just into hiding. Working abroad and sometimes working within limited genres at home, the radicals picked their spots to rework some basics.

Some of the best efforts of the day could be seen on the London stage of the "Angry Young Men," so it was no surprise that blue-collar themes could also be found in the contemporary British genre of B-films that looked a bit like 1940s American noir with British accents. Cy Endfield, who had guided *The Underworld Story* (1950) and *The Sound of Fury* (aka *Try and Get Me*, 1950) before fleeing, made a game effort to resume working as a director with *Hell Drivers* (1957). It was hardly more than a petty crime drama, but it did have moments of extreme realism about truckers' daily lives. For the next decade Endfield kept trying genre pieces with indifferent success. Then he hit cinematic paydirt with *Zulu* (1964), a spectacular reenactment of nineteenth-century colonial warfare starring Stanley Baker, and *Sands of the Kalahari* (1965), a vastly more radical treatment of ruthless mineral extraction in Africa and the collapse of civilized behavior. Like Losey, also working the lower genres, the Endfield of the 1950s had been preparing the way for better British (and British-American) efforts.

A considerably more significant breakthrough in France can be traced to a community of comrades and their circle of sympathizers within the powerful French Communist Party and beyond. The British Left, always smaller and operating mainly through the unions and the peace movement, provided a certain warmth, and a few of the exiles did exceptionally well in English film. But they also tended to feud among themselves and to scatter into disparate milieux. The French Left by contrast was very large, culturally very keen and eager to receive new personalities regarded as victims of the Cold War's punishing effects on art. Unlike the exiles in Italy, the French also did not have to contend with Ambassador Claire Booth Luce breathing down their necks, demanding the expulsion of the unacceptable American artists. Not only Dassin but a handful of others received in Paris what could be regarded as a hero's welcome, with many opportunities for interviews in the press and public appearances. Even if none of this provided ready opportunities to actually make films and to make a living, it meant a lot.

Jack Berry did well in Paris, at least for a few years—so well that his subsequent collapse in the French film world must be regarded as one of the bigger disappointments in the early era of exile, apparently due more to tough luck than to U.S. State Department machinations. He was, at least, never lonely for Americans: his adopted world included Dassin for a few years, but in a more sustained way Lee and Tammy Gold, Ben and Norma Barzman, Hollywood screenwriter Vladimir Pozner, occasionally Joseph Losey, and a handful of French comrades, including Jacques Prévert, Yves Montand and Simone Signoret. Only in France could cultural events have brought Hollywoodites into receptions with Picasso, Léger or Braque. The French also had cine-clubs, politically minded local operations that showed classics and less-known recent films, frequently offering new life, at least in a small way, for otherwise forgotten left-wing American movies. All in all, as Norma Barzman wryly remarked, it was easier to meet like-minded people in Paris cafes and boulevards—from left-wingers and film folk to columnist Art Buchwald—in a few months than she had managed to meet in decades of Hollywood social life.[21]

Berry's first job, landed through friends, was for a script mostly written by Ben Barzman and produced under impossible conditions. The partners were mistakenly convinced that a film shot quietly in French and English might escape a ban on screenings in the United States. Swarmed around, on the set, by sympathetic French reporters gathering to do stories about a film by blacklistees, it fell apart. At one point Berry hid himself in the bathroom, giving directing orders to an assistant through the door, while the forever snoopy and red-baiting Louella Parsons visited the set. The result, *C'est arrivé à Paris* (1953), was an admitted disaster.

Then Berry landed a job directing *Ça va barder* (1954), a film that made a large impression on French filmgoers for several reasons, but especially because of its lead. A most improbable European film star whose face on billboards would become as familiar to Parisians for decades as Humphrey Bogart's, Eddie Constantine was actually an average American movie type whose transatlantic story mirrors the fate of the blacklistees and suggests how politics could be subordinated to opportunity. Born to Russian Jewish immigrants in Los Angeles in 1917, he was trained in Vienna as a singer, worked as a film extra and followed his wife, a talented French dancer, back to Paris, where he became a protégé of singer Edith Piaf. He landed his signature Lemmy Caution role thanks apparently to his American accent and his resemblance to the veteran gangster character actor (and reluctant friendly witness) Marc Lawrence. Cast in the Dashiell Hammett mold of the detective who took no lip and shot his way out of tight corners, he was the perfect campy American countertype in a culture that mixed anticapitalism and anti-Americanism.

Over time, Constantine made some 13 of the Caution films, and still more with essentially the same character but different monikers, all the way to 1991.[22] The most famous was doubtless *Alphaville*, directed in 1965 by Jean-Luc Godard, a stylishly avant-garde feature that over the next decade filled the seats for campus film societies. But it was *Ça va barder*, a decade earlier, that had earned Constantine acclaim from French critics and audiences, thanks in no small part to Berry's co-script and direction. Formally based on one of the Peter Cheyney novels in the *Série noire*, the original story treated an Englishman and a French lover whom he rescues from prostitution after vindictively placing her in the life. Berry rewrote it from top to bottom, saving almost nothing of the original.

Berry mixed noir atmosphere with a French sense of detachment, making fun of film clichés while advancing the plot toward a foregone conclusion. This private dick wangles, punches and shoots his way through a fleet of tropical freighters to win back old girlfriend May Britt, now hooked up with the smuggler boss. *Ça va Barder*, a tramp steamer of a film carrying a strange cargo of French left-wing existentialism, crypto-Marxism American style and low-budget popular culture, could also be called the representative project of the exiled devotees of left-wing high modernism in urgent need of ready cash.

If *Ça va barder* was a hit, *Je suis un sentimental* (1955), the followup that Berry once again co-scripted and directed, proved one of Constantine's best. Written in part by fellow blacklistee Lee Gold, whose career had not taken off before exile and who spent the better part of the next 30 years writing for French television, it was a funny film about friendship, ambition and a murder that turns out to have been perpetrated by the son of a millionaire. That is to say, it was close enough to Hollywood memories to offer revenge, if not a vindication. French critics admired *Je suis un sentimental* as audiences applauded, but it never crossed the Atlantic.

This lack of success may have predicted Berry's downfall in France—even if, as we have seen, he found an American ghetto audience for the neorealist *Tamango*.[23] Berry's friend and collaborator Ben Barzman, who had contributed to *C'est arrivé a Paris* and co-scripted (with director Dassin) *He Who Must Die*, had a more significant contemporary role in French culture, mostly as a public intellectual representing a distinctively left-wing American view of films.

Not that Barzman had an easy time. Landing in France after the completion of *Give Us This Day* (1949), he dipped into the Parisian milieu, worked with Lewis Milestone in an unsuccessful attempt to make a film adaptation of Dostoyevsky's *The Idiot* and enjoyed the warm reception given *The Boy With Green Hair* (1948) as well as *Give Us This Day*. Winning best picture and best screenplay at the Czech film festival for the latter was an enormous morale boost. But film jobs were still scarce, and the Italian experience with *Stranger On the Prowl* had been profoundly discouraging.

He had a constituency waiting, if not necessarily a career. Reporters from the French left-wing papers and cultural magazines found in Barzman a witty insider to the Hollywood he had left behind, and public forums proved his real métier. He seemed to carry controversy along with him, eventually going head to head with Jean-Luc Godard over film techniques, the American as eclectic and the Frenchman as purist bitterly opposed to the continuation of old Hollywood narrative styles. Years later, Barzman became the first screenwriter honored by the Paris Cinemateque with a retrospective.[24] The French had all along appreciated his left-wing Americanness, probably more than his films. Perhaps Barzman's decisive (but uncredited) contribution to the structure of Costa-Gavras's Z (1969), placing the assassination at the beginning of the film, was the high mark of his influence.[25] Success more commercial than artistic returned to him with international features like The Fall of the Roman Empire (1964), The Blue Max (1966) and The Heroes of Telemark (1965), all written for the big screen.[26] He never wrote another art film like Give Us This Day, and he never regained what he had lost in Hollywood.

The same was more or less true, of course, for nearly everyone who went abroad, notwithstanding a dozen or so successful writers and directors. Leonardo Bercovici, a successful radio writer/producer on the verge of million-dollar contracts in Hollywood before his banishment, reflected later that he became an intimate of Italy's great directors and still never did much more than rewrite dialogue. He, like the rest—with the partial exception of women writers who had not been able to establish themselves in the United States—never stopped yearning for a successful return to Hollywood.[27]

Shooting outside the United Kingdom or France was nevertheless a premonition of the truly international wave of production that was just on the horizon. Paul Jarrico and Michael Wilson had been looking hard for a film project to star the banned Paul Robeson, if only Salt of the Earth had succeeded. Wilson settled for the moment on a little crime-and-gender film made in Germany, Party Girls for Sale (1954, aka They Were So Young, aka Violated), written with Dalton Trumbo and made from a documented story of German blue-collar girls transported to South America for sexual exploitation. It was an interesting (and exploitable) theme, but the film was made on a shoestring and had poor distribution. Besides, assorted blacklisting agencies were not about to allow a film with those writers onto American screens.

Back at home in real-life Hollywood and New York during the middle fifties things were yet more difficult. Some few fortunate screenwriters, thanks mainly to their low profiles, would not be picked off by the blacklist until relatively late in the game. Others managed to get a screenplay or two or three—occasionally more—produced, using a front or assumed name. Most scrambled for something and failed to find it. Flesh and Fury (1952) thus paired fledgling screenwriter Bernie Gordon with rising Method actor Tony Curtis, born Bernard Schwartz in the Bronx. Gordon, rewriting on the set, found in Curtis a feeling for the screenwriter's best material, through the revisiting of the deaf, disadvantaged slugger redeemed by the love of a good woman.

Unfortunately, serious bottom-bill B-melodramas were on their way out—cancelled by the very television shows that brought home the tales of gritty slums to new audiences—and so was Gordon. *Crime Wave* (1954), just about the last film for a decade made under his own name, was his best in this vein. When an ex-con is blackmailed back into crime by his former partners, the background dialogue of a delightfully sleazy L.A. bar scene quickly becomes more interesting than the plot. By the later 1950s, Gordon was working for Philip Yordan, the one-man producing team who eagerly exploited blacklistees and often misappropriated writing credits but managed to pump out film after film for audiences not too particular in their tastes.

If Yordan had any artistic vision at all, one could say that his best efforts had been aimed toward the first film version of James T. Farrell's *Studs Lonigan* (1960). Adapted by fellow blacklistee Arnaud D'Usseau and directed by yet another blacklistee, Irving Lerner, with a big boost (mostly restructuring in post-production) by Gordon, this version of the classic Irish-American trilogy by a 1930s anti-Stalinist left-winger (since become an avid conservative and *National Review* columnist) sought to reinstate the view of blue-collar suffering and sense of identity in ethnic America before race decisively redrew the lines.

Class themes worked better paired with gender. Even as McCarthyism fell over Hollywood, *A Place in the Sun* (1951) drew raves and Oscars—although rewrites forced on Michael Wilson's script made the proletarian murder victim (Shelly Winters) plainly annoying and her upper-class romantic rival (Elizabeth Taylor) so enticing that the audience could sympathize with the murder. *I Can* *Get It For You Wholesale* (1951), written by Abraham Polonsky and directed by future friendly witness Michael Gordon, offered a garment center romance-melodrama with Susan Hayward as the hard-charging woman entrepreneur and Sam Jaffe as her proletarian conscience. Reviewed sympathetically, it disappeared into the blacklist.[28]

But *Roman Holiday* (1953)—an original scripted by Dalton Trumbo, hiding behind Ian McClellan Hunter, himself about to go on the blacklist, and collaborating with John Dighton—offered proof positive that the scattering reds knew how to put a gendered message across at the other end of the class spectrum. The film also had the inestimable advantage of direction by their old ally, William Wyler. And who better than a princess (played by a vulnerable but lively Audrey Hepburn, her first big film as well as her first Oscar) to demonstrate the old Shakespearean notion that the weight of monarchs and monarchy is too much for any human to bear? Who better than a couple of Hollywood's unindicted political progressives of note, Gregory Peck and Eddie Albert, to play respectively the American reporter who romances her for an interim, and the pal who helps maintain the cover for the hopeless affair? It was a charmer all the way through, one of the industry's biggest hits of the year, decades later listed as one of the American Film Institute's top ten American romance films of all time.

Opportunities to repeat this kind of triumph disappeared, with rare exceptions along the way. Take the case of Jean Rouverol Butler, a child and teenage supporting cast member in W. C. Fields comedies, Hopalong Cassidy westerns and assorted light fare during the 1930s. Later a radio actress and fiction writer for slick magazines, now in need of work to support the family, she wrote *So Young, So Bad* (1950), a tale that joined teenage rebellion with women's themes by way of melodrama in a home for female juvenile delinquents. In a way, *So Young* was a continuation of the women's prison film, a thin vein mined by assorted progressives and left-wingers—later, mostly exploitation filmmakers with drive-in audiences—to make a larger point about social ills. The movie is now remembered, if at all, for the film debuts of Anne Francis, Anne Jackson and a luminous Rita Moreno.

So Young has plenty of drama. Revolting against authoritarianism, seeking the guidance of an understanding and proper psychologist (Paul Henreid) in place of the monster (Grace Coppin), the girls struggle to find themselves. Moreno, playing a Latina victim of social circumstance and the first of the girls to become fully aware of her own sexuality, is sacrificed in the process. Their collective pain is real enough, even if in the end the school authorities learn the necessary lessons.[29]

Butler's unpretentious next screenplay (in collaboration with husband Hugo) of parents' initial experience with a baby (*The First Time*, 1952) was followed with a potential blockbuster directed by that intimate ally of the blacklistees, Robert Aldrich. *Autumn Leaves* (1956), written from family exile in Mexico, had to be organized behind a unique double blind: Jack Jevne, an old friend, took the screenwriting credit, giving "Jean Rouverol" (by now she had dropped "Butler") story credit. *Autumn Leaves*—the film title borrowed from the popular song rather than vice-versa—was the perfect vehicle for Joan Crawford. An aging superstar in angular ways more beautiful than ever, already cast as the tragic figure of a deranged (and masochistic) deserted woman in *Possessed* (1947), Crawford was ready to play the older lover for the younger man. Cliff Robertson is the one who comes into her life, sweeps her off her feet and then as husband turns out to be a psychotic. Aldrich's direction brilliantly captures her as a woman on the verge of middle age, a typist reaching out for her sexuality at what seems to her the last possible moment, then discovering that her grasp is empty.[30]

 Tainted by her family blacklist connection and raising a house full of children in Mexico, Jean Butler managed nevertheless to create an interesting, complex character in the antifascist action picture, *Face in the Rain* (1963), which she wrote with husband Hugo for an Italian production. The woman (played by Marina Berti) had during the war simultaneously provided a hiding place for an American partisan and protected her family by becoming the lover of a powerful Fascist official. Now she must face the implications of her husband's return and her own domestic crisis when the husband grows desperately ill. It was a strong film, but instantly obscure.

Aldrich meanwhile directed a teleplay on the *DuPont Show of the Week* about a missing actress-celebrity. *The Legend of Lylah Clare* (1968) that was translated strangely into cinema, highlighting Kim Novak's over-the-top performance as the ingénue stage-managed by a fading but still-tyrannical director (Peter Finch) to resemble his late wife. All the usual Hollywood clichés could be found here, but so would the lesbian sub-theme whose day had finally come (or nearly), and whose presence in the final scenes is unmistakable. Hugo Butler had meanwhile died by the release date. Jean Butler found her own most commercially successful writing years on *The Guiding Light,* one of television's soap opera mainstays, largely treating women's agonies for women viewers.[31] One is tempted to say that she wrote better than she knew in the era before feminism opened eyes and opened up fresh themes.

A decade earlier, with the first modest easing of the blacklist, *That Kind of Woman* (1959) remade *The Shopworn Angel* (1938), originally written by Waldo Salt. In the first version, an innocent falls for a sexually experienced actress as he prepares to go off to likely injury or death in the First World War. In the newer version, this time under the direction of Sidney Lumet, Sophia Loren meets Tab Hunter on a train and the two fall for each other before she subsides into the arms of her domineering bourgeois husband, played to the hilt by George Sanders. Even by 1959, *That Kind of Woman* was a drama almost too adult for exhibitors and pressure groups, if definitely not for the audience. Screenwriter Walter Bernstein, just in the process of rehabilitating himself in Hollywood, was evidently the guilty party. The film demonstrated that if the romantic couple cannot resist animal magnetism, it also cannot overcome the practical power of the checkbook.[32]

Heller In Pink Tights (1960), from a script by Bernstein and once again starring Loren but this time for her husband (producer Carlo Ponti) and director George Cukor, drove toward something like the same point, albeit through comedy. Discovered by Ponti and overnight made into one of Italy's favorite stars, Loren was personally close to several of the Hollywood exiles and in pursuit of serious acting roles. Here, along with former child star Margaret O'Brien and Anthony Quinn, she is touring the West of the late nineteenth century in a fly-by-night theatrical troupe whose performances are just this side of risqué and just one step ahead of the law. Bernstein's co-scriptwriter was the once-famed Hollywood liberal, Dudley Nichols; their adaptation of a Louis L'Amour novel was funny enough to sustain credibility for a film with more action and setting than plot.[33]

Much of the rest that left-wing writers managed to do in gender themes was even lighter material, because farce and family comedy could become slightly edgy in sexual suggestiveness if it ultimately returned to safely wholesome values. Edward Chodorov, a highly esteemed writer-producer from the 1930s to the blacklist, had his last hit in My Sister Eileen, a play written from New Yorker short stories by Communist novelist Ruth McKenney and adapted from the 1940s stage hit as a new musical in 1955, albeit with Chodorov's name quietly removed.[34] Chodorov made a soft landing on Broadway, his real home, but he returned to film for the farcical adaptation of his play, Oh, Men! Oh, Women! (1957). Here, a shrink played by Tony Randall (a progressive actor making his film debut), dispenses advice to neurotics Barbara Rush and David Niven on how to save their marriage.[35] A well-liked figure in movie circles and a close advisor to magnum producer Sam Spiegel, Chodorov had somehow escaped the American Legion's watchdogs.

Happy Anniversary (1959), another film version of a popular Broadway play written by Chodorov, was further risqué fare for the day—this time husband Niven and wife Mitzi Gaynor turn out to have lived together before their marriage, albeit now more than a decade earlier. This discovery sets off shocks among the growing children of the family and produces some laughs, although the film is probably best remembered for Niven's law partner, played by Carl Reiner.[36] Its director was friendly witness Michael Gordon. After his testimony, Gordon emerged as a studio favorite for modern, harmless titillation. Pillow Talk (1959) and Move Over, Darling (1963) fairly typified the newer style of romantic comedy of romance as war between the sexes, with a perky Doris Day standing in for Katherine Hepburn or Ginger Rogers.[37]

Careful viewers could even detect an unintentionally hilarious appeal by Elizabeth Taylor, as Cleopatra (1963, written in part by an uncredited Sidney Buchman) pleading to save the library of Alexandria from fire and plunder. Like the actress, a recent Jewish convert, the Queen of the Nile was evidently no deep thinker but knew an intellectual edifice when she saw one. In fact, for all of its overwritten qualities, Cleopatra could be called (by Bosley Crowther) "one of the great epic films of the day," a four-hour marathon that somehow worked, thanks to magnificent casting (Richard Burton, Rex Harrison and Hume Cronyn were particularly good), production and co-scriptwriting by Joseph Mankiewicz (more likely, Sidney Buchman and Ronald MacDougall did the heavy lifting of adapting "ancient sources" and C. M. Franzero's Life and Times of Cleopatra).[38]

Ten thousand would-be patrons rushed the premiere, a record turnout marked by the excitement of the stars' appearance (the Burton/Taylor off-and-on screen romance was a particular lure) and even pickets (a small group of African Americans complaining, with a degree of justice, that Cleopatra should have been shown as African herself). The payoff of a million dollars to Elizabeth Taylor meanwhile typified for many the excess that was ruining Hollywood. Critics' complaints were said to lower the value of Fox shares on the market by $2 overnight—

an omen.[39] After the excitement had passed, *Cleopatra* turned out to be one of the bombs that almost finished off the staggering studio system.

Perhaps not much more was possible in gender matters in this period, and perhaps the underground or barely overground left-wing writers were simply not the ones to get the call in any case. In another time, Marilyn Monroe (a cheery proletarian lass in *Clash by Night*, an adaptation of an Odets play) might have been a magnificent actress in the strong parts she never got. Likewise, a potentially crusading Jean Seberg (she only got to crusade mythically, as Joan of Arc in *Saint Joan*, 1957) and even an ingénue like Audrey Hepburn might have learned about their hidden strengths. It hardly happened at all. Personally tough and gutsy Shelly Winters, to take a contrary case in point, came to play overweight, insecure females, and with one or two exceptions, these were her best roles.

ACTION FILMS

Accepting assignments as they came and grateful to have them whether at home or abroad, blacklistees fell as unnaturally into westerns as they did naturally into revivals of wartime bravery and idealism. As we've seen, the turn toward the anti-western had come first in the pro-Indian tales and disillusioned gunfighter epics of the later 1940s and in some of the best of the more-or-less serious drama on television during the 1950s. Neorealism had played out these themes *in extremis* and would continue to do so, though more abroad than at home. But there was a larger middle zone for the more old-fashioned and less risky western film, properly adjusted to domestic tastes through melodrama. The same was true, more or less, of the war films that now, like some of the movies in this genre of the late 1940s, recognized as much of the horror as the honor in antifascist combat.

Thus *The Lawless Breed* (1952), written by Bernie Gordon, brought back the restless outlaw theme under Raoul Walsh's direction. John Wesley Hardin, in Rock Hudson's debut as a star, here emerges rather ineptly as a misunderstood rancher driven into a life of crime. Producer William Alland reassured Gordon of his sole screenwriting credit just as he informed the writer that he had been fired by the studio and now faced the longest night of his career. After 1970, Gordon moved mostly into line-producing, sometimes for his lifelong friend Julian Zimet, most notably in *Horror Express* (1972) but also in *Pancho Villa* (1973), another made-in-Spain subclassic actioner with Pancho as a colorful rascal (played by Telly Savalas) and his nemesis, the arrogant invading American general John J. Pershing (played by Chuck Connors). Pershing ends up hilariously head-to-toe in hospital plaster after a CinemaScope train crash whose special effects used up most of the film's non-star budget.

The big talent of old-time Hollywood writing hardly did better. Marguerite Roberts, tagged back in the forties as a cowboy writer, closed her restarted career in a mini-flourish of oaters. The films were clearly not her choices, and with the exception of *True Grit,* she never had a chance to make films approaching her outstanding features of the 1940s like *Escape, Dragon Seed* or *Sea of Grass. Five Card Stud* (1968) could easily have been a better picture, but star Dean Martin could not take himself seriously as an actor and proved insufficiently charming as a drinker. *Shoot Out* (1971), with Gregory Peck as a vengeful ex-con and single father falling for a widow who can help him create a family, had a stale feeling, mirrored by Roberts's own sense that westerns of that kind had become archaic for a film industry that couldn't sell those types of morality tales any more.[40] *Red Sky at Morning* (1971), the best received of the three, departed from the formula by putting its characters in World War II Nevada, where the West had become something very different without altogether losing its sense of place.

True Grit (1969), for which John Wayne won his only Oscar, was truly another story. Wayne badly wanted the Chuck Portis novel as a vehicle, producer Hal Wallis bought the option and assigned Roberts, one of his favorite writers. Wayne knew of her status, refused to be bothered by it, and director Henry Hathaway made one of his own best pictures. A lynch mob with a crowd of typical Americans deliriously happy, a scene that might have badly upset Cold War sentiment a few years earlier or in the frame of a dissenting picture, here came through unconstrained, as the badly aging lawman played by Wayne helps an adolescent track down her father's murderer.[41]

War, at least the Second World War, may have become the last redoubt of real heroes, but with a difference. Bernard Gordon wrote the script for *Cry of Battle* (1963), an acute rendition of the guerilla war against the Japanese in the Philippines (based on the realistic novel *Fortress in the Rice* by Benjamin Appel), with progressives Van Heflin and Rita Moreno in the second and third leads. In one sense, it was a remake of *Back to Bataan* (1945), a Ben Barzman–scripted war action film directed by Edward Dmytryk emphasizing the struggle of the Filipinos themselves, albeit led by Duke Wayne. Twenty years later and just as determinedly antiracist, *Cry of Battle* rested on the same action premise: A businessman's son (played by James MacArthur) finds himself by joining the guerillas. And like its predecessor it was mostly action, although nothing like Moreno's nude bathing scene had spiced up the original. By now, the racial element had become anything but secondary.

The Thin Red Line (1964), Gordon's best credit and the first film rendering of James Jones's World War II novel, also had plenty of action but was more in line with the style of the 1940s war film, now updated. The assorted traumas of battle and preparation, the cravings (clear enough in a pre-battle scene where a willing

GI goes into drag and, after a dance scene, is nearly assaulted sexually by several others) and the endless fear were played out good and gritty. Keir Dullea as the sensitive soldier and Jack Warden as the sadistic sergeant proved, production dollar-for-dollar, an interesting contrast to the moody, 1998 Sean Penn version. By contrast, *55 Days at Peking* (1963), for which Gordon managed to get a co-script credit, was simply dreadful, a Yordan production directed by Nicholas Ray, where embattled westerners find themselves in barely civilized China during the Boxer Rebellion, surrounded by a cast of thousands.

Seen in the rearview mirror from the standpoint of MASH and the various Vietnam epics of disillusionment, *Men in War* (1957), ably directed by Anthony Mann and written by Ben Maddow under a pseudonym, may have been the best predictor of the style of war drama that was yet to come. Korea offered the backdrop for acts of courage among men who are brave enough to protect each other but tortured by the misery of combat and unredeemed by the prospect of some great victory. A cast headed by the exquisitely tortured Robert Ryan brought the message home that war really *is* hell. A simple message, perhaps, but the essential one.

RACE

Race issues, pressed upon a young American communist movement by the equally young but vastly more powerful and prestigious Communist International, had been important for the Left since the early 1920s. The Cold War, the rising resentment of African Americans at their conditions, the cooptation of unions into the mainstream, and most of all the rise of anticolonialism across Asia, Africa and the Caribbean brought the issue home with force. Hollywood communists, who had always wanted to make hard-hitting films about race and to some extent during the 1940s actually succeeded, now found themselves out of the picture but not entirely without hope or contacts.

Paul Jarrico aimed to film a version of the Scottsboro story, but the project failed with the *Salt of the Earth* debacle. Nothing in the United States until the very end of the decade, not even *The Defiant Ones*, carried the message of smoldering black rage—with one exception: *Odds Against Tomorrow* (1959). This story begins properly with Harry Belafonte.

Born in Harlem but raised mostly on his father's home island of Jamaica in extreme poverty, Belafonte came out of wartime service in the Navy a progressive, militantly antiracist actor and singer who moved quietly into the surviving Popular Front milieu, a close friend and protégé of the much-persecuted Paul Robeson. The Dramatic Workshop, another Group offshoot, solidified his network of friends, and under less severe political conditions the startlingly handsome and multitalented Belafonte might have gone into acting as a career. Instead, he jumped onto the then-small boat of Caribbean music beginning to sweep the Manhattan club scene and personally carried calypso to hitherto unimagined heights, even gaining spots on television variety shows. He became an instant sex symbol, the first American male of color to do so, in his signature sunglasses and windbreaker. He thus reached what Robeson had attained in the early 1940s, successfully soft-pedaling his own version of left-wing politics.

Hollywood seemed to promise Belafonte much but delivered little. His film debut, *Bright Road* (1953), playing a schoolteacher opposite Dorothy Dandridge, was deeply sincere and very small; no theater chain would put a film starring a black man and woman at the top of the bill. A remake of the Bizet opera, *Carmen Jones* (1954), produced and directed by Otto Preminger, with Dandridge, Pearl Bailey and the voice of Marilyn Horne, could have been a major musical success, but not in white America.

An adaptation of Alec Waugh's best-selling novel *Island in the Sun* (1957), produced by Darryl Zanuck, directed by friendly witness Robert Rossen and written by Alfred Hayes, allowed supporting star Belafonte, in a drama about colonial struggle in the Caribbean, to resent racism but not to actually do anything about it. The film touched off a small controversy within Hollywood and among reviewers because the issues seemed so daring (a visiting reporter asks Belafonte what the biggest problem on the island is, and he answers, "Color!"). Doubtless it was photogenic Barbados, during its era of fast-expanding regional tourism, that was intended to be the real subject, as suggested by Zanuck to interviewers; the social qualities of the film were perhaps purposefully kept vague and murky, the pacing slow.[42] Like *Pinky*, Zanuck's production with Elia Kazan a decade earlier, it demonstrably failed the test of an honest, compelling treatment of race. The film was also a commercial failure.[43] Belafonte's next film outing, *The World, the Flesh and the Devil* (1959), a post–nuclear war disaster film, placed him with fellow survivors Inger Stevens and Mel Ferrer in a nearly destroyed Manhattan. Here, albeit glancingly, moviegoers experienced some of a black man's frustration, as well as white rage directed at him (and complicated by the implications of interracial sex) before the film fell apart in the middle.

If this unhappy career saga does not sound unusual for any actor's first years, when set against Belafonte's spectacular singing success it suggested that only a more moderate-sounding Poitier could make any headway in Hollywood. Independent production, Belafonte hoped, could go further. As he told an *Ebony* interviewer, it was high time "to make films that show Negroes just as we are . . . working, succeeding, failing, loving, hating and dying."[44]

Thus Belafonte put together his own funds with the backing supplied by several prominent Hollywood liberals, including promises from Paul Newman and Joanne Woodward, for his HarBel Productions. The plan was to make three or four films in as many years, showing that tough racial themes, properly put together, could win popular audiences at home and abroad. To that end, he bought an option on a realistic interracial crime novel by former policeman William P. McGivern, brought on board director Robert Wise and snared the writer that he wanted: Abraham Polonsky.

Polonsky thoroughly transformed *Odds Against Tomorrow* (1959) and disguised his own identity behind novelist John O. Killens. Robert Ryan played the southern-born racist who believes that he "understands" black people, Shelly Winters his insecure live-in girl friend and progressive actor Ed Begley the ex-cop purged from the force by minor corruption and station-house informers. Belafonte, in his best film role, is the third of the criminal trio, a musician-singer so far in debt to a bookie that he will finally agree to a caper that seems (and is) suicidal.

Unlike *The Defiant Ones*, there will be no gestures of racial reconciliation here. The bank job in a small upstate town misfires. Trying to escape, Ryan's and Belafonte's characters run toward giant oil tanks, shooting at each other until an explosion all but obliterates their bodies and a county coroner cannot differentiate the races of the two dead criminals. As the film closes, there's the moral—highlighted with musical commentary from the Modern Jazz Quartet, providing the first complete jazz score for an American film.

Precious little commercial room existed for *Odds Against Tomorrow*. Most reviewers considered the movie too bold and garish and it barely made back costs. With this commercial failure went the larger project—most immediately a second and much tougher feature about racial and sexual conflict in the antebellum South, dramatizing the implications of interracial sex, the emerging wage slavery of contemporary northern factory workers and all in all the need for drastic social change everywhere in the society. Probably it was unrealistic to expect contemporary Americans to look their own history so starkly in the face. According to insiders, Paul Newman pulled out, uncertain about the project and the implications for his own career. The HarBel dream collapsed.[45]

There are so many losses here that simply to add them up would be difficult. Still writing under pseudonyms and still struggling to make a living in Mexico, Hugo Butler co-scripted a second low-budget film for Luis Buñuel, *The Young One / La Joven* (1961), with a narrow melodramatic plot organized around a jazz musician (Bernie Hamilton) on the run. He escapes to an island where a young Lolita (Key Meersman) and her racist father (Zachary Scott) live an insular existence. It was black-versus-white and possessed the usual Buñuelian virtues in depicting a set of lives hanging by invisible threads—and it, too, was a commercial failure.[46]

With help from the Ford Foundation and some fellow blacklistees (notably film editor Carl Lerner and co-star Zero Mostel), Belafonte put together one more film company ("Belafonte Productions") for *The Angel Levine* (1970), an adaptation of a short story by Bernard Malamud. Belafonte himself took the role of a recently dead black hustler who remains on earth with a celestial mission as the black and also Jewish Angel of Death for the female half of an aging Jewish couple, Yiddish stage veteran Ida Kaminska (Zero Mostel as her husband, at his own theatrical best). Like the film's angel, it didn't fly and now Belafonte had nowhere to go.[47]

The films that might have made a difference in the civil rights era would not be made until it was over, the potential stars who might have been on hand to realize the goal never escaped type-casting and, save for Poitier (who left Hollywood in disgust after several giant hits in the 1970s), achieved little of their potential. Dorothy Dandridge, who got an Oscar nomination for best actress in *Carmen Jones* and showed her worth for a last time in *Tamango*, died of a drug overdose in 1965. Not so incidentally, her final film, the British-made caper drama *Malaga* (1960), had been written by blacklistee and exile Donald Ogden Stewart during the final phase of his own attempted comeback. Belafonte returned to the stage, his film career as good as finished by the time director Robert Altman cast him, in support roles, repeatedly in the 1990s.[48]

One more commercial failure is richly worth redemption: *Black Like Me* (1964). A project launched by Carl Lerner and his wife, Gerda Lerner, it starred James Whitmore in the screen version of a best-selling true-to-life story by a northern journalist who dyed his skin and "passed" for black in the South of the civil rights era. Co-starring blacklisted Will Geer as a racist, and with a collection of African American actors as the folks who he comes to know in daily life, it revealed the small and large humiliations faced by southern blacks, the white hatred at the prospect of integration and the warmth of the southern black community. Held back by a poor initial script, an extremely low budget that forced overly fast shooting and a nonexistent promotion, the courageous and artistically experimental film died quietly.[49]

The always-narrow margin for experimental or artistic projects, even narrower in the case of left-wing African Americans, remained the norm for most of the blacklistees, not to mention graylistees like William Marshall. Another semi-protégé of Paul Robeson, he would be called to the studios only when they "needed an angry African." Disgusted, he worked abroad on stage, until summoned home for the blaxploitation films *Blacula* (1972) and *Scream, Blacula Scream!* (1973). A distinguished and strikingly handsome Shakespearean actor "discovered" in the early 1950s by Hollywood, he had been meant, surely, for something better. But it never happened.[50] In a way, Carlton Moss had been luckier. The original blacklisted black Hollywoodite, Moss had written (without credit) and starred in *The Negro Soldier* (1944), a "Why We Fight" documentary with Joe Louis, repeatedly censored—no African American could be shown holding a gun—and then shown only with trepidation that white GIs might somehow be insulted by the patriotic depiction. Moss spent the rest of his career making documentaries about African American life for young people and, like Marshall in later life, teaching film.[51]

Liberal African American images guided by blacklistees played better on television drama or comedy, and in counterpart films done on strictly limited budgets. Jack Berry's *Claudine* (1974) was a light-hearted effort with James Earl Jones as a garbage man wooing a single mother (played by Diahann Carroll) with six children. Critics complained, in that era of conflict, that it was *too* light-hearted and the ending is forced (the couple are married as white police pursue a son, Lawrence Hilton-Jacobs, as a nonviolent disturbance erupts). But it was *sui generis:* It lacked even a genre. *Sister, Sister* (1982), directed by Berry and written by Maya Angelou and placed on the shelf years before finally coming out as a TV film, delved into the lives of three black sisters (with the lead going again to Diahann Carroll) sorting out their problems in the shadow of a dead patriarch—who only happens to have been a black labor hero suspiciously like A. Philip Randolph. It was the black version of family-TV drama, eloquent if not especially dynamic.

In *Boesman and Lena* (2000), its post-production nearly finished by director Jack Berry when he died suddenly, Danny Glover and Angela Bassett play a couple fallen on harder days because their tarpaper shack and their community have been destroyed. They wander, emotionally as well as physically homeless, along deserted beaches of South Africa. It's a talky film but it gives Glover a chance to work out his political commitments as an unembarrassed successor to the part of the Old Left in Hollywood and Broadway that was black—that is, to Belafonte, Ossie Davis, Ruby Dee and all the others. True to the end to the vision of his youth, Berry had made his last days count for something. His work, standing for that of so many others, embodied a vanished but noble effort.

CHAPTER SIX

THE LONG CLIMB BACK

DURING THE COLD WAR, BIG CHANGES WERE AT WORK in the neighborhood movie theater. Looking back more than a half-century later, it's not all that difficult to see why attendance at the traditional downtown Bijou dropped heavily from 1947 to the 1960s and why the major studios so often seemed flummoxed. Lots of sensible sociology has been advanced to explain the decline, including competition from bowling and assorted nighttime TV sports viewed at home or at the bar, new mortgages, growing childcare duties and so forth. But there are at least two other equally plausible reasons why audiences fled to the art houses and the drive-ins: sex and politics.

In the "sure-seaters" (the *Variety* term for art houses, because of their presumably steady audiences), the sex was onscreen and the politics were elusive because the dialogue was in a foreign language. In the drive-ins, the sex was inside the cars and the politics often sunk so deep in the narrative that most of their meanings could not be excavated for decades, as with the ambiguities in *Invasion of the Body Snatchers*.[1] But in unpredictable ways, for an increasingly fractured audience, a kind of experimentation flourished.

There had been only 50 independent production companies in 1945, sharply reduced in number from a few years prior, partly because of the wartime shortage of film stock. By 1950 the independents had more than doubled, with many of the new outfits filling the demand for B-films, including westerns.[2] A good number of those B films played in the new "ozoners" (another *Variety* term), or drive-ins, which increased in number from 102 in 1946 to almost 1,000 in 1949. As the Cold War deepened, drive-ins continued to spread through the expanding suburbs, reaching 3,000 in 1954.[3] Meanwhile, the art theater, devoted largely to the exhibition of foreign films, emerged in major urban areas. These became established enough that by 1950 about 80 first-run art theaters were operating successfully around the country. Not a large number by drive-in standards, it was nevertheless an important sign of audience migration.

By 1963, both the year that the blacklist seemed broken and the moment when the college film society developed in earnest on U.S. campuses, there were no fewer than 450 theaters devoted to the exhibition of art and foreign films.[4] The impetus for the growth of an entirely new kind of exhibition in the United States was to provide audiences with a regular supply of Italian, French, British and Swedish neorealist films. It was common for the owners of art theaters, who did not have to pay attention to industry censors, to advertise the most solemn explorations of the human condition as opportunities to ogle prodigious Euro-bosoms.[5] It was also true that the Europeans, then as now, were a good deal less anxious about the expression of human sexuality and better informed about the political and economic condition of the rest of humankind.

If the studios viewed all this as a threat, it may have been because they were unable to satisfy the demonstrable hunger for a different kind of movie, or even for adequate current versions of beloved genres. The expulsion from Hollywood of many of its best writers and directors had little directly to do with the exodus of the audience from traditional movie venues, but the overall decline in quality was evident.

Not all friendly witnesses did less interesting work after naming names, although most did. It is generally accepted that the films of Elia Kazan were for a few years artistically stronger after he testified, thanks in no small part to his cachet as an actor's director and his political prestige (thus his creative control) in Cold War America. Robert Rossen, although his remaining films were few compared to his earlier output, retained much of his original artistic vision. In fact, the films of both men would be among the favorites of the campus film societies, whose influence by the middle 1960s was beginning to reshape the tastes of U.S. audiences. Around the middle of the decade, film societies began to outstrip the art theaters not only in the number of European art films and American Popular Front movies recovered for exhibition: they also emerged as centers of a thoughtful criticism in the form of mimeographed or printed "film notes."

The inaugural issue of the monthly journal *Film Society Review* noted in 1965 that the cinema society movement had started from "slow beginnings" in 1920s Europe and reached the United States in 1955. Actually, on leading campuses such as UCLA and the University of Wisconsin in Madison, where bohemian and left-wing tastes had been established during the Depression if not before, film societies arose in the late 1940s, with a sophisticated GI Bill audience clamoring for foreign productions. Further development did take years, however, and it was not until 1955 that the American Federation of Film Societies (AFFS) began to publish a newsletter for members, including reviews of particular selections.[6] Little

understood at the time, this was the process by which the budding U.S. film scholars and critics of the 1960s began to come to terms with the neorealist revolution
and with it the last articulations of the European Popular Front. The AFFS, tabu-
lating the results of the 2,500 questionnaires sent out to its affiliates, estimated a
campus film society *membership* of a half-million, with the audience of casual filmgoers who attended estimated at perhaps ten times that. Allowing for exaggeration, it was enough to make Hollywood take note of something new in the history
of U.S. film: an organized audience.[7]

This was an exceptionally well-informed audience, thanks in some part to insights diffused from student journals (drawing in turn upon readings of foreign—
especially French—journals), in other parts to the radical sentiments sweeping
campuses at large, especially those with well-developed avant-garde audiences. A
real canon of film society movies, formalized in a handbook for society organizers,
was published in 1973, less than a decade before these groups (who had always relied on 16mm prints) faded away with the popularity of the video cassette
recorder.[8] If the handbook reflected actual practice, only about 300 of the 800 titles widely exhibited were foreign films. Unlike U.S. productions, a majority of
which were comedies or unintentionally hilarious camp (like *Reefer Madness*), the
list of foreign features was heavily weighted, with directors like Ingmar Bergman,
Jean-Luc Godard, François Truffaut, Luis Buñuel, Federico Fellini and Akira
Kurosawa among the favored. Most of the rest were French and Italian directors of
the new wave and neorealism, including Roberto Rossellini. The shortness of the
list suggests an audience intent on pursuing the directors' work to a depth that
could be called scholarly.

Meanwhile, campuses that combined left-wing leanings with a cerebral
cineaste culture were notorious for the revivals of the Popular Front film. The repeated viewings of not only *Casablanca* and *Citizen Kane* but *The Little Foxes*,
Woman of the Year, *Sahara* and other baby-boomer favorites doubtless begins here,
at low admission-price grassroots. To the extent that the blacklistees were indeed
finding their way back it was thanks to an audience, sometimes the children of the
Old Left, whose tastes would help reopen the space to work in. No wonder Abe
Polonsky affectionately called his *Willie Boy* "a testament for the New Left." Hollywood had tuned in, slowly and reluctantly, to the new audience that had virtually created itself.[9]

REBOUND

The studios, as suggested above, had mostly survived the winding down of the
1950s and the initial challenge from television (a few of them buoyed from
shrewd investments in TV production). The most inventive of the major studios,

the comparatively small United Artists (UA), deftly divested itself of physical holdings and converted its operations almost exclusively into finance and distribution, sinking corporate investments into such hot prospects as the James Bond films, the Pink Panther series with Peter Sellers, spaghetti westerns and Beatles films. Like Roy Huggins and the strictly exploitation-oriented film independents such as American International, the execs as UA had figured out the youth market, forecasting the need for film innovators to plug further into rebellious themes. But UA was no major player, and the bigger studios continued to bank on big-screen spectaculars from musicals to war action films and westerns, with somewhat stronger sexual suggestion.[10] Not much more could be claimed.

For the moment, stars like Rock Hudson and Doris Day, or living remnants of another time like Cary Grant and John Wayne, commanded larger salaries and percentage shares than ever before.[11] The industry that in a few decades was to become allergic to anyone over 35 was still, in the 1960s, at its top levels pretty close to the opposite: run by those who had collected salaries and survived various setbacks since the catastrophic decline in filmgoing. Despite the steady addition of drive-ins to make up for the erosion of urban theaters, attendance hit an all-time low of 15.8 million in 1971, roughly an 80 percent drop-off from the figures a quarter-century earlier. More than a few saw the end at hand.[12]

Two would-be auteurs named Stanley, each powerfully connected with a Left that they never themselves joined, played key roles in the revival. The elder one was Stanley Kramer (1913–2001), a Manhattan-born film editor who spent his military years in the Signal Corps, not coincidentally with many left-wing veterans. Heading for Hollywood, he soon formed an independent production company known for its "message" pictures until forced under economic discipline to reorganize as a unit of Columbia—an artistic straitjacket that Kramer escaped by going independent in the middle 1950s. Carl Foreman had been his best writer (*Champion*, *The Men*, and *Cyrano De Bergerac*), and left-wingers were clearly pained when Kramer ordered the writer off the set of their best collaboration, *High Noon*.[13]

A few years later, Kramer took what must have been a considerable chance in hiring "Nathan Douglas" (Nedrick Young, working under a pseudonym, as Kramer must certainly have known, since Young made a brief appearance in the film) to co-script *The Defiant Ones* (1958). It was not Kramer's artistic best, but certainly his most influential liberal picture and Hollywood's most determined statement on race to date. The anti-nuke *On the Beach* (1959), scripted by the Left's old friend and frequent collaborator, John Paxton (perhaps with some unacknowledged assistance), was followed quickly by the treatment of the Scopes "Monkey Trial," *Inherit the Wind* (1960), once more co-scripted by Ned Young.

The Defiant Ones had, of course, been the most important to the blacklistees. Sidney Poitier, the first of the African American actors to gain star stature and stay in the big time for decades, already had had a leading role in the anti-apartheid *Cry, the Beloved Country* (1951), written behind the front of novelist Alan Paton by John Howard Lawson, as well as supporting roles in *The Harlem Globetrotters* (1951, written by the blacklistee Al Palca after he had earned his only credit), director Richard Brooks' *Blackboard Jungle* and several other liberal films. As Poitier liked to tell the backstory, *The Defiant Ones*, showing himself and fellow (but white) convict Tony Curtis as equals under the skin, was exceptionally brave for the time. If Poitier never actually knew that co-writer "Nathan Douglas" was blacklistee Ned Young, he must have been aware that close friends and contacts like Harry Belafonte and Katharine Hepburn were part of a submerged tradition considerably larger than himself.[14]

The framework of the film centered on the two escaped convicts' ambivalent feelings of mutual hatred and cooperation. Curtis played a disappointed blue-collar worker guilty of craving luxury and Poitier a tenant farmer who bashed the white man coming to throw him off his land. As the two make their way through woods, then a rural settlement and the shack of a single mother eager to escape her environment, Curtis seems ready to sell Poitier out for the sake of his own escape. Lon Chaney, Jr., as the moral figure of the rural settlement (himself a branded former convict), appearing to dare his lynch-happy fellow citizens to expose their brutality, actually sets the proper example of a higher standard in a scene that comes as close as the film ever dared to suggesting the hysteria of the Hollywood blacklist. But even the pursuing southern sheriff, improbably played by Jewish folksinger Theodore Bikel (at the time an important Hollywood/New York supporter of civil rights causes), who refuses to make the pursuit a racial matter, seems on the side of the angels. Escape was never really possible. Late in the film, Curtis does the right thing rather than leave Poitier in the lurch as bait for the dogs.

The final moment of *The Defiant Ones*, destined to become a Hollywood cliché, shows black and white hands intertwined. Poitier reaches out unsuccessfully to help Curtis up to a moving railroad car, then, after jumping down to take care of him, passively awaits the arrival of the hounds and the sheriff—when he could easily have left "Charley Potatoes" behind. It was not exactly an enactment of the old communist slogan, "Black and White/Unite and Fight" (although a favorite communist logo that showed joined black and white hands perhaps suggested the ending to Young), but it did make mutual recognition the proof of humanity.

So heavily did Hollywood congratulate itself on the film that Lenny Bruce devised a standup routine around wealthy Beverly Hills liberals inviting Poitier up to polish their limousines. But it wasn't easy to go further in 1958, and probably wasn't even possible in big-budget, mainstream Hollywood. The New York Film Critics Circle voted *The Defiant Ones* best of the year in three (rather than the usual five) ballots, also naming Kramer best director, and the script by "Nathan E. Douglas" and his collaborator Harold Jacob Smith was voted best screenplay.[15] Bosley Crowther had prepared the way by hailing the film on its appearance a few months earlier, praising Kramer for returning for the first time since *High Noon* to "the kind of 'idea' picture-making" he had done "when he was breaking his own trail."[16]

Judgment at Nuremberg (1961), which posed the painful question of collective and individual guilt, was next for Kramer. Then came the arm-twisting antiracist liberal comedy of manners *Guess Who's Coming to Dinner* (1967), with Sidney Poitier and the reunion of Hepburn and Tracy (in his last film), its success showing that earnest movies could still make money.[17] One of Kramer's last films, *Bless the Beasts and Children* (1971) was in essence an eco-feature, written by friendly witness and veteran radio-television comedy writer Mac Benoff, a weak version of the themes of *Born Free*.[18] Kramer lived long enough to get a Lifetime Achievement Award from the academy in 1991, no doubt adding a certain extended vindication of themselves in the minds of the many left-wingers who, for all their differences with the producer-director, had in many ways made his achievement possible. It is safe to say that without them he would never have been either a great success or a cinematic artist.[19]

Younger Stanley Kubrick's connections with the Left were both more personal and more oblique, but his impact upon the remaking of Hollywood was rather more decisive. Born in 1928 and raised in the Bronx, Kubrick, like Kramer, was the descendent of Jewish immigrants, although his father was a well-to-do physician. Kubrick learned photojournalism in high school and joined the staff of *Look* at the remarkable age of 17. In 1950, he abandoned the magazine to work in films of his own, at first thinking of making documentaries. Soon he ran into Faith Hubley, who was working with her husband, John, in the small studio set up after the repression of the *Finian's Rainbow* project. As Kubrick's biographer cautiously records, the young man "spent a lot of time" with her in the cutting room, talking about filmmaking and learning how to do his own cutting.[20] On the basis of these skills and ideas, he moved on to small-budget industrial films.

. Building up from minor projects, Kubrick made the noirish *Killer's Kiss* (1955) and the stunning antimilitarist *Paths of Glory* (1957), both praised for their artistry but neither successful commercially. Kubrick was getting himself ready for great things as Hollywood became more daring. In 1959, when Kirk Douglas dumped Anthony Mann in the first weeks of filming *Spartacus*, Kubrick took over the helm—the salvation of the project that brought the most famous blacklisted writer back from the blacklist.[21]

Hollywood might have been Kubrick's oyster. Still, despising artistic conditions in the film capital, he moved his base to Britain, returning to the mainstream with the most condemned film of the time, *Lolita* (1962), and then the explosive and radically antiwar *Dr. Strangelove* (1964) and the ambitious *2001: A*

Space Odyssey (1971). His later films reflected artistic more than political commitments.[22] But he had shown Hollywood new cinematic possibilities.[23]

And he was right. Warren Beatty, Peter Fonda, Francis Ford Coppola, Dennis Hopper, Mike Nichols and Robert Altman joined such canny, emerging writers-cum-execs as Robert Towne (with Carole Eastman, a student in Jeff Corey's playhouse of the early 1950s) in similarly daring projects. Towne later scripted *Bonnie and Clyde, Chinatown* and *Shampoo,* and with collaborator Bert Schneider showed himself interested in art cinema but especially quick to cash in on the rebellious-image youth market.

Bob Rafelson, another member of this group, made a shrewd early move in creating those wild but well-meaning boys with long hair, The Monkees, as ersatz Beatles, for ABC. Rebellion felt good: in 1970s Hollywood, despite the cynicism and outright hedonism of the business, it was popular to be against the war in Vietnam and even to feel guilty about the extreme privileges enjoyed by the grandchildren of impoverished immigrant Jews. This was the crowd that introduced the rock 'n roll soundtrack in feature dramas and shaped the images in so many films following *Bonnie and Clyde* that dumbed them down to the lowest levels of teen exploitation, like *Wild in the Streets* (1968) and *Angel, Angel Down We Go* (1969).[24]

The industry had another crisis ahead. By the early 1970s, five of the remaining seven major studios were in serious trouble, due in no small part to the restructuring of filmmaking around "packaging" by talent agencies skimming off huge quantities of cash for themselves and production costs ballooning nearly out of sight. The recession deepened the general dismay but it also changed bottom-line priorities. Conglomerates cut costs drastically and eliminated at least some of the old-fashioned wasteful bureaucracy, putting fresh-faced corporate types in control. More to the point, they followed UA's strategy of consolidating assets through global production.[25]

Not that the old dynasties died out entirely. For scions who made themselves masters of successful projects, the money was incredible and the creative influence strangely familiar. Within the same decade as Hollywood's near-nadir, producer Richard Zanuck could admit that what he made on *Jaws* alone added up to more than his famous father had earned in a lifetime of Hollywood hits and misses. The same young Zanuck had earlier given Fox the okay to proceed with *MASH,* a relatively low-budget project but politically the riskiest to appear in Hollywood for decades, and arguably the first intentionally controversial mainstream film to re-hire a blacklistee under his own name.

An extraordinary adventure followed. Even the editing was New Hollywood, which is to say more open to experiment and even to a certain playfulness. Young Zanuck, much inclined to cut director Robert Altman's directorial excesses, which included inaudible mumbling as well as much sexy raucousness to expose the moral hypocrisy and naked lust of pseudo-patriots, finally yielded to the enthusiasm of the screening audiences. Pauline Kael, reversing her almost perfect consistency in red-baiting or otherwise scorning the films of blacklistees, evidently set aside co-scriptwriter Ring Lardner, Jr.,'s pivotal role and fell in love with Altman's style. Lobbying other reviewers to praise the film, she may have helped make it larger in the studio's marketing than its producer or directed had expected. Somehow MASH was not, in her mind—as it was in everyone else's—the "message" picture that she claimed to despise as a cinematic category.

MASH finished behind only Love Story and Airport in that year's box office receipts, winning five Oscar nominations and playing huge in foreign markets. There, its appearance was taken as a welcome Hollywood position against the war in Vietnam and against the Cold War culture that spawned it. A New York Times critic uneasily described MASH as the first American film to ridicule God (probably because of a faux Last Supper tableau), which was surely not true, but the charge was indicative of how the film roiled movie traditions.[26] Perhaps its most important and certainly its most lasting accomplishment was in the younger medium of television where, with the addition of a few asterisks in the title, M*A*S*H became by the measure of later residuals the most successful and the most peacenik television series of all time. Finally, MASH the film allowed Hollywood to come of age—or come of age again, after 20 years of general if not unrelieved regression.

Many of the other emerging super-hits and super directors, writers or producers owed next to nothing, at least nothing consciously, to left-wing traditions. It would be hard to attribute any such to George Lucas and his Star Wars series or to Peter Bogdanovich, Paul Schrader or mild avant-gardist Hal Ashby, at least until Ashby directed Shampoo, the Woody Guthrie biopic Bound for Glory and Coming Home, all within three years beginning in 1975.[27] Steven Spielberg's connections with the blacklistees were strictly personal, although important to his early career, and his films were almost from the beginning humane if not in any apparent way rebellious.[28]

The case of Ashby, however, suggests that the situation is more complex, the connections more difficult to pin down and analyze in an era when rebellion often meant good box office and when many of the leading film personalities (Vanessa Redgrave, Julie Christie, Jane Fonda, Donald Sutherland and Bruce Dern, to name a few) openly identified themselves with a variety of radical causes. The subtleties of relationships and friendships, here and elsewhere, were often missed because the more spectacular moments belonged to a rather condensed period of effort. Peacenik youngster Richard Dreyfuss hung out with an underground Abbie Hoffman, and exec Steve Blauner along with Bert Schneider actually spirited an on-the-run Huey Newton to Mexico. Jane Fonda took to the road globally with

New Left savant Tom Hayden, headlining antiwar concerts for GIs. Such things had never happened before, certainly not in the high days of red Hollywood, and, short of a major social upheaval, were not likely to happen again.

However short-lived, the cumulative impact of this moment was nevertheless lasting on particular artists, directors, producers and executives. A handful of well-known radical intergenerational figures like cinematographer and director Haskell Wexler provided continuity. Continuing connections including such later stars as Martin Sheen, Susan Sarandon, Alan Arkin, Christopher Reeve, Margot Kidder, Mandy Patinkin, Ed Begley, Jr., Jeff Bridges, Danny Glover, Tim Robbins and Rubén Blades. It could be described as an accident of careers and generations, but this would be inaccurate, because plenty of helpful older types, including such guilt-ridden erstwhile friendly witnesses as Lloyd Bridges, had been on hand to advise on career choices and to pass the liberal message along.[29]

It would be equally difficult to dismiss out of hand the symbols of a virtual Hollywood-wide embrace of George McGovern in 1972. The South Dakota peace senator first got his political bearings as a supporter of the 1948 Henry Wallace campaign, which practically opened with Katharine Hepburn's Hollywood Bowl rally endorsing the former vice president in early 1947—the moment before it collapsed along with the Hollywood Left in the face of accelerating repression. Nor can one ignore the moment of Oscars night, 1975, when Bert Schneider and Peter Davis, accepting the award for the antiwar documentary *Hearts and Minds*, simultaneously accepted on stage a celebratory telegraph from the Provisional Revolutionary Government of Vietnam, a scarce few weeks before the South Vietnamese puppet regime fell and, amid worldwide celebrations outside the United States, the first major military defeat in American history became final. (Frank Sinatra and Bob Hope, backstage, wrote a repudiation on behalf of the Academy. They had no authorization, but it certainly laid out the divisions in the film capital.)

Something more subtle but also more important took place in what Peter Biskind has described as the "Manhattanization" of Hollywood but what may be better seen as the reinstatement of New York (and Method acting) influences after the removal of television production to Los Angeles in the later 1950s. Martin Scorsese and Francis Ford Coppola, recreating a film studio base in and around Manhattan, would naturally draw upon theatrical actors and the ambience of Method and its successors. Scorsese avowed, in later years, that Abraham Polonsky's films had been crucial to his own developing film sensibility.[30] Coppola had personally sought to revive *Finian's Rainbow* by directing a film version. It had the distinct honor of being banned in South Africa, evidently for promoting interracialism.[31] *Rainbow*'s reception was otherwise mixed at best: ridiculed by reviewers, it was received by audiences more kindly (then and later.[32])

Artistically, the reopening of Hollywood might be traced in the story of a single film (*Midnight Cowboy*), its screenwriter (Waldo Salt) and its lead actor (Dustin Hoffman). It would be difficult to exaggerate the young character actor's outsized influence at the time the film was made, for Hoffman was the living embodiment of *The Graduate* (1967), whose rebellion, without being in any way consciously political, was that of an over-privileged young man with no conscious craving except for an equally over-privileged girl. His sin was to be seduced by her mother, the famed Mrs. Robinson (real-life avant-gardist liberal Anne Bancroft) of Simon and Garfunkel theme-song fame; his radical act was to lock a church door with a cross to spirit his dream girl away from her wedding ceremony.

Director and former stand-up comic Mike Nichols, whose only previous film was the taboo-breaking *Who's Afraid of Virginia Woolf* (1966), had shrewdly, and contrary to Hollywood tradition, turned a novel's characters from WASP to Jewish, emphasizing the nouveau riche qualities and casting the unknown method actor Hoffman rather than Robert Redford as the lead. Nichols himself eschewed political commitments, although his own grandfather was the famed German anarchist Gustav Landauer, martyred by protofascists during the uprising of 1919. The film's cast also happened to be full of Actors Studio graduates, from Norman Fell to Hoffman, and even the walk-ons, including two then-unknowns destined to be notable Hollywood progressives, Mike Farrell and Richard Dreyfuss.[33] This was obviously rebellion in a different key, opening up the industry to seemingly uncharismatic "ethnic" leads like Hoffman—in any earlier era certain for mere character roles. Its magnum success gave Hoffman the star power, with veteran progressive TV director John Schlesinger and neophyte radical actor Jon Voight, to launch the most daring film of the moment and arguably of any moment in Hollywood history.[34]

Absent Hoffman's prestige and performance, *Midnight Cowboy* would not likely have been seen all that much by audiences. In the rebellious year of 1969, not even an off-screen blowjob (by a male) and an "X" rating could keep audiences away or distributors from extending theatrical runs. *Cowboy* got Oscar nominations all around, for director, writer and actor. More than any other film of the time, it threatened to turn the industry's ideas about potentially successful films upside down. All this seemed to friendly witness and television-production mogul Roy Huggins the bitter proof positive that, notwithstanding the loss of employment for the vast majority of victims, the reds had finally taken over Hollywood.[35] The blacklist, which supposedly wiped out all such influences, had evidently backfired!

Huggins' was an absurd conclusion, but one that seemed to be shared by not only political conservatives (who considered the film an abomination and wanted it banned) but by liberal critics like Andrew Sarris as well. No "second viewing or even second thought" was required for the "unpleasant and dishonest" images of Voight and Hoffman created by the infernal writer Waldo Salt and director Schlesinger. Worst of all, warned Sarris, it was Marxism warmed over, bearing the stain of the older cinema.[36] In short, *Midnight Cowboy* marked a most unwelcome return of the repressed.

Sarris' visceral attack on the film and its artists carried no weight, thanks to the growing admiration that screenwriter Salt had earned in the industry. His 1987 death, following years of tutoring young would-be screenwriters, prompted the Sundance Film Festival's annual prize for outstanding screenwriter to be re-named the "Waldo Salt Award." In FBI terms dating back to the 1940s, he had been the only one of the formerly "top dozen" Hollywood communists able to make the comeback that eluded almost every other blacklistee, even those with a single triumph, like Ring Lardner, Jr., or those with a string of fairly lucrative commercial contracts, like Dalton Trumbo. The three subsequent films written or co-scripted by Salt before his health gave way were the hard-hitting *Serpico*, about dirty cops; *Coming Home*, one of the strongest of the antiwar films directly taking on Vietnam; and what may be the most artistic of all the films made by blacklistees after they returned to Hollywood, *Day of the Locust*.[37]

THE FOREMAN FILE

Carl Foreman (1914–1984) acquired as much prestige as any blacklisted screen-writer by moving on from screenwriter to executive positions, returning to screen-writing only intermittently and with mixed success at best. On the other hand, that a *persona non grata* could become president of the Writers' Guild in Britain, governor of the British Film Institute and Queen-appointed Commander of the British Empire was only a little short of astounding. That his credits during the blacklist included *Bridge on the River Kwai*, *Born Free* and (indirectly) the early anti-nuke farce, *The Mouse That Roared*, not to mention several well-received war films, made him living proof that high-prestige comebacks were possible.

None of the younger writers emerging in later 1940s Hollywood had more po-litical and commercial promise. Growing up in Chicago with a Russian-Jewish im-migrant family, Foreman dutifully attended college and law school before plunging himself into the life of a carnival barker and publicist en route to Hollywood. Join-ing the Communists and quickly entering their all-purpose writers workshops, where screenwriting technique was taught by some of the best (and where invalu-able personal connections were made: he broke into films with Bowery Boys sub-features), Foreman was slowed down only by a hitch in the U.S. Army Signal Corps. After the war, he became the key writer for young producer-director Stanley

Kramer. No one at the time, it is fair to say, wrote better for leading men like Burt Lancaster and Gary Cooper, none tackled racial issues or the situation of the returning GI more boldly and none had delivered a film more central to American cinema than *High Noon*.

Under a cloud, Foreman headed from Hollywood to London.[38] It proved an artistically propitious move, up to a point. *The Sleeping Tiger* (1954), written under a pseudonym with director Joseph Losey, was a small gem. Three years later, Foreman co-wrote, with playwright Michael Gazzo and former folksong lyricist-radical Alfred Hayes, the advanced and realistic heroin-addiction melodrama *Hatful of Rain* for director Fred Zinnemann, an adaptation of Gazzo's highly regarded Actors Workshop original about the world of the addict. By giving closed-session testimony about himself only, Foreman had been redeemed, but only slightly.

Foreman next worked on *Bridge on the River Kwai* with uncredited fellow exile Michael Wilson, for the brilliant director David Lean and an equally brilliant cast headed by Alec Guinness. It could be taken as a psychological study of the military mentality, as Guinness plays the British commander of POW prisoners who determines to do the job assigned to him, even if it will help the Japanese. It could also be viewed as an American military adventure, because the officers who subvert the plan are led by heroic American William Holden. Or it could be taken as an all-time classy action feature in which the political or ethical plot plays second fiddle. Neither Foreman nor Wilson lived long enough to receive the screenwriting Oscars eventually awarded to them for the film (the producers used novelist Pierre Boulle as the front), but the seven Academy Awards boosted the pair's standing hugely among those in the know.[39]

Frustrated as a writer, Foreman turned producer and was arguably victim to the need for box-office hits. With a notable exception or two, his films would hereafter be big budget, action-packed adventures, especially war adventures with big stars, but thin on script. His Open Road production company, launched in 1958, was no doubt dependent upon these kinds of successes and in trouble when it did not deliver them. The psychological tension and character development that marked his pre-blacklist phase seem to have vanished; nor did the films have any great political punch.

Acting more as executive rather than director or writer, he made one fine exception possible. "Carl Foreman Presents," with Foreman as uncredited script contributor, turned a contemporary satirical, anti-nuke novel into *The Mouse That Roared* (1959), with sci-fi veteran Jack Arnold—no friend of the blacklistees—as the most unlikely director. Jean Seberg, pursued furiously (some say to her death) by the FBI for her political connections with American Black Power activists, co-starred with a 1950s British radio phenomenon from *The Goon Show*, the then little-known (in the United States) Peter Sellers. It was a send-up so good that Kubrick's *Dr. Strangelove* (1964)—including, of course, Sellers as the pivotal cast member—should be seen as a lineal descendant.

In *Mouse*, Sellers plays multiple roles as monarch (female), political leader and military chief of a tiny and anomalously English-speaking European duchy that declares war on the United States, counting on its own quick defeat and lots of financial assistance afterward. The Army (a few archers in chain mail) crosses the Altantic on a normal passenger ship, lands by accident in Manhattan during an A-bomb air raid drill, and just happens to capture the scientist (along with his daughter, played by Seberg) whom everyone believes has perfected the ultimate weapon—shaped just like a football. In the merry adventure to follow, the invaders return home with the bomb, and the duchy insists that small countries hereafter control the ultimate weapon, while the major powers take up activities more peaceful than preparing to destroy each other and everything else. The bomb happens to have been a dud the whole time, just as most of the world wished the real-life bombs might be.

Mouse thus uses the apparent powerlessness of the mini-nations to explore the powerlessness of the modern citizen everywhere, especially in the life-or-death issues of militarization and war. *Dr. Strangelove* brilliantly reversed the valence (with a vastly larger budget), offering a parable of bigness and military-technological madness gone utterly out of control, but *Mouse* cheered scattered peaceniks then involved in a global campaign against nuclear proliferation—and offered an opportunity for Foreman to make a little money.

Of Foreman's own action features, *The Guns of Navarone* (1961) was easily the best. Starring Gregory Peck, David Niven, Anthony Quinn, a hardly acting crooner James Darren and contemporary British favorite and frequent collaborator with left-wing projects Stanley Baker, it was a sort of antifascist caper film, as Brits and (mostly) Americans set out to sabotage new German weapons. Taken from a novel by Alistair MacLean, *Guns* won its Oscar for special effects, attracting a large audience and sparking a renewal of the big-budget films about the "good war." *Force Ten From Navarone* (1978) with Robert Shaw and a young Harrison Ford was a colossal bomb of a sequel. *MacKenna's Gold* (1969), which Foreman scripted and produced, was intended to be a satire of American cupidity and a comment on the individual fates of the men of Hadleyville who had refused to support the sheriff in *High Noon*, but it lacked inspiration and quickly sank from sight.

Foreman had more success with a different kind of war film reminiscent of Danny Kaye's old features, supplying heroes but also a satire of sorts on the John Wayne–style swashbuckler. He directed *The Victors* (1963) with an international star cast, about GIs fighting en route to victory in Germany—sometimes fighting a drifty and stilted script along the way. Foreman produced *The Virgin Soldiers*

(1969), about British lads (even a young David Bowie) in Singapore learning about sex and war, which was still more predictable, but no less pleasant, especially for British filmgoers.

Around this time, Foreman had also come more and more to play the industry executive, assuming leadership of the British Film Institute from 1965 and the Writers Guild from 1968. With this degree of influence, he had the leverage to make a different kind of film, now with an old friend who had had no luck on the gray market. Foreman thus notably served as executive producer for *Born Free* (1966), drawing on Joy Adamson's bestselling novel about a lion cub raised by a couple in Kenya.

Screenwriter-adaptor "Gerald Copley" was in fact Lester Cole, the unrepentant left-winger who hadn't had a film since his heyday with war features in the 1940s. With the benefit of an Oscar-winning score and title tune, and with brilliantly cast if little-known actors Virginia McKenna and Bill Travers, *Born Free* instantly became the new standard for the lovable animal film, anticipating such future features as Mike Nichols's *Day of the Dolphin*, in which dolphins were threatened to be used in a secret government program, and *Free Willie*, not to mention assorted sci-fi films and telefilms with benignly intelligent and almost terminally cute aliens, including Spielberg's *Close Encounters of the Third Kind*.

The couple in *Born Free* successfully save the cub and, true to the emerging logic (or lifestyle) of the counterculture, must learn to love and let go. During the film's final moments, as they return to Kenya for a visit and find the lioness raising her own cubs, the benevolent former colonialist couple experience something close to a recognition of the environmental consequences of Western civilization's economic expansionism. (They also take up with the Royal Society for the Protection of Animals, a large constituency in the United Kingdom.) Cole was certainly no ecologist; but as a Marxist, he knew perfectly well that the side effects of colonialism and what would become known as (neocolonialist) globalism had to be remedied or even reversed. Four years before the first Earth Day, Cole, director James Hill and Foreman had found the appropriate metaphor. The sequel, *Living Free* (1971), for which Foreman again served as executive producer, was thin soup by comparison. But Foreman had surely made his contribution to the developing political sensibilities.

Foreman didn't have much more to say, and his return to the United States with an independent production company (wishfully called "High Noon") in 1975 can only be seen as a disappointment. *When Time Ran Out* (1980) with Paul Newman and a host of others, including veteran progressives Eddie Albert and Burgess Meredith, was a catastrophe of a film, despite a script by Foreman and television veteran Stirling Silliphant.[40] After a long run, Foreman's career was over.

SAM SPIEGEL

No other blacklistee approached Foreman's influence as a producer, and in this respect the semi-rehabitated Left found itself much as before the blacklist: dependent on the whims of powerful figures. Sam Spiegel (1903–1985), one of the oddest characters in all of Hollywood, made some things possible and other things absolutely impossible as art or commerce. Michael Wilson, never to be recognized as among the best dramatic writers of his age while he was alive, personally owed to Spiegel the fact that he was able to return to Hollywood at all.

Wilson and Spiegel could not have been more different. A Jewish-Galician merchant's impetuous son, Spiegel had made his way to the United States in the 1920s, served five months in jail for writing bad checks, then worked in the European film industry one step ahead of the authorities.[41] Back in the United States, Spiegel bamboozled his way into producing *Tales of Manhattan* (1941), created a left-leaning salon for his own purposes (which always included a supply of women as well as a supply of cinematic collaborators) and produced for Orson Welles on *The Stranger* (1946) and for Losey on *The Prowler* (1951). Undaunted by failure, Spiegel mortgaged his house to produce *The African Queen* (1951) and soon was producing *On the Waterfront* (1954), a political two-step that presented no problems for him, even in those controversial times. His personal dealings, secretive but deft, carried a good deal more financial clout than anything the Hollywood Left could pull off at the time.

Spiegel's biggest cinematic triumph, by most assessments, remains *Bridge on the River Kwai* (1957). He knew perfectly well that he was hiring Carl Foreman, who had bought the first option, and probably knew that he was hiring Michael Wilson as well. The two writers-on-the-run made a decisive change in the original, creating the heroic American who brought down the famous bridge. Expensive and difficult to shoot in Ceylon, and at 161 minutes in CinemaScope, *Bridge* simply had to be a blockbuster, and it was. It won seven Oscars, from director to scoring (famously, the soldiers whistled the "Colonel Bogey March"), offering proof that a film backed by an American, if not quite an American film (it was in several respects more British) could point the way to a better cinema in Hollywood, even with the familiar theme of World War II.[42]

Faced with the equally daunting project of *Lawrence of Arabia* (1962), Spiegel once again called Wilson into action, this time without the powerful Foreman, and for that reason among others ended up with something more distant from

Wilson's hand and left-wing intent by the time production had finished. The other writer, playwright Robert Bolt, was actually imprisoned for anti-nuclear demonstrations and for refusal to recant his beliefs; he was well matched to Wilson in this respect, and they shared an ambivalence toward the British adventurer who had written that ultimate Orientalist tract, *Seven Pillars of Wisdom*. In such matters, Spiegel ultimately prevailed, brilliant in the formidable logistics of production, shooting in Jordan with the meticulous (that is, slow) David Lean in the director's seat again. Strictly a fictional portrait but with Peter O'Toole perfectly cast as Lawrence and a host of brilliant supporting actors (Alec Guinness, Jack Hawkins, Omar Sharif and Anthony Quinn, to name a few), it hit the public fancy from the United States and Britain to Europe, Asia and Latin America.

Sadly for the blacklistees, that was more or less the end of Spiegel. As his friend the blacklistee Edward Chodorov observed, the producer could not restrain himself from interfering ever more in production as he gained prestige, and that made his doom inevitable.[43] His great failure was *The Chase* (1966), made badly from a rewritten Lillian Hellman script by way of Horton Foote. It can be seen as the ultimate 1960s film, depicting a society out of control—or a film out of control, thanks in no small part to the mismatch of Jane Fonda, Marlon Brando and Robert Redford, as well as to Spiegel clumsily re-editing director Arthur Penn's own cut.[44]

VINDICATION OF JULES DASSIN

Jules Dassin, working in a tiny Greek film industry, briefly came the closest to the kind of global status that a magnum filmmaker achieves in a single film. *Never On Sunday* (1960) was more than a movie. It could be described as the first real cinematic event for the exiled blacklistees. It was also a unique and shrewdly devised commercial film, based on a then-controversial premise of a happy whore encountering a confused American searching, as so many were in their real-life European travels, for some timeless truth apparently lost within modern materialism. The film's radiance owed much to Dassin, who wrote and directed and also played the American innocent. But it owed even more to its star and Greece's emerging film goddess, Melina Mercouri. Not since the days when Donald Odgen Stewart and Ring Lardner, Jr., were writing for Katharine Hepburn had there been such an opportunity to explore the self-emancipated female. Despite the iconic presence of Barbra Streisand, Jane Fonda and others in subsequent films written by rehabilitated left-wingers, there would rarely be one of Mercouri's stature again.

Melina Mercouri was the granddaughter of the mayor of Athens and his favorite; she was also the daughter of a royalist imprisoned with the coming of the republic. The return of royalty in 1935 with semi-fascist partners had prompted a heroic underground workers' movement, setting off a civil war. In the defining act of the Truman Doctrine, the Americans funded ex-fascists considered enemies short years earlier, and counterattacking partisans were now suddenly treated as agents of Stalin, who meanwhile actually cut off Russian aid. The Partisans lost, but the class war only abated within a dubious democracy. A politically naïve Mercouri, a young actress/bohemian, toured Europe and made a small name for herself—while hardly ever acting in Greek dramas, considered hopelessly old fashioned.[45] History soon caught up with her, twice over.

Mercouri's transformation took place within a left-leaning artists' world, but specifically within a milieu of lyricists and musicians urging "Greekness," a return to roots and to the *bazouki* music shunned by the Greek upper classes as "Turkish" (meaning insufficiently European). A subgenre called "rembetiko" had come to Greece during the 1920s from Asia Minor; it was associated with lawlessness and was banned by the government but "discovered" by avant-garde Greek intellectuals of the 1950s, much as jazz had been "discovered" in the United States. Mercouri played a Greek free spirit in *Stella* (1955), her defining film. A cabaret singer who seems to fall for men until they demand she marry them, she shows herself utterly unwilling to accept subordination to a male-dominated culture.[46]

At the showing of *Stella* in Cannes, Mercouri met Jules Dassin and both their lives changed. Together they shot *He Who Must Die* in Crete, under the most difficult conditions (including a minimal budget), using villagers as actors and inspiring local death threats. The film won a handful of international prizes, served as France's entry at Cannes—and lost money. A few years later, the film was screened in California, with Dassin and Mercouri sudden celebrities. At this late date, when Dassin refused to sign a declaration repudiating his political past, only Richard Brooks, Gene Kelly and Walter Wanger among the glitterati bothered to show themselves at the premiere. The old lines or at least the old intimidation held.[47]

Rehabilitation came with success, and in *La Legge* (The Law, 1958, aka, *Where the Hot Wind Blows!*), starring a young Gina Lollobrigida as the mistress of a rich tourist, Dassin edged closer to making the film that would become *Never On Sunday*. *Never* was made on the merest of budgets, in black and white, shot in and around a ship yard. But as an evocation of a time and place, it was perfect. The plot had jolly proletarian shipbuilders and a parallel small army of sex workers, each surviving thanks to the latest stages of the ancient Greek water-transport commerce. Mercouri's whore cheerfully serves the men except on her "day of rest," and eventually leads the other women in a walk-out against the local vice boss when it is discovered that he is trying to run her out of business for her independence. Modern capitalism has arrived, but the masses have conquered—in their own Greek fashion.

Failing to nail down any proper American star (Van Johnson was the final try), Dassin winningly played the part himself. Mercouri's old friend and bazouki music maven Manos Hadjidakis contributed the award-winning title song that held the film together (the Greek musicians, true to the film, did not themselves read music but were guided into an improvised triumph). Dassin personally conspired, on money from United Artists, to bring a bazouki orchestra to Paris for the Cannes Festival, and the film took off spectacularly.[48]

Phaedra (1962), the first of Dassin's modern versions of classic drama—in this case Euripides' Hippolytus—was in box-office terms also mainly a vehicle for Mercouri herself. But the plot had a maddened Anthony Perkins seduced by and falling hopelessly for his stepmother (Mercouri), wife of a modern-day shipping magnate. Raf Vallone played the paterfamilias, a heartless bourgeois who cares nothing for the working people who have made his fortune, and who proves his indifference as a shipping accident leaves him cold to the widows and orphans waiting hopelessly in line at the corporate office for compensation. This family also collapses in tragedy, although American viewers might be forgiven for best remembering the sex scenes, Mercouri's suicide and Perkins driving his slinky white Aston Martin over a cliff with Bach's Toccata and Fugue in F-major pounding in his ears. The film barely made back its costs and Dassin's plan to make a film about Socrates and the rise of imperialism could not be made, even (perhaps especially) in Greece.

Topkapi was intended to be another pot-boiler, a caper film descended from Rififi, with subthemes of police repression and black humor stronger than the caper. Mercouri won the Donatelli Prize and this film made money.[49] Amazingly, Dassin came to be an admired cultural figure, beloved of left-wing Greek unionists in ways that he could only have fantasized about American workers during the 1930s and 1940s.[50] Then came 1965 and the Greek military coup, which put the fascists back in charge. The celebrity pair went into exile and, in an unexpected, remarkable way, enjoyed the greatest cultural-political influence that any of the blacklistees would ever achieve.

Once more Mercouri was the key. Her appearances in the capitals of Europe, but especially in the United States, rallied attention to the junta and excitement around a democratic movement regarded by the State Department and the CIA (which had been quietly supportive of the junta leaders even while calling for "democracy") as dangerously left-wing. It was her initiative to rally opponents around Andreas Papandreou, a socialist with left-wing supporters, particularly in Greece's trade unions, but with no political obligations to the Moscow-oriented Communist Party. As an icon, she could not be effectively demonized. With the triumphant return of democracy, Mercouri found herself culture minister under Papandreou. Dassin, for his part, launched the Mercouri Foundation. Together

THE LONG CLIMB BACK / 171

they helped create a Greek Film Center, lifting up the local efforts, and she personally spearheaded a successful drive to save the Plaka historical district of Athens from developers. Even tourism in general continued to owe heavily to the pair, because her "cultural capitals" public-relations campaign threw fresh light on the lasting pleasures of "Old Europe."

Dassin's film career had suffered badly in the meantime. His own favorite project, a film to be called *The Rehearsal*, was never released. Made in New York during 1973 while Greece writhed under the dictatorship, it reenacted the occupation of the Polytechnic University in Athens by students and the murderous invasion of the campus by tanks. The cast actually included Dassin's friends Arthur Miller, Lillian Hellman, Maximilian Schell and Laurence Olivier, among distinguished others. But the junta fell in July, distribution plans collapsed, and postproduction was never completed.

Five years earlier Dassin had been invited to Hollywood to create a new version of *The Informer* centered on the struggle of African Americans. His version was rewritten whole cloth by actress Ruby Dee and future screenwriter Julian Mayfield, who ended up with a role in the film. Shooting in Cleveland was actually halted, in the midst of a year punctuated by riots and assassinations; it finished in Los Angeles, and the resulting *Up Tight!* (1969), unmistakably about the police pursuit of the Black Panthers, might be regarded as one of the most interesting political failures in that period of Hollywood history. It might be, that is, except that it disappeared immediately, like most of Dassin's other post-blacklist films.[51]

Circle of Two (1980), a play adaptation with former child star Tatum O'Neal playing opposite Richard Burton, was supposed to be about a teenager in love (platonically but dangerously tipping toward something else) with a famous but spiritually broken painter. But this time O'Neal's acting powers were failing, and the director tried to back out of his contract and in the end sued unsuccessfully to have his name removed. The results stood for themselves, and Dassin at age 69 drew the logical conclusion from his recent American failures. Artistically, he became for the rest of his career an American director working in the Greek theater; politically, he ran the Mercouri Foundation, which had one last, large role—demanding the return from Britain of the historic Elgin Marbles.[52]

In retirement from cinema, Dassin left behind one final remarkable film. Only he could have had the audacity to write, direct and produce *A Dream of Passion* (1978), using a literal Greek chorus speaking the dialect of antiquity behind a modern feminist remake of *Medea*. Ellen Burstyn played the American who, mentally tortured by her brutal husband, kills her three children; Mercouri is the Greek journalist who takes up the case, forcing a reluctant Burstyn to explain her actions. If the production of *A Dream of Passion* did not reach its aspirations despite Burstyn's strong performance, the reason was almost certainly the impossibility of the task. It marked another failed effort to make theater work on film. It reached no wide audience—least of all in the United States, where its themes might have had the most chance—and Dassin himself has chosen not to speak about it.

TRUMBO AND TARLOFF

Dalton Trumbo, the only figure comparable to Dassin, Foreman or Wilson in his succession of post-blacklist hits, had been the only blacklistee to make a real living in Hollywood during the 1950s by writing under a series of pseudonyms and fronts until *Spartacus* set him free. Producers had badly wanted his talent all along. In the decade following his pseudonymous triumph in *The Brave One*, he continued to write prodigiously: *The Boss* (1956), *Cowboy* (1958) and *Career* (1959), none of them under his own name; *Exodus* (like *Spartacus*, 1960), *The Last Sunset* (1961), *Lonely Are the Brave* (1962), *The Sandpiper* (1965), *Hawaii* (1966), *The Fixer* (1968), *Johnny Got His Gun* (1971), *The Horsemen* (1971), *F.T.A.* (1972), *Executive Action* (1973) and *Papillon* (1973). It would have been an impressive lifetime output for any screenwriter; in projects good, bad and indifferent, Trumbo had usually managed to place his own stamp of realism and iconoclasm, offset somewhat by the idealism he recuperated from happier days and applied to rebels in the present.[53]

Interestingly, Trumbo had never been a writer of westerns in his pre-blacklist years. His best credits of the time were domestic dramas like *Kitty Foyle* (1940) or *Our Vines Have Tender Grapes* (1945), and war films like *A Guy Named Joe* (1943) and *Thirty Seconds Over Tokyo* (1944). If not high art, they were prominent contributions to the humane output of Hollywood and, to be generous, earned Trumbo his $3,000 weekly paycheck, a considerable portion of which went to leftist causes. *Papillon* was his last, and in some ways the most satisfying of his later films, with Trumbo himself playing the commandant of the Devil's Island prison that Steve McQueen and Dustin Hoffman must escape from. Adapted with Lorenzo Semple, Jr., from the autobiographical bestseller of Henri Charrière, it permitted itself a length that none of Trumbo's wartime films ever could have.

In between, Trumbo wrote moneymaking big-budget films that might easily have been better—if only stars like Elizabeth Taylor had bothered to act (as in *The Sandpiper*, where she plays a free-spirited single mother on the bohemian beaches of Big Sur),[54] or if the story line of colonialism and eco-destruction had not been sabotaged by cinematic tricks and long pans of scenery (as in *Hawaii*, an adaptation with Daniel Taradash that even director David Lean could not save).[55]

Breaking the blacklist with *Spartacus* had been no small matter, even if it had little immediate effect on others under proscription. It was as much a natural subject as Robin Hood and perhaps more so: the slave-hero had not only robbed from the rich of the Roman Empire, he had struggled to build a free society with his assembled army, weakened the empire and bid fair to change history.

The theme had been rumored for years to be a subject of an upcoming big movie. The property first considered likely was the Arthur Koestler novel, *The Gladiators*, in studio discussion for direction by Martin Ritt, starring Yul Brynner.[56] Abraham Polonsky was actually commissioned to script it, and had it worked out, Polonsky rather than Trumbo might have emerged early from the blacklist and Ritt might have won the big-budget clout that always eluded him.

But as the Polonsky-Ritt *Gladiators* hung fire, Kirk Douglas moved ahead, turning down an initial script from Howard Fast, who had written the novel, and turning to Trumbo. The depths of current intrigue prompted this most famous blacklistee to work behind a front to fend off possible public attacks from either conservatives and/or Cold War liberals that might yet KO the production. Meanwhile, actors Laurence Olivier, Charles Laughton and Peter Ustinov signed on, all but assuring the film major appeal; Tony Curtis successfully lobbied for a part and blacklistee Jeff Corey came in as an acting coach. Shot at huge expense in manpower and sets in California and Spain, interrupted in post-production when Trumbo submitted an 80-page critique and Douglas agreed to have sections reshot and re-edited, the film fell partly into the hands of yet another blacklistee, Irving Lerner (suggested to Kubrick by his old confidante, Faith Hubley). *Spartacus* went on to take four Oscars, for supporting actor Ustinov (personally a well-known peacenik), costume design, art direction and cinematography. It had, perhaps, succeeded as a spectacle more than as a narrative, but it certainly succeeded.

Perhaps the blacklistees had hoped for too much in a single project. But Fast and Trumbo were not destined, in any case, to feel entirely vindicated either politically or artistically. They both had in mind, consciously and unconsciously, a cinematic riposte to *Viva, Zapata!*, a film that left-wing Hollywoodites regarded as suffused with the idea, comfortable to politically obliging intellectuals, that revolutionary romantics must and *should* fail if they are not to be corrupted.[57] *Spartacus* let them down somewhat with hints at Zapata-like conclusions, but also with the deletion of an unsubtly homosexual scene featuring a gay Tony Curtis (Anthony Hopkins dubbed the voice of Laurence Olivier for the restoration). The placement of actor Woody Strode as a black gladiator was nevertheless the kind of movement that the reds had intended for decades, and much of the rest of the film satisfied the urge to see a great rebellion enacted. If *Spartacus* fell short of the movie that the Hollywood Left had craved, it nevertheless went a long way.[58]

By contrast, *Exodus* (1960), produced by Otto Preminger with Trumbo's script, was a glittering success at a moment when Israel enjoyed maximum prestige in Europe and the United States, but the film is a disappointment with the passage of time. It was the hit of Cannes, with a Broadway premiere that could turn out celebrities from Sal Mineo to Myrna Loy, Adlai Stevenson and Kennedy brother-in-law Peter Lawford. But Leon Uris' bestselling novel, as later commentators would document, advanced a monumental revision of Israeli history, placing all the blame for the Middle East conflict upon wickedly conspiring Arabs while ignoring the plight of Palestinian families driven from their ancestral homes. Even the quasi-fascist Irgun, bitterly opposed by Israel's founders, got the romantic treatment here, as if real-life military aristocrats such as Ariel Sharon had not conducted campaigns of human-rights abuses and mass murders that shamed Jewish liberals. The best scenes had Jewish refugees fleeing Europe in hopes of finding a homeland; some of the worst combined mismatched resistance leader Paul Newman and gentile nurse Eva Marie Saint in a sappy romance.[59]

The Fixer (1968) was by contrast a superb Jewish story—its production ardently condemned by American Jewish conservatives—based on a Bernard Malamud novel and surprisingly well cast, with Alan Bates as the handyman in Czarist Russia who finds himself entrapped and on trial for a crime that he obviously did not do. Dirk Bogarde played against casting as the good lawyer, and supporting actors Jack Gilford (still returning from the blacklist) and others might be described as unable to drag the story from the internal monologue of Bates' character. All in all, it was nevertheless a powerful humanist film with a message of resistance and courage, making it insufficiently Jewish for its critics but Yiddish enough for its admirers. In a remarkable turnabout, gentile Trumbo, surrounded since his earliest Hollywood days by Jewish comrades (and bitterly opposed by Jewish moguls), practically finished out a career with the films that might logically have gone to Jewish screenwriters.[60]

Executive Action (1973) stirred a bit of a fuss when it was condemned by critics as speaking in the same conspiratorial tones that would become the standard charge to Oliver Stone's *JFK* (1991): it, too, applied a light coating of fiction and sought to lay the blame for the Kennedy assassination on the right wing. It is remembered mainly as Robert Ryan's final film.[61] *Johnny Got His Gun* (1971), Trumbo's own adaptation and direction (his one time in the director's chair) of his powerful 1939 antiwar novel about World War I, was to have been the screenwriter's personal triumph and redemption. Informally produced by John Bright, one of the pioneers of 1930s left-wing screenwriting, it was extraordinarily modernist in presentation. Trumbo's device was to mimic the blindness of the near-fatally injured 1917 draftee (played by Timothy Bottoms) as he lies vegetating in a hospital bed by intercutting a dark screen with glimpses of his past and future, including a demure version of the hitherto rare frontal nudity, in the fiancée role played by Kathy Fields, and cameos by Jason Robards and Donald Sutherland. Hardly anyone would call it entertaining. With scenes actually shot in and around Trumbo's 1930s apartment in Los Angeles, it could only be deeply personal, and it came off as incoherent if heroically sincere.

Trumbo, who had held off joining the Communist Party until the 1940s and spent the rest of his life in resistance, had at least proved that he possessed movie-writing talent undestroyed by the ravages of McCarthyism. Not the greatest of artists, he had abundant skill and plenty of mettle. He had surely done his share of shlock, and veteran cold warriors (more liberal than conservative, in this case) would never tire of calling him middlebrow, doubtless because he had audiences vastly larger even than their own idols, like Saul Bellow, could claim. Trumbo also went out with courage, having written as many serious films as any writer in the history of Hollywood.

The tale of other former blacklistees who achieved real success in subsequent years can be seen as a simple struggle for survival with professional dignity. Those who were successful in the struggle had been fortunate in contacts made before the blacklist but were also successful in adapting skills to different kinds of projects. Frank Tarloff stands as a good example.

Tarloff was, as we have seen, the one influential sitcom writer in the crowd, but also the one who managed a return to films and grab an Oscar. Self-consciously the artisan rather than artist and most skilled at light comedy, he had few film credits prior to the Cold War, the best of them *Behave Yourself!* (1951), a Runyonesque comedy about a dog. Despite his insider reputation in television's *Danny Thomas Show* or (according to Tarloff himself) because of it, at first he got nowhere when he sought to return to film. For that reason, and for a little adventure, he headed for London at the close of the 1950s, where he got himself introduced to a veteran Hollywoodite, if no political exile, Hal A. Chester. By now, the former Bowery Boys character actor turned producer of low-budget 1940s Joe Palooka movies was a player in British films looking for low-priced talent.

Chester saw his opportunity in the blacklistees. Britisher Stephen Potter had written a series of satirical bestsellers about contemporary business practices, and Carl Foreman picked up an option, together with Chester. A script for the film that would become *School for Scoundrels* (1960) had been written before Tarloff turned up, but not written well enough for production. It needed restructuring and considerable rewriting, for which tasks the sitcom veteran was perfect.

Perfect in his way also was the gap-toothed comic lead Terry Thomas; *School* came to be known as one of the most British of comedies, an early (and unmusical) version of the Broadway and Hollywood smash *How To Succeed in Business Without Really Trying*. Enrolling in an academy that teaches "oneupsmanship" in the corporate world, the protagonist learns trickery, and tricks himself before the inevitable conclusion. Tarloff, on the set all through the shooting, knew just how to keep the gags rolling.

Tarloff got neither credit nor full payment from the scheming Chester, but he did get something far better. Chester bought a story that at first glance looked very much like a poor man's *African Queen*, with an interesting bum romancing a fancy lady in an exotic locale somewhere in the Pacific during World War II. Calculating the possibilities, Tarloff introduced a pseudo-family: orphans that needed to be cared for. He also offered a *deus ex machina* by which the humanization of the rough-edged character would be realized. Chester took the idea to Hollywood and snared Universal for what would become *Father Goose* (1964), destined to be one of the most beloved of war films.

Cary Grant as the lead was decisive, of course. This, his seventy-fourth film, could hardly have failed at the box office. To make sure, Universal picked Peter Stone, hot from *Charade*, to do the final rewrite. Often happiest cast as a "spiritual bum" (in Grant's own words), this time the actor dressed like one—the history professor who has abandoned civilization to live alone and unbothered but is ensnared in civilization's ultimate debacle. Willing to man a listening post in the Pacific, he suddenly becomes the reluctant guardian of seven children and their teacher, played by the oh-so-French Leslie Caron.[62] The old battle of the sexes, with a background of lush scenery and Japanese bombers, yielded what Hollywood and audiences wanted. The film won a screenplay Oscar, shared by Stone and Tarloff.

Meanwhile, Tarloff had sold Chester a script of his own, perfect for a Paul Newman outing and very much in the same World War II satirical vein. It would become *The Private War of Harry Frigg* (1968). One of those rebel-makes-good films about an officer-hating private who nevertheless manages to carry out his own plan to free five captured generals, it was considered to have modest potential when Chester sold the package to Universal and once again brought in Stone for rewrites. This time they didn't work. The lead character was cleaned up and his character development sacrificed for gags, leaving Newman with one of his weaker roles.

By now Tarloff was nearing the end. The writer's last real success, *A Guide for the Married Man* (1967) was a harmless sex comedy, full of gags and star cameos, with Tarloff's old friend Walter Matthau as would-be cheater and Robert Morse as his coach. Another progressive pal, Gene Kelly, got the directorial nod, thanks to Tarloff's pull. It was enough for one career.[63]

COUNTERATTACK

One cannot easily say what the best of these theatrical releases and made-for-television dramas might have done with a friendly press. On the one hand, the returning blacklistees tended to write and/or direct old-fashioned sorts of films, at least by contrast to the extreme modernism of the French. On the other hand, they specialized in just the kind of movie storytelling to which Hollywood and its sympathetic practitioners across the world would return, time and again, long after the blacklistees had vanished.

The blacklisters of the early and middle 1950s had only been interested in getting rid of the guilty parties—almost never, except in extreme cases, in the films themselves. Thus old favorites written or directed by proscribed artists actually gained large new audiences on television. Cold War criticism from the later 1950s onward struck a distinctly new note. Key reviewers of the later 1950s to 1970s, especially Pauline Kael and Andrew Sarris but also Stanley Kauffman, were far more concerned with identifying the films that the returned radicals actually made and, in a variation on the HUAC practice, ensuring the films themselves of an unfriendly reception. In this respect as in most others, Kael was first and last. Acclaimed as the leading critic of American films from her appearance in *The New Yorker* in 1958, she often opposed Sarris' auteurism. But she had also apparently resolved from earlier days to finish off Hollywood's Old Left, declaring, in her first published essay, Chaplin's *Limelight* to be "slimelight."

It was her condemnation of *Salt of the Earth*, however, that proved her signature. Contrary to the known hopes and expectations of the group that made *Salt*, in her view the film was *never* intended to make money and thus render possible the creation of an independent film company on the Left. No: since the filmmaking communists were "not likely to envision" the overthrow of American capitalism, they must have something entirely different in mind—the sneaky Russian strategy of discrediting the United States abroad, among the Europeans and former colonial peoples who also happened to go to movies.[64] Moreover, *Salt* was not even intended to depict real working people, let alone real Mexican-American miners. "If we want to know something about the treatment of minority peoples in the United States, we don't look at one community, we examine and compare data in various communities . . . integrated as well as unintegrated communities" and interethnic warfare among communities, Kael insisted.[65] Of course, no Hollywood film had ever seriously attempted it.

Kael was surely bothered by the filmic description of Anglo racism (common in Hollywood's later left-leaning treatments of Mexican Americans). Even if she had (evidently) never actually visited a mining town during a strike and never seen a history of ethnic solidarity blend in with labor solidarity, she nevertheless knew better. This story couldn't be true because the workers were too good, the bosses too evil, the whole project so "ridiculously and patently false" that its very creation pointed to certain "dangers in a commercialized culture."[66] Kael did not specify the nature of the dangers here, but as arch defender of film art against communism on the one hand and commercialism on the other she felt herself upon high ground indeed.

Europeans, more casual about and accustomed to communist connections to the film industry and for whom the accusation of someone holding "Un-Italian" or "Un-French" views was unimaginable, had their own disagreements, and sometimes sharp ones, with *Salt*. But when British critics in *Sight and Sound* responded to Kael's invective, she rejoined that her own freedom of speech (or at least of criticism) was now being threatened. She insisted that since she had never proposed that anyone be prevented from making films—although she had never defended the blacklistees from being blacklisted, or protested the campaigns to keep their films off American screens—she had the perfect right to attack propaganda directed at America as a racist society.[67]

Kael had thereby fairly established the standpoint of the newly minted Cold War reviewer and set it off from the standards of the *Times*' Bosley Crowther and the assorted critics who, more often in the daily press than elsewhere, cheered films they enjoyed straightforwardly without recourse to suspicions of certain writers and directors. Indeed, overthrowing Crowther and his generation of critics came more and more to be Kael's fondest aim. Her fellow thinkers were especially exasperated by films deemed so critical of American customs and political leaders (such as *Dr. Strangelove*) that they bore evidence of "nihilism" and neglected to provide the useful and intelligent criticism that world leaders needed from artists. Andrew Sarris, who often disagreed with Kael on other matters, generally chimed in on the same note when it came to film politics.[68]

One of Kael's longest essays in her long career was devoted to *The Group* (1966), not really a left-wing film at all but a novel by Mary McCarthy translated to film by Sidney Buchman, then directed and transformed by director Sidney Lumet. Kael didn't like Buchman one bit and admitted slamming his last script (for *The Mark*, 1961), but it was Lumet who had carried the stain of the Old Left's commitment to 1930s-style realism and bore the blame.[69] Kael announced that the real purpose of her analysis was to show, in something like auteurist fashion (although she wouldn't have put it that way), "why America isn't producing great film directors."[70] Lumet might never have been a communist (at least not since his teen days in the Young Communist League) but there was virtually nothing that was *not* wrong with him. He represented the television director—itself a proof of low artistic ambition—in that he liked to work fast, and he was (in Kael's disdaining tone) the semi-educated New Yorker who had "no intellectual curiosity of a more generalized or objective nature." In short, Lumet was a showbiz "genius" of the type that Kael despised even as she defended assorted American practices against the disloyal critics of the business society.[71]

Whatever Lumet and Buchman ("a very tired and cynical sixty-three") did in putting together *The Group* was therefore wrong and often worse than wrong; it was deeply malign. Casting had evidently been confined to selecting losers. The two auteurs, in her estimation, were not even thinking of the movie when they made it, but projecting ahead to "future hoped-for Howard Fast and John Hersey projects"—even worse versions of realism, socialist or otherwise. They never understood the essential complexity of the book upon which the film was based, remaining wedded to what Kael called the "basic cheat of Hollywood message films," which meant the "preposterous mixture of wanting to do good but evading the real problem."[72]

Kael reflected that she had personally "warned" Lumet that he couldn't make a film that did not reflect the television style of a few main characters alone on the screen. "Sidney, you can't do that," she recalled saying. Unwisely disregarding the warning of an important critic like herself, he fecklessly went on "faking it."[73] No wonder he failed—in her eyes. Lumet made it still worse by translating the subject into 1930s Method terms, creating a memory close to his own and marked by "a basic emotional vulgarity."[74]

Kael had to admit that the film was actually sympathetic toward its female subjects. Nevertheless, Buchman and Lumet had "betrayed" women by their sympathy, "treating the girls as poor, weak creatures" rather than making them perversely powerful. They came off as compassionate rather than insightful, even if the men in question were even less sympathetic. It was certainly not the film that a "good women's director" would have made. And this failure was symptomatic of, if it did not actually bring about, the "death of what we now still know as the art of the film." Lumet had just the genius to make popular television into popular film without the mass audience noticing the "absence of beauty" and "loss of visual detail." This was the truly subversive danger.[75]

Kael's indictment could have no possible (or at least reasonable) answer, but it was one to which there would be virtually endless additions. *The Group* was indeed a mediocre film, confused and drifty for the same reasons that film adaptations of famous novels often are. The auteurs, far from being auteurs, feared tampering with the original. But malign or dangerous? Only Kael thought so.

She had, however, pinned down the means for condemning the Hollywood Old Left as both too left-wing (un-American) and too Hollywood (too American, as the world sees America), simultaneously too unartistically literal and also too commercial. *Lawrence of Arabia* was therefore awful (Michael Wilson would have agreed in part, but for very different reasons) because cinematic form had trumped all else;[76] *Bridge on the River Kwai* was "flawed" at best, because of its "spectacular" content;[77] *A Funny Thing Happened On the Way to the Forum* (which, as we may recall, brought several blacklistees out of the blacklist) was ridiculous not because it mocked the idea of empire but because it didn't allow the vaudevillian quality of the acting to shine through—a fair charge but a huge over-reaction;[78] *The Sand Pebbles* (1966), directed by progressive Robert Wise and regarded as an antiwar film close to the blacklistees' sentiments, was particularly contemptible because the parallels with Vietnam were too much for her to bear.[79] Hardly anything could be worse for Kael than Lumet's classic, *The Pawnbroker* ("a terrible movie"[80]).

One gets a further run-through of what Kael really hated in her passing pronouncements on *The Big Knife* ("thoroughly immoderate"[81]), *Casablanca* (amazing "how entertaining a bad movie can be"[82]); *Citizen Kane* (she was "disappointed by the shallowness of the film's political treatment"[83]); *Edge of the City* ("reduces the human values to a quick fix"[84]); *Grapes of Wrath* ("gross sentimentality"[85]); *High Noon* ("primer sociology passing for dramatic motive"[86]) and *A Place in the Sun* ("full of meaning-charged details, murky psychological overtones . . . and overlapping dissolves designed to affect you emotionally without your conscious awareness"[87]). Even the much-loved *Born Free* was repellent, entirely the wrong kind of family film for young viewers.[88]

More than her colleagues, she also felt a desperate need to condemn certain telltale elements of the modernism greatly admired by art film crowds. Losey's *Accident* was unoriginal and *Rififi* ("I had the uncomfortable feeling that the film was directed by a gangster . . . I can't think of any other reason to make *Rififi*") vastly worse.[89] *The Daily Worker* had never been quite so predictable.

Sarris, the American champion of *nouvelle vague* and of auteurism more generally, was only slightly more moderate. Lumet and Ritt proved the favorite directorial butts of his attacks, but Waldo Salt was sure to be attacked as a dreadful writer, just as surely as left-wing folksinger Joan Baez, a descendent of the old Pete Seeger school of the Popular Front, was equally destined to be "conventional," uninspired and thoroughly uninteresting on camera.[90] Sometimes, as with Kael, Sarris slipped up because a favorite film of the pre-1950 period like *The Southerner* was actually written in large part by an uncredited future blacklistee.[91] Occasionally, as we shall see in detail below, one of Martin Ritt's films was also deemed acceptable (Kael approved *Sounder*, Sarris liked *Norma Rae*). But the only blacklistee they disagreed seriously about was Joseph Losey, and only because Sarris loved *The Servant*.[92]

These critics increasingly concluded that they, or at least their values, were under assault by something worse than the Old Left: a sinister combination of Hollywood salesmanship and disloyalty from the younger generation. What effect did their stinging criticism have on the filmmakers and their films? It's hard to say, even now. Left-inclined films like *The Pawnbroker* were indeed almost killed by a lack of attention and quick evaporation from the theaters, although the influence of that film has, by any standard, been longlasting, especially for Jewish filmmakers and audiences.[93]

Perhaps *Johnny Got His Gun* could not have been saved by the friendliest criticism (although far less coherent films attracted respectable attention and some audiences) and *Cleopatra* surely did not deserve to be saved. The most telling effect was on the little-seen neo-noirs that were ignored to death, valuable oddities like *Short Cut To Hell* (1957) or *The Last Mile* (1959). But the worst these critical attacks on Ritt and Lumet could accomplish was to slow down the directors' advance, make them more cautious and more overly attentive to the box office. If the revolution of the new filmmakers in the 1960s and 1970s did not last, it was in no small part because their foundation in Hollywood film history remained weak and could not be strengthened. Hollywood filmmakers, with all of their self-celebration, rarely had the self-confidence to make films that they could themselves take seriously; the effects of the blacklist and the premeditated attacks on the "silenced generation" had, in this way, triumphed after all.

CHAPTER SEVEN

THE HOLLYWOOD ART FILM

HOLLYWOOD'S NOTION OF THE ART FILM during the cinema revival of the late 1960s and afterward owed less to the ambitious work of blacklisted exiles like Joseph Losey and Jules Dassin than to the Golden Age studio projects of the 1930s and 1940s. It may have owed even more to the reshaping of the expectations of audiences for a higher realism and producers for higher profits after *Bonnie and Clyde* (1967). Still, for filmmakers on the blacklist, the central problem of making intelligent, ambitious or even artistic movies remained pretty much what it had been before 1950—matching possible projects with financial backers. Now, however, the problem was recast increasingly outside the studio context. If the blacklistees were suddenly freed of the worst kinds of censorship, particularly if they were discreet about sex and revolutionary rhetoric, they were just as dependent as ever on dependable financing and bankable stars.

How far could serious art go in the film capital? Losey and Dassin had been off-center for Hollywood, as much by personal inclination and fate as by artistic design. Even at their most radical and tolerant, the studios as constituted probably would have remained unequal to the tasks that the pair of distinguished emigrés wished to elicit from the film art. Lillian Hellman might have been the one artist who had been right for the old era and right for the next. It didn't work out, for reasons worth exploring. Instead, it was Martin Ritt who most faithfully represented Hollywood's version of the art film in the next phase—the beating heart of the moralistic, occasionally uplifting melodrama that at its best transcended the merely melodramatic through the refinement of narrative detail, visual composition and depth of characterization.

Significantly, Hellman and Ritt both chose the South as their favorite location. Just as significantly, both the scenarist and the director reached the peak of their art and influence during the public disillusionment with the system and the parallel upswing of social criticism, optimistic interracialism and feminism. The serious work that Ritt took during his earlier years, turning Faulkner into middle-high drama in *The Long, Hot Summer* (1958) and less successfully in *The Sound and the Fury* (1959), was arguably the true Hollywood version of filmed theater. Hellman, a distinguished playwright since the 1930s, proved herself always more the screenwriter-as-dramaturge, never really in creative control of her material in the film versions but highly skilled in rendering her material filmable. Unfortunately, most of it was butchered anyway.

And then there was charisma. Ritt as much as recreated television star Sally Field from a Flying Nun to the heroine of *Norma Rae*, a role the actress understandably aspired (but with little success) to reinvent in her subsequent career. By contrast, Hellman remained the literary persona in the world of New York letters and theater, a world in which famous and powerful personalities paid court to her at work and play. She did have one film counterpart: Vanessa Redgrave as Julia in the film of that title, reaffirming the old antifascist standard once again in bravura form.[1]

Ritt and Hellman even shared the same enemies, including inveterate cold warriors, as often liberal as conservative, longtime supporters of the blacklist grown older but no more contrite. Seeing in the public triumphs of the old radicals a renaissance of an un-American Left, contemptible for their appeal to the culturally tasteless as well as unpatriotic younger generation, these critics inclined toward the hysterical. Some rising younger critics who placed themselves firmly within the auteurist avant-garde but admired the liberal cold warriors' cinematic sentiments joined in the fray, plainly looking for patronage. Sometimes Pauline Kael and Andrew Sarris also seemed to make themselves the enemies of a new Hollywood liberalism (or radicalism) that they disliked quite as much as the despised, semi-rehabilitated reds. Using every rhetorical weapon at hand to savage *Hud*, *The Spy Who Came In from the Cold*, *Julia* or *The Way We Were*, they aimed unmistakable blows at American films seen as similar "message" successors to Old Left projects. The partisan qualities of the battle, waged with the contemporary ferocity of the struggles in the wake of the Vietnam War and Watergate, often threatened to drown out discussion of the films themselves.[2]

At the end, by 1980, it was clear that all the old combatants were returning to the margins, but they never left the stage entirely. Their shadows continued to flicker in the press, the cultural journals, film revivals, even home videos—in short, everywhere that cinema continued to cast its influence.

THE GROUP ON FILM

We've seen how Martin Ritt, veteran of the Group Theatre and early television drama, edged toward the film mainstream with a sophisticated remake of an acclaimed teledrama, *Edge of the City* (1957). Even before his disastrous (in his view) trip abroad to make *5 Branded Women* (1960), he had found the backer for a more successful path.

Jerry Wald, producer of Ritt's *No Down Payment* (1957), was the key. Born in Brooklyn in 1911 as Jerome Irving Wald, a dry-goods salesman's son, Wald wrote a newspaper radio column after dropping out of New York University, and on the strength of connections sold Warners on a series of shorts featuring current radio stars. He later swore to friends that he was *not* the model for Budd Schulberg's alarming 1941 novel, *What Makes Sammy Run?* And indeed Wald made a point from the start of working amiably with left-wingers, either because he admired their work or appreciated the career opportunities that their work provided. Most likely, he made no distinction between the two. After a series of social-minded hits at Warners during the 1940s, he formed a production company with Norman Krasna in 1950, then moved on to Columbia, and finally struck out on his own once more with Jerry Wald Productions. He died prematurely in 1962.[3]

Wald played a crucial role, for a mixture of personal, artistic and political reasons, in reintroducing the artistic social film to Hollywood. Bankable after his production of *Peyton Place* in 1957, he could afford to make heavy payments to literary masters he admired—above all to William Faulkner, whom he had known personally at Warners in the 1940s. On screenwriter Irving Ravetch's recommendation, Wald chose Ritt to make *The Long, Hot Summer* and *The Sound and the Fury*.

Wald had a task for Ritt to complete before he got to the big time. *No Down Payment* (1957), a film practically lost to later viewers, was the toughest of the iconoclastic social commentaries, more common in television drama than in films, about the alienation and inequities of much-idealized suburban life. In this case, a California suburb dependent on defense spending hides alcoholic commuters (Tony Randall in his first serious film role), alienated housewives (Joanne Woodward, in a role that she described, in a 1959 interview, as her best in films thus far) and assorted bigots and depressives. Studio chief Spyros Scouros looked at the final rushes and meditated on suppressing the film altogether—it was considered especially embarrassing for its bold suggestions of American racism—but settled for a final scene around a church, somehow bringing balm to so many troubled lives.[4] Shot on a tiny budget, *No Down Payment* had the look of a television drama, but was in some important ways a fair predictor of what lay ahead.

By now, Wald considered Ritt ready to helm multi-million dollar productions shot in color and CinemaScope. This alone gave the fledgling film director clout, including casting options that included some of the most important young, progressive-minded actors, especially Paul Newman (who had personally studied with Ritt at the Actors Studio) and those fellow studio vets Joanne Woodward, Anthony Franciosa and Lee Remick. The promotion from B- to A-budgets also contained unseen risks for Ritt.

In *The Long, Hot Summer*, for the first time, Ritt providentially went to work with the husband-and-wife team screenwriting team that, along with his old friend Walter Bernstein, gave him the best material for nearly all his subsequent career. Irving Ravetch and Harriet Frank, Jr., were in some ways a curious choice. Ravetch, a young writer of westerns who had collected his earliest credits in films like *The Outriders* (1950) and *Ten Wanted Men* (1955), had been a youthful Communist who held onto his profession by giving friendly testimony. (As a near-nonentity, he was apparently directed to give only a few names, and had little to say about himself.[5]) Harriet Frank, Jr., the left-leaning daughter of screenwriter Harriet Frank, had no credits before the blacklist and had been spared the ritual. If the testing of Ritt as a rehabilitated (but never supine) ex-red may have included the hiring of a "friendly" screenwriter, the relationship was nevertheless enduring. The team delivered not only the two Faulkner adaptations but *Hud*, *Hombre*, *Conrack*, *Murphy's Romance*, *Stanley & Iris* and above all, *Norma Rae*.

There was one more fascinating and historic left-wing connection in *The Long, Hot Summer*. Very near the end of his brilliant but ultimately disappointing Hollywood career, Orson Welles was first opposed by the studio for the film but successfully lobbied for by Wald. This was a decision fraught with Hollywood symbols. Welles had been the very emblem of the Golden Age, at once its chief and bad boy rebel. *The Long, Hot Summer* was never destined, by a long shot, to become a *Citizen Kane*. But Wald and Ritt, who sparred with Welles before the two settled down to an amicable relationship, unquestionably shared a seriousness of intent then rare in American movies.

The result was a Faulkner so heavily interpreted that it was considerably indebted to Tennessee Williams but even more to a synthetic view of southern social life seen through theater and novels since the 1930s. It was also markedly sympathetic, unlike the images of racism and repression that fill most of the liberal and left-leaning films made about the South from the 1950s to the 1970s (Ritt's own *Sounder* is another exception, but thanks only to its focus on black life).[6] The film's success was wrapped up in every sense with Newman as the lovable rascal Ben Quick. In the opening shot he is already on the move, falsely accused of the tenant sabotage known as barn burning.[7] He arrives in the small town of Frenchmen's Bend and rents his little piece of land from a property-rich veterinarian (Welles).

He woos and marries the patriarch's daughter, a sexually frustrated teacher played by Woodward. As in the Faulkner short story "Hamlet," from which the film was mostly drawn, Newman wins fair lady (albeit a different one from the book version) by demonstrating his adeptness, and the climax arrives when he tricks an unsavory rival into buying land by salting it with false treasure.

Somehow, in *The Long, Hot Summer*, it all works out happily for the major characters, with multiple marriages and Newman's character amiably reconciled to Welles'. But Ritt and the screenwriters were savvy or quietly radical enough to add an attempted lynch scene, reminding audiences of the friendly South's other side, and then to get Newman out of the way of a noose thanks to Welles' Big Daddy–like gesture.[8] Newman won Best Actor at Cannes, and although the film failed otherwise to achieve awards, it proved a modest money-maker.

Ritt and Wald, high on southern success, as much as stumbled into *The Sound and the Fury*, likewise a Faulkner original rewritten by Ravetch and Frank, Jr. This time Wald chose to shoot in the studio, an enormous disadvantage for Ritt, and this time Margaret Leighton unconvincingly played a Blanche DuBois–style character seeking freedom and self-development, tragically pulled down by the continuing decay of the rural South.[9]

The Sound and the Fury may well have been less interesting as film than for the critical furor it inspired. In 1958, when the orthodoxy of the New Criticism in literary studies was hardly a decade old, Faulkner's novels had a prestigious following armed with a defense that the novelist might not have shared—the identification of nonwhites and women as the chief sources of moral collapse in the backwater, post–Civil War South. Faulkner's version of modernism, a break from the traditional novel's narrative into a modernist, individual voice, had also seemed perfect to empowered critics who sought in the text an implicit repudiation of the more social-minded readings of American literature typical of the era just past, the 1930s and 1940s. The film version was therefore an unholy betrayal, perhaps even an artistic return of the Popular Front. By giving the narrative over to the *woman* character, it overturned the thesis of the novel. Notwithstanding a great deal of narrative confusion, Ritt had successfully subverted Faulkner.[10] Still, the effort had all been in vain, for Universal pulled *The Sound and the Fury*, which died with hardly anyone to lament its passing.

A Ritt project after *5 Branded Women* was *Hemingway's Adventures of a Young Man* (1962), intended as another arty adaptation and based loosely on the novelist's *A Farewell to Arms*. The film was not a success, either financially or artistically. Looking beyond failure, Ritt looked back to the Group, alive in the Actors Workshop. And he found Paul Newman, who had turned away from Belafonte's financially doubtful race-film production company, ready to make films about mainstream (i.e., white) Americans facing up—or not facing up—

to an assortment of other social dilemmas. It was doubtless a weighty decision for Newman, based at least as much on box-office potential as on film art. Salem Pictures, formed as a three-cornered deal with Ritt, Newman and Paramount, was thus promoted to feature "a reflection of our American way of life"—or quietly put, the promise of progressive and artistic filmmaking.[11]

One of the most important consequences of the break from Wald was Ritt's ability, much in the tradition of Abraham Polonsky and some of the best of the Left writers and directors from the Golden Age, to make films with strong women. In the context of American film emerging from the 1950s to the 1960s, this alone would be practically revolutionary.

Sally Field, an Actors Workshop veteran, later testified that Ritt had discovered her in lesser dramatic roles before casting her as Norma Rae, bringing out more than she had previously been able to demonstrate or even to understand of her potential.[12] In the budding era of the legitimated feminist personae, Ritt hit the main point again and again with Joanne Woodward in *Paris Blues*, Patricia Neal in *Hud*, Samantha Eggar in *The Molly Maguires*, Sally Field again in *Back Roads*, Mary Steenburgen in *Cross Creek* and Barbra Streisand in *Nuts*. The female characters are not always the main focus of the narrative, but they are nearly always the characters who provide the moral fulcrum.

Other directors and writers working in film from the 1960s to the 1980s and beyond made the obvious points more polemically, sometimes more artistically as well. But in the social melodrama, the story told in the traditional frame in ways most familiar to its audience, no one was more effective than Ritt, particularly when it came to the representation of working-class protagonists.

Hud (1963) was the first grand result of Ritt's labors. Paul Newman, the son of a Jewish sporting goods store owner in Cleveland and a Hungarian Catholic mother, and a radio operator in the World War II Pacific theater, had grown up from the early success he achieved in *Picnic*. Soon he had become the Marlon Brando–like rebel but a more restrained version, a quietly left-leaning actor who mixed humor with psychological depth and charismatic good looks. He and Joanne Woodward, married in 1958, made for a decidedly left-liberal pair in a conservative era. Salem Pictures was therefore his opportunity as much as it was Ritt's, a preparation for the rest of his career. Newman, perfectly cast, was indeed Hud. But who, really, was Hud?

Pauline Kael was sure that she knew the answer. Entertaining *Hud* undoubtedly was—one of the few such films released in 1963, according to her estimates. But it also was, for Kael, at the very least terribly contradictory and at worst horribly deceptive: an anti-American film with the cleverness to fool not only audiences but other critics who naively saw it as a straightforward criticism of materialism. Meanwhile, the studio men, the director and the producer (Newman himself) had obviously intended to reveal Hud's depravity, but just as obviously allowed the viewer to enjoy it. Kael had enjoyed similarly mannered if superficial movies from old Hollywood (she significantly named *Casablanca*), but those films had been *purposefully* transparent in their supposed moral claims rather than sneaking in the message like the films of the 1940s and 1950s that she despised (*Best Years of Our Lives, A Place in the Sun* or *Gentleman's Agreement*—all left-liberal to the core). Above all, she hated moralism.

Everything about the film except Hud himself therefore struck Kael as hopelessly phony and pretentious, the best example imaginable of a terrible Hollywood film. In a momentary flashback, she described her own father as an adulterous, politically conservative Republican ranch owner who nevertheless proved his virtue by inviting his Mexican and Indian ranch hands to eat dinner with him! It was not the sort of thing that Europeans, Easterners or left-wingers, New or Old, were ever likely to understand and appreciate.[13]

The plaudits laid on the film by other reviewers (especially in the older generation, Bosley Crowther above all) left her further enraged and, perhaps more to the point, all the more eager to assert her own particular views. Dwight Macdonald, *Partisan Review* veteran, enemy of both popular culture and the Popular Front, was on Kael's wavelength and proclaimed the film "stupid"—but even he, according to her estimate, didn't penetrate the depths of the film's deviousness. Spelling out her contempt for Ritt and for the most skillful of other left-written or left-directed films that she so disliked, Kael insisted that "*Hud* is so astutely made and yet is such a mess that it . . . is redeemed by its fundamental dishonesty," that is, redeemed as entertainment, but not as a film, to say the least.[14]

It must have been strange for Kael to read that Ritt, Newman and others were actually stunned to learn that audiences liked the man that they were supposed to hate. Hud's character had been strictly secondary in Larry McMurtry's novel, *Horseman Pass By* (1961), on which the film script by Ravetch and Frank, Jr., was based. But McMurtry had intended a drama of the modern West, depleted of romance, and had originated the crucial Lonnie character, a coming-of-age figure experiencing disillusionment but who, according to Kael, was far too innocent to exist anywhere in the real West.

Newman's charm certainly offsets some of the distastefulness of Hud's character. But no audience could miss the meanness of spirit or the shadow of death when a cattle disease prompts the mass slaughter of an entire herd. That hit audiences hard. Yet Kael described it as phony and downright anti-western, a send-up of the Holocaust. There is no mistaking the meaning when Hud's father, Homer, an Olympian figure played unforgettably by aged liberal Melvyn Douglas, himself a victim of HUAC congressmen's jibes, declares that "you keep no check on your appetites at all. Men of your sort have come to be the heroes of our age." In a

sharp ending, Ritt and Newman choose to have Hud inherit the ranch and in effect disown Lonnie. And so Hud emerges at the end as unredeemed and no wiser,
indifferent to the wishes of anyone else and perfectly ready to sell off the land, exploit it for oil or whatever else will suit his purposes. (The studio objected that the
ending was too harsh; Ritt and Newman won.)

Hud reaped international praise and a half-dozen Oscar nominations, including Ritt's only one for best director. Patricia Neal, playing a housekeeper, won best
actress, and veteran progressive James Wong Howe won his final award for cinematography. It lost best picture to How the West Was Won, demonstrating that decisions of the academy remained politically conventional this close to the
imminent explosion of the cinema of youth rebellion.[15]

Ritt had a half-dozen fine films ahead and more in the hit-and-miss category.
Hombre (1967) was the last guaranteed success, because it starred Newman again,
and because it was arguably the strongest film about white–Indian relations made
since before the blacklist, when Broken Arrow (written by Albert Maltz, using future witness Michael Blankfort as front) and Devil's Doorway (written by Guy
Trosper), had shocked sensibilities by reversing the usual narrative in the struggle
between townsfolk and Indians.[16] In these three films, as in the real Old West,
tribes were struggling just to exist, and whites were more likely to be involved in
lynch mobs than peace missions. Past Indian good deeds, like fighting for the
Union in the Civil War or signing treaties, were meaningless in the ongoing
white land grab, and one way or another—often by forcibly removing youngsters
from tribal homes when outright extermination had proved an impractical solution—the new power-brokers had determined that the mythicized "disappearing
Red Man" was indeed to disappear.[17]

Hombre's protagonist, played by Newman, is a white man raised by Apaches
on the San Carlos reservation in Arizona, someone who knows the land but has
also inherited a boardinghouse in town. The novel, written by a young Elmore
Leonard, is a Bildungsroman narrated from the viewpoint of a townsman who has
come to bring the Indian-raised white back to civilization. The shift in the point
of view makes all the difference.

So does the referential nature of the picture. Ritt had in mind Stagecoach
(1939), as he later told interviewers, unarguably the most famous western of all.
Ford had made the film in a moment during the Depression when even he was
under suspicion of communist sympathies, and it stressed the New Dealish themes
of community among strangers on a journey in close quarters, showing that after
much difficulty, American life will proceed with a certain rough dignity and justice. Hombre's characters, by contrast, don't see any light at the end of the tunnel.
The town with the boardinghouse, called in double irony "Sweetmary," is plainly
dying, and, as in so many dying factory towns of middle America in the 1970s, al-

most everybody wants out. Rather than surviving a rough trip, the stagecoach in which they have been traveling together is abandoned after an outlaw attack, and Newman's character unwittingly finds himself leading the other passengers on foot through rugged terrain. Danger ennobles none of them except a middle-aged woman (played by Diane Cilento) who consistently acts to alleviate suffering but has scant effect on the outcome.

Our protagonist this time around is endangered by the woman's appeals, destined to be killed for practically nothing, and in this twist the film echoes sheriff Gary Cooper's quandary in *High Noon*. There, the town itself did not want to be saved and would rather have Cooper banished than risk a violent clash that would presumably hurt its business-first reputation. By the time of this re-revision, even unwanted redemption is out of the question. No wonder so many reviewers (although not the admiring Bosley Crowther) considered *Hombre* too tough and Newman's character not real at all, merely "alienated" and "masochistic," in Kael's carefully poisoned adjectives.[18]

Ritt made a real flop in his effort to remake as a western the Japanese classic that made Akira Kurosawa famous, *Rashomon*. Written for the stage by Michael Kanin, produced (as *Rashomon*) on Broadway by David Susskind, the film version, *The Outrage* (1964), starring Claire Bloom, Paul Newman and Edward G. Robinson, just didn't hold together. The intent to show the same incident from different points of view badly confused audiences and, worse, simply bored them. It was not the last of Ritt's failed transformations of stage drama into film.

The Spy Who Came In from the Cold (1965) was something altogether different. Ritt bought the rights to John le Carré's novel immediately after seeing the galleys, a move financially possible only because the spy novelist was still at the threshold of his international success. By the time the book achieved bestseller status, the tale had become a Cold War narrative in a vein very different from the James Bond thrillers. Ritt also produced the film, probably a crucial factor in getting the astronomically paid but frequently tippling Richard Burton (after failing to get Paul Newman or Burt Lancaster) for the lead. Guy Trosper scripted a first version, followed by Paul Dehn, whose main achievement was to recover the novel.

Burton, under Ritt's direction, nevertheless proves perfect as the unromantic spy. He believes in nothing at all, and he goes into East Germany with what he believes is the purpose of unveiling a double agent, only to learn at the end that he is being set up by his own intelligence chiefs. Like the Newman character in *Hombre*, he is destined to die without glamour, for no real purpose in a struggle in which neither side can claim much virtue. He takes down with him a British Communist idealist, played by Claire Bloom, who innocently asks the right questions about political morality in the Cold War era and is given the genuine answers (spies of either side, insists Burton, are "silly, squalid bastards . . . playing cowboys and Indians to brighten their rotten, little lives"). Ritt had no surviving illusions about Stalinism but none about capitalism, either. In his only noble act, the spy chooses to die with his lover instead of escaping. The cinematography of a fictional East Germany, in the architecture and courtroom, is perfect for the flatness of this brilliantly stark black-and-white film.

The public reception of *Spy* was generally quite good, but Andrew Sarris took the lead in the counterattack. "Brilliantly cast," it was nevertheless a failure, he thought, because of Ritt's direction. Any really brilliant director could have made it the film of the year; Ritt's "uninspired mannerism" was so confusing that "any imbecile" could apparently have done better. "Thus though everything we know and feel about contemporary politics," Sarris concluded, "asks us to come in from the cold, a lack of meaningful style in the presentation of the narrative makes us sniff suspiciously at a sanctimonious odor of self-sacrifice."[19] Which is to say: the events of 1965 suggest that the Cold War had scant nobility on either side; nevertheless, simply pointing out the difference between reality and rhetoric in the West was beyond the pale artistically and politically unacceptable to boot.

Ritt followed quickly with a mob film, *The Brotherhood* (1968), thanks to the urgings of the studio and of Kirk Douglas, who played the role of a mob patriarch. The director tried hard to emulate a classic tragedy but achieved a film keyed so low that it seemed badly out of date.

The Molly Maguires (1970) was next, and it may well be Ritt's best cinema art. It surely was Walter Bernstein's finest, both as producer and screenwriter, an epic working-class history seen through the lens of aging master cinematographer James Wong Howe, with one of Sean Connery's best performances. It was also destined for an undeserved obscurity. Never before had a film attempted a rich study of the lives of embattled nineteenth-century working-class Americans, in this case Irish-American coalminers, and never of course had this particular episode of nineteenth-century industrial relations been explored, with conspiracies on all sides ending in the hanging of ardent unionists.

Harris plays an agent of the industrial secret police come to flush out the members of the "Molly Maguires," violent troublemakers of the Pennsylvania coal district grown strong thanks to terrible wages and working conditions and the violent repression of all attempts to form unions. He worms his way into the tough working-class society and wins the heart of a widow (played by Samantha Eggar) who would do almost anything to get out of coal-town misery. In the end, leaving town with the informer is the one thing that she will not do. Although the agent is successful in his task, he is exposed as thoroughly amoral in his purpose and in the end must face his own disappointment. He is an empty man.

Some of the most brilliant and complicated cinematography, according to Howe himself, was scrapped in condensing an overly long (ultimately, two hours plus) film, but that was not the heart of the problem. Getting ordinary viewers interested in a story about a scoundrel with precious little charm was too much. Besides, the historical depth of the film all but demanded an audience of near-Ph.D.s. for whom a scrupulously accurate depiction of blue-collar social history would be compelling. If Ritt called The Molly Maguires his favorite film, perhaps the most revealing comment was made by Stanley Kauffman (who mostly, and altogether predictably, hated it). He compared it to John Ford's sentimental classic, How Green Was My Valley (1941), a portrait of happily singing Welsh coalmining families somehow spared the degradation of Ritt's mines.[20] Ritt's portrayal of oppression and misery was unacceptable because it happened to be historically accurate.

Kael seized the moment to pour out her contempt on the screenwriter (without naming Walter Bernstein) for manipulating audiences by writing about the condition of nineteenth-century workers when the current situation of rioting African Americans was, for her, the only real subtext for any film of this kind. Ritt's workers were mere stand-ins, she insisted, and The Molly Maguires therefore was "too somber and portentous for the rather dubious story it carries," more "lifeless and lugubrious than evocations of the past generally"—even if it was an "impressive failure" because of the cinematography. No fan of labor lore, Kael didn't seem to be aware that the Molly Maguires really were no small story within American working-class history.[21]

The Great White Hope (1970), an unsuccessful theatrical adaptation of black boxing champion Jack Johnson's life, recalled Ritt's own theatrical origins in the Group with Golden Boy and featured the all-powerful James Earl Jones in the lead. Jones is indeed great at times, replicating his Broadway triumph. The rest of the film is not strong enough to support him, and probably viewers were also simply unprepared for the kind of black hero Jones represented.[22] As if to compensate with a less confrontational, more filmable project about African American life, Ritt next contracted with a shrewd producer to adapt a bestselling pastoral novel of the 1930s South, with Cicely Tyson, Paul Winfield and 13-year-old Kevin Hooks playing the black family in hard times. In the novel, the dog of the title is shot dead as he tries to protect the family of sharecroppers against a brutal police assault. In Sounder (1972), as in so many other doggy features, the animal must survive, and the family gains stature by its relationship with the canine star.

Sounder, based on a children's novel by William H. Armstrong, was a story that surely would have proved too much for Lassie's or Rin Tin Tin's screenwriters. The imprisonment of the sharecropper father, the boy's odyssey in pursuit of him, the classroom experience with a black teacher (echoing the Mexican classroom experience of The Brave One) and the sudden maturation of the boy all made for a reassuringly liberal message without losing the film's militant, antiracist edge. The cinematography was more lush, perhaps, than any film about an African American family had ever been. Taj Mahal composed a sound track that, like the Modern Jazz Quartet's score for *Odds Against Tomorrow*, was unique and interesting in itself, if not as full as it might have been.

Perhaps only in 1972, a few years after Martin Luther King, Jr.,'s death and a few years before the wildly successful production of *Roots*, could this low-key film have been greeted with so much critical and popular enthusiasm. Ritt's usual critics did not even bother to attack it. As in *Conrack* (1974), the tale of a white teacher reaching out to nearly illiterate black youngsters in an insular island off South Carolina, Ritt succeeded in making excellent liberal family fare, and it was recognized as such even if none of the films after *Sounder* were big hits. *Pete 'n Tilly*, released in 1972, had Carol Burnett and Walter Matthau playing against type as middle-aged parents of a child with fatal leukemia, trying to live with themselves and each other. Arguably miscast, and like *No Down Payment* set in the dark suburbs for which Ritt had no sympathy, it had nowhere to go.[23]

The Front (1976), made possible by the surprising box office success of *Conrack* and the nearly universal praise of *Sounder*, was ultimately destined—but only after the mass ownership of the VCR—to be a livingroom favorite. The story, as we have seen, really begins with Walter Bernstein, a veteran of several highly praised outings (especially *Fail-Safe*, 1964) and looking for a way to air the blacklist issues. His old friend Ritt was more than ready, and the two of them had devoted many informal discussions during the making of *The Molly Maguires* to the details of such a film. Ritt set the scene by opening with glimpses of 1950s mass culture, including bomb shelters and Joe McCarthy, set against the sounds of Frank Sinatra's "Young at Heart." No one could miss the politics.

Most critics, like most fans, nevertheless treated the film as a Woody Allen serio-comedy, perhaps not quite a satisfying blend but interesting and weighty enough in subject matter for an industry that for so long had avoided looking in the mirror. Reviewers in the literary set responded differently, and the *New Republic*'s Kauffman probably spoke best for Kael (who only hooted at it as an out-of-date, 1940s-style film), Sarris and others. Kauffman, a bit unique in this respect, claimed that he actually admired both Ritt's training as an actor and his political commitments—even if he found *Sounder* "facile," *Hud* and *The Spy Who Came In from the Cold* "graceless" in many respects. He admired the good acting and the astute "guiding intelligence" characteristic of Ritt's best efforts. But this flattery was a preparation for saying that he found *The Front* utterly unendurable.[24]

There was no reason for *The Front* to have been made at all, in Kauffman's view—except that it could be made. If the Allen character's unwillingness to testify was the inevitable conclusion of such a film, it was unbelievable because, given his lack of political commitment, why would he? Kauffman had answered his own question earlier by peevishly complaining that most of the blacklistees shown were "plainly Jewish"—exactly why, because of the Jewish proscription against informing, a nonpolitical writer or actor would nonetheless refuse to testify, and why a handful of those never even in the Popular Front milieu as well as otherwise embittered ex-communists did refuse. (There was one more point missed here: in strictly Allenesque terms, refusing to testify also meant he got the girl.) By Kauffman's familiar conclusion, no one sympathetic to the Soviet Union in those years deserved real sympathy, even if the associated legal persecution and harassment had been "indefensible" and the McCarthy types who led the witch-hunt unpalatable.[25]

Ritt might have deceived himself, as directors (and not only directors) often do, in thinking that *The Front* could somehow have escaped this kind of attack. It is still more unlikely that he anticipated the influence of *The Front* on Woody Allen's cinematic persona. Perhaps he only confirmed one part of Allen, the part that had been with him all along, the legacy of the Jewish lower-middle class or working-class past ready to ridicule the pretensions of an upwardly mobile and increasingly hypocritical Jewish present.

Allen had broken into big-time comedy writing in the 1950s, it might be remembered, thanks in part to connections made for him by a distant cousin, Abe Burrows, at a moment when Burrows was a celebrity writer but also one of the nastier friendly witnesses. Early on Allen worked for Bob Hope, already a key Reagan ally in the purged Screen Actors Guild.[26] Never one to take strong political stands, Allen made amends from the moment of his highly publicized stage appearances and subsequent literary exercises in *The New Yorker*, skewering the cultural pretensions of those Cold War liberals who had ignored or actually supported cultural repression at home while jetting around the globe to proclaim the independence of the intellect. Allen could get away with it because of his enormous popularity among young people and his emerging status as the leading filmmaker in New York, the city he took as his subject (sometimes in exquisite detail). He also memorably depicted popular entertainment and celebrity as it was seen from the inside; that is, the largely Jewish world of stage and film that he had made his own. In some of his best strokes, he brilliantly recalled the undercurrents of Jewish popular life of the 1930s–1940s in films like *Broadway Danny Rose* (1984) and *Radio Days* (1987) through the reconstruction of the experiences of the Jews without money—their lives, follies and dreams, from the Borsht Belt to Sheepshead Bay.

Allen's skillful use of older character actors underlined his feeling for those lost decades of popular culture egalitarianism. So did his political jibes at such establishment favorites as Vietnam hawk Albert Shanker in the sci-fi sub-classic *Sleeper* (1973), where the union bully had brought down civilization by personally setting off a nuclear weapon. Even the gags were intimate, like the *Sleeper* protagonist who says of another, "I love him like a brother—David Greenglass." The reference to the Rosenberg case must have flown right past the vast majority of viewers, but it would have been entirely at home in a Jewish Popular Front standup act, if one had ever existed. *Crimes and Misdemeanors* (1989), which earned Allen Oscar nominations for director and screenplay, offered an especially penetrating commentary on the Jewish generation that made fortunes by fiddling with the books, all the while claiming public status as philanthropists or even idealists.

For Allenophiles around the world—and they could be counted in the millions as the last U.S. troops withdrew from Vietnam—*Annie Hall* (1977), an Oscar winner for best picture and with two more awards for Allen personally, would likely remain the apex of his accomplishments. (Left-wing viewers reveled in a deathless Allen line delivered about the imaginary merger of *Dissent* and *Commentary*: a new journal to be titled *Dysentery*.) Like the best moments in his other films, but sustained virtually throughout, *Annie Hall* was about romantic hopes and disappointments, modernity, loss of self and identity (ethnic or otherwise) and the acceptance of that loss without any compensating faith in religion or nationalism.

Perhaps in a different Hollywood and a different world, this was more or less where the more wistful elements of the blacklistees' imagination would have taken them as well. But it was Woody Allen whom Bernstein and Ritt developed in *The Front*, with the memories that had become common stock for all those who could make use of them. In Woody's world, the blacklisters and their apologists were and would always remain "nogoodniks," just as lower middle-class Jews sitting around automat tables and making dour jokes about capitalism would remain a cherished memory of the generations vanishing with their neighborhoods. In these many ways, he had repaid the favor to the Old Left of being taken into the showbiz fold; and he helped in no small degree to make the further projects of his auterist counterpart, Martin Ritt, possible.[27]

Norma Rae (1979) stands so tall that it is in danger of overshadowing practically all of Ritt's other work, and with good reason. Representing union struggles onscreen was an old, old dream of Hollywood radicals but a theme banned from Hollywood until the 1970s (doubly banned in the case of *Salt of the Earth*), and when the breakthrough finally came in director Paul Schrader's *Blue Collar* (1978) the wonderfully realized blue-collar life was framed in the context of rigid union bureaucracy. *Norma Rae*, by contrast, remained true to the original dream, and if there was an opportunity to tell the tale it was in this story of this Carolina mill town. Here in the South, "Operation Dixie" had been promised during the 1940s as the means not only for unions but left-of-center social movements to enfranchise black voters, overthrow the Dixiecrats and reorient the Democratic Party from an amoral coalition (liberal North with the racist South) into a real liberal movement. Popular Fronters as much as originated the strategy, and, with their allies in left-led unions like the Food and Tobacco Workers, had been the only ones to create successful community-based, interracial unions in postwar southern towns.

In the real-life story behind *Norma Rae*, the historically progressive Amalgamated Clothing and Textile Workers had merged with the ferociously anticommunist (and now badly reduced in numbers) International Ladies Garment Workers Union (ILGWU). As northern jobs continued to move south, the Amalgamated belatedly began to pick up organizing where it had left off during the red scare. In real life, the effort was only marginally successful, although those successes were still bright compared to the drought of victories for unionization elsewhere. Norma Rae's racially integrated but still mostly white textile mill might have been one of the successes, even if in reality the priorities of the labor movement lay mostly elsewhere—especially at the leadership level, where the Vietnam War and the Cold War continued to be chief obsessions.[28]

It could not be entirely true, then, to say, as Ritt's best biographer does, that the director became interested in the theme only after reading an essay about real-life southern union activist Crystal Lee Jordan.[29] As a radical repeatedly discovering and rediscovering the South, Ritt had been interested in the theme all his adult life and only found the proper object now. But it is true that he finally found the hook upon which to hang his interest: a youngish woman straight out of American life who braves all the vagaries of employer threats, ostracism and male chauvinism to lead a successful strike and ballot for union certification. As Adele Ritt recalled later to us, the effort to find a mill owner willing to allow production was daunting and ultimately drove the production team from Georgia to the little mill town of Opelika, Alabama. Oddly, the former segregationist champion, presidential candidate and self-avowed tribune of working people, Governor George Wallace, had intervened to make it happen.

The genius stroke in *Norma Rae* was in casting Sally Field, scarcely known beyond her kitschy television work.[30] Field's Actors Studio background suggested why Ritt thought Field had the requirements for the leading role, but he had to insist over studio reservations that she be given the chance. Field responded in ways that still seem astounding, because of the sincerity and also the empathy she expressed in working-class characters, including some with less-than-loveable traits. She was perfect as a working woman with a couple of children, a dependent mother with enough sexual abandonment to prompt an affair with a married man, and just as good as the illegitimate mother and occasionally battered woman who finds in the union cause and in the union organizer a purpose and a mentor.

The organizer and the activist do not become lovers, however, and this is a key point. The union organizer, Ron Leibman playing "Reuben Warshawsky" in a definitely Jewish key, had Actors School credentials and a strong progressive streak but had almost never played a lead in stage or films. Usually cast as an oddball, here he is the Jewish organizer as oddball in the industrial South, a creature known there only by the reputation that conflated "labor," "New York," "communist" and "Jew." He remains firmly in love with New York and with another woman (a "lefto" whom, he notes, his mother also loves), so that a real romantic connection with Norma Rae is impossible. A potential erotic tryst—the likely moment arrives when they go skinny-dipping together—is pointedly avoided. Instead, he patiently recruits her and then recasts her as activist-agitator and consequently helps her become the self-confident person she has never been. We see him largely through her eyes, as she leaves an anti-union father and marries, more for security than love, a man (Beau Bridges, another member of the progressive Hollywood family) who opposes her union activities but does not stop her. At a crucial moment of the film, Leibman speaks straight out of the playbook of Norman Thomas and the Popular Front, recalling his grandfather's funeral at which black and white, Jew and gentile, gathered to remember their fellow union member. Not a bit saccharine, but undoubtedly didactic, it is an articulation that offers a moment of solidarity across classes that is rare in American commercial cinema.

Norma Rae's ultimate strength comes neither from the union-organizing outsider nor from the paternalistic figures around her, but from her fellow workers, especially women workers (with a sprinkling of black men). We see, from the first moments of the film, that they are a potential community, actualized at last by her firing, which brings about a strike and a National Labor Relations Board election. As so rarely happens in real life, the workers win without having to confront years of mostly fruitless legal maneuvering. Other movies and good ones were made during the 1970s and 1980s about working-class women, in particular Silkwood (1983), directed by Mike Nichols and starring Meryl Streep (with Cher in vivid support). Yet Ritt made Norma Rae without either star power or a large budget.

Murphy's Romance (1985), adapted by Ravetch and Frank from a 1980 novel about the modern West, by contrast certainly had the star power—thanks to Field's growing reputation but mainly thanks to James Garner, that perennial television favorite. Field created her own production company and served as executive producer to get it made; Ritt fought Columbia to cast Garner, whom he saw as an underrated screen actor. It was a shrewd move, aesthetics apart: Garner got a best actor nomination, the closest he has come to an Oscar. Field plays a divorcee with a son and an ex-husband, handsome but no good, whom she brushes aside when he comes around trying to take over her life again. In a small western town where the Garner character is the community druggist and a much-sought-after widower, Field struggles to keep a small ranch going, tries unsuccessfully to borrow money from him and ultimately falls in love. Shot to emphasize the picturesque moments in a setting that contemporary films (like *The Last Picture Show*) more often portrayed as scenes to escape, *Murphy's Romance* has a warmth and personal quality that evade political categorization. The film took off briefly at the box office before sinking into the so-so range. Perhaps it also marked, lamentably, the onset of Fields' cinematic decline.

Back Roads (1981) had suggested, a few years earlier, the weakness of her persona. Released by CBS Films in a doomed attempt by the network to market its own dual-release productions, it co-starred Tommy Lee Jones as the loser who, with erstwhile prostitute Field, leaves the South to head toward a change of luck in California. Made for more than $7 million (nearly twice the ticket on *Norma Rae*), a fumbled combination of *It Happened One Night* and something out of a Nelson Algren novel about the dispossessed, it simply disappeared. Working on yet another film with Field after *Murphy's Romance*, Ritt pleaded ill health and backed out. His best work was nearly over.

But not quite. Robert Radnitz, the producer of *Sounder*, sold Ritt on the idea of making a film from novelist Marjorie Kinnan Rawlings' memoir of living in rural Florida during the 1920s and 1930s. A much-beloved popular author, Rawlings left behind something that needed special handling to translate into film, above all close attention to the appropriate location. Striking out from her Manhattan literary life, Rawlings had sought to rediscover the undiscovered, much as the New England regional women writers from the 1880s to 1890s described a culture of their own imaginative creation. The casting of Mary Steenburgen was inspired. A Neighborhood Playhouse protégé of Sanford Meisner, she had already won an Oscar for best supporting actress in *Melvin and Howard* (1980) and played another supporting role in Woody Allen's *Midsummer Night's Sex Comedy* (1982)—although she had precious few good roles ahead. She was splendid, at any rate, in Ritt's *Cross Creek* (1983).

A liberal Democrat if hardly an articulate feminist, Steenburgen was cast at the center of *Cross Creek* as a writer learning to write while engaging with the community of rural folk around her. The key character is a neighbor, played by Rip Torn, whose world she must enter, including that of his family and a doomed pet fawn. As in her literary imagination, Rawlings/Steenburgen must come to accept the idea of community, including a local suitor (played by the radical actor Peter Coyote). But the plot, if minimal, is less important than the visualization. This is the American pastoral—if that term can be applied to "unproductive" swamp land—according to Ritt. "The earth may be borrowed, not bought," in the testimony of Rawlings. The film seems to say that nature possesses the possibility of redemption for those who understand its message, making of Ritt somewhat of an ecologist without ever using the word. It marked the Popular Front film updated; "poetry" according to his friendliest critic.[31]

Suffering from a deteriorating heart, Ritt was near the end of his artistic energies when he directed *Nuts* (1987). It is one of the strongest films ever made about sexual abuse and its psychological effects—and one of Barbra Streisand's best dramatic efforts as well—but it could not please him. The diva had first wanted to direct the film herself, on a huge budget and with a script that she had revised to suit her own star status. She turned reluctantly to Ritt, for whom she had great respect, but she obviously intended to keep a guiding hand. After much indecision, they pinned down Richard Dreyfuss as co-star, the public defender who will work with the prostitute and uncover the real story of her past. The distinguished cast was rounded out with Karl Malden (who remained, despite attachments to Kazan and hostility to all politics, past or present, Ritt's friend from Group days), Maureen Stapleton, Eli Wallach and James Whitmore. It was almost a survivors' dream team, in an era when most of the blacklistees had died or retired.

According to Ritt, Streisand stole the picture. It's a good argument, despite strong performances from Dreyfuss and others. As a self-confessed killer whose suicidal impulses are stilled if not conquered by heavy doses of Thorazine, Streisand looks suspiciously like those film stars of the 1930s who waded through battlefield gore with their hair still somehow perfectly coifed. Her moral innocence is never in doubt, although the revelation of childhood sexual abuse by her stepfather in a respectable upper-middle-class home could still come as a shock to that large portion of American society in which such problems were perceived as part of the impoverished life. Like a television movie about a female victim, driving the point home with daggers and clubs (but in this case blessed with quality production values and delightful supporting actors), *Nuts* was somewhat misplaced. But in Reagan's America, it wasn't half-bad.[32]

Ritt's last effort, *Stanley & Iris* (1990), had the odd status of being Jane Fonda's last serious movie and a favorite of First Lady Barbara Bush, who screened it at the White House to publicize a reinvigorated literacy campaign. Adapted by Ravetch and Frank from a Pat Barker novel, *Union Street* (1983), about blue-collar misery in modern New England, it was uneven at best. Fonda does not quite convince as a working-class woman with a difficult life, including a dead-end job at a bakery, a troublesome teenage daughter, an abusive brother-in-law and a sister who takes the abuse. To that add a potential boyfriend and fellow blue-collar worker played by Robert De Niro, who also does not convince as an illiterate who needs help but is too ashamed to admit it. Filming had to be moved from Connecticut to Toronto when several veterans' groups raged against Fonda. Perhaps the contradictions were too much to carry for a little film that could not be advertised as a love story without losing its didactic virtues (and vice versa).

It was an unsuitable ending, as in most cinematic careers. But Ritt had accomplished a great deal. Despite unremittingly hostile critics, the political points had been made decisively. Kael had earlier mused that one could liken *Hud* to *Streetcar Named Desire*, but if *Streetcar* was real theater, *Hud* was something straight "out of Lillian Hellmanland." For Kael, of course, no more hellish location could be imagined.[33]

HELLMAN: A HOUSEHOLD WORD

The New Republic's Stanley Kauffman wrote of Lillian Hellman on the appearance of *Toys in the Attic* in 1963 that she was "the most overrated dramatist of the century." It was an early indication of things to come. The butt of critical attack was not any particular film as such but Hellman the persona. As Bernard Dick pointed out, she didn't actually *write* the movie that Kauffman attacked.[34] It was, rather, the *memories* of the triumphant *Watch On the Rhine* (1943) and *Little Foxes* (1941) or the less triumphant but intriguing and more recent *The Children's Hour* (1961) that actually stirred the reviewer's ire. Everything about Hellman brought up unpleasant recollections in some circles, memories destined to flare into culture wars with the appearance of *Julia* (1977), the veritable high tide of fashionable "Hellmanism" at the corresponding low tide of Cold War (conservative or liberal) prestige.

The idea of Hellman and her place in the culture had always been given too much baggage, but that came with the particular territory she occupied alongside her longtime partner (sexual companion but more important, writing and drinking comrade), the still more legendary Dashiell Hammett. *Dash and Lilly* (1999), an HBO film directed by Kathy Bates and starring Sam Shepard and Judy Davis, followed the two literati from their first meeting in 1930s Hollywood through the war years and on to his imprisonment for refusing to testify, reviving the charisma and capturing the tone of a time when both figures enjoyed favorable media coverage. Shepard was no Jason Robards (who played Hammett in *Julia*), but Davis was more convincing than Jane Fonda, while Bebe Neuwirth of *Dash and Lilly* managed by far the best version of Dorothy Parker so far. Added to the acting, Bates' crisp direction made *Dash and Lilly* one of the more memorable history-based HBO films.

The reputation of the couple stood in marked contrast to the world of highbrow anticommunist liberalism so much in vogue from the early 1950s until the expansion of the U.S. war in Vietnam. Whenever the thirties intellectuals came into the picture, the legacy of the Popular Front seemed always to return to the same divisions among the same competing intellectuals. Notwithstanding literary talent, public reputations and the enthusiasm of reviews in the pages of the prestige publications, there was nothing similarly romantic about Lionel and Diana

Trilling or the rest of their circle, a lamentable fact driven home by the rise of the New Left and the dwindling reputation of the literary giants. When intellectual life returned to something like normal on the campuses after the 1960s, undergraduates in English courses were far more likely to be assigned Alice Walker or the rediscovered Zora Neale Hurston and Tillie Olson than, say, Saul Bellow (practically the only one of the New York intellectuals ever treated fictionally in Hollywood—in a quickly forgotten movie[35]), and this contrast grew more complete as the decades went on. It rankled.

Hellman, by contrast, seemed to come back again and again, with fresh and multiple constituencies, from *New York Times* film commentators to Harvard seminars and film crowds. If film was indeed the political document of the 1970s, as Peter Biskind insists, *Julia* had to be the one film that literally connected the old resistance to capitalism with the new resistance, and Hellman as its source was fashionable once again.

Hellman's popularity in this particular light was ironic because so much of the supposed adventure of Hellman and Hammett must be seen precisely as a response to the pair's bitter disappointments in Hollywood. None of the projects given to him by the studios satisfied, and Hammett hated all the adaptations of his work save the *Thin Man* series (whose screenwriters rapidly outstripped the original) and the second remake of *The Maltese Falcon*. Hellman had several big hits (especially *The Little Foxes*), and the two of them collaborated on *Watch On the Rhine*, but soon enough the scene darkened. She had been set to write an adaptation of the famed Theodore Dreiser novel *Sister Carrie* and was offered one million dollars and an eight-year contract with Columbia that specified no interference with her creative control—if she would sign the loyalty oath personally handed to her by Harry Cohn. She declined and, arguably, had exactly one good film offer during the remainder of her life—a quarter century later.

Hellman continued to work in theater, although without anything like her previous fame, until the 1970s. She was best known as a memoirist during her last 20 years. But she was overwhelmingly best known from the early 1950s onward as a resister to McCarthyism, the naysayer who put the issue most quotably when she wrote that she would not "cut my conscience to fit this year's fashions." This phrase stayed in memory after the choice phrases of the other side (like Sidney Hook's pamphlet, *Heresy, Yes, Conspiracy, No!*, demanding the immediate discharge of disloyal college teachers) were put aside as examples of the embarrassments of the era.

Hellman's initial return to film should have been a decades-delayed bombshell, *The Children's Hour* (1961), recuperated from its heterosexual dilution as *These Three* (1936). William Wyler, who had directed the original and escaped the blacklist with dignity, reprised his role. Wyler took on the producer's task as well but without a script by Hellman, who had backed out in order to care for the terminally ill Dash. John Michael Hayes, whose recent credits had included *Rear Window*, *To Catch a Thief* and *The Man Who Knew Too Much*, stepped in, which was a mistake.

The moment was right, or perhaps only almost right, for the homosexual victim to become a legitimate protagonist. Suggestions of homosexuality had become by that time an avant-garde gesture, although more boldly in British films (*Oscar Wilde* and *The Trials of Oscar Wilde*) than American. The Production Code had actually been changed in 1961, formally allowing homosexuality within tasteful limits because, as is usual in these matters, several major productions were already underway and not to be halted. *The Mark* (1961), written by Sidney Buchman and produced in the United Kingdom, had made a paroled sex offender/pederast the protagonist who did his time, achieved a satisfying heterosexual relationship and still faced the hatred of a fearful, misunderstanding community that was alerted to his presence by the same kind of newspaperman who in the noirs of a decade earlier had inflamed crowds of Californian rednecks. But *The Mark* had no run in the United States, possibly due more to Buchman's own standing than to the controversial nature of the subject.

Female homosexuality was another matter, of course. *The Children's Hour*'s Shirley MacLaine, a more daring actress than she had been allowed, but already cast as a mistress type and destined to become famous as the hooker in *Irma la Douce* (1963), possessed the courage to be the first sympathetic, mainstream Hollywood butch. MacLaine is boyish Helen, whose best friend and school-teacher/partner, Karen, played by Audrey Hepburn, is repressed and severely feminine. (According to MacLaine's later reflections, the two actresses did not even discuss lesbianism off camera because it was considered too difficult by all concerned.) James Garner is the intervening man who lacks the cultural interests of this pair but will win Karen over the anguished protests of Helen. As the drama plays out very much like the original theatrical version and a *Bad Seed*-type child seeks to escape punishment by accusing the two women of sexual relations, the teachers are pilloried and lose the careers they had planned together. Helen then confesses her real feelings and hangs herself (in the play, she shoots herself). In taking in the full weight of the tragedy, the naïve Karen nearly comes to grips with the possibility that she may have had similar stirrings, along with devotion to a friend, and that her feelings ran deeper than any she had for any man, including Garner.

Critics didn't appreciate this film version much, not even in New York, where growing agitation for homosexual rights (nearly all of it phrased in male terms) had gained the quiet sympathy of city officials and prepared the way for the incipient gay liberation movement. Perhaps the mistake lay in the overweening effort to do the old film again and get it right—without the censorship, as Wyler later confessed. Perhaps the subtlety of the intention that had made the Broadway original such a smashing success in the thirties could not be recaptured, at least not by hands other than Hellman's own. Then again, lesbianism itself continued to be a commercial loser, outside of exploitation films made for men, for another 20 years or so. When Kael remarked sarcastically about the film that lesbians deserve sympathy because "there isn't much they can do" (as though they lacked a way of consummating their desire), no voices cried out against the canard—or perhaps none that cried out were heard.[36]

As if to further demonstrate the case, The Fox (1968), adapted by Howard Koch from a D. H. Lawrence novella and directed by Mark Rydell, got no critical credit (and did precious little business) with erotic scenes between feminine Sandy Dennis and butchy Anne Heywood. It was not at all badly done, despite some predictable overacting by Dennis. Their partnership in the wintry woods, broken up by mysterious intruder Keir Dullea, leads to a similarly tragic end, although they accidentally kill him off after he has already spoiled their little heaven through the familiar means of luring the more feminine of the two away from her soulmate. The small-budget, Canadian-made feature seems never to have had a chance.[37]

The next film adapted from Hellman's pen, at any rate, must have been still more disappointing because it was based upon the grand success (her biggest since 1949) on Broadway of Toys in the Attic (1963). Here, she returned to the South she knew as a child and young woman, this time setting it considerably closer to the present than the play and films she had done about the post–Civil War days. Once more, her southern characters scheme relentlessly through an unfolding domestic drama, with the women fortifying their positions at its center. It has often been said by Hellman's admirers that she always was more interested in character than context and that she secretly admired her villains for being so interestingly seductive. Nowhere was it truer than here.

Hellman's 1950s dramas, The Autumn Garden and Montserrat, were both critically admired and both commercial failures. Michael Wilson had tried to recast the latter for film but it went unproduced—a loss, he insisted to an interviewer, of one of his best efforts. Toys followed another small success (The Lark, her adaptation of a French drama) and captured Broadway audiences, running for more than 450 performances. With the worst of the Cold War over and civil rights very much on the agenda, it seemed her time to write about the South had come again.

Once more Hellman fashioned a domestic drama with subtle political lines. A bounder returns home with his childlike wife, "Lilly," and settles in with his two unmarried sisters whom he overburdens with presents and promises of boat-tickets to Europe. Soon enough it becomes clear that he is a swindler and a cheat:

his mistress has a mulatto heritage, a southern "dirty little secret" revealed during the last moments of the play and film. The plot draws to a terrible conclusion as the wife, all too obviously the projection of New Orleans–raised Hellman, relentlessly pursues hidden truths with her husband (a projection of her businessman-father) and the aunts, representations of real if far more benevolent aunts who shared her childhood household.

It is difficult to imagine that even under the best of conditions the film version of *Toys in the Attic* (1963) could have survived the casting of Dean Martin as the lead, although Geraldine Page was brilliant as one of the two scheming aunts and Yvette Mimieux surprisingly credible as the child-like wife. Whatever chance it might otherwise have had was lost, in any case, in the script adaptation by James Poe, a highly skilled writer who had done well for director Robert Aldrich in the screen version of Clifford Odets' *The Big Knife* (1955) and more recently had lived up to his nineteenth-century namesake in his adaptations of southern gothic novels by Tennessee Williams and William Faulkner. This time, though, it was pure stereotype; in Bernard Dick's characterization, the soggy saga of a South reduced to heat and sex.[38] Reviewers were not kind, although for the most part not as aggressively hostile as Kauffman in *The New Republic* nor as determinedly unwilling to grasp that the writer had been deprived of the creative control that might have realized the point of her work.[39]

Hellman reentered film work as a screenwriter in 1959 on a Horton Foote play (written in 1952, with a novel following in 1956) called *The Chase* (1966). The support team should have been perfect: Arthur Penn, who had guided *Toys* on Broadway and whose *Bonnie and Clyde* lay immediately before him, was to direct, and the estimable Hollywood veteran Sam Spiegel produced. Spiegel's own notion was daring, to say the least: metaphorically, the film was about the assassination of John Kennedy, in the sense that the misunderstood convict returning to his home digs will be murdered by an unsympathetic mob, representing (if the viewer could possibly take this in) America at large.

The play had been somewhat of a flop, but the novel was slightly more successful. Hellman tried to straighten out a plot that, quite apart from its ungainly allegory, was both a southern character study and a 1930s–1940s style social drama of a poor boy unfairly treated as a child and now become an embarrassment for the town that would rather forget about him. The decision to have the film cover a 24-hour span offered pitfalls. Casting overshot the mark. Robert Redford, for the best political but all the worst cinematic reasons, served as the returning non-hero "Bubber," Jane Fonda was his nervous wife and Marlon Brando the persistently overacting sheriff. The supporting talent of E. G. Marshall, Robert Duvall and Miriam Hopkins (co-star of *These Three* and the evil aunt in its remake as *The Children's Hour*) was practically wasted.

The film had a few fine or at least well-intended moments. When Christ-like Redford is discovered in a wharf junkyard, the crowd descends on him, amid firecrackers, flares and burning tires in an unmistakable reference to the napalming and carpet-bombing of Vietnam's forests. Like the visuals of the miserable town itself, this is a look at the America of the 1960s exposed after decades or generations of hypocritical self-deception. But a *New York Times* critic was not wrong to call the total result an overheated mess of civil rights themes set in Peyton Place.[40] Perhaps it all came down to the artists' own confusion and despair over the middle 1960s and an evocation of the tragic sense of the era, above all of American democracy's failure to advance over the deaths of victims and martyrs.[41] Hellman herself remarked, after seeing the film in its final form for the first time, that "it is far more painful to have your work mauled about and slicked up than to see it go in a wastebasket," an experience that taught her never again to trust her "old and foolish dream" that a writer could pen a screenplay with the same integrity or self-sufficiency enjoyed in a novel or play.[42]

All the more surprising, then, was the reception a decade later for *Julia* (1977) and the praise, indeed celebrity, heaped upon an aging Hellman by the *New York Times* and all the critics save the hard-bitten Cold War faction. Apart from the film itself, the response was no doubt a combined reflex from Vietnam and Watergate, *MASH* (both film and television) and the sentimental look back at the Old Left that was perfectly realized in *The Way We Were*.

The cold warriors would have their revenge upon Hellman one last time, but not for another decade; by then Vietnam was in the past, Reaganism at full tilt and the Soviet Union nearing collapse. For the moment, however, Hellman was riding high, a literary personage lauded as a civil liberties heroine and senior literary don—quite despite the contested quality of *Pentimento*, the semi-fictional autobiography from which the film was adapted or drawn.[43] Fred Zinnemann, agreeing to direct, made the best imaginable helmsman for her work since William Wyler had guided her southern epics of the 1940s. An émigré Jew sympathetic to his left-wing collaborators since his own breakthrough in the late 1940s and early 1950s, Zinnemann understood the best of her purposes. Screenwriter Alvin Sargent, a television veteran, followed the memoirist as closely as possible. And the casting was considered something of a miracle because British leftwinger Vanessa Redgrave, then at the height of her fame, agreed to play a supporting role, something stars at the time considered almost inconceivable.[44]

Another small miracle: Jane Fonda, in the lead as "Lilly," hewed to her characteristic nervous or hesitant style but with good effect this time (*Coming Home* and *The China Syndrome*, made in the following two years, were her other politically strongest films; she was on a roll that ended with *9 to 5* in 1980). Jason Robards, who might properly be called the Method actor as heavy drinker, proved a near-perfect Dash. But the real center of the film was the friendship of the two women, described admiringly by the *New York Times*' often unsympathetic Janet Maslin as "flawless and astonishingly so."[45]

In *Pentimento*, Lilly gets to grow up as an artist, through Dash's tutoring, and simultaneously learn about fascism, as in *Watch on the Rhine*. The self-sacrificing good German (aka, antifascist red) is not a fatherly Paul Lukas of 1940s vintage but a sisterly Redgrave as "Julia," a Viennese bohemian who had spent college in a Seven Sisters school with the overprivileged Lilly and tried to explain socialist politics as well as (a highly gendered) personal courage to her. The first time it didn't take, except perhaps as an unattainable ideal. Then came Hitler, the *Anschluss*, and renewed contact between them. Lilly is asked to be a courier for the antifascist underground at a certain risk to herself (but not too great: she is still an American citizen, and the United States is not at war with anyone). The Julia who meets her this time in Vienna is a prematurely aged figure with a wooden leg ("no tears," she tells the suddenly distraught Lilly, noticing the artificial limb). The next message from afar to Lilly back home will reveal that Julia has been killed; attempts to locate her child, perhaps saved from the Nazis or perhaps not, will fail.

Nothing remains but memory and what memory means. True to *Pentimento* in successfully simplified form, *Julia* manages to slice back and forth across time and circumstance without losing coherence—a remarkable achievement for any ambitious Hollywood film. No doubt Zinnemann's restraint, both visual and dramatic, contributed greatly to this success. The images seem never tempted to overwhelm (the same, of course, can be said of Sargent's script). Most remarkable as well as most remarked upon is Redgrave, who won an Oscar for best supporting actress.[46]

Inevitably, the two stars were accused of portraying a potential lesbianism, though in this case with no more evidence than Lilly's teenage crush on an idealized role model. Maslin had nevertheless accurately observed, "seldom have two more admirable women loved each other so selflessly on the screen"—as if what had been lost in *The Children's Hour* had been gained back in spades. By this time, such references were considerably less daring than they had been at the dawn of the 1960s. Once more on the cutting edge, Hellman and her celebrity rankled. Perhaps it was a coincidence that Redgrave was savaged for her support of "post-Zionist" multicultural Israel only a few years after Hellman's final memoir, *Scoundrel Time* (1976), brought the wrath of the fading but potent New York intellectuals upon her. Or perhaps, for them, Redgrave was already as guilty of treason as "Hanoi Jane" by her mere appearance in *Julia*.[47]

Manifestoes against Lillian Hellman predictably flared up in the neoconservative press. But the critics were considerably weaker and less influential than they would have been 10 or 20 years previous. This was due not only to the passage of

time and disappearance of personalities since the events described in the movie
but to the difficulty of defending Cold War positions at a moment so near the end
of the Vietnam War. Even Pauline Kael seemed to yield to the spirit of the times
in praising Fred Zinnemann's direction, Jane Fonda's acting and above all Redgrave's queenly presence as Julia. The critic saved a small dose of venom for the
end of The New Yorker essay, suggesting that the movie lacked the necessary anger
of the written story and that, because of the film's constraint on this point, the
quest for "perfectionism has become its own, self-defeating end."[48] In short, it was
beautiful but a failure anyway, doubtless (although she didn't say so) infected
somehow with her old bogey, leftism. Considering Kael had regarded all Popular
Front antifascism as a fraud, this judgment was itself remarkably restrained. It remained mostly to old rivals of female radicalism or liberalism, Mary McCarthy
and Diana Trilling, to rail at the elderly, ill but definitely still on-stage Hellman.

The same critics had one more large and bitter pill to swallow: the films of
screenwriter Waldo Salt. Raised by a depressive, near-suicidal mother and a conservative businessman father in Chicago, Salt had escaped early, graduated from
Stanford at the extraordinary age of 16 and plunged into the Junior Writers division of the Hollywood film colony, where his close friends were all on the Left.
After The Shopworn Angel (1938), his assignments had been so-so, his reputation
as a leading communist intellectual more impressive, to insiders at least, than his
credits. His value had risen sharply just before the blacklist with an Oscar nomination for Rachel and the Stranger (1948) and even higher for The Flame and the
Arrow (1950), a Robin Hood–style action movie starring Burt Lancaster. Producer
Harold Hecht had as much as promised him writer-director status and lots of
money if he could come up with more such films. Then the subpoena arrived, and
he spent the decade drinking as well as bringing out a play (with the collaboration
of fellow blacklistees Earl Robinson, Howard da Silva and Arnold Perl) that did
nothing for his broken career.

Salt earned his way back into film credits with another action picture, Taras
Bulba (1962), featuring Tony Curtis and Yul Brynner in a decidedly upbeat (silly,
actually) adaptation of a Gogol novel. Flight from Ayisha and Wild and Wonderful
(both 1964) followed, and Salt hated them, too. He took little satisfaction in
writing serviceable dramatic television episodes for East Side/West Side and The
Nurses.[49] Then came Midnight Cowboy (1969), the first X-rated film to achieve
mass distribution and one of the most daring Hollywood films ever made.

The impact of Midnight Cowboy on the possibility of an American art film can
hardly be overestimated. Not that there hadn't been artful and successful films
made in the United States before 1969, but who could imagine that Hollywood
might create an art house cinema that could also pack 'em in on Saturday night? If
this possibility did not begin with Midnight Cowboy, then it was certainly crystal-

lized within that screenplay Salt fashioned out of James Leo Herlihy's 1965 novel. It is as though Salt had found the moment when everything was prepared for a radical change in sensibility, starting with himself.[50]

Vowing never again to do hack work, the screenwriter plunged back into familiar territory with Cowboy, this time in a tale of an earnest cowpoke adrift in the big city and the women he meets there who've seen it all.[51] It's really about a little boy in a cowboy suit who never grew up because no one ever taught him how. Somehow, even into his mid-twenties and after a tour in the army (all covered in a single three-second flashback), Joe Buck, played with extraordinary skill by Jon Voight, believes the popular image of a cowboy is still so powerful that he will escape from a lonely life in the Southwest to New York, where well-off women will pay him considerable sums of money to give them pleasure. There he meets Ratso Rizzo (Method actor Dustin Hoffman, in his most challenging and arguably his greatest role), a deformed street hustler who first deceives Joe and then finds in his fellow outcast a last, tenuous connection to humanity.

In the end, the adolescent cowboy who knows how to screw but not how to touch or be touched learns about both by coming to terms with what it means to take responsibility for another person. In these two social castaways humankind is, for a few moments at least, redeemed. Buck, unlike the bewilderingly cruel and deceptive society that surrounds him, learns how to grow up.

The real meaning of Salt's success in transforming the Herlihy novel may be best understood within the decades-old historical battle between screenwriters and studios (or producers) over the importance of dialogue. Since Salt's own days writing Shopworn Angel and before, Hollywood leftists had struggled for artistic control over dialogue to acquire some of the same authority that playwrights in New York, through their guild, had customarily enjoyed. Protection of their dialogue came to represent the full possibility for art and integrity. In Midnight Cowboy, Salt overthrew all of that.

In a very real sense Salt emancipated film from dialogue narrowly conceived by seizing on the stage directions and turning them into a systematic visual exposition of the narrative. These were no longer just helpful asides in the script aimed at a director who was accustomed to cutting the film around the spoken language. This was the screenwriter taking hold of the visual sequencing of the story, in effect calling the camera setups and shooting angles and virtually pre-editing the film in his own mind with the purpose of creating an integrated and detailed representation of what ought to appear on screen. The most highly paid writers sometimes exercised something like this kind of authority, but it was rare, and it had never been granted to a has-been returning from the blacklist.

With this new narrative authority sunk into the artwork (and, not incidentally, into the budget, once approved), the screenwriter could weave new patterns using familiar devices, such as the flashback and the montage, or by inventing new variations on them. In *Midnight Cowboy*, for example, Salt recovered the first half of the novel by presenting it in tight glimpses of memory exhibited against the continuous present of the main narrative, which is entirely derived from the second half. The flashbacks become longer and more complicated, culminating in one particularly complex display of distorted memory (as though from a child's point of view), until Joe Buck's history and motives finally emerge, plain and obvious as a county fair. In another transformation of a familiar device, Joe Buck is seen walking down the same slice of New York sidewalk in four identical two-second shots, given in jump cuts, back and forth from night to day, an extraordinarily simple montage that shows the passage of forty-eight hours in a few heartbeats.

Toward the end of the movie, Salt's screenplay lays out a series of flash-forwards to establish a sense of urgency as the crisis of Rizzo's death approaches, giving the narrative a sense of propulsion and lift in the drive to the resolution. Here was the vindication of the ambitious use of flash-forwards that Harold Pinter would devise for Joseph Losey just a year later in *The Go-Between* (1970) but would be rejected by Losey's producers.

Perhaps what it all added up to, self-consciously or not, was a stab at fulfilling the promise of Abraham Polonsky's "Manifesto for the Screen," published a few years earlier in a French film magazine. The master noiriste argued that in the ideal film, the set of images depicted in the screenplay "would not exhaust the set of images in the film but be the literary paradigm for the work of the director . . . In the end we might escape from the paralysis of naturalism which has for so long distorted the reality of our condition on the screen."[52] Part of Salt's movement toward images and away from dialogue derived from the fact that he was a visual artist of some accomplishment. His screenplays often began as charcoal drawings or as a series of inked figures in scenes doodled on artist's sketch pads, with scraps of dialogue scattered here and there over the images. More often than not the mood of these sketches was dark, but it was also original and internally coherent.[53] This seems to have been the practice that finally led him to his breakthrough in the screenwriting method that was his chief contribution to the Hollywood art film.

Needless to say, this accumulation of narrative authority in the hands of the screenwriter required an unusually generous director, and he was found in John Schlesinger. Schlesinger was so loyal to the project that during some of the difficult later scenes, when Hoffman and Voight struggled to find the right note in the dialogue, the director would sometimes send for Salt to coach them through their effort.[54]

What was it about *Midnight Cowboy* that attracted its considerable audience? The better question might be, what was it about the audience that made a project like *Midnight Cowboy*, hardly a date movie, such a hit? The answer may be found in the fact that it was right around this tumultuous time that the audience, when it came to the cinematic arts, had already had some of the Joe Buck knocked out of them. Tens of thousands of them had been to the art house, had attended a film society screening and had had available to them a few of the newer critical film journals and movie reviews in the rapidly emerging underground press that expressed a sensibility not yet at odds with but somehow different from the often covertly hostile attitudes of mainstream film critics.

In short, there was a new audience for whom cultural issues, at least in popular culture, were often only slightly less important than political issues. With the continuing military draft, these issues could be a matter of life and death. Struggles over that generation's mass art were a struggle for control of politics and culture, including one's life and limb. In *Midnight Cowboy*, then, this audience understood the representation of the dark side of the U.S. society, that the film was speaking the unspeakable, breaking out of "the paralysis of naturalism" and into something new and hopeful.[55]

Only one other movie written by Salt qualifies as art cinema. Undertaking the most explosive and original of the many Hollywood insider novels, by fellow leftist (and until his untimely death in 1940, unsuccessful screenwriter) Nathanael West, and working again with John Schlesinger, Salt undertook to reinterpret the Hollywood he had seen in the 1930s while remaining as loyal as possible to West's highly experimental story. It would not be possible, under these circumstances, to show any real sympathy for any of the main characters.

The casting was superb. A forlorn William Atherton plays the painter who makes himself over into a set designer and comes to Los Angeles to live in the typical colony of bungalows and casitas. Karen Black is the unattainable, screwed-up neighbor who would do anything for a break in the movies but is uninterested in sex. Golden Age Hollywood progressive Burgess Meredith has one of the best roles of his life as her father, a dried-up boozer and vaudevillian turned door-to-door salesman, a racist and an anti-Semite to boot. Donald Sutherland is also at the top of his game as a dumb local hopelessly drawn to the Karen Black character. Meanwhile, rich portrayals in cameo abound, including Geraldine Page as evangelist/hustler Aimee Simple McPherson.

At 144 minutes, *Day of the Locust* (1975) can be a lot to absorb. But most critics considered it a major accomplishment from the moment it was released. The ruthlessness of the studios has never so artfully depicted as here, when the moguls are aware that a set may collapse but indifferent to the consequences. In the depiction of suffering—and on this point the screenplay differs from the novel—Salt and Schlesinger clearly intended to suggest the imminence (from the perspective of 1936) of world war and Holocaust, an impression confirmed by the drawings that artist Atherton makes of faces twisted in agony, and heads like skulls. But the short term is bad enough. In a climax hardly equaled in Hollywood history, a riot breaks out in the midst of a Cecil B. DeMille premiere and the crowd of fans turns into a lynch mob, ripping Sutherland's character limb from limb, dragging stars out of their limos, revealing finally that they are seeking revenge for their own lack of celebrity.

This is, all too clearly, not only a look at Hollywood or Los Angeles but also a look at modern hell, just as West intended, and not something that most fans even two generations later were likely to "enjoy." But Waldo Salt and the rest had something different in mind from the usual popcorn-pushing entertainment. America of the 1970s had to attend to its sins, hubris being high among them. Salt's dark view, the way the world looked to so many sensitive left-wingers after the Cold War destroyed 1940s optimism and the Russian invasion of Hungary ruined old hopes for Eastern Europe, might well have been the America that Joseph Losey would have captured, if only he had been able to work at home.[56]

A *New York Times* reviewer, Vincent Canby, approached the film with something like awe. Rarely had a more faithful reading been given to a great American novel, especially not to one so unyielding in its criticism of Hollywood and the society that nurtured its carnival of artificial values. "Less a film than a gargantuan panorama," showing an endless care for detail on "second-rateness as a way of life," so full that even two hours plus seemed hardly enough to contain it. The actors seemed reduced to "functions of the director and the screenwriter," but managed beautifully nonetheless. When was so great a scale, so many extras, such attention to set, period and costume devoted to capturing "a vision of futility"? Answer: never. Canby was naturally inclined to attribute most of this to the director and the literary source, but the screenwriter was a close third.[57]

Locust was thus a remarkable evocation of film as art. And so it was opposed not only by political conservatives (some of whom considered the film an abomination and wanted it banned) but by critics like Andrew Sarris and Stanley Kauffman. Salt and Schlesinger were guilty, for Sarris, of Marxism warmed over, the stain of the older cinema.[58] Kauffman despised it, too. Lacking so much as a "shred of aesthetic and psychological consistency," *Locust* was horribly cast, directed as if Schlesinger's talent had entirely vanished and in short a disaster that utterly failed to capture the American nightmare of the literary original.[59]

The attacks on *Day of the Locust*, so much like those on *Bonnie and Clyde* at its release, carried no apparent weight either within the industry or outside it. During these years, indeed, Salt made a revitalizing connection with the young Hollywood circles that included his daughter, actress Jennifer Salt, her roommate Margot Kidder and their friends, including Brian De Palma, Martin Scorsese, Donald Sutherland, Richard Dreyfuss and Bruce Dern, among others.[60] It was the first moment of what would become a close interaction with younger film people leading to years of mentoring screenwriters at the Sundance festival.

In this late period, offers came to Salt for many projects, although his notorious perfectionism made him a difficult catch. *The Gang That Couldn't Shoot Straight* (1971), adapted from a Manhattanesque novel by newspaperman Jimmy Breslin, was cast intelligently with Jerry Orbach, Robert De Niro and ex-blacklistee Lionel Stander among the bumbling crooks. It somehow got misdirected and was edited badly. But it was Salt's last failure.

Serpico (1973) was shocking at a time when films about serious and deep-rooted police corruption rather than the occasional rogue cop were rare; films about the honest cop who is hated by his fellow officers were hardly known since 1940s film noir days. The story could hardly be more real, with veteran cop Frank Serpico nearly shot dead for giving testimony to the Knapp Commission, then fleeing abroad. The ex-cop returned long enough to sit in on story conferences with Salt and his collaborator, Norman Wexler, director Lumet (hired six weeks in after producer Dino DeLaurentiis fired a predecessor) and star Al Pacino. Filmed largely in Manhattan stationhouses with the cooperation of the police, and with Lumet urging actors to make creative contributions, the film had the grittiness of urban modernism, including the reality that only low-level corruption is ever likely to be punished. It bore as well a barely muted version of the documentary style found in contemporary films like *Z* or *State of Siege* and the moral energy of Lumet's own directorial film debut, *12 Angry Men*. It boosted Pacino's reputation with an Oscar nomination, likewise screenwriters Wexler and Salt.

Coming Home (1978), co-scripted by Salt with Robert C. Jones and Nancy Dowd and directed by Hal Ashby in the single best film of his career, examined the effects of the Vietnam War on the home front, and the Oscar awarded to the screenwriters could not have been more political. Based on hundreds of one-on-one oral history sessions with Vietnam vets, the result was a depiction of the crisis of maleness after the injuries of war. In something of the spirit of *The Men* (1950), written by Carl Foreman, but freed of sexual censorship, the film had Jon Voight as a vet, paralyzed from the waist down, drawn into a romance with volunteer Jane Fonda who is alienated from her gung-ho vet husband (played by Bruce Dern).

In *Coming Home*, there is no community outside the stricken. Gathered in a rehab center, they painfully find a voice for their absolutely pointless loss, and the returning super-patriot hubby gets his just desserts. He walks into the ocean, a suicide, the loss attributable to American macho "can do" determination to win the war no matter who has to be killed in the process. It was a brilliant success and struck the final note. Salt, seriously ill, never got to make another film.

By 1981 and the presidential inauguration of a B-actor and FBI informer who seemed sincerely convinced that he had actually taken part in the history that he only played on the screen, an epoch seemed to have passed. Neoconservatives who had blasted away at Hollywood and especially at the revived Old Left in Hollywood were invited to the White House, part of the cultural wing of the new team. Good movies were still being made—although now only a few were written or directed by the victims of the blacklist—but they faced increasingly long odds in a Hollywood once more hooked on spectacles. The avant-garde of young directors, including Ashby, Peter Bogdanovich and Paul Schrader, faded almost as quickly as the victims of the blacklist had decades earlier, and with them many of the best opportunities for left-leaning screenwriters. Everything would have to be reinvented once more, but the record of past accomplishments counted for a great deal. Their successors would not have to start all over.[61]

CHAPTER EIGHT

THE LUCID OUTSIDER: JOSEPH LOSEY

ONE OF THE MORE INTRIGUING MOMENTS in the 1991 HBO film *Guilty By Suspicion*, which had been adapted from a screenplay by Abraham Polonsky about his experiences on the blacklist, was the announcement by a director, "Joe Lesser," that he was abandoning Hollywood for England. Accused like the others of being a communist, "Lesser" (played by Martin Scorsese) explains, "Hey, I *am* a communist," thus "guilty," unlike the heroes and heroines of film treatments to come. Without a doubt, Lesser was Losey, and he did indeed make the same trip rather than recant or testify.

More than any other filmmaker on the Left, Joseph Losey overthrew the melodrama as the preferred narrative form for communicating with popular audiences. By the end of that task, accomplished especially (but not exclusively) with the collaboration of British playwright Harold Pinter, Losey rounded off the idea that he had been working toward implicitly throughout most of his career: film as avant-garde, radical theater. His movies may often have expressed a bitter and jaundiced view of the modern human situation, but his autopsies of an empire and a civilization eating away at itself from the inside would stand as among the finest accomplishments of the blacklist generation.

Losey had a background more privileged than most of those in radical theater. Son of a lawyer from La Crosse, Wisconsin, he attended Dartmouth and Harvard, and, like Waldo Salt, would remain very much the gentile in artistic and radical milieux known for their Jewishness. Abandoning a half-started medical career after a near-simultaneous conversion to Marxism and the theater, he plunged into the most popular dramatic forms of the day. During the Depression he directed the Living Newspaper troupe, which under his hand evolved a considerably more sophisticated dramaturgy than the street-corner agitprop of its origins. This early success left its mark on the rest of his career. In one early interview, Losey said that while he had closely studied the theory and practice of the stage, he had never bothered with film theory beyond shooting angles of "certain films."[1] The stage practice that had influenced him most and which he applied to the Living Newspaper had been learned on a visit to Moscow in 1935, where he watched rehearsals directed by Vsevolod Meyerhold. Meyerhold, as we've seen, had been the presiding spirit of the revolutionary stage in the Soviet Union, and it was he who, in 1929, overthrew agitprop in a search for an authentic proletarian drama that also refused to retreat into melodrama.

Losey shared the Meyerholdian impulse with Bertolt Brecht. The two maintained a prickly relationship over most of their lives, even though they never met in person again after the German playwright fled from the United States in 1947. It is this relationship alone that some of Losey's breezier critics use to assert the idea that the theatrical qualities of Losey's films are attributable to Brecht's influence. It would be more accurate to say that Brecht and Losey shared the same Russian radical theatrical tradition, which they applied independently to the stage and film arts, respectively. Meyerhold's theory of "the grotesque" provided the wellspring both for Brecht's epic theater and for Losey's cinema. If the grotesque was only one of the influences on Losey, it provides the continuity between his work as a stage and a film director, stylistically and politically linking the early Losey of Hollywood to the low-budget British features, the mid-career masterpieces with playwright Harold Pinter and finally to the mature films of the late, international Losey.

NEW YORK

During his final years in exile, as Losey struggled past one bad review after another from New York critics, it must have been difficult for the director to remember a much different time and place; during the Depression, the *Times*' Brooks Atkinson had praised Losey's direction of Sinclair Lewis' Civil War play, *Jayhawker*, for its "pleasant air of roguery and mischief," and "lusty feeling of roaring, ranting men."[2] His famous 1936 productions of the Living Newspaper, *Triple-A Plowed Under* and *Injunction Granted!* also were given careful and sympathetic attention, although complaints were made about his "Moscow stylization."[3] A little over a decade later, Losey was laying the foundation for his own kind of art film.

Losey's direction of Brecht's *Galileo* for stage productions in Hollywood and New York in 1947 proved his last significant theatrical effort and the main source of much subsequent characterization of him as a Brechtian (particularly after he directed the film version of *Galileo* in 1974). If Losey did little to discourage this kind of talk, it was because he was eager to be associated with Brecht in any way he could.[4] Aside from predictably hostile Hearst notices, the Hollywood production received respectful reviews. *The New York Times'* L.A. critic, a noted war correspondent, described Losey as "long a disciple of Mr. Brecht's novel ideas on dramatic presentation, who invoked some of them for his late New York Federal Theatre living-newspaper productions."[5] This, of course, was backward; it was Meyerhold, hardly Brecht, who had inspired Losey's approach to the Living Newspaper.

As the Cold War began to close in, the New York production opened (in December), and shortly after Brecht dissembled (without giving names) in front of the committee and slipped out of the country. Losey soon found himself working in exile and under pseudonyms; he would become intimately familiar with the principle that, for the artist in particular, knowledge is a form of suffering.

In the tradition of the European theater, the notion that the first principle of drama is the depiction of *action* is carefully counterbalanced by an equal and contrary principle. The opposite of the verb "to act" in drama is the verb "to suffer," that is, in the older English sense—to be acted upon, to *react*. A firm understanding of this principle had a transforming effect on the American theater in the 1930s as Europeans fled fascism for New York and Hollywood. In film, the thinking actor can be so cunning in his ability to react that he can steal a scene with nothing more than his eyes (giving rise to the saying, "Theater is action, film is reaction").[6] Before this, action in American theater had been largely a matter of depicting action as spectacle in the highly calculated stage realism called melodrama.

The principles of action and suffering go to the very heart of dramatic structure. The playwright's choice of which characters do most of the acting and those who do most of the suffering (though of course all characters must do both) is the social core of the drama. In a broad sense, the answer to the question of who is acting and who is suffering is the same as the answer to this question: which characters know and understand the action and how it affects them, and which do not? There is a third element: the audience. Sometimes it is only the audience that understands the meaning of the action, while the characters remain unenlightened, at least until the end. Broadly speaking, this is comic irony, the formal structure of comedy. If, on the other hand, the characters have a deeper understanding of the action than the audience, it is called tragic irony. And so the question of how much the characters understand the meaning of their own action and suffering, compared to how much the audience is given to understand it, is the key to the drama's social intention.

The art of Joseph Losey resolves this tension between action and suffering in ways uniquely his. For Losey, a character's ignorance—which is to say, his lack of understanding of his own behavior—is a form of dramatic action because it is voluntary, a stubborn refusal to awaken. Ignorance is a *choice*. Many of Losey's films depict this stumbling and confused condition of characters who insist on compounding their ignorance rather than permit themselves to awaken to their social situation.

In short, Losey's chief critical instrument as a dramatist is his persistent use of comic irony for entirely mirthless ends. In *Monsieur Klein,* as we will see, the protagonist's action is his indifference to the effects of his behavior on others. "This does not involve me in any way," he says over and over as circumstances conspire to insist that he awaken. On the other hand, to know—which is to say, to understand how society organizes one's own behavior and the behavior of others—is, in dramatic terms, to suffer. To stop acting in ignorance means to understand how one is acted upon, to be pushed by the pressure of light to the social margin and beyond it, to the status of permanent outsider. As Losey himself found, to know is to pay a price. Ultimately, this knowing is in an unspecified artistic sense the equivalent to the Marxism that he adopted early and never abandoned for softer forms of humanism.

This, then, is Losey's persistent theme. In David Caute's paraphrase of the filmmaker's best critic, English writer Raymond Durgnat, "Losey made the soul 'a battleground' where victory was lucidity."[7] The director never found a way to translate these dramatic issues into explicitly political terms, no doubt because he had relied upon the political Left—until the crisis of Communism in the 1950s— to define those things for him. Abroad, his rage tended to be expressed as a kind of simmering anger at the British class system. He told an interviewer in 1967 that class was "*the* major problem. Almost everything else stems from it."[8] But his more complicated views of class relations were nearly always expressed in dramaturgy.[9]

In the practical elements of the drama, the Meyerholdian impulse showed up right from the start. Losey's first feature film was *The Boy with Green Hair* (1948), a social fantasy (much in the spirit of what the film critics in the French Popular Front had called the *fantastique sociale*) that was co-written by future blacklistees Ben Barzman and Alfred Lewis Levitt. The hair of a "typical American boy" turns green after he learns that he has been orphaned in a London blitz. From this distance it is easy to forget that the film appeared just 24 years after the production in Moscow of Meyerhold's *The Forest,* in which the Russian director mixed naturalism and fantasy in a nineteenth-century setting using nothing more than mismatched period furniture and costuming, achieving his effect by dressing the protagonist as a young woman in an ordinary nineteenth-century dress and putting her in conflict with a young man in a white tennis outfit—and green hair.[10]

Losey's four film features before he fled Hollywood involved the mystery genre that by then had evolved into film noir, and which the Left had refashioned in the late 1940s for its own purposes. All bear the stamp of an impatient but highly skilled artist who badly wanted to break out of the popular formalism of the Hollywood melodrama and connect with something closer to the avant-garde. "I was working in, knew only, the Hollywood mold," he recalled later, "and didn't know that very well. I protested, within myself, against certain aspects of it, but this is what I used . . . up to and including *Blind Date*, at which point, I think, I left it entirely."[11]

Whether he appreciated melodrama or not, Losey was awfully good at it. *The Lawless* (1950) and *The Prowler* (1951) brought the American crime mystery in this period as close to successful neorealism as any director in Hollywood. *Stranger on the Prowl* showed that, even deprived of Hollywood's conveniences, Losey could still put his art across.[12] After *Stranger*, Losey spent most of the 1950s struggling to remain a filmmaker while resisting the familiar forms of Hollywood storytelling. His frustrations with this period poured out in a long and bitter 1960 letter to Adrian Scott in which he compared his situation to that of other blacklistees who were beginning to make some headway in the industry. "I am older than all of you . . . and at the same time younger in the business because I came to Hollywood much later—only after the war."[13]

EARLY YEARS ABROAD

It was true. Moreover, as a director, it was more difficult for Losey to remain anonymous than for writers, and because his films had to make money, he was in a squeeze at once financial and political. The result was a string of 1950s British films, each competent enough in its own right but nothing like *Stranger on the Prowl* in sustained stylistic achievement and with few hints that major films lay just around the corner.

There are, however, several interesting signs of struggle against the received clichés of melodrama. One is the remarkable atmosphere of political menace conjured by *Time Without Pity* (1957, co-scripted with Ben Barzman), in which a desperate journalist, an alcoholic, tries to save his son from hanging for murder. The other, *The Intimate Stranger* (aka *Finger of Guilt*, 1956, co-scripted with Howard Koch) is the story of a film editor who has left Hollywood under mysterious and apparently not altogether honorable circumstances and is drawn into an elaborate blackmail plot by a visiting young American actress who threatens to expose their sexual affair. In both films the conventions of the whodunit are simply dispensed with. The temptation is to read into these two films something of the situation of the director himself, who was notoriously given to bouts with the bottle among other indiscretions—and certainly many of the films have about them an autobiographical aura including more than a little self-criticism, relieved here and there by striking moments, as in the worshipful cinematography of Constance Cummings, his inamorata, in *Intimate Stranger*.

All of these departures from the normal business of cranking out potboilers for the B markets in England and America seem like efforts by a gifted artist to distract himself from the constrictions of the form. There were two exceptions, one often discussed and the other hardly at all. Dirk Bogarde, a little-known actor destined to become the most important homosexual film star in the English-speaking cinema, began his upward climb with *The Sleeping Tiger* (1954), continued with Losey in *The Servant* (1963) and arguably reached his personal best in the often overlooked *Accident* (1967). As Bogarde suggested in a memoir, his relationship with Losey was always uneasy, but Losey early on caught the actor's talent for revealing the dark side of social relations by combining class and a glimpse of the gay assessment of straight gender roles.

The first film after *Stranger, Sleeping Tiger* portrayed an apparently well-meaning psychologist who takes in a petty crook, convinced that psychological support and understanding can cure him. Bogarde's character seduces the wife (played by Alexis Smith), whose betrayal of her husband reveals more about the pretenses of conventional morality than the actions of the seducing rascal. It is the wife who has lost control of herself and dies in a climactic auto crash, while Bogarde's seemingly wicked character remains quizzical at worst. At one level dime-store Freudianism, *The Sleeping Tiger* is best seen as a 1950s counterpart to the Hollywood Left's noir of the previous decade.[14]

These Are the Damned is the most interesting of this group of initial British efforts, though hardly for the reasons commonly cited. What is memorable about the film is admittedly the imagery of radioactive children locked in an underground vault by a national security madman of a still all-too-familiar type. Their radioactivity, expressed as an extreme coldness of the hands, is thought to give them some kind of immunity to the effects of the inevitable next war. The social allegory is unfortunately rather clumsy because the equivalences can only be guessed at. Yet it points infallibly toward some shared fate in the lives of the characters and the audience that lies beyond the cinema doors. The damned come to understand their fate thanks to the intervention of a courageous figure from the Old Left (Macdonald Carey), an exile who, like Losey himself, has washed up on the shores of Britain.[15]

The Damned is actually two films. The inside story is about the kids with updated versions of green hair, and the outer story concerns a bunch of motorcycle teddy boys led by none other than Oliver Reed, who plays a thug incestuously jealous of his attractive sister, whom he uses as bait for his gang to roll tourists. His jealousy, we are indirectly informed, is a compensation for his inability to consummate his own sexual desires. In this spirit too much of the film is spent on Reed slapping around the much older Macdonald Carey for his attention to the sister (Shirley Ann Field). Carey—middle class, lonely and perhaps a bit lecherous—finds Field eager to get out of the confinement of an English port city. The situation is strongly reminiscent of the two lovers in Losey's *Blind Date* (retitled *Chance Meeting* for the U.S. market) of just a few years earlier. In that film, a young Dutch artist succumbs to the seductions of a much older woman, only to discover that she has used him as bait to lure her husband's mistress into a murderous trap. While the relation between prey and predator always has a sexual dimension, Losey insists, no matter how elaborate the game, that the prey is invariably a form of property. Meanwhile, the artificially created younger generation of the atomic age is doomed twice or three times over, whether scientifically prepared for all-out war or left to drift (the teddy boys) in the larger fate of the post-industrial working class. Survivors will be few and not happy—except perhaps to have survived.

FILM ARTIST

With *Eve* (1962), Losey the unsentimental and personally often unsympathetic Marxist begins to heave into view. Now he is fully emancipated from the conventions of melodrama, partly by the film's entirely new jazz rhythms. The film is also full of silences and *longeurs*, annotated by a jazz saxophone which, as the sole American note in his films of this period, is rather like the brooding presence of the director himself far in the background.

Eve is also self-conscious and highly mannered, closer to Fellini and Antonioni in tone than to anything Losey had done before or would indulge in later. It has about it the flavor of the European genre that Pauline Kael described as "the-come-dressed-as-the-sick-soul-of-Europe parties."[16] But if Losey in *Eve* was not yet emancipated as an artist (he was still mostly an inexpensive hire for producers looking to exploit the blacklist), he had come close to it. To the extent that a single event can be said to commemorate that moment, it was the appearance in September 1960 of a special issue of the presiding film magazine of the day, *Cahiers du Cinema*, on the works of Losey. Here, the reputation-making editors collectively swooned over his mastery of *mise en scène*.

This was the critical attention that launched what remains, after all these years, of the Losey cachet. It allowed him to raise the money to make *Eve* and along the way to hire the trendy French composer Michel Legrand (who had worked with *nouvelle vague* auteurs, including Jean-Luc Godard). He also had on hand the interesting Welsh actor Stanley Baker, who had earlier appeared in Losey's *Blind Date* (1958) and *The Criminal* (1960) and had formed a close attachment to another blacklisted American director, Cy Endfield, in a half-dozen of his features, culminating in Endfield's best, *Zulu* (1964) and *The Sands of the Kalahari* (1965). Baker was perfect for the male lead in *Eve*. The actor's brother had died of black lung acquired from the coal pits and his father lost a leg in them. Politically as well, he was compatible with the director: After the actor's death, his widow, in an interview with a popular biographer, casually referred to her husband's "terribly profound commitment to Socialism."[17]

The moment was prepared, then, for a sexy, stylish and intense film cut to the cinematic equivalent of a black cocktail dress, and that's what *Eve* was, at least before the producers had it recut. After viewing the most complete version available in 1966, English critic Kenneth Tynan considered *Eve* the equal of *The Servant*.[18]

Here's the story. Some while before the action of *Eve* begins, a Welsh miner has apparently drunk himself to death after finishing a first-rate novel. His brother (played by Baker) puts his own name on the book and reaps the rewards of both the novel and the subsequent film. At the height of success, after he has bought a mansion on his own Italian island and become engaged to the exquisite Verna Lisi, he meets the figure of the title, a high-class prostitute played with great slyness and understanding (she loves American blues and jazz records) by Jeanne Moreau. She is insolent, cynical, wise and corrupt—even more than the Baker character, and thus the only other person in a position to understand him or to forgive him, since he is far too corrupt to forgive himself for stealing his brother's life. He throws himself at her a half-dozen times, like a series of waves breaking on a shoreline, until, rejected and humiliated by the time the movie shudders to a halt, the Baker character has lost everything (including Verna Lisi) and become an alcoholic slave to a hooker. So ends Losey's social allegory about the fate of the working class, with perhaps more literalness than might have been strictly necessary.

But as *Eve* looks back at *Blind Date* and *The Damned*, it also looks forward to *King and Country*, *The Servant* and *Accident*, Losey's best and most enduring films. *Eve* represents his aesthetic fulcrum, marking the first appearance in full of Losey's grand theme, namely that bourgeois sexuality is an acting-out of property relations. This dramatization evokes not only the Meyerholdian grotesque but at times touches on the grotesqueries of another tradition, the Grand Guignol, a form of low realism that amused the Parisian ruling class and haute bourgeoisie in the back streets of the late Victorian/Edwardian era.[19]

Jean-Pierre Coursodon is typical of those critics who recoiled from Losey's depiction of sexuality, calling it the "masochism [that] finds its way into all his plots under one guise or another." *Modesty Blaise* (1966), Losey's big-budget pop fantasy taken from a comic strip with scarcely a plot in sight (lead Dirk Bogarde tries to make the best of a bad situation, and sex star Monica Vitti is simply embarrassing), was for the astute Coursodon no more than "one S&M fantasy after another."[20] And it's true that sexuality was playing an ever more important role in Losey's films. But the same was true of the rest of U.S. and European cinema in this period, not merely to please the crowds but, as the cultural counterpart to the political movements of the time, a rebellion against the stranglehold of the Cold War on the libido.

Practically unique to Losey, however, is the use of sexuality to describe class relations. If there is an air of self-disgust in some of Losey's work, it is matched by his disgust for just about everyone else, from his representation of twitty and effete ruling-class characters to the calculated mutual exploitations of the middle classes, and the febrile working class unable to act in its own interests. Precisely here Losey is least understood, because it is in sexuality that he brings to bear the full armament of the grotesque.

Losey loves to display for his audience all of the pleasures of bourgeois manners, and then, after the gradual insinuation of one slightly disturbing element after another, raise the lid from the system of class relations for which the drama or comedy of manners is merely a culinary distraction. *Eve* also introduced Losey's second grand theme, which he shared to some degree with the disillusioned socialist dramatist of the 1950s' "Angry Young Men" in theatrical England, Arnold Wesker; namely, the backwardness, weakness and displaced patriarchal violence of a working class that missed the opportunity to rid itself of its oppressors and now wanders about the stage of history in search of a narrative.[21]

It is hard to say which of these themes in *Eve* and the rest of this cycle of films is developed more contemptuously or more effectively. It was a style of filmmaking forged on the anvil of political failure, the fear of poverty and the personal humiliation of an already irascible and not particularly likeable artist who was hounded out of his home and profession and sometimes even the editing room (as when the hackish Hakims, producer-brothers with a bankroll for outré projects, brought in their own cutter to dismember the first version of *Eve*). The result is a style of film noir unmediated by any of the accustomed virtues of melodrama at its most disciplined—the proletarian happy ending, the celebrations of a darker eros—and is instead subtended by a neorealism stripped of Rossellini's spirituality, a realism unleavened with compensating uplift about the class struggle. It is just this: a cold, hard look.

That *King and Country* (1964) is a masterpiece of antiwar filmmaking is evident from the moment of the last pistol shot. And we must discuss the ending first, for the entire film rises and falls on its last few moments, when the fate of the soldier Hamp (played in his best proletarian style by Tom Courtenay) is decided after members of a firing squad have refused to kill him. The job is taken over by an officer, Captain Hargreaves (Dirk Bogarde), who cradles Hamp's head in one hand and then shoots him in the mouth with his regimental pistol. It is an act of extraordinary cold-bloodedness, for the officer is none other than the lawyer who has argued the case against the death penalty for Hamp, explaining that the soldier accused of desertion deserved forgiveness because he was disoriented by the exhaustion of too many years at war and bad news from home. This brutal ending is prefigured by an exchange at the end of the trial when Hamp thanks his lawyer for "having spoken the truth so well." The answer comes like a pistol shot from Hargreaves, who remarks, philosophically, "I only did my duty—a pity you didn't do yours."

The officers' panel decides that Hamp must be made an example of; they are organizing another attack, after all, and the boys must be "encouraged" to keep up discipline. In the final scene, some of the soldiers mount a modest mutiny by shooting past the figure of Hamp, bound with ropes to a wooden chair that has fallen over into the mud. When one of the officers peels the blindfold off Hamp's eyes and finds that he is still alive, Hargreaves steps forward and asks the wounded soldier, "Isn't it finished yet?" Hamp responds, "No, sir. I'm sorry." And with that, Hargreaves dispatches the boy with his sidearm.

Among the many antiwar films made by the blacklistees and their immediate circle of sympathizers—Dalton Trumbo's *Johnny Got His Gun*, Robert Aldrich's *Attack*, Waldo Salt's *Coming Home*—Losey's *King and Country* comes closest to an uncompromising dramatic production that preserves the power and immediacy of theater on film and very much *as* film. This is the fulfillment of the old promise and dream of the Depression of a film medium that reaches beyond the middle classes to the people it takes as its subject.

Whether most of the viewers, in their normal movie house search for escape from the anxieties of daily life, really understood the intentions of *King and Country* is another question. But the average recruit or a young man contemplating his fate in a wartime draft (for the British lad, the Suez Crisis was just a few years earlier) would come away from this film with impressions entirely different from those harvested by some middle-class critics. "Horrific as that moment is," observe the co-authors of *The Films of Joseph Losey* about the shooting of Hamp through the mouth, "the anguish here is as much Hargreaves's as Hamp's."[22] One would have thought that, in the act of perishing, Hamp could claim rather more of the anguish than his executioner. But the point of this moment in the narrative has less to do with either character's anguish than with Losey's disgust for the ruling class' willingness to subordinate every shred of decency, everything within the circle of its authority, to the close-order drill of established class relations. It is also Losey's farewell to the working class that, in the pitiful figure of Hamp, apologizes for any inconvenience it might have caused on its way to oblivion.

This is surely rough stuff for the traditions of Hollywood's Old Left. But perhaps it instigated in its younger male audience a round of conscientious objection. If Losey is open here to any spiritual critique it is that, in his despair, he has lost faith not only in the working class but in history as well.

King and Country has about it more of a sense of exasperation than accumulated wisdom. It is too outraged to be content with wisdom, and that may be its greatest strength. Here, Losey summed up several decades of work. Now it was time to move on to a larger exploration of the grotesque. The opportunity arrived in the person of a playwright just as angry and frustrated as he, in an artistic collaboration that was to be the highpoint of Losey's career.

ENTER PINTER

"Those of us who enjoy private incomes, however small, or the affluence of relations, cannot know the insecurity which haunts those who have no money and no refuge."
—Robin Maugham, "The Servant" (1948)

The author of those words, written without the slightest irony, was the son of a Lord Chancellor, First Viscount Frederic Herbert Maugham and nephew of novelist W. Somerset Maugham. By the time Harold Pinter had finished with the screenplay, Maugham's fable would be transfigured from a dark little tale of jealousy and resentment against the lower orders into an unforgettable representation of an upper class whose every step had grown dangerous because of the rot in the floorboards.

Harold Pinter was still up and coming when Losey saw the playwright's first TV production and immediately offered him the chance to do the screenplay for *The Servant*. Both the spareness of the story and its subject matter were very much Pinter's cup of tea—which he promptly inverted, looking at class relations from the bottom up (and from the outside in). It was this relatively brief but intense relationship with Pinter that completed the arc of Losey's ambition to raise the radical theater to the peak of its dramatic and critical powers and to take the result directly to the masses. It would also represent a kind of reconciliation of high modernism to popular art.

Within a few years after the collaboration began, Pinter would be recognized as one of the central figures in modern English theater. He has been called a leftist who embraces conservative aesthetics—a useful enough characterization, but one that hides a larger truth. Pinter embraced a certain kind of literary modernism at about the same time that many other artists and intellectuals had discovered its power to emancipate writers from the cant of a language too often sunk in the left-wing equivalent of melodrama and uplift.

Pinter was an autodidact whose education derived for the most part from the years he spent knocking about England and Ireland as an actor in repertory theater. After mouthing the lines of standard characters in whodunits and comic romances, the stripped-down language of Samuel Beckett made an extraordinary impression on him. When he began to write, he followed Beckett by throwing out all of the elements of dramaturgy except space, time and what little dialogue was necessary to create the context for dramatic action. As aesthetic practice, it seemed conservative because of its extreme formalism. But in practice, it evolved into something quite different. "From the start, Pinter was alert to the political power, as well as the distress, of silence," his biographer acutely observed.[23] Put simply, all of his plays would consume their characters in a struggle for power.

Both of Pinter's parents were Russian Jewish immigrants, one of whom was devotedly secular and the other mildly observant, with a deep interest in the arts. The future playwright grew up in a working-class area of London to which he always remained attached, and he was poor for nearly the first half of his life. In 1948, he became a "conchie"—a conscientious objector to war. During the war in Vietnam, Pinter became one of the most outspoken British critics of U.S. policies and he remained so down to the U.S. wars of 2002–2003 on Afghanistan and the Middle East. But Pinter enjoyed the boisterous vulgarity of American popular culture even as he disdained the Pentagon and the presidents. One critic, making a point about music hall comedy, noted shrewdly that the ideal casting for the two men in one of Pinter's most famous plays, The Dumb Waiter, would have been Bud Abbott and Lou Costello.[24]

Pinter and Losey had two things in common: an aversion to the habits of the middle class and a love for expressing it aggressively, forcefully and even brutally in the large and small narrative displacements of the grotesque and its exaggerations. In addition, Losey had a special regard for the English aristocracy, whom he seemed to admire for its carelessness, adolescent cruelty, self-deluded ability to live outside society's all-consuming cash nexus and, at least in its own circles, within a kind of loony democracy. Raymond Carr, an Oxford figure knowledgeable about the events depicted in Accident, may not have been far off when he called Losey "a cinematic Proust, fascinated by the upper crust, even a snob."[25] For an American used to a society largely ruled by a corporate class with lower-middle class tastes, the aristocracy was very likely at the very least a welcome change of pace.

In the original version of The Servant inscribed in the Maugham novella, Tony (the James Fox character) is an officer very much like Hargreaves. He has served as a tank commander in World War II North Africa, and he takes on a "manservant" to look after him while he devotes his energies to studying for the bar. Barrett, the servant, is a servile sort with pretensions to an advanced taste in everything from food to flowers.[26] He understands how to manipulate everyone around him by giving them exactly what they secretly desire. In Tony's case, it's the repose of creature comforts. Barrett even changes the socks on his master's feet.

After Tony has become utterly dependant on Barrett, the servant plays his trump. He introduces his 16-year-old "niece" to Tony, and she moves in. As Tony is incautious when it comes to drinking, it is not long before he and the girl excite each other's passions—considerably helped in her case by the fact, again asserted with no trace of irony by Maugham, that she is a "nymphomaniac." Now Tony is twice dependent. By the end, Barrett has begun to supply a steady stream of other 16-year-olds for his own and Tony's mutual pleasure, with Barrett seizing control over Tony's private income.

It is rather startling, reading the source novel against the Pinter and Losey film, to realize that Maugham's conclusion to the tale of The Servant is darker and altogether more sordid than the filmmakers'. Pinter removed the temptations represented by adolescent girls and set Tony and Barrett at each others' throats in a kind of psychotic descending fugue into indolence, confusion to squalor. The only thing that rescues the pair is Barrett's own pathetic clutching at the remnants of his lower-middle class pretensions. The film's "orgy scene," implied more than depicted, restores the story to the social dimension with one of the most shocking kisses in cinematic history. Barrett, the drunken and impudent servant, kisses his master's girlfriend—and the squeamishness of the audience is provoked nearly to nausea when it becomes obvious that his daring has actually aroused her. Nothing of this sort occurs in the book.

Maugham's novella also provides an answer to lingering speculations about homosexual content in The Servant. In the novel, homosexuality makes an appearance in silhouette in the backstory, but only as a suggestion in the friendship between the narrator and Tony, and never in connection with the servant himself. Before he died in 1981, Maugham wrote at least two novels with frankly gay themes (The Last Encounter and The Sign, both published in 1973), but in his 1948 novella the matter was handled with the kind of casual tact that gentlemen with public school backgrounds hardly needed to enunciate.

What Pinter preserved from the novella was Maugham's revulsion at Tony's degradation—but in Pinter's hands the degradation was no longer entirely or necessarily sexual. Much more terrifying, in Maugham's original notion, was the utter incapacity of either the gentleman or the manservant to maintain their class relations. This failure turns them into monsters. Together they create a void into which the emotional wastewater of the class system trickles, then pools then sumps. By comparison with this fundamental "corruption," sexuality of any sort is merely symptomatic and incidental. Of course, what Maugham presents as horrifying, Pinter depicts as grandly ridiculous, one of the best applications of the stage practice of "the grotesque" in all of film history.

Then as now, *The Servant* is listed as among the top two or three films of 1963, and its effect on filmmaking and on the culture at large was (and arguably, remains) enormous. Writing in the *New York Times* in 2001, film historian David Thomson called it "a movie that altered England's sense of itself."[27] Stylistically, the film referred to many elements of left-wing filmmaking of the preceding 25 years, including French poetic realism and the *social fantastique*, Italian neorealism and Fellini and even a bit of Hollywood noir. But it was more than the sum of these many parts because of Pinter. The seamless collaboration between the writer and director raised for the first time the prospect of an art cinema at once intelligent and uncompromising and as political as it needed to be. *The Servant* was, then, correctly seen as a hammer blow to the class system and would place it among the most memorable Marxist films ever made.

Losey biographer David Caute states flatly, with no need for insistence, that the pair's next collaboration, *Accident,* is the director's best film.[28] Not many students of Losey's films would dispute this judgment. There are defenders of *The Servant,* and even a few holdouts for his filmed version of Mozart's *Don Giovanni,* a masterpiece of a much different kind. But *Accident* holds a special place for its technical perfection and its dramatic power.

Again, the text is from the hand of an aristocrat of sorts, although that is hardly the most interesting thing about the author. Novelist Nicholas Mosley was the son of the third baronet of Staffordshire—Oswald Mosley, the famous leader of the British Union of Fascists. When the novel *Accident* was published, Nicholas Mosley considered himself non-political and an ardent Christian.[29] In fact, he intended it to be a tale of "spiritual improvement," according to his autobiography.[30] Instead, it suffered the same ironic fate as Maugham's story.

Once more it is necessary to start with the ending, for in true film noir fashion Losey opens the film close to its resolution and then tells the rest of the story in flashback. In the dead of night, on a remote rural road, a car crashes and overturns in front of the home of Stephen, a philosophy don at Oxford (Dirk Bogarde). When the don investigates, he finds the unconscious figures of two of the undergraduates he has been tutoring, a young man and woman, both aristocrats. The young man is dead. Stephen helps the Austrian princess Anna into his home and calls the police, and when they arrive he neglects to inform them that Anna, the drunken and unlicensed driver of the car, has passed out in his bedroom in a state of shock.

And so the moral question is posed: is it a lie to withhold critical information if one is never asked about it? Close to the end of the novel, Stephen and his close friend and fellow don, Charlie (Stanley Baker), debate this question at some length in what Mosley considered the moral heart of his story.

The question was complicated by the erotic facts of the case. The married Charlie had been having an affair with Anna, and the young aristocrat lying dead in the car, William (Michael York), had been engaged to marry her. Stephen, too, lusted after Anna despite the fact that at the moment of the accident his wife was giving birth to their third child in a hospital in another town.

In the novel, Stephen never achieves his seduction, and neither he nor Charlie reveal to the police the truth of who was driving the car. Their silences cover for—but do not cover up—Charlie's affair with Anna and Stephen's complicity in it, for the philosopher had played the pimp by providing his home for their assignations while his pregnant wife was away. His unmistakable motive had been the hope that he could cadge a bit of sex from Anna as well.

If Stephen's help in the coverup of Anna's culpability in William's death seems an unlikely example of "spiritual improvement," Mosley claimed that his own religious conversion owed to his surprise in discovering that, despite his youthful revulsion at the adultery in his parents' social circle, he too had succumbed to the practice. And so the novel presents the web of betrayal and bad faith with such eerie casualness (much like Maugham's novella) that Mosley seems to have assumed that his readers would find in his story a familiar part of their own lives. If that were true, *any* movement toward self-restraint could be characterized as "improvement."

Imagine, then, the effect on the story when Pinter throws out the concluding scene between Stephen and Charlie, Mosley's intended moral fulcrum of the novel, and instead has Stephen copulate with the helpless Anna, in a state of clinical shock from the collision, on his wife's bed: an obvious act of sexual blackmail for protecting her from the police. It is very close to a rape and not without a hint of necrophilia. It is also one of the single most powerful scenes in any of Losey's films, for it completes the critique of bourgeois sexuality that had until now only been implied. This is the undisguised sexuality of property relations, a colonialism of the body and the senses, a marking of territory distinguished from the habits of canines only by its privacy. In short, *Accident* has become the Mosley story with the skin off. The result was no act of spiritual improvement but of revelation and class revenge.

After two such extraordinary films, Losey and Pinter had one more production together. The themes were similar in many ways, but the treatment was quite different. This time, the hallmark was subtlety. In a way, it had to be.

One could hardly blame a craftsman like L. P. Hartley, author of the 1967 novel that was to be Losey and Pinter's next project, for his initial horror at the idea that the auteurs of *The Servant* and *Accident* were about to fasten on to his work. He needn't have worried, as Hartley realized after he read the first draft of Pinter's screenplay. Pinter was respectful of a story that several times had moved him to tears. The playwright's treatment was, Hartley pronounced, "splendid."[31]

The Go-Between is the Proustian recollection and reflection of a man in his mid-60s about events in the summer of 1900, the year he turned 13 years old. The man has discovered his schoolboy's notebook from that year and reconstructs from it his month in the country visiting a schoolmate, whose beautiful older sister drew him into the role of messenger in a forbidden romance that has consequences over three generations.

The sister, Marian (Julie Christie), is in love with a tenant farmer (Alan Bates), and both lovers rather carelessly use the boy as a courier to carry notes of assignation back and forth. During the course of this passionate affair, Marian becomes engaged to an aristocrat, the Viscount Trimingham (Edward Fox), whose family line, now fallen on hard times, built the estate on which Marian's family lives. The marriage is commanded not only by Marian's mother but by every convention of English society, for it will provide the viscount ownership of his ancestral home and Marian with a title. Marian fully accepts this. There is no lunge toward American melodrama, in which true love will somehow find a way to triumph over the barriers of class. On the contrary, Marian understands that the pleasures of her affair with the farmer are her due for entering agreeably into a lifelong relationship that will have many comforts but little passion.

The climax of the story comes when Marian's mother, upon discovering her absence from a family celebration, suddenly confirms her suspicions about her daughter's affair and, under the pretext of ordering the schoolboy to guide her to the trysting spot, drags the protesting child there by the arm. When they find daughter and farmer *in delicto*, the mother loses her senses. The farmer, meanwhile, goes home and kills himself with a shotgun. The boy is so badly traumatized (we find out later in a kind of epilogue) that he remains a virgin for his entire life. Meanwhile, Marian and the viscount emerge from the revelations without a scratch. Their social position after the marriage protects them from any consequences more serious than gossip—even though Marian, seven months after the wedding, gives birth to what must be the farmer's son.

Some 50 years later, the man who was that messenger boy returns to the country town to uncover the details of the fate of the people in the story. He finds Marian, now in her seventies, unrepentant; her grandson, the latest edition of the Viscount Trimingham, resentful of ancient sins and hesitant to marry, not out of guilt but apparently because of the biological compromise to his family of the interloping farmer's genes.

The film did not depart from the story in detail or in spirit. In technique it offered something very new—too new for the industry's decision-makers. Once again Losey found himself the victim of nervous producers, although what they proposed was hardly the butchery that had been performed on *Eve*. This time, he may even have acquiesced to the cuts because of the tantalizing realization that he might have a hit on his hands.

Pinter's screenplay had broken up the novel's epilogue of the old man's return to the town into a series of brief scenes with no dialogue that were to be inserted throughout the narrative. These foreshadowings, all of which were cut, were to serve as a counterpoint to the action and to have the gradual effect of revealing the old man as the storyteller, or more precisely, as the possessor of the memory unfolding on the screen. These foreshadowings were intended to relieve the march of the story, using a technique the filmmakers called "flash-forwards." Clearly, Pinter and Losey were looking for an alternative to the hackneyed voice-over narrator. They sought to use the oneiric advantages of film to show how memory is interleaved with the present, how the past inhabits it and sometimes imprisons its best possibilities. It was a most Proustian ambition.[32]

Losey got the long-postponed hit his career (and his fortunes) so badly needed. But the cost to the film was considerable. There may be worthier film restoration projects, but surely a reconstruction of *The Go-Between* based on Pinter's screenplay is high on the list. In its current form, the film's ending trails off into ambiguity: yes, the old man continues in his role as a go-between to the very end (by negotiating with the aged Christie over her interpretation of the past), but he also resumes his role as an utterly clueless narrator of his own history. Meanwhile, Marian's romantic egoism magnificently asserts the right to pleasure but ignores the consequences of her behavior in a rigid class society, whether in the ancient "boy" before her or in the farmer's suicide. The flash-forwards would have preserved the comic irony, which was designed to bring the audience to an understanding of events that lay well beyond the capacity of the characters (the old man most particularly), since their imprisonment in the social system made it impossible.

One point unites the three films of this great collaboration. While all three obviously take as their cinematic meat the consequences of sex across class lines, the larger unity is in the incomprehension of the characters about themselves as social creatures. It is this utter lack of understanding that makes them incapable of tragic stature. Taken as a whole, the three films mark the highpoint of Marxian filmmaking of the blacklist era and the definitive reconciliation of high modernism with radical theater.

If there was a way of summing up the political point in *The Servant*, *Accident* and *The Go-Between*, we can look to Walter Benjamin: "Proust describes a class which is everywhere pledged to camouflage its material basis and which for this very reason is attached to a feudalism lacking any intrinsic economic significance but all the more serviceable as a mask of the upper-middle class."[33]

LATE LOSEY

That the Losey-Pinter collaboration had not been exhausted is evident in *The Proust Screenplay*, an ambitious attempt to contain the sense of À *la recherche du temps perdu* in 455 shots over some 3 hours. But the project would exhaust the commercial limits of filmmaking then as now, for while the screenplay has been adapted for the stage, it has never been produced as a film. On paper, there is a sense that the flash-forwards cut from *The Go-Between* had opened some doors for the filmmakers that they wanted to explore. In the unproduced screenplay, no fewer than 35 scenes—the slightest intimations of what is to come—are intercut before a single line of dialogue is spoken. The direction for a "momentary yellow screen" appears several times without explanation, until finally in the fourth or fifth such shot the camera pulls back to reveal that the color is a patch of yellow wall in a Dutch painting. But to whom does the perceiving eye belong? The cinematic question has never been answered cinematically.

Although he afterward made a number of good films, many of them were unanswered questions. *Modesty Blaise* (1966), *Boom* and *Secret Ceremony* (both 1968), all of which he had turned out between *King and Country* and *The Go-Between*, had the air of projects that started out with high hopes and then were shuffled through listlessly when disappointment set in over the quality of the raw material. Some of that must have had to do with his brush with the Burtons, Richard and Elizabeth, who enter the scene at this point, though their first mention in the same breath with Losey was (however improbably) as proposed cast members for *Accident*. If filmgoers were spared that, however, they were not protected from their appearance in *Boom* which, because of a highly attenuated Tennessee Williams screenplay, was a botch. (It boiled down to this: death is a thief.)

Modesty Blaise, a sort of pre-feminist satire on the popular James Bond films, captured a bit of the popular optimism in the youth culture of 1964–1967 but yields no mysteries to patient study, only a latent sympathy for the Arab situation under British imperialism (and the wonderful joke at the end, when villain Dirk Bogarde, his limbs staked to the sand and his lips cracking, calls deliriously, "Champagne! Champagne!"). *Secret Ceremony* had a subdued Elizabeth Taylor playing the ersatz mother to a disturbed young heiress, Mia Farrow, in another tale of mutual dependence in a fantasy world. If it sounds like an echo of *The Servant*, it was, but the genre was strictly commercial gothic.

One of the puzzling things about these projects is that Losey, who for many years seemed anxious to turn out careful work even under pseudonyms and labored to free himself from the conventions of melodrama, now assumed an air of such insouciance. "I stopped somewhere along the line—I guess at *Eve*, maybe—making that kind of picture," he told an interviewer in this period, "and have been much more interested in pictures of provocation."[34] Perhaps that was explanation enough. But what could explain the indifference to his subject in his next film?

In 1972, Losey was 62 years old, and while he had some bad luck, it was nothing compared to the train wreck of his next film, a biopic of Trotsky. The failure seems to have derived from his weariness (perhaps even his ambivalence) over old political battles. While he had reveled in skewering the upper-middle class, particularly when he could use the aristocracy as a foil, it was something altogether different to use his prominence to wade into the internecine battles of the Left itself.

The Assassination of Trotsky was written and shot rigidly, in the spirit of a docudrama. By all accounts, it had started out rather more promisingly as a quasi–Popular Front melodrama dealing with one of the worst crimes of the once-admired Soviet leadership. The first draft had been written by another blacklisted (former) U.S. communist, Ring Lardner, Jr.'s old friend and frequent collaborator, Ian McLellan Hunter, in the Hollywood noir style—but was rejected after the French star Alain Delon expressed his misgivings and after Hunter returned to the U.S. because of illness.[35] Then Losey, in a fatal error, called on Nicholas Mosley, a writer even further out of his depth for this subject than Losey himself. The director insisted that he had wanted to remove from the script any unmouthable (for an actor) "Marxist jargon"—though nothing of this sort ever showed up in the rest of Hunter's writing—and so he turned to the least political, not to mention least experienced, screenwriter he knew. The mistake must have been somehow deliberate, even if unconsciously.

Losey's state of mind before shooting started is revealed in his response to the thousandth well-intentioned suggestion, from another left-wing friend, on the course he should take: "I can absorb no more."[36] He had been buffeted on all sides with advice about the sectarian disputes of twentieth-century socialism and seems to have gone into production, with the dreadful miscasting of Richard Burton as Trotsky, in a fatalistic mood that guaranteed a static and nonpolitical result. Trotsky was indeed often egotistical and personally overbearing, in some small measure the author of his own political downfall. But he was also fundamentally correct about the disaster that Stalin had perpetrated upon the world revolution. Even if his strategic alternatives persuaded few and even prompted continual splits (over the precisely correct political positions) among his scattered followers, still he knew betrayal when he saw it.

Burton was merely incoherent, as if Burton the working-class aesthete who despised both Brecht and the political Left were actually playing Burton the millionaire-celebrity blowhard rather than a sophisticated Marxist theorist and former commander of the Red Army.[37] Only the assassin seems on the mark, because only a psychotic could carry through such a task, regardless of ideology.

The internal evidence of his later films, particularly *Roads to the South*, shows that, despite his reputation as a growling Stalinist reprobate, Losey had actually come to terms with the New Left critique of bureaucratic state communism.[38] Perhaps, like most other leftists who felt the point had been obvious for decades and who refused to join Cold War liberals and conservatives in the flogging of a horse that was so obviously deceased, he simply preferred to err on the side of subtlety and silence.

Vastly riper with real rather than imagined political opportunities was another film from this period, an adaptation for the screen of Henrik Ibsen's *A Doll's House*, with Jane Fonda in the lead role. Decades later, it remains one of Losey's most widely available and accessible films—its success attributable in great part to the director's skill at avoiding staginess and to Fonda's equally skillful and openhearted depiction of Nora. By the time an astonished Torvald (David Warner) manages to squeak out his closing plea, "I have the strength to change," Nora is on her way to slamming the famous door on the nineteenth century and effectively asserting once again the power of Ibsen's drama. Despite the widely reported tumultuous sexual politics on the set during filming, the success of the production was never really in doubt. Given the film's extraordinary depth of talent, not much more was needed than a serviceable version of Ibsen's script.

It was the screenplay that was the heart of the famous struggle for artistic control between Fonda and Losey. The best account of this dispute depicts a rather aloof actress sweeping into the production and handing out new pages for the actors with changes in dialogue.[39] Losey is shown as on the defensive—mostly defending Ibsen's intentions, that is—while personally flattering Fonda and trying to isolate her from her feminist retinue. A few of the changes described by a Fonda biographer do seem to have altered Ibsen's intentions somewhat (notably the attempt to write Nora's flirtatiousness out of a key scene).[40] But there is also little doubt that Fonda's insistence on restoring some of the lines that had been deleted by screenwriter David Mercer, including one that underscored the fact that a woman could not lawfully borrow money without her husband's consent, did strengthen the political content of the film.[41] However indiscreet she may have been about handing out pages, the evidence shows that Fonda was nonetheless defending Ibsen as best she could.

The film's production history, then, captures or encapsulates the spirit of the time, in the collisions between radical old men who understood feminism rather abstractly and radical young women who felt it viscerally, between those who helplessly watched the progress of a vicious war from a distance and those who had thrown themselves, as they believed, on the barbed wire of history. Just before filming started, Fonda had been traveling with a stage troupe called F.T.A., for Fuck the Army, rendered shortly afterward into a low-budget film (with script credited to Dalton Trumbo) as *F.T.A.* Losey, of all people, was hardly in a position to accuse her of having "little sense of humor," as he told a newspaper interviewer during post-production of *A Doll's House*.[42] It was around this time that Fonda started to ask for some control of her projects for all of the familiar reasons—as a thinking actor in the Stanislavkian tradition and as a socialist and a feminist. At that moment, she was fighting for control of a founding artifact of modern feminism.[43]

Adaptation of great theater to film is always a tricky business, of course. Along with *Mother Courage*, *Galileo* is probably Brecht's most famous play, a piece moreover that he presented in three distinct versions: the original he worked out in a burst of creative energy over 16 days in 1938; the first revision for the American production in the United States in 1947; and the final rewrite for the last production during his lifetime, presented by the Berliner Ensemble in 1953. The differences between the three scripts do not involve large structural overhauls but subtle changes in emphasis that reflected Brecht's hardening views over that decade and a half about the subordination of science and technology to the needs of the modern security state. In dramatic terms, this concern comes to a head in the epilogue, when Galileo utters the line to his scientific assistant, "Welcome to the gutter." Then follows this remarkable speech, which does not appear in the 1938 version: "I have come to believe that I was never in real danger; for some years I was as strong as the authorities, and I surrendered my knowledge to the powers-that-be, to use it, no, not use it, abuse it, as it suits their ends. Any man who does what I have done must not be tolerated in the ranks of science."[44]

A good deal has been written about the legitimacy of Brecht's worry about the atomic bomb and his growing belief that Galileo's capitulation to church authorities meant forever after that the development of theoretical physics, unlike the rest of the natural sciences, would be governed by the interests of the state. Liberal Brechtians tended to support the 1938 text, which seemed to imply that Galileo was wise to accept the humiliation of recanting his beliefs because it bought him time to continue working. They also point to the fact that in any case Brecht's effort to deposit responsibility for the full horror of modern atomic weaponry on a seventeenth-century intellectual can only be an artful exaggeration.[45]

But as Marxists, Losey and most of the Hollywood blacklistees tended to agree with Brecht—and that's why Losey ended the film with Galileo's unambiguous self-mortification. The blacklisted filmmakers had other reasons to support Brecht's position, however, for to them the issue was deeply personal. By this time, the church represented the House Committee on Un-American Activities—director Irving Pichel's church-funded *Martin Luther* (1953), made in Germany, expressed it most literally—and they were not alone in that interpretation. At least one Hollywood film worker who had capitulated to the committee, talented composer David Raksin, found solace in the idea that Galileo's was a vindicating slyness because it allowed him to continue working.[46] What Raksin overlooked, of course, was that Galileo had faced the threat of physical torture and, unlike Raksin, he still had had to work through a front—to smuggle his work out of Italy—despite his act of contrition.

For that matter, Abraham Polonsky, the most sophisticated of the Hollywood Marxists, had had the unique opportunity for his version to be seen by millions on television, in *You Are There*, naturally working behind a front. In 1953, the same year Brecht was putting on his last production in Berlin, CBS broadcast "The Crisis of Galileo." Polonsky also ran into some of the same problems as both Galileo and Brecht, when a startled CBS executive, William Dozier, after reading the teleplay, hand-carried a copy to acquaintances in the New York Catholic Archdiocese, with the result that several changes were ordered in the text.[47]

Unlike the Brecht play and the Losey version, Polonsky has the old physicist read into the record his humiliating confession of error and then, upon returning home, bury his weeping face in his hands. The Brechtian point—more Brechtian than Brecht, in this case—is made when CBS cuts to a reporter in London who is trying to get a reaction from William Harvey, the discoverer of the circulation of blood in the body. Harvey glares into the camera and says, "I reject the action of Galileo Galilei as a betrayal of the work of his life and the truth about nature and the universe which we scientists must defend no matter what the personal consequences."

Polonsky's *You Are There* episode naturally lacked the *mise en scène* of Losey's rendition, as well as the rehearsals and so on. But it appeared at the right time in television history and confronted surprisingly little censorship, for a variety of reasons. Losey's version, put on as a prestige art-house American Film Theater production, may be thought to have appeared at the right time as well, in the midst of the Watergate scandal and barely after the high point of "Enemies Lists," FBI/COINTELPRO operations against the domestic Left (including local underground newspapers surviving from the 1960s, a prime source of alternative views), and the closing years of the Vietnam War. But, like Losey's troubled 1947 stage version, this one was somehow off.

Casting Topol as Galileo could only have been an invitation to melodramatic excess. Others in the cast, including Edward Fox, Margaret Leighton and John Gielgud, were so good that they almost made up for this mistake: but not quite. Losey's *Galileo* constituted a sturdy theater piece on film, just at the moment when artistic experimentation in the popular American film was peaking. It could uplift, but only for those who wanted uplift; it could not entertain.

Losey did better with narratives about sexual politics, no doubt because that impulse was so important to the era. *The Romantic Englishwoman* (1975) and *La Tru-*

ite (1982), although separated by seven years, share many of the same impulses and a good bit of what remained remarkable in the last phase of the director's career.

Englishwoman pairs the strong actors Glenda Jackson and Michael Caine in a screenplay by British playwright Tom Stoppard. Here we are plunged back into the world of Loseyan irony, but in Stoppard's screenplay the characters are not only given no understanding of themselves, they are allowed no dignity. If the comedy seems broader, it is only because the irony is sharper (even mocking), and very close to satire. Yet the comedy is still essentially humorless. This is a world of bourgeois saps who don't understand a thing and will be exposed as the authors of all their own problems.

Jackson plays a bored and frustrated wife, a woman of middling years married to a jealous and wealthy writer of romantic pulp novels. He has so little talent that he must steal his dialogue and plot points from the lives and conversation of the people around him. Since those lives belong mostly to suburban twits, he cannot get anything interesting out of them unless he bullies them, makes passes at the women, or forces them into situations in which they must perform like trained monkeys. And so he rants at a female friend of his wife until she delivers the pearl, "Women are an occupied country," which he promptly appropriates for his own purposes.

Jackson flees for an unsupervised weekend to Baden Baden, where she meets a handsome young drug dealer, played by Helmut Berger. After he carelessly loses the stash he had planned to sell, Berger must flee from his suppliers, who now want him to pay up or die. He pursues Jackson to England, where her suspicious husband invites him for a stay at the house to provide him with some occasion for marital jealousy and thus material for his next novel.

The tone is struck right at the start of the film when a customs agent checks Berger's passport and sees that he has identified his occupation as "poet." "*Ach, ein Dichter sind Sie,*" sneers the uniformed agent with undisguised sarcasm, "*wie nett.*"[48] Jackson's character is revealed as a hopeless fuddyduddy in her choice of Baden Baden as an escape as well as in her choice of gown to wear to the gambling tables; it manages to be both dowdy and ridiculously virginal. Caine himself gets to strike poses as the outraged husband when his wife finally accepts his dare and has it on with Berger in plain sight, in an oddly transparent glass gazebo next to the swimming pool. It is all played quite straight, except for the mysterious and very gothic few seconds of the final scene, in which the married couple return home to find the "the help" (it is not really clear who it is) drunk and disorderly and in possession of their home. This movie is the closest Losey came to recidivism in the matter of melodrama, and the last scene has the feel of a late and unsuccessful lunge to rescue the film with something suggestively ominous. But it falls flat, at best some sort of private joke.

Englishwoman has its defenders. Losey was not among them. "I think it is a piece of junk," he told an interviewer.[49] The film is better than it deserves to be because Losey knew how to give even a slight story some visible weight. *La Truite* was similarly troubled. That the problems were near-fatal should have been evident to Losey right from the start of the project, when he ignored the advice of screenwriter Frederic Raphael, who declined to write the screenplay from Roger Vailland's novel.[50] Nearly a quarter-century earlier, Vailland's best-known novel, *La Loi*, had been made into a highly successful film by Jules Dassin (*Where the Hot Wind Blows*, 1958). But Vailland's view of Aphrodite had darkened considerably between the appearance of Dassin's exuberant Gina Lollobrigida, who took what she wanted, whether sex or property, and Losey's Isabelle Huppert, for whom no distinction between sexuality and property was either possible or necessary.

Once again the story is about sexuality across class lines, but there is a sense that Losey has exhausted his subject. The story concerns the rise of a cynical young beauty who takes it as a birthright to exploit the desires of old men for money and in the process to gain enough knowledge to succeed as the head of a multinational corporation. She is as cold-blooded as a freshwater fish in an alpine stream—and utterly implausible except as an idea, or perhaps an act of literary revenge by Vailland against a younger love of his last years.

What is best about *La Truite* is the technical quality of the storytelling. Each scene is a leap out of the narrative, the result of action that is never seen and barely implied. Like *Englishwoman*, it is technique superior to its subject. Losey did better with his last efforts at political expression: less technique, more content.

Monsieur Klein, Losey's account of the famous roundup of French Jews by the police in 1942 and their deportation to Germany, was the first and also the most ambitious of his three French-language films, at least measured by the size of the budgets. The fact that in the final scene he could command 2,000 extras and 18 makeup artists, 23 hair specialists and 20 first assistants behind 4 cameras was a measure as well of the respect that was still afforded Losey in France. It was the last big budget (18 million francs) of his career, for a meticulously well-told story with many superb moments, rich with the director's famous gift for *mise en scène*. It was also one of his most intensely political movies, though its real theme was well hidden.

Monsieur Klein is ostensibly about the madness of the Holocaust, which in a sense makes it uncontroversial. On issues of this sort, leftists could make few errors. As some filmmakers used to say, Marxist statements in Hollywood movies were always acceptable as long as they were something liberals agreed with, and this was certainly one of them. But there is a deeper theme here, one about the resistance of Jewish communists to fascism and how their methods of resistance were based on a clear understanding of the ways in which French society was organized. In other words, there is another side of this movie, as though it were being watched by another audience on the unseen side of the screen, perhaps in a post-revolutionary society. The other film, the one on the invisible side of the screen, is an action movie about the techniques used by a group of resistance fighters in identity theft, infiltration of German defense plants near Paris and the stealing of munitions for sabotage. This is the movie that we are not permitted to see but must discover for ourselves on this side of the tapestry, the lucidity we achieve with Mr. Klein about the true nature of the movie we are watching—though of course it is he who pays the price.

The movie presented on our side of the screen gives us Robert Klein (Alain Delon), a fastidious little haut bourgeois with manners that are as silken as his dressing gowns. He has a casual predisposition to fascism. He literally confines his mistress to his bed and makes a living buying paintings from distressed Jews at cut-rate prices. His motto is, "None of this has anything to do with me." But one day it has very much to do with him. He discovers a Jewish newspaper on his doorstep, the first clue that his identity has been appropriated by someone of the same name who wants to disappear into the cover of his identify and who is, as he learns eventually, an enemy of the state.

The rest of the film is a chase to unmask the thief and turn him over to the Gestapo so that the "innocent" Klein can vindicate himself from the fatal charge of being a Jew and a communist. Along the way, as he gets closer to finding the "other" Robert Klein, the bourgeois gradually awakens to the social horror around him. As he loses his social position and property to friends who betray him and steal from him, he begins to devour newspapers and take ever greater risks to meet the man who is now becoming the "real" Klein, a man whom he has even secretly begun to admire. By absurdly following what he imagines is his quarry into what turns out to be a cattle car bound for Germany on the day of the police roundup, he throws away his last chance of escape and discovers that in some sense he is the "real" Klein every bit as much as the other man. When he achieves this lucidity, it turns him into the ultimate outsider: a man doomed to die in a concentration camp.

Although *Monsieur Klein* has sometimes been called a melodrama with elements of film noir, it is closer in spirit to the thriller genre, particularly the conspiracy film, fulfilling Frederic Jameson's definition of the type of movie that explores the mystery of "a potentially infinite network, along with a plausible explanation for its invisibility."[51] It was written by Franco Solinas, who wrote screenplays for Rossellini before turning out a half-dozen highly prized Marxist spaghetti westerns and a few of director Gillo Pontocorvo's best films, including those global New Left favorites, *The Battle of Algiers* (1965) and *Burn!* (1969). The high point of his career was probably represented by a pair of screenplays for

Costa-Gavras, the brilliant *State of Siege* (1973) and *Hanna K.* (1983). *Monsieur Klein* was surely among his most intricately argued narratives.

The conspiracy (in Jameson's sense) is unambiguously identified as the state in its capacity as an occupying power over humanity itself. Its "invisibility" is its commonplace quality as the ordinary brutality of quotidian life—official suspicions followed by quiet disappearances in the marketplace, inquiries taken as proof of subversion: paranoia about the very act of breathing. Many of the same qualities are found in Solinas' other late screenplays, particularly in those he wrote for Costa-Gavras, who used the power of the documentary style to alert his audiences to the possibility that they, too, could be the object of a roundup outside the theater after the show. But in Losey's hands, now grown subtle at the end of a long career, the story is told in a narrative that cuts deeper into the brain—Klein's as well as the audience's. By the last shot, the exact nature of the conspiracy that put Klein in the cattle car no longer matters. All that is important was that he and we be lucid about the act itself.

Among the few U.S. critics who dealt with *Monsieur Klein*, Vincent Canby stepped forward once again. Aside from a gratuitous slap at the lead actor, Canby was restrained. Nonetheless, "Mr. Solinas and Mr. Losey are not as interested in the workings of the plot as in matters of identity and obsession. . . ." There was "a hole in the center of the canvas," which was in turn a painting "concerned with ideas that are fashionable without being at all disturbing."[52] This was rapidly becoming the favorite conceptual ground of the budding neoconservatives. Radical ideas and styles had taken over the mainstream, uncomplicating that which urgently needed to be complicated. It was not a full-throated attack of the kind Kael could be counted upon to make upon Martin Ritt, but it was enough, suggesting that the film may have been too difficult for pop audiences after all. *Monsieur Klein* disappeared.

A sign that Losey was a bit on the defensive in approaching his late masterpiece, *Don Giovanni* (1979), is the motto scrawled as though on a stone wall by an urgent hand in the film's very first frame. It was taken from the *Prison Notebooks* of the anti-Stalinist Marxist, Antonio Gramsci, and in the previous decade had often been quoted by New Left activists. Here it was pressed into dubious service: "The crisis consists precisely in the fact that the old is dying and the new cannot be born; in this interregnum a great variety of morbid symptoms appears." Never mind that the well-known aphorism was written in the 1930s, the "morbid symptoms" referring specifically to the rise of fascism. Or that Losey, no theorist, had to have English novelist John Fowles look up the reference for him.[53] As a metaphor for the birth of the socially misshapen and the monstrous, it was apt enough for any age and had the advantage of managing to invoke despair and hope at the same time.

The Gramsci quote is the only overtly political gesture made in a film that hardly needed one. The whole purpose of the production, according to the man who conceived the project, was to bring into a movie theater the ordinary viewer who could not afford to buy a ticket to the opera house. Here, the magnificence of the music (recorded on 16-track tape by some of the finest voices then available, including a young Kiri Te Kanawa) would be matched by the sumptuous *mise en scène* and the accessibility of singers who could really act. It was Rolf Lieberman, director of the National Opera Theater of Paris, who urgently sought to step around the traditional elitism of such stage productions and bring Mozart to the masses, precisely the kind of project that had always animated Losey. Together, Lieberman and Losey pulled it off: the most revolutionary opera of the European canon was properly placed on film by a revolutionary or two.

Not that any of the prestige critics, particularly Canby, seem to have noticed. Missing the key points entirely, Canby argued that one of the principles "opera depends on" was that its audience "remain fixed, stationary and not go wandering around on the stage, poking its nose into the faces of the performers."[54] Apparently he had never heard of the eighteenth-century practice of seating aristocrats on the stage with the performers for this very purpose, a privilege abolished by the middle class but now democratized by the camera. In his weekend column, Canby went further. "Here is a movie to blacken the name of intellect," he wrote. Sounding like *New Leader* critic John Simon on a bad day, Canby went on to attack the physiognomy of the singers. "With the exception of Te Kanawa," Canby wrote, all of the voices "belong to singers best seen in the kind of long shots we get in an opera house, not in close-ups of the movie screen."[55]

Canby's comments set off a flap in Europe. Bernardo Bertolucci had already complained that because of the *Times* and the unique political role it plays in the United States, New York was a "slaughterhouse" for European films. Losey wrote Canby a letter bitterly complaining about what he perceived as unfair treatment. Given the opportunity to respond in an interview with the editors of *Cineaste*, Canby was predictably nasty: Losey's *Don Giovanni*, he said, "is a joke. He attempted to do something and he did it very badly. I thought what he did to it was scandalous."[56]

It's true that Losey's efforts to open up the proscenium in all directions, outward as well as inward into various kinds of close-ups and two-shots, are sometimes overly self-conscious (Canby's point without Canby's animus) and lead to the occasional excessive gesture. For example, when Te Kanawa sinks to a knee bench to deliver an aria as though it were a confession, Losey shoots her through the confessional screen in a visual trope lifted directly from *The Romantic Englishwoman*, when Glenda Jackson peered through the metal slats of the elevator in

Baden Baden. It jars because, just for a moment, the audience takes the point of view of a priest, narratively a non sequitur.

Still, Losey's *Giovanni* is ripe with a social and aesthetic energy that was until then almost unknown in filmed opera. It is at least comparable in quality to Ingmar Bergman's version of *The Magic Flute* (1975), the *Parsifal* of Hans-Jürgen Syberberg (1982) and even the German-Austrian production of Herbert von Karajan's *Don Giovanni* (with Samuel Ramey) telecast from the Salzburg Mozart festival in 1987. In fact, many a reasonable opera fan, if forced to choose, will prefer the Losey version, with music directed by Loren Maazel, to von Karajan's, despite the fact that Losey drains from the figure of the Don all traces of rococo charm and movie star seductiveness, preferring to exploit the serpentine leer of Ruggero Raimondi to assert the personality of the ruthless aristocrat whom the director so admired, the egoist who expects to be cleaned up after by the sort of people who are eager to do that sort of thing (particularly, in this opera, Don Ottavio, the nattering proto-bourgeois).

This theme was Losey's meat—the proleptic value of aristocratic sexuality for a working class that could only emancipate itself by legitimizing its own desire. Where he had earlier seemed to have given up in despair on the working class, with *Giovanni* Losey began to reexamine this attitude. He was no longer as concerned about sex across class lines as with the class character of sexuality itself.

It was of course a stretch (not to mention a silly anachronism), for Losey in an interview to refer to the Don as "an anarchist rebel," the first articulation of a theme he was to explore quite often in his last films.[57] Mozart's Don Juan may well have represented the last gasp of feudalism. But there was no necessary contradiction between that and Losey's implicit view that the Don was also the ultimate antibourgeois who refused to cave in to the rising institutions of middle-class social control, including a Calvinized church and a middle-class notion of love that replaced pleasure with the proprieties of ownership.

Les routes du sud (*Roads to the South*, 1978) is one of Losey's least known films and one of his most personal. For a director who never wrote any of his own screenplays, Losey somehow found his way to subjects that were too autobiographical for coincidence—or was it that his experiences as an exile were close to those of so many other people in his part of the twentieth century? The screenplay for *Roads to the South* was written by the highly regarded Jorge Semprún, who had worked extensively with left-wing directors Alain Resnais and Costa-Gavras—he had a credit for *Z* (1969), and another with Ben Barzman for *The French Conspiracy* (1972). Semprún even served as the minister of culture for the social democratic government of Spain in the time following the events portrayed in *Roads to the South*, which deal with the last days of the Franco government as the old dictator lay dying in his bed of Parkinson's disease.

The screenwriter tied the historical to the personal and political by asking the very specific question, "Who was the last person to die in Spain in the 40-year resistance to fascism?" In this story, the answer is a middle-aged, happily married woman, a Spanish exile in France who is killed on the highway to Barcelona while acting as a courier for the Communist Party. Left behind in France to mourn her are her husband, a novelist and filmmaker (Yves Montand), and his son (Laurent Malet), who has brought his girlfriend (Miou-Miou) to his father's home to help guide him through the painful task of communicating with his grieving father. The lovely young girlfriend remains behind after Laurent suddenly leaves the house. She seduces the much older man, whom she accompanies to Barcelona to witness the end of fascism. In an eerie scene close to the story's end, Spaniards are seen gathering in absolute silence around newspaper stands to read the news and listen to radio broadcasts, still too intimidated to rejoice at their emancipation.

This is a film determined to capture a particular moment in its fullness, and both director and writer accomplish the task masterfully. As the film opens, Montand is obsessed with a screenplay that he begins this way: during World War II, a German soldier who is also a Communist Party member risks his life to cross the battle lines and warn his comrades in the Red Army that they are about to be attacked. The Russians listen to his story and then kill him without another thought. This allegory for what his son later calls "the cult of Stalinism" hangs over the rest of the film. Montand (himself, as actor-activist, and like his more famous wife, Simon Signoret, by this time politically disillusioned) plays an intellectual contemplating the fact that he devoted his life to a cause that ended badly, notwithstanding its supporters' courageous roles in class struggles large and small, its (sometimes grudging) support for anticolonialism and, most memorably in France, its resistance to fascism.

If *The Assassination of Trotsky* was a failure, *Roads to the South* succeeds in contemplating the crisis of conscience without resorting to the usual symptoms of disillusionment or the uncritical acceptance of parliamentary capitalism (under ultimate U.S. control) as the best of all possible worlds. The screenwriter is not ashamed of having been a communist, certainly not of the heroic support given to an antifascist underground in Spain for decades, or of providing crucial assistance to political exiles. The irony is that the old system of fascism, like Franco, dies of natural causes, and Spaniards themselves do not quite know what to make of it. In real life, of course, Spain becomes a major tourist destination with long-treasured coastlines turned into ecological disaster areas, as the Spanish themselves become Caribbean-like servants of their richer neighbors. Socialists in government, as the communists might gloomily have predicted, actually promoted the takeover and transformation by foreign capital.

In the film, the dialogue hits a political high point when son asks father why his movement, the resistance, didn't just assassinate the dictator. Smacking his forehead ironically with his fist, Montand shoots back, "Why didn't we think of that?" as if it had not been contemplated all along. In frustration, he confronts his son about his arrest by the Paris police at a demonstration in which he was agitating against the execution of five antifascist activists in Spain, accusing him of naiveté. The son resents the lecture but is grateful that his father's influence got him out of jail.

And so the story reveals the conflict between the Old Left and the New, with affection on both sides—even respect and love—but also poverty of communication. Each generation is painfully aware of its own and the others' failures in changing the world, and the sense of personal betrayal, mirroring the betrayal by history itself, runs deep. The son is shocked to find a diary in his mother's hand commemorating her affair with another comrade, and shocked again to discover that his father knew all about it and did not object.

At the center of the story is the spirit of the revolution, the beautiful young woman—seductive and independent and just out of reach—whom the father and son share, a skillful dialectician (she gets most of the best lines) who explains the ways of the son to the father and vice versa. In the end, she abandons both of them and moves on. Her elusive memory nevertheless beckons the father to "start again" and commands him to offer his son solidarity in whatever struggle may lie ahead.

If there is an elegiac tone to the film, it is hardly surprising. This is Losey's last major political statement: a look backward, an accounting of the appropriate regrets as well the legitimate hopes of his generation.

The director had just one more film to go, *Steaming*, and he labored on it through illness and production problems. Arguably more of a period piece than anything he ever did, it remains memorable for what it attempted if not for what it accomplished. Losey's last wife, Patricia Losey, who came into film work as screenwriter Hugo Butler's secretary, would get the screenwriting credit—probably the main purpose for Losey's involvement in the project not long before his death. But it was surely not the only reason.

Steaming (1985) has something of the air of John Ford's apology to the Indians in his last western (*Cheyenne Autumn*, 1964). After years of hectoring strong actresses and feminists in his films, beginning with Jane Fonda in *A Doll's House*, Losey gives the impression in *Steaming* of conceding the error of his prejudices. But even here he had a difficult time getting along with Vanessa Redgrave, ostensibly because she was loath to grant him the nude shot he wanted (and eventually got, from the back). Losey admired Fonda, Christie, Jackson and Redgrave personally as courageous artists, but more important, shared their critique of sexuality as property. He also seemed to regard them with the same suspicion, sometimes anger, that Yves Montand reserved for Miou-Miou in *Roads to the South*. They belonged to a new generation that hadn't lived through the 1930s and 1940s; if he had often been accused (or celebrated) for substituting style for political substance, perhaps he could not help projecting some of that charge onto them.

If *Steaming* was supposed to launch a screenwriting career for Patricia Losey, it was not successful. But her screenplay for Nell Dunn's two-act theater piece, no doubt revised in the shooting by Losey himself, nevertheless was in some ways an improvement on the original. For one thing, there was never much of a story. It was more of a premise that provided a voyeuristic opportunity for the vivid discussions of a half-dozen women of different classes in a shambling London neighborhood's Turkish Bath, threatened with extermination by the geniuses of urban renewal. Dunn had adapted her original novel with little attention to dramatic structure, but Patricia Losey managed to rearrange and edit the play into something more pointed and more serviceable for the purposes of cinema.

Dunn's real talent lay in the way she captured the speech of working-class women in all their variety, from the blowsy, hypochondriacal older woman with her stockings rolled up to her knees to the youngish woman whose husband has been sent to prison for stealing jewels and who insists on taking what she wants when she wants it: "When I want to get drunk, I get drunk; when I want to fuck, I fuck." This is Josie (Patti Love), an updated version of the scandalous "Poor Cow" of another Dunn novel of the same title, published in 1967 and made into a film by Ken Loach the same year.

In a sense, Josie is also Doña Giovanna, contrasted to the watery and remote bourgeois, Nancy (Redgrave), confessing that not only did she never take what she wanted, she never even learned how to ask for it, "even in bed." Redgrave is effective in the role, as when she laughs inappropriately (thus proving the point), while Josie lays into her for her self-pity and passivity. Josie, by contrast, is the embodiment of the virtue of taking all the things she pines for, even "if I've got to steal them"—until finally, it is implied, it is the promise of revolution, of women's liberation, that has been seized, a last gem in the diadem of Josie's inventory of jewel thievery. Gender, in the most socialistic versions of contemporary feminism—and more for the United Kingdom than the United States—was to intersect with class, prompting blue-collar women (at the head of a column with their more privileged sisters) allied with people of color to overthrow the patriarchs of class once and for all. The dream—a nightmare for conservatives and many liberals as well—died, although never entirely. *Steaming* was a revolutionary manifesto of sorts when the class side of the social movements was already in retreat.

Steaming was not well received, and not only because of its politics and its unusually frequent technical flaws (the editing is particularly jarring). Vincent

Canby had decried the play as "junk," the "kind of societal cross-section one used to find in William Saroyon's barrooms," now thrown together in a bathhouse to "sweat out their psyches." In his view, the movie, despite a few compensations, was no improvement on the play.[58] This judgment was altogether predictable on political lines alone. But it also separated theater and film from life, in which feminism was the great moving force of artistic inspiration, even if rarely realized artistically. The film *Steaming*, like the play, successfully captured the essence of the historical moment when middle-class women, in the first flush of that generation's discovery of feminism, insisted on the right to a sexuality defined by themselves alone and found new sympathy for their working-class sisters. They may have entered the theater feeling like Nancy, but they left like Josie.

Throughout filming and until he died in 1984, Losey remained what he had long been—arrogant, often drunk, sometimes foolish and angry but always unrepentant, a Marxist lion heartbroken over the insufficiency of history and an artist disappointed by the inadequacy of his art to make up the difference. In *Steaming* at any rate, Losey rediscovered the working class and found a way, reluctantly and ungraciously, toward a sense of affirmation and optimism. Despite his battles with some of the best feminist stars of the day, when he died it had been this new generation of radicals with whom he made his most hopeful films.

All of these films, including *A Doll's House*—the only one starring an American actress—had to be shot in Europe because Losey remained more or less in involuntary exile for almost all of his life. There was never any doubt that the real cause of that exile was that U.S. critics and most producers never ceased to regard Losey as a dark angel of the cinema. Like Orson Welles, Losey was always a most inconvenient talent.

The last word in his *Variety* obituary was given to Losey to comment on his inability to make movies in his homeland: "I've been asked if I'm bitter. I'm not bitter at all. But I profoundly resent the lack of opportunity to comment on my own society, my own roots, my own country."[59] Critics could put that on his epitaph.

CHAPTER NINE

AN ENDING?

AT THE 1977 ACADEMY AWARDS CEREMONY, members gave Lillian Hellman a standing ovation for writing the novel that became the screenplay for *Julia*, and a year later *Coming Home* won Oscars for screenwriter Waldo Salt and the film's leading actors, Jane Fonda and Jon Voight. *Coming Home*'s none too cryptic protest against America's Vietnam fiasco might be said in these awards to have received its vindication. In 1979, one of the most enduring of the blacklisted screenwriters, Walter Bernstein, saw the favorite of his own films, *Yanks*, appear to good if not spectacular reviews. Under the amiable guidance of director John Schlesinger, *Yanks* offered a look back at the social experience of the war against fascism as told by a real live blacklisted veteran and journalist of the conflict.

Promising assignments still awaited on television, especially for Bernstein, who was winning Emmys into the middle 1990s and still earning credits at the dawn of the new century.[1] A few other veterans had also gotten in their last shots, although in projects that were mostly dissatisfying and occasionally disastrous. Age had taken its toll. After 1980, Hollywood's Cold War victims were all but finished as film writers, directors or producers. Only a handful of aged actors (notably John Randolph) held on, and not for much longer.[2] What remained was untold tale and legend, like the classroom "lesson" of Richard Dreyfuss in an episode of *The Education of Max Bickford*, in which he played prime-time television's college professor in the 2001–2002 season, teaching the history of McCarthyism, with the blacklistees representing something larger than themselves.[3]

The martyr's role had been foreshadowed in real life by untimely deaths. Enemies portrayed the blacklistees as script hacks—generally ignoring the fate of actors, directors and technicians altogether—who were rudely pushed into some other, equivalent hackish employment, or left to work in the same kind of dishonorable scribbling under pseudonyms and at lower pay. The reality was often a good deal grimmer; this was driven home, if only for the blacklist community and its sympathizers, by the fate of Nedrick Young, dead of a heart attack in 1968 at age 54.

Raised in a Russian-Jewish family in Brownsville, Brooklyn, trained as a World War II staff sergeant who wrote orientation and training films, Young was handsome and dashing enough to be regarded by the studios as the next suave swashbuckling adventurer (he had supporting roles in non-classics like *The Gallant Blade* and *The Swordsman*, both 1947). He was also versatile enough to have written a handful of successful scripts for family films before 1950. Then the blacklist came, and suddenly Young was for years reduced to blue-collar jobs in and around Los Angeles, including assembly-line auto worker, parking lot attendant and bartender.

Young had not yet lost everything. As we've seen, with Harold Jacob Smith he co-wrote the screenplay pseudonymously for *The Defiant Ones* (1958), from Young's original story, for producer Stanley Kramer. Delivering an additional jab at the blacklist, Young had actually cast himself in the opening scene above the credits as the van driver for Sidney Poitier and Tony Curtis, the convicts who were about to escape and, despite their mutual hatred, go on the run for the duration of the film. Bosley Crowther, like other critics emphasizing the importance of director-producer Kramer, seemed to sense (and perhaps knew secretly) that something had begun to turn around since the deepest freeze of the Cold War.[4] At any rate, the issue of race, still unresolved and now growing increasingly urgent in a world of emerging former colonial peoples, would inevitably provide the key for reopening the old doors in Hollywood.

Kramer had in Smith and Young the talented writing team he needed, and he set out almost immediately to film *Inherit the Wind* (1960), an adaptation of a Broadway drama about the Scopes "Monkey Trial" of 1925, which effectively put the teaching of evolution on trial. *Inherit the Wind* offered a reprise, in a broad sense, of every left-wing film involving a raging right-wing crowd ready to tear innocent victims, liberal lawyers and their supporters limb from limb. It was set in the South but, like television's *You Are There*, sizzled with more than allegorical anti-McCarthyite sentiments. Liberal Gene Kelly, who badly wanted this kind of part, was miscast as a fictional journalist closely resembling H. L. Mencken (who had covered the trial, in acid prose, for the northern press); Spencer Tracy was defense lawyer Clarence Darrow; the redoubtable Harry Morgan was the hanging judge; and former Popular Front idol Fredric March played against type as William Jennings Bryan, once a great radical-of-sorts and antiwar crusader but long since gone to seed as defender of southern racism and right-wing Christianity.

The year before the appearance of *Inherit the Wind*, the academy rescinded its 1956 bylaw forbidding an Oscar nomination for any artist who had refused to answer the questions of a congressional committee. But the change did the scrappy Young no good. In the face of studio objections, he successfully claimed screen credit for the original story behind the drastically altered screenplay for *Jailhouse Rock* (1957), a prison drama that had evolved, after Young's separation from the project, into a musical vehicle for Elvis Presley. In the world of Elvis aficionados, *Jailhouse* nevertheless remains the King's best film. Along with *Wild in the Country*, the last script Clifford Odets delivered, and *Flaming Star* (1961), in which Elvis plays a halfbreed suffering racial discrimination, *Jailhouse* captures the rock n' roll great most empathetically as a southern prole struggling to realize himself. How much of *Jailhouse Rock* one can attribute to Young's work is difficult to determine, but it remains a fascinating and unexpected intersection of U.S. popular culture. In 1958, the blacklisted writer even managed to appear under his own name (actually as "Ned Young") in the highly curious western, *Terror in a Texas Town*.

This credit in particular cost Young dearly. The American Legion went after him and others by name, renewing the appeal to all members to write letters urging film studios to boycott anyone who resisted the blacklist. Young deepened his own hiring dilemma by joining 11 other actors and writers in collectively suing several studios for continuing to use a blacklist. This attempt to utilize the Sherman Anti-Trust Act—if successful, it might have ended the blacklist outright— was refused a hearing on appeal by a plainly hostile U.S. Supreme Court (although the Motion Picture Producers and Distributors Association paid attorney fees and $80,000).

On a personal level, the continuing emotional ravages of the blacklist had already cut too deep for Young. He spent his savings traveling to Japan to look at the sites of atomic warfare and lost his gamble when the Japanese government showed no more interest than Hollywood in financially supporting a production of the film script that he'd written from the popular novella, *The Flowers of Hiroshima* (1959), by Edita Morris. He also wrote a screenplay, never produced, for John Frankenheimer, and the two tentatively agreed in 1963 to form a new production company. It might have been Young's salvation.

Then Young's wife, Frances Sage, a blacklisted actress who could not work behind a *nom de plume*, committed suicide, and the Frankenheimer plan fell apart. Increasingly weary but still game, Young managed to write an early script for Burt Lancaster's World War II vehicle, *The Train* (1964). The next year, however, the writer suffered his first heart attack. He got his literal final credit with a stroke of irony: three months after his death from a second attack, ABC premiered the made-for-television *Shadow on the Land* (1968) about a military coup that brings a fascist dictatorship to the United States. The timing of the production could not have been planned, but might easily have been regarded, in the aftermath of Nixon's election a month earlier, as revenge against the noted California red-baiter and anti-Semite whose administration was about to engage in the worst political repression since the early Cold War.[5]

If he was among the earliest, Young wasn't the only premature fatality of the blacklist by a long stretch. Outright suicides remained relatively rare (among screenwriters, the aging comedy writer Howard Dimsdale committed suicide with his terminally ill wife in 1991). But premature strokes and heart attacks were fairly common, along with heavy drinking as a form of suicide on the installment plan. Arnold Manoff, his career lost after pseudonymous success with *You Are There*, succumbed in 1960, only 51. Gordon Kahn, better known as an editor of the Screen Writers Guild's house organ and as the earliest historian of the blacklist than for his commercial success in writing the first Roy Rogers/Dale Evans movies, died before Manoff, following a failed effort to rebuild a screenwriting career in Mexico (and a desperate attempt to support his family as a furniture salesman in Massachusetts). Actress Mady Christians, banned from television, died of an early cerebral hemorrhage, the respected character actor J. Edward Bromberg of an equally early heart attack. Hugo Butler, who had better prospects in Mexico (where, as we've seen, he worked with Luis Buñuel on two films) and in Europe (where he worked with both Robert Aldrich and Joseph Losey), never got all that far, either, and died in 1968 of a stroke at age 54. Dorothy Parker, active in the Hollywood Left until the last moment, passed away in 1967, willing her estate to Martin Luther King, Jr., and the Southern Christian Leadership Conference. And so on. The fate of most of the others who were never so famous or so well connected was less dramatic but no less depressing.[6]

A small handful, as we have seen—prominently Jules Dassin, Joseph Losey, Jack Berry and animator John Hubley—actually got a push from the blacklist in a creative direction they probably would not otherwise have taken. But as Dassin acidly observed decades later, being forced to start over, especially in a new cultural context, still could not be construed as a blessing in disguise or any kind of blessing at all.[7] A very few others, television writer Frank Tarloff the most notable, had managed to suffer scarcely at all. The vast majority simply lost their profession, or at a minimum their best years.

And there were the hidden personal losses, less dramatic than death and obscurity. Anne Froelick, with several credits (the best was *Harriet Craig*, a remake of *Craig's Wife*) before the blacklist, afterward became an alcoholic—very likely the most common fate, affecting certain later phases of the lives of Ring Lardner, Jr., Dalton Trumbo, Michael Wilson and many more.[8] It was, after all, the martini-and-highball age.

Not that the tragedy was confined to those who refused to testify. Robert Rossen was dead at 58, in 1966, less than a decade after several apparent heart attacks that, to be generous, had helped prompt his transformation from un-friendly to friendly testimony in 1953. *The Hustler* (1961), with Paul Newman as the thinking prole, was Rossen's apotheosis, the film he had planned for decades to make—but also practically his final note.[9] Leopold Atlas, who suf-fered two heart attacks after co-scripting *Story of G.I. Joe* (1945), the best of the war films, gave friendly testimony in 1951 and died after years of creative frus-tration, in 1960.[10] Sterling Hayden, who told a reporter in 1963, "I was a rat, a stoolie, and the names I named of those close friends were blacklisted and de-prived of their livelihood," was widely believed to have drunk himself into a near-suicidal depression decades before his 1986 death. Perhaps Hayden had gained a personal salvation, if at all, in *Terror in a Texas Town* (1958) and in *Dr. Strangelove* (1964) and other hard-hitting, post-testimony liberal films in which he played character roles. Anecdotes are legion among other friendly witnesses who considered their testimony the worst thing they ever did in their lives, their careers saved by betraying friends.

Even Elia Kazan, the most pugnacious and apparently least repentant friendly witness, confessed at the time of his Lifetime Achievement Award in 1999 (an award protested, to be sure, by dwindling survivors of the blacklist) that he had "probably" done the wrong thing in dropping the dime on his friends. If Kazan's tenacious champions, most prominently Arthur Schlesinger, Jr., continued to hail the director's public testimony, and accompanying full-page ad in *Variety* to an-nounce his apostasy, as supremely heroic and patriotic, the director himself appar-ently no longer agreed.[11] Confession had saved a career in films for his best work, but had been altogether unnecessary for a vital role in American theater, which could not have been denied him any more than it was denied to non-testifier Arthur Miller. A *New York Times* editorial of 1999 confirmed public sentiment ex-tending deep into the liberal community: McCarthyism still left a bad taste after all these years. Tale-tellers like Kazan should be forgiven personally, the *Times* sages observed, but not vindicated for their betrayals during the red scare, what-ever their personal artistic merits.[12]

A quarter-century earlier, in 1974 at a Hyatt Regency gala in Los Angeles, Burt Lancaster had served as master of ceremonies for the "Bill of Rights Program" honoring Albert Maltz, with special awards to Nixon victim Helen Gahagan Douglas and her husband, Melvyn Douglas, who had been baited by the commit-tee for his Jewishness as well as his friends.[13] During the two decades before his 1990 death, Lancaster was said to have paid repeatedly for a table at the celebrity banquets honoring local left-wingers, most of them victims of persecution in one way or another. He had a personal reason. At the moment of crisis in the early

1950s, he had sealed his partnership with friendly witness and producer Harold Hecht and gone silent on the blacklisting of some of his best writers—and best friends. During most of the banquets, he sat alone and silent. In his own fashion, he was repaying an old debt.[14]

The Academy Awards ceremony of 1996 offered another giant, Kirk Douglas, a moment to take the stage and make his peace with the past. As Steven Spielberg narrated the history of Hollywood's most ethical films on social issues (thus seeking to refute Tinseltown's reputation for immorality, an old charge recently renewed in Congress and the news media), the film clips that the celebrity audience watched and cheered revealed a strangely familiar pattern. Most of the films chosen—including *Home of the Brave*, *Champion*, *The Defiant Ones* and *Spartacus*—had been written by victims of the blacklist for Douglas and other outspoken liberals like him. No one said so in front of a microphone, but in that audience, everyone except the most dim-witted undoubtedly knew.

Recovering from a severe stroke, Douglas determined to make his appearance at the ceremony and listened respectfully while Spielberg narrated the Lifetime Achievement Award he was about to hand the old star. "He's directed, he's produced and, in the process, he helped to hammer the blacklist to pieces!" Recalling that historic moment years later for *Parade* magazine, Douglas reflected that his success in breaking the blacklist was "the one thing I was really proud of."[15] No more absolute statement could be made, no more decisive refutation possible of the familiar counter-charge that the blacklistees deserved their fate and that Hollywood had lost nothing in the bargain.

And so it all came to an end in a trailing off of events, including a widely publicized series of Writers Guild decisions restoring a few dozen credits and creating a small special pension fund for surviving blacklistees. A Hollywood-funded memorial sculpture was installed at the University of Southern California. A January, 2002, remembrance night of the academy (coinciding with an academy exhibit of blacklist materials, with a smaller sister exhibit at UCLA) and a series of associated scholarly events capped these developments in the opening months of that year.[16] The hard news, a thinning stream of obituaries in the *New York Times*, *Los Angeles Times* and the *Hollywood Reporter*, seemed to end the tale. Or did it?

Not surprisingly, the Hollywood backstory made for better or at least more productive film fiction than film documentary. A few months before the Writers Guild and Actors Guild events, in October, 2001, the Boston Jewish Film Festival saw the theatrical premiere of *One of the Hollywood Ten*, a 2000 HBO film about the making of *Salt of the Earth*, starring Jeff Goldblum as director Herbert Biberman and Greta Scacchi as his wife, actress Gale Sondergaard; it was written and directed by Karl Francis, with the financial backing of the Arts Council of Wales. After the film's reappearance in the New York Jewish Film Festival and Film Society of Lincoln

Center in December and January, it attracted respectful critical attention—even if the film itself missed theatrical showings and went straight into cable.[17]

Sondergaard was one of several dozen Oscar-winning actors whose careers came to a crashing halt. Fittingly, in terms of historical celebrity, the biopic begins (after a newsreel clip of the *Triumph of the Will* premiere in New York) with Academy Award night, 1937. Scacchi, as Sondergaard, is nervously awaiting the announcement of the best supporting actress (a new category that year). Sitting with Goldblum as Biberman, she waves to mogul Jack Warner, who badly wants to lock in her services for his studio. As she accepts the award and graciously thanks the studio and her husband, she seizes the moment for an antifascist commercial, inviting everyone to join the Hollywood Anti-Nazi League. Here, dramatically if not literally, the American Popular Front is born.

Cut to: FBI headquarters, 1946, where an intrepid agent (played by Chris Fulford) has begun the case of his career. He convinces his superiors that the Hollywood reds are not invulnerable, however high they may be riding at the moment. A year or so passes and we see Biberman (a masterful theatrical director who showed only a little promise of success in 1940s Hollywood) thrown out of his job and his friend Michael Wilson (played by Geraint Wyn Davies) all too aware that his own Waterloo cannot be far behind. They travel with 18 unfriendly witnesses and many supporters to Washington, D.C., in August, 1947. Goldblum's Biberman is making the trip under a subpoena and Wilson as an observer. Once in town, their erstwhile backers (notably Jack Warner and Humphrey Bogart), faced with a barrage of negative press, quickly dump them. Years pass, Fulford's character is still avidly on the job but obviously more influential, FBI harassment intensifies, homes are bugged and Goldblum-Biberman goes to prison for his refusal to testify. He emerges with a career in shambles, and by now the blacklist has spread far. A veritable colony of Hollywood talent is scraping along, looking for work.

From here on, the story becomes a frame for the movie-within-a-movie. There are some fine portrayals of Hollywood Left personalities apart from Biberman and Sondergaard, notably Wilson's brother-in-law and producer of *Salt*, Paul Jarrico (played by John Sessions), and especially Wilson, along with many touching moments as the Latino community of the mining town of Silver City, New Mexico rallies behind (and performs in) the movie.

Some of the best moments of the film come with Ángela Molina as Rosaura Revueltas, the real-life Mexican actress who was deported during the shooting. In real life, Revueltas was blacklisted in her homeland, and she would die in poverty decades later—a fate suggested in Molina's weary look. Kael had absurdly accused Revueltas of being too glamorous to be credible as a community leader. The critic's other accusations—the purported inauthenticity of the Latinos and the mendacity of un-American communist propaganda—now seem, more and more in this retelling of the story, part of a distant and receding era when wild McCarthyite charges of conspiracy were as common as they were devastating. Meanwhile, the film has endured.

One of the Hollywood Ten is unique in another sense as well. Wilson and Jarrico, still the real leaders of the Hollywood Communist Party at the time of the filming of *Salt of the Earth*, were not "innocents" of the sort usually cast as protagonists in films about the blacklist era—not even as innocent as Hammett, who hardly played any political role at all except as public personality in antifascist and, later, domestic legal defense campaigns. But neither were Wilson and Jarrico anything like the stereotypes of the communist apparatchik. Serious artists in a popular medium, intellectuals jealous of interference with their artistic freedom, they were Hollywood types, after all. If they were guilty of anything, it was not for writing dreadfully unbalanced and unfair treatments of race relations in the United States, as Kael had charged, but of a political kamikaze action in making a film like *Salt of the Earth* at the height of the Cold War mania.

It would be years before there would be advances on the themes raised in *Salt of the Earth* of racial minorities in revolt, and when they did appear some of the best would take curious shapes, their roots in Cold War politics disguised or ignored or severed altogether. One of the most curious would be *Malcolm X* (1992), by director Spike Lee.

The issues naturally began with Malcolm himself. There were good reasons, beyond the obvious one, that Hollywood had for decades feared to show an angry black man with a weapon in his hands. But if the sympathetic treatment of petty criminals was old hat in Hollywood, the sympathetic treatment of black criminals who evolved into revolutionaries remained utterly unknown. And the real story of Malcom Little was more explosive even than that.

Converted in prison to Islam, like many other black men, Malcolm had resisted the draft at the height of the Cold War. His lawyer, Conrad Lynn, was a veteran Harlem Marxist who handed the prisoner revolutionary texts on request.[18] The text that reportedly piqued Malcolm's interest, *The Revolutionary Answer to the Negro Problem in the USA*, happened to be a pamphlet made up of historical documents from the Socialist Workers Party, a Trotskyist group on the left of the regular Communist Party. He was naturally drawn to the ideas of SWP's chief theorist on the issue, C. L. R. James, a black Trinidadian-born scholar, activist and pan-Africanist who had outlined to Trotsky personally, in Mexico, a synthesis of Black Nationalism and Marxism. In the final years before his assassination, as Malcolm moved away from the Nation of Islam, he moved toward his own version of internationalism and even toward a partnership of sorts with these Marxists.

Here was a mixture of nearly everything about the Cold War and the 1960s that large numbers of Americans, especially those in power, would rather forget.[19]

Racial, political and social themes of this complexity would have been difficult to weave together by the most gifted screenwriter, even if the outline of Malcolm's life and death offer the temptation for melodramatic exploitation. Indeed, the story of how the screenplay was put together is itself a complex tale not entirely free of drama, but one worth telling because it shows how the politics of the blacklist continued to affect filmmaking even into the last decade of the twentieth century.

In 1967, two years after Malcolm X was assassinated and just a year after *The Autobiography of Malcolm X*, written by Alex Haley, became a bestseller, Haley and Elia Kazan approached the playwright James Baldwin to ask him whether he was interested in adapting the *Autobiography* for the stage. After Baldwin won the blessing of Malcolm's sister and widow Betty Shabazz for the project, he retired to the country with Haley and Kazan for a week to work out some of the details. Baldwin's relationship with Kazan had begun a decade earlier while he was preparing the theater piece *Giovanni's Room* (1956) for production and the older man took him under his wing. By the time Baldwin had acquired a measure of fame, he had become skeptical of the value of the Kazan relationship (because of what a Baldwin biographer called "lingering political doubts" over the director's role in the blacklist), withdrawing from a wider partnership, but perhaps as consolation agreeing to work on an adaptation of the Haley book.[20]

In 1968, producer Marvin Worth bought the rights to the *Autobiography*, took it to Columbia Pictures, and offered Baldwin the first chance at writing the screenplay. After a great deal of soul-searching, Baldwin agreed and set out to transform the beginnings of his stage play, *One Day, When I Was Lost*, into a film script. But things went badly from the start. At one point, Columbia sent Baldwin a memo that he was to "avoid giving any political implications to Malcolm's trip to Mecca." As to his suggestions for a lead, Billy Dee Williams was out and perhaps even Charlton Heston, "darkened up a bit," would be offered the part.[21] When Baldwin balked at this kind of treatment and made little progress, Columbia insisted on bringing in another writer to help finish the job: none other than Arnold Perl, not long from his controversial stint on *East Side/West Side*.[22]

It was no mystery why Baldwin had been chosen early on to engage the story of Malcolm X. Although the gay, lyrical and rather high-strung playwright might have seemed at first glance an unlikely choice to tell the story of the person who represented, as Ossie Davis had put it in his eulogy, black manhood itself, Baldwin had always admired Malcolm. They also shared a certain sympathy for the Trotskyists, with some of whom the playwright was personally close and under whose banner he had actually marched, his youthful thinking influenced by the same C. L. R. James.[23]

Baldwin's recommendation of Perl remains somewhat puzzling. Until the middle 1950s, Perl was a typical Popular Front writer, a passionate opponent of racism but characteristically for men of his race and politics disdainful of black nationalism. But feelings for Malcolm had warmed in those quarters after his death, and Perl possessed the well-known ability to adapt almost anything, from individual or multiple sources, into a coherent drama. He had been a frequent contributor to the TV show *The Big Story* (1949–1957), whose gimmick was to dramatize the newspaper writings and backstories of big-city reporters.[24] As we have seen, he had also written for some of the best dramatic anthologies on television in the sixties. The two men worked on the screenplay together until, in March of 1967, Baldwin finally abandoned Hollywood in disgust (according to another version, he left for Paris with a lover). Columbia then sold the Baldwin-Perl property to Warner Brothers. Marvin Worth and Perl followed the project to the new studio, where Perl drew on his earlier work to direct a one-hour documentary, also called *Malcolm X*, that relied heavily on newsreel footage. Warners, apparently regarding the result as inflammatory, kept its name off the print and effectively buried it.[25]

After the documentary, cinematic silence descended on the subject. But it would only be a matter of years before the rising influence of progressive black actors in Hollywood, true to the older pattern of liberal-left white actors, began to assert itself in fresh new projects. When Worth was able to interest Denzel Washington in a feature version and elicit a commitment from him, a dramatized version of Malcolm's life became a virtual certainty. The biggest uresolved question was, who would direct?

By this time, the Malcolm of ferocious black nationalist lore and probable victim of a police conspiracy had receded and been replaced by an updated figure of respectable black pride. Rap groups, Clarence Thomas and even Dan Quayle could mine the speeches of Malcolm to grind their own axes. Meanwhile, in Spike Lee's account of the affair, the feature version of the Baldwin-Perl screenplay languished at Warners until the studio entered into a deal with Norman Jewison. The producer-director looked over their catalog of studio properties and settled on *Malcolm X*, hiring novelist and TV dramatist Charles Fuller to do a rewrite.[26]

An agitated Lee, watching these developments from the sidelines and no doubt emboldened by James Baldwin's own publicly expressed unhappiness in dealings with studio execs on this matter earlier, encouraged a press campaign against the notion that someone other than an African American should handle the assignment. The resulting publicity and pressure led to Jewison's removal in favor of Lee. The studio was finally vindicated in its gamble of placing the responsibility for a major production in the hands of a younger director whose previous films had been modestly budgeted. But it was touch and go for awhile.

Lee himself raised a chunk of the needed money from pre-release merchandising, including T-shirts, baseball caps, trading cards, refrigerator magnets and even air fresheners, licensed directly or indirectly to the director's own Forty Acres and a Mule company.[27] Even that might not have been enough to cover the $40 million tab if not for financial donations from Magic Johnson, Janet Jackson, Bill Cosby, Oprah Winfrey, Michael Jordan and others. Black film had never seen anything like it. Nor had Lee: a reporter called the evolving *Malcolm X* a "career-defining project."[28] In the meantime, Marvin Worth, who accepted a demotion to co-producer with Lee and two other money men, had been able to claim a series of hits with two other biopics, *The Rose* (about Janis Joplin) and *Lenny* (Lenny Bruce). Worth insisted that production was on the mark even when a bond company tried to seize control of costs and keep the film to no longer than 135 minutes. Warners' execs also sweated, keeping a close eye on Denzel Washington and insisting on watching the rushes with Lee. The outstanding young black actor in contemporary Hollywood, Washington's own considerable reputation was also said to rise or fall—for an extended moment, anyway—on the outcome.

Lee successfully brushed off complaints that the film was more interested in dramatic effects than in historical accuracy, defending it as an epic. Critics mostly responded in the same vein, obviously pleased or relieved at the closing scenes in which inflammatory radical (and racial) rhetoric was put aside for appeals for a transnational brotherhood. It also helped that images of an Islamic brotherhood were vastly less controversial than they would be ten years later. Lee was praised, perhaps most accurately, for underplaying the melodrama and letting the story tell itself.

Aside from his credits as co-producer and director, Lee also took a co-credit with Perl for the screenplay. The question of just how much Lee actually contributed as a writer remains a sensitive one. Lee has asserted that he rewrote the script and would "take full responsibility" for it.[29] But according to Perl's friends, Lee added the early scenes in and around the Roseland ballroom (in which Lee conspicuously wrote himself into the film as the sidekick Shorty), the entirety of the hero's visit to Mecca in the very last part of the film—and little else. The dramatic construction of many of the major scenes in the film are clearly discernable in Baldwin's original screenplay, *One Day, When I Was Lost*.[30] But Perl cut much of Baldwin's overlong and rather stagey dialogue, eliminated many scenes and compressed and rearranged the rest for the sake of the larger continuity—leaving little doubt that Perl's contributions accounted for the lion's share of the final screenplay. According to Writers Guild standards, at least 25 percent must be added for a screenwriter to receive co-credit. Of the nearly 200-minute film, it seems likely that Lee fell considerably short of the necessary 50 minutes to qualify for the credit. And if Lee, why not Baldwin?[31]

What did it suggest, to take a more recent Hollywood backstory, that definite non-leftist Spike Lee, his reputation raised a large notch by using a forgotten blacklistee's major film script, paid special public tribute to Budd Schulberg (who has supplied a script for the biopic of Joe Louis to be directed by Lee) for introducing him to Elia Kazan? Was it art or politics as usual in the new Hollywood, where insiders like Jim Carrey (star of *The Majestic*) could feel a distinct sympathy for the blacklistees while self-defined outsiders like Lee might be looking for a leg up into the Hollywood Establishment, 1950s style?

BARBRA

Hilton Kramer had sought to deliver the death blow to Cold War revisionism shortly after the premiere of *The Front*. Behind the muckraking of cold warriors he insisted, in a *New York Times* essay, that he perceived the effort "to acquit '60's radicalism of all malevolent consequence . . . by portraying 30's radicalism as similarly innocent . . . benign, altruistic and radical." *Some* people, he admitted, had indeed been unfairly smeared and even damaged in the McCarthy Era. But the charges against blacklistees were "not all false" by a long shot.[32]

This was a familiar revival of an old view. As a *Partisan Review* essay by philosopher Sidney Hook had acutely put the issue near the height of the HUAC hearings, a witch trial is not inherently mistaken, let alone unethical, if real witches actually exist. Perhaps the crones accused in Salem were really guilty and a threat to Puritan society (this presumably in response to the hated Arthur Miller's current theatrical hit, *The Crucible*). Certainly their modern counterparts had thrived in Hollywood, threatening subversion. Besides—Kramer here returned to another familiar line of thought—the blacklistees had themselves to blame for much of the anticommunist hysteria, by refusing to admit they were communists and demanding constitutional protections obviously unavailable in the Soviet Union. It was they, therefore, at least as much as the committee, the tabloid press, the FBI and so on, who had actually "created an atmosphere of havoc and hazard for the truly innocent."[33]

If Kramer's concise statement recapitulated the general line of Cold War liberal (by now neoconservative) thought, he seemed, in a philosophical sense at least, to have practically finished it off as well.[34] The New Left and the larger peace movement, also the movements for Black Power, Red Power and so on, had effectively taken the place of communists in Hollywood as well as outside it—notably decades after younger activists had utterly renounced Russian-style communism. The political effects of the sixties, evidently demoralizing American foreign policy to the point of defeat in Vietnam, had been bad enough. The cultural effects were even worse, promoting everything from cultural illiteracy to feminism, weakened patriotism, widespread drug use, single-parent families and so on. All this, as Kramer and his colleagues at *The New Criterion, Commentary, The New Republic, The Public Interest* and *The Wall Street Journal* were to explain at length, had roots in a massively deceptive revisionism according to which former communists and other insufficiently repentant members of the Popular Front had been demonized and treated badly. Repeated so often that it had grown tiresome by 1970, these charges nevertheless resurfaced endlessly, right down to the Hollywood commentary of *The Weekly Standard* in the next century.

The chief newer source of cultural controversy, women's liberation, had been one of the complaints against the New Left least attributable to the Popular Front (with regard to its equally hated counterpart, multiculturalism, the Popular Front was definitely more guilty).[35] Feminism's glamour in contemporary social movements, novels and films seemed to call into question, albeit from an angle scarcely related to Russia and the old controversies, the accomplishments and even the dignity of the now-senior critics whose world, despite the presence of a few important women, had been one of heavily male-defined intellect and art. Hollywood, always considered a chief source of kitsch undermining real culture, was once again a chief culprit here. Jane Fonda and Vanessa Redgrave offered a natural target, by virtue of their up-front leftism. But so did the most unlikely feminist icon of Jewish Hollywood: Barbra Streisand.

The Way We Were (1973), the first of the major Hollywood revisionist films, seemingly proved the conservatives' case beyond any doubt, connecting the Popular Front and its Hollywood wing with the infernal reappearance of the radicals' disloyalty to civilized values. Streisand in turn became, through this iconic film, something more and different than she had been before: not a bubble-headed comedienne, not a diva on film, but "Katie," the irrepressible personality and committed left-winger. The film's novel basis and a portion of its script were from the pen of the gay, graylisted writer Arthur Laurents, last seen as creator of the "book" for multicultural *West Side Story.* He, too, personally and proudly epitomized yet another case of the revenge of the repressed in Hollywood.[36]

By the time Streisand delivered a speech in L.A.'s LaBrea Park against the Israeli invasion of Lebanon in 1982, provoking a barrage of rotten vegetables from Jewish conservatives on hand, she had long since become a staple of liberal Jewish chic. A Brooklyn-born former theater usherette and Off-Broadway singing actress, she made her breakthrough in 1964 on Broadway in *I Can Get It For You Wholesale,* a theatrical remake of the forgotten feminist film scripted by Abraham Polonsky in the early 1950s.[37] Following a New York Critics' award, Streisand landed the lead in another stage musical, *Funny Girl,* and never looked back. Her film debut was in the same vehicle in 1968, and this time the screenwriter for *Funny Girl* was the regretful friendly witness, Isobel Lennart.

Lennart, known only for her screenwriting contributions to 1940s musicals like *Anchors Aweigh,* had pleaded with friends that, pregnant and divorced, she had no choice but to testify. It did save her career, mostly for material on the lighter side (*This Could Be the Night, Merry Andrew, Please Don't Eat the Daisies, Fitzwilly*) but occasionally also for melodrama (*Love Me Or Leave Me*) and the picturesque (*The Sundowners*). *Two For the Seesaw,* an adaptation of a contemporary play, was a borderline soapy treatment of adultery and abusive behavior. But in the hands of director Robert Wise, guiding Shirley MacLaine and Robert Mitchum, it could be called at least proto-feminist.

Funny Girl was something else: the treatment of Manhattan's own Fanny Brice, premiere Jewish comedienne of the 1910s through 1930s. After a triumphal run of the play version on Broadway—the apex of Lennart's slight career in writing for legitimate theater—it went to Columbia, to William Wyler, to Sidney Buchman (still a London exile) for a first script try, and then back to Lennart for the final version.

In many ways, *Funny Girl* proved less a film than an event. Its Manhattan opening featured a charity setting for the city's elite, a tent party staged in a theater district parking lot. This gala actually had been preceded a few months earlier by a Plaza Hotel fashion show of outfits (including a retro "Henry Street Look" of vintage proletarian pride, with flannel knickers and a middy blouse) "inspired" by the play and anticipating the forthcoming film.[38] The ticket prices at the film opening were the highest ever charged in New York, and charged successfully: it was a smash and made Streisand a superstar and a multi-millionaire with good prospects to become her own producer-director.

In one of those classic show-business ironies, the play had nearly died of bad notices before reaching Broadway. Only two things saved it: the choreography of friendly witness Jerome Robbins and the drawing power of Streisand.[39] By an odd but less than total coincidence, Brice had in real life been a feature performer for the Hollywood Anti-Nazi League, the first glittering Hollywood "front" of the Popular Front. Streisand, instinctively liberal, was on her way to being the feminist and peacenik that conservatives and outright antifeminists simply loved to hate.

Her performance won Streisand an Oscar, in a rare but significant tie with the leading actress who was still resented by right-wingers for her support of the blacklistees after so many years—Katharine Hepburn. In 1970, a special Broadway Tony named Streisand "actress of the decade," a reputation that helped keep her a star and her films hits at the box office despite a run of poor scripts and overly familiar roles as the ingénue destined to overpower the cute guy through a combination of humor and klutzy sincerity. She arguably reached her peak as a dramatic actress (barely) under Martin Ritt's direction in *Nuts* (1987), as we have seen. Nevertheless, *The Way We Were* (1973) would be her lasting triumph. More than *The Front*, more than any other film on the subject, it was destined to remain for popular audiences *the* film about the blacklist experience.

Not that critics were wrong to complain at the packaging of Streisand in an old-fashioned Hollywood romance. Arthur Laurents had constructed his novel and the film script from the Hollywood lives of Jiggy Schulberg (a popular Hollywood personality, but not an actress) and her second husband, Peter Viertel (son of Salka Viertel, a German exile in whose salon the Hollywood Popular Front was virtually hatched).[40] Laurents was initially fired and 11 other writers, including Dalton Trumbo, were invited to rework the script. In the end the job came back to Laurents and back to the real Hollywood problem: crafting the right vehicle for the chosen stars, Robert Redford and, above all, Streisand herself.

Streisand fought to save the "Katie" of the first version of the script, and for good reason; she, like Laurents, had in mind a feminist heroine. In the film, she is a campus antiwar leader of the 1930s, while Redford plays a gentile athlete-hero (far more of a hero than in the original). They fall in love and go to Hollywood. Katie remains on the Left, if politically inactive. Redford the novelist becomes a screenwriter and wants desperately to be successful, so he declines to join the defense movements of the day, indulging in a cynicism that he had always only half-disguised.

Katie naturally flies to Washington to defend the Hollywood 19—we could almost imagine her in the chartered plane with John Garfield, Humphrey Bogart, Lauren Bacall, Marsha Hunt, Abraham Polonsky, Danny Kaye, Michael Wilson, Waldo Salt and the unfriendly witnesses themselves—in the film (if not the novel), and returns upset at her reticent husband. After a confrontation with an unfriendly crowd at the airport (Laurents correctly observes that an authentic L.A. crowd, even in 1947, would more likely have wanted autographs than political revenge), she lays it on the line when she argues that people are more important than principles: "People *are* principles." The line was cut from the script, then returned at Streisand's insistence. It had become, in Laurents' retrospective assessment, "the political point of the whole picture."[41] Without it, the politics would have been lost. Katie leaves her husband to protect him from falling into HUAC's trap of guilt by association. She raises their daughter by herself as a working mother but also an unbroken political person back in New York. Former husband and wife meet at the end, in a gut-wrenching moment that many viewers probably remembered better than any other in the film.

The chemistry between stars Redford and Streisand, more than any political point, made the film a hit. Director Sydney Pollack and others on the scene actually cut Laurents' intended climax (again, not in the novel) in which Streisand would watch her daughter lead a rally on campus protesting the Vietnam War, mirroring her own youth. It was lost, although the final scene as it appears in the film—Katie herself handing out antiwar leaflets as Redford's character meets her again, still unable to be with her although loving her—was for most viewers meaningful enough.

The strain of Streisand striving to be Streisand being Katie, with Redford more modestly trying to be Redford but also her fictional lover and husband, upset discerning viewers who wanted the novel's characters rather than star turns, and it upset Laurents, too.[42] But it fulfilled a certain personal and generational agenda. Laurents recalled about himself that as a Jew growing up in an era of anti-Semitism, he had developed certain sensitivities. Through Marxism (and doubtless through his homosexuality as well), he broadened his sympathy toward underdogs and against the rich who think "they deserve the world."[43] It was an old, old message, reflavored by a relatively new one.

Decades after *The Way We Were*, the image of Katie remained vivid. Not that left-wing politics had become a lifestyle—far from it. But the kinds of commitments that Cold War liberals, neoconservatives and outright antifeminists had made to traditional sex roles (and their economic counterparts) had remained unpalatable for most educated or just spunky women, even in highly conservative times. Even so, global conflicts and stock market booms would bring a new generation of cultural conservatives a media adulation generated by their increasingly powerful allies. By that time, nearly all of the older Cold War intellectuals had died or gone into retirement, and not even cartoon-like action films with U.S. presidents prepared, Rambo-like, to take on the world managed to convey the cerebral cold warriors' interior values. Society had moved on.

RECAPITULATIONS

After *The Way We Were* and *The Front*, the next project of blacklistees themselves to reinterpret the blacklist experience came from yet another experienced writer (and victim), Abraham Polonsky, who from the 1980s until his death in 1999 was considered pretty much the ideological savant of the surviving community. His novel of the red scare, *A Season of Fear* (1956), had its main impact though a translation for European audiences and was carefully if elusively framed by the experiences of a Los Angeles civil servant rather than a Hollywoodite. But a noted French director knew of it and considered Polonsky ideal for a serious film about the blacklist. The script Polonsky delivered to Bernard Tavernier in the middle 1980s was very much an artistic treatment of his own recollections: a screenwriter returns to Los Angeles from France (as Polonsky did in 1950, after completing an

earlier novel) in the hope of resuming a screen career despite the unfavorable political conditions, only to find his world unraveling. The opening scene was to be
a flashback from the rapping of a congressional gavel, and after much political
trouble and personal turmoil, at the end of the film a return to the gavel scene for
the Polonskyan character who defies the congressmen and their stooges. By coincidence or otherwise, Polonsky's was exactly the ending a dozen years later chosen
by the writer and director of *The Majestic.*

Tavernier turned to other projects, and producer Irwin Winkler, a money
man who produced some interesting and controversial as well as commercial
films with fellow producer Robert Chartoff (notably *The Split, They Shoot Horses,
Don't They?, The Gang That Couldn't Shoot Straight, Raging Bull* and *The Right
Stuff,* not to mention the last four *Rockys*) seized the opportunity to become a director for the first time. But with friends high in the Reagan administration,
Winkler looked back on McCarthyism as an unfortunate misstep in an otherwise
defensible global war against the enemy. Polonsky, for his part, insisted upon a
film that did not hide behind an innocent: there had been enough films about
misunderstood liberals. The two parted company after Winkler unsuccessfully offered Polonsky a great deal of money to stay in the credits, and the film played on
HBO for the 1990–1991 season.[44]

The resulting *Guilty by Suspicion* had many sparkling moments, however
much they might have been undercut by Winkler's direction and revisions of the
screenplay. Robert De Niro even looked rather like the young Polonsky returning
to Hollywood full of confidence (if lacking the wry, cerebral humor of the original
and, unlike Polonsky, suffering a collapse of marriage and career). The director
finds his friends in something approaching emotional paralysis, the FBI on the
trail and a particularly repugnant attorney (based on real-life attorney Martin
Gang, played by blacklistee Sam Wanamaker as "Felix Graff") eager to encourage
contrition-by-confession. In the end, the De Niro character turns on his persecutors. The protagonist had not only never been a communist, he had not even
been a front, just a friend; no wonder he can be vindicated in the viewer's eye.

By the time this bastard creation appeared in 1990, another odd project
about the blacklist had already been made in the United Kingdom, and also produced for HBO. *Fellow Traveler* (1989), written by Michael Eaton and directed by
Philip Saville, starred Ron Silver, Hart Bochner, Imogen Stubbs, Katherine
Borowitz and, a surprise in the role of heavy, television actor Daniel J. Travanti,
familiar to audiences as the liberal cop with a conscience in the acclaimed "quality" series *Hill Street Blues.*

A better effort in some ways than the Winkler-distorted *Guilty by Suspicion,
Fellow Traveler* is set at roughly the same historical moment, with Silver as the
screenwriter matched or contrasted with a childhood friend, Bochner, a Jewish

proletarian by origin (he wears a star around his neck and sports a Brooklyn accent) who has become a screen sex idol. Here, through an effective flashback to the 1940s, widespread support for the Popular Front is dramatized in a gala fundraising event that evidently Jewish Hollywoodites hold to support the war effort. As Bochner tells the gathering around the inevitable pool, they have been vindicated: Hollywood is theirs, or at least they think so. Interestingly and quite on the button, their reddish politics has a mixed flavor simultaneously reflecting the ghetto past of parents and grandparents and embracing the anti-fascism of the moment, with its longed-for future world of peace and prosperity. They are the outsiders who have made their way inside without losing the outsider's faith. Then comes 1950, the investigations intensify and Silver heads for London, where he can write for the production company of *The Adventures of Robin Hood*. And there is Stubbs, Bochner's lover in the happy Hollywood past, now a British peacenik returned home in the onset of the powerful "Ban the Bomb" crusade, led in real life by British Marxist historian E. P. Thompson.

The *Robin Hood* section is definitely the better part of the film. Then comes the tragedy: separated from his family by thousands of miles, Silver has a failed fling with Stubbs, and learns the awful news that her ex-lover and Silver's intimate comrade has committed suicide—after spilling his guts to the committee. In the aftermath, Silver struggles to come to grips with the personal and historical dimensions of the situation. He is also tortured by other, vaguer childhood memories that he had been trying for years to expunge or at least neutralize with psychoanalysis. His shrink (Travanti), we learn in the climactic scene of the film, has been quietly coaxing the Hollywood reds to give the committee what it wants, and successfully persuaded Bochner—indirectly but unquestionably provoking the suicide.

This is one of the most interesting twists in a movie that otherwise might be memorable mainly for its Jewishness, its somewhat realistic recreation of the production of *Robin Hood* episodes (the film's British producer is politically indifferent, very much in contrast to Hannah Weinstein) and its treatment of psychoanalysis as part of the Hollywood Left equation. Too bad that *Fellow Traveler* died even more quietly than *Guilty by Suspicion*, shadowed rather than made more memorable by the ongoing collapse of the Soviet bloc and literal collapse of the Berlin Wall.

The new situation, an astute critic of popular culture observed, revisited familiar issues most curiously. New York intellectuals, those ultimate enemies of the blacklistees, had spent decades simultaneously opposing Popular Frontism and television, to them the twin markers of totalitarianism and conformism. When consumerism at large and television in particular succeeded in overwhelming what had withstood a half-century of rhetoric and madly accelerating weaponry in the Eastern Bloc, the militant highbrows were dumbfounded. Had they won or lost, and what about their old enemies?[45]

No one could say for sure. Support for and opposition to Kazan receiving a lifetime award from the academy in 1999 was marshaled in the main by people a generation or two younger than the blacklistees, most of them eager to praise the artist with as little as possible said about the fellow travelers of the blacklist. After antagonists Dmytryk, Polonsky and Lardner, Jr., all died in the 18 months after that ceremony, hardly any original combatants remained on either side.

THE LAST WORD

It may, then, have been a distinct surprise in post–9/11 America, with prospects of a new McCarthyism in the air, with studio heads rushing to make patriotic statements and promising an era of red-blooded films, to see that the most politically intriguing movie of a dull Christmas 2001 season happened to be *The Majestic*.

Clearly, this film had been made as a vehicle for Jim Carrey, the hottest comedy star in Hollywood. Carrey had one previous deadly serious role, as the self-discovering star of *The Truman Show*, depicting a world where all images are manipulated. *The Majestic* unmistakably revisited the seasonal television favorite, *It's a Wonderful Life*. Few fans of that Jimmy Stewart classic directed by Frank Capra would know that several screenwriters soon to be on the blacklist had drafted or redrafted the script, leaving their mark upon its cultural politics. Screenwriter Michael Sloane and director Frank Darabont of *The Majestic* gave them more than a few clues about the historical connections of the subject.

The Majestic includes a famous bit of footage. Hollywood screenwriter John Howard Lawson is cross-examined by the House Committee on Un-American Activities in October 1947, and attempts to respond by insisting upon his constitutional rights to free speech. Moments before, Carrey is seen in a 1951 studio story conference discussing inane plot points recommended by an anonymous producer off-camera. Soon we learn that the apolitical or vaguely liberal writer played by Carrey has been named as a red, then fired and forcibly escorted off the studio grounds. When the writer also loses his starlet girlfriend, he drives drunkenly north out of L.A., plunges off a bridge and, after a rescue on the beach, finds himself in—Lawson, California. His rescuer happens to be played by James Whitmore, in real life one of Hollywood's most prominent veteran progressives.[46]

Little Lawson is the Bedford Falls of *It's a Wonderful Life*, now removed distantly westward and a few years forward in time. The current trauma is no longer the threatened return of Depression economics, with a bank failure roiling the local economy and quality of small-town life, but something worse. Lawson of

1951 continues to suffer under the gloom of having lost its best men in the war against fascism. Now, as we learn with the townsfolk, the freedoms retained at such cost are threatened again, this time by the Cold War's clampdown on civil liberties. Real-life screenwriter Sloane, in a follow-up essay in *Scripting.com*, noted, "I've been known to refer to the blacklist (figuratively speaking) as 'the entertainment industry's own Vietnam War,'" a dark, divisive period that damaged nearly everything it touched and changed everything afterward.[47]

Director Darabont and Sloane chose something only a little less supernatural than an angel to move the plot along. The movie's screenwriter has total amnesia and looks a lot like the town's favorite son, lost in the Pacific theater and presumed dead all these years. It's a miracle. The townsfolk obviously convince themselves to believe in the miracle because they need to believe in themselves again. The restored son will bring the town back to itself, specifically by reviving the town's movie palace, which had obviously been the center of local culture. The hero's father (played movingly by Martin Landau) is physically failing, but capable of one last burst of energy and hope. The hero's erstwhile fiancée, now training to become a civil liberties lawyer, not only believes Carrey but adds steel to his backbone. And so he becomes a political stand-in for the lost legions of American dead who died fighting fascism abroad and, the movie implies, might have fought it again if they had been able to return home.

Near the end, the screenwriter recovers his memory (triggered when a B-film that he wrote is playing at the local theater) and, more or less simultaneously, the FBI along with a voracious daily press move in on him. From the red hunters' angle, the dangerous character who disappeared is now at work nefariously somewhere in middle America, in disguise and carrying out god-knows-what Russian schemes. Only the audience and the theater's custodian, played by Gerry Black, have grasped the truth of the situation all along.

It is perhaps a given that our real hero will refuse to regain his professional standing by submitting himself to the committee (to name the names handed to him). But the matter is handled interestingly by the revelation that the former would-be girlfriend who named him, apparently a genuine active leftist back in the forties if perhaps never a communist, was simply protecting her new career as a TV producer. Now the writer can get off the hook similarly by doing the same to someone else. And what would that gain him? We see that the story conferences are still the same as before he left; the voice of Rob Reiner as the producer is heard, proposing or actually demanding that a script "add a dog" to work out the melodramatic complications. The writer would be just another Hollywoodite—exactly what he wanted to be when the film opened. Here, *The Majestic*, like most of its predecessors, unfortunately eludes the central issue of Jewishness that powered the Popular Front and shaped artistic creativity as an independent factor; the identification of the outsider with other outsiders and the mass-culture artist with the possibilities of popular entertainment that was also popular resistance. The lapse could not have been incidental, even if Martin Landau, as theater-owner and father of the war hero, seems strikingly Jewish, albeit thoroughly secular like so many Jews of his generation and later.

Charitably viewed, *The Majestic* needs the presence of this absence because the film's mainly happy ending sees the townsfolk of Lawson rejoice at the return of their newly adopted "native" son, notwithstanding his political notoriety. In real life, WASPy small towns, especially amid the hysteria whipped up during the Korean War, were more likely to be part of the McCarthyite constituency that viewed red screenwriters as "those Jews" and deserving any punishment they received (or worse). Perhaps if the victims had been known personally and affianced to a native daughter an old civil liberties spirit would still prevail? Perhaps. But maybe not if he were Jewish.

The Majestic is hardly great art. Friendly critics cheerfully and accurately recommended it as a film for the season of family viewing, especially that particular Christmastime, as threats against civil liberties multiplied and the prospect of endless global warfare seemed to roll far out over the horizon.

More obvious than the success or failure of *The Majestic* in artistic or box-office terms was its continuation of this book's central themes. Although more than half a century has passed since the onset of the blacklist, the underlying issues seem as alive as ever, with the Hollywood victims as perfect (and charismatic) examples of the culture's self-inflicted tragedy. Probably it was a given all along that the suffering of the poor—an inevitable subject as the division of wealth came in the 1980s and after to replicate 1910s levels—would serve the needs of the popular narrative less effectively than the suffering of the middle-class idealist, existentialist, lover or rascal. Writers and directors, as intellectuals of a sort, treat their own kind most effectively. And even when they do look in the direction of the poor or the working class, it is not likely to be to the humble but to such larger-than-life personalities as fighter Muhammad Ali (as in Michael Mann's biopic *Ali*) who are regarded as possessing a stature suitable for narrative treatment.

Still, there is far more to the memory of the 1930s and 1940s than this. The filmic tribute to the "Greatest Generation" of World War II also constitutes a tribute to the last idealistic war—and not the hypocritical one for a redefined "freedom" of open markets everywhere or for the invasion of an oil-rich former U.S. weapons client, transformed into an enemy of biblical proportions. The collective memories of Hollywood's Golden Era, endlessly re-edited and replayed on American Movie Channel in film-clip documentaries, embodies a disappeared time when movies provided a transforming world of enormous creative energy and a rich social imagination. Never mind that stale narratives and predictable directing and acting, corruption and mob influence dominated Hollywood at its most golden. Something about those days and in those films remains more vital, more imaginative, more real and ultimately truer to the country, at its best, than what came afterward.

Hollywood was always about money. It is still is. But at its best it was and eventually might once again be something a great deal more—a glimmering of a democratic art form returning the embrace of its vast audience with equal sincerity and the sense of a common fate.

NOTES

INTRODUCTION

1. David Caute, *Joseph Losey: A Revenge on Life* (New York: Oxford University Press, 1994), 169–70.
2. These were, after all, men whose political power largely derived from the fact that great numbers of their citizens were *prevented* from voting. For a brief account of Wilson's intentions in turning Rod Serling's original screenplay into a satire, see Joe Russo et al., *Planet of the Apes Revisited* (New York: Thomas Dunne Books, 2001), 33–34.
3. Lucille Frackman Becker, *Pierre Boulle* (New York: Twayne, 1996), 76. Boulle's novel, *La planète des singes*, was published in 1963.
4. Hunter said she was removed from the blacklist after an unidentified person wrote a letter to *Planet* producer Arthur Jacobs telling him that he would be provided the reason for Hunter's blacklisting in exchange for $200. The person's boss was said to have been upset that the blackmail had been put in writing and removed Hunter's name from the list. Russo, *Planet of the Apes Revisited*, 50.
5. Any lingering doubts about Wilson's allegorical intentions are resolved by a rarely noticed bit of dialogue, when an older chimp researcher complains to Dr. Zira that he is little more than a "vet" in her laboratory: "You promised to speak to Dr. Zaius about me." Dr. Zira: "I did. You know he looks down his nose at chimpanzees." Older doc: "But the quota system's been abolished! You made it. Why can't I?" The mention of a "quota system," underscored in Zaius' own later slur against the chimpanzees as "perverted scientists," are references to the *numerus clausus*, the academic practice of limiting the number of positions available to particular ethnic groups, notably Jews, that was once practiced formally in Germany and more informally in the United States.
6. Wilson also wrote *Friendly Persuasion* (1956), starring Gary Cooper, a much-admired account of a pacifist Quaker's soul-searching over the Civil War, but received no credit until 1996, when several of his key credits were restored posthumously. Thanks go to Becca Wilson for allowing us to examine the original scripts of these and other films (made or never made) in the Michael Wilson Collection, UCLA.
7. "Author's Comment," following script for "Noon On Doomsday," in A. S. Burack, *Television Plays for Writers: Eight Television Plays with Comment and Analysis by the Authors* (Boston: The Writer, Inc., 1957), 353–59. The sponsor of the television drama series, *The U.S. Steel Hour*, which broadcast the play, insisted upon various changes and Serling submitted, adding that he believed that a central point, the

evil of prejudice, still received serious treatment. See also William Boddy, *Fifties Television: The Industry and Its Critics* (Urbana: University of Illinois, 1990), 201–204, for a retrospective look at the significance of the controversy around the show.

8. Two comparable films were written by semi-rehabilitated blacklistees: *Fail-Safe* (1964), by Walter Bernstein, had an American president cowed by the military into dropping a hydrogen bomb upon New York City to prevent all-out nuclear war; and *Executive Action* (1973), written by Dalton Trumbo, featured a military-backed plot to seize the presidency.

9. Arthur Laurents, *Original Story By: a Memoir of Broadway and Hollywood* (New York: Knopf, 2000), especially 263–85.

10. Christine Gledhill, "The Melodramatic Field: An Investigation," in Gledhill, ed., *Home Is Where the Heart Is: Studies in Melodrama and the Woman's Film* (London: BFI Books), 5–39.

11. Interview with Abraham Polonsky by Buhle and Wagner, 1994.

12. Characteristically, Renata Adler viewed the allegory as a confrontation between "Neanderthal flower children who have lost the power of speech" and apes representing "police brutality." As she concluded about the movie, "It is no good at all." *New York Times*, February 9, 1968.

13. W. McNeil Lowry, "A Writers' Congress and Its Credo," *The New York Times Book Review*, September 24, 1944.

14. Theodore Adorno, *Prisms*, translated by Sam and Shierry Weber (London: Neville Spearman, 1968), 122–23.

15. Significantly, Crowther spent five years on *The Times'* drama desk before turning to film criticism, 1932–37. See Frank Eugene Beaver, *Bosley Crowther: Social Critic of the Film, 1940–1967* (New York: Arno Press, 1974), 7.

16. Samuel Johnson, from the preface to his *Dictionary of the English Language* (London: 1755).

CHAPTER ONE

1. See Gabriel Miller, *The Films of Martin Ritt: Fanfare for the Common Man* (Jackson: University Press of Mississippi, 2001), 153–54.

2. See the final chapter for an accounting of these nearly half-dozen films, spanning a quarter century in production.

3. Polonsky liked to refer to anonymity on the show as "Keeping it from Arthur," a sly reference to Arthur Schlesinger, Jr., who would presumably have taken satisfaction in the firing of himself, Manoff and Bernstein.

4. Jeff Kisseloff, "Another Award, Other Memories of McCarthyism," *New York Times*, May 30, 1999.

5. Walter Bernstein, *Inside Out: A Memoir of the Blacklist* (New York: Knopf, 1996), 21.

6. See Daniel M. Czitrom, *Media and the American Mind* (Chapel Hill: University of North Carolina Press, 1982), with reflections upon the fluidity of each new medium and its ultimate monopolization.

7. Ball noted in her autobiography that she had also told HUAC interrogators about being registered as a Communist in 1936: "It just didn't seem like such an awful thing to do, the way it does these days . . . it was almost as terrible to be a Republican then." Lucille Ball, *Love, Lucy* (New York: G.P. Putnam's Sons, 1996), 226.

Walter Winchell continued to hound her, but the sponsor of her show, the board chairman of Philip Morris, considered her too valuable to lose. As she observed about not being blacklisted, "I was one of the lucky ones." Ibid., 231.

8. Even *Hee Haw* boasted the occasional presence of John Henry Faulk, the first tele-personality to sue an agency blacklisting him and win.

9. The uncertain and utterly weak position of the television writer of the 1950s is re-called in "'Wild, Wild West,' as seen by Old TV Writers," *New York Times*, July 8, 1999.

10. Stefan Kanfer, *A Journal of the Plague Years* (New York: Athaneum, 1973), 121–22.

11. David Marc and Robert J. Thompson, *Prime Time, Prime Movers* (Syracuse: Syracuse University Press, 1992), 119.

12. Edward Braun, ed., *Meyerhold on Theater* (London: Metheun, 1969), 269.

13. David Garfield, *A Player's Place: The Story of the Actor's Studio* (New York: McMillan, 1980), 21, thus expresses the common view that Strasberg, who "was reading a great deal of Marx, Lenin and Trotsky" in the late 1920s, "defined the actor's problems in Marxist terms" of the theater as a commodity and the typing of the actor as a characteristic form of specialization as exploitation.

14. Ira Levine, *Left Wing Dramatic Theory in the American Theater* (Ann Arbor: University of Michigan Press, 1985), 16.

15. Thus, as we will see below, Group drama drifted toward the personal. Its would-be final production of 1941 would have been Odets' *Clash By Night*. Financial backer Billy Rose pulled out and the poetic ending misfired. Rewritten for film by former Communist Alfred Hayes, it was a powerful statement on the end of a working-class era. See David Garfield, *A Player's Place*, 41, and Paul Buhle and Dave Wagner, *Radical Hollywood* (New York: The New Press, 2002), 326–27.

16. Garfield, *A Player's Place*, 180–81.

17. Many thanks to Prof. Robert Hethmon for compiling this list.

18. Garfield, *A Player's Place*, 277–80. Many "graduates" enjoyed playing down Method as such, insisting that immersion was a simpler explanation for good acting. One of the most famous to make the claim was Rod Steiger. See Richard Severo, "Rod Steiger, 77, Oscar-Winning Character Actor Known for His Intensity and Versatility, Dies," *New York Times*, July 10, 2002.

19. Just to name some of those younger actors taking lessons from Corey or involved in the intimate Stage Society, which produced plays in a renovated two-car garage near Corey's Los Angeles home: Carol Burnett, Dean Stockwell, writers Robert Towne and Carole Eastman, Richard Chamberlain, Robert Blake, James Coburn, Jack Nicholson, Rita Moreno, Sheree North, John Gavin, Pat Boone, Peter Fonda, Candice Bergen, Ellen Burstyn and even superstar Gary Cooper, who came to Corey to improve his acting. Jeff Corey interview with Patrick McGilligan, in Patrick McGilligan and Paul Buhle, *Tender Comrades: a Backstory of the Hollywood Blacklist* (New York: St. Martins, 1997), 188–96, and Douglas Martin, "Jeff Corey, Character Actor and Acting Instructor, 88," *New York Times*, August 20, 2002.

20. Interview with Paul Jarrico by Larry Ceplair, UCLA Special Collections. Other actors were not so inclined toward teaching and not so lucky. Jean Muir, dropped from *The Aldrich Family* in the 1950 season, was the first known blacklistee of the medium. In 1953, after the SAG officially passed a loyalty test for its members, the blacklist rapidly picked up. Only 36 actors appeared on the list of those who had refused to answer HUAC questions, but hundreds had been graylisted from films or television. See David F. Prindle, *The Politics of Glamour: Ideology and Democracy in*

the Screen Actors Guild (Madison: University of Wisconsin Press, 1988), especially 37–62.

21. Joseph Papp (still Papirofsky) was hired as a stage manager by CBS in 1951, thanks to his friend and teacher Morris Carnovsky, already blacklisted and in charge of the Neighborhood Playhouse. By the time he was called in front of HUAC in 1957, Papp was stage manager of *I've Got a Secret*. See Helen Epstein, *Joe Papp: an American Life* (Boston: Little, Brown, 1994), 73–76.

22. Arthur Penn, in "The Crucible, an Oral History by Peter Biskind," *Premiere*, "New York" special issue, 1994, 104.

23. Penn later, of course, made many other important films of the 1960s. See p. 22.

24. Thanks go to the late Yiddish poet Martin Birnbaum, a Pindar of the 1930s sweat-shops (as well as an admired lyricist), for explaining "the ghetto is warm" as the reason for his own reclusive career within the Yiddish-speaking Left rather than writing poetry in English, which he knew perfectly well.

25. Interview with Adele Ritt by Paul Buhle, Los Angeles, 1992.

26. And not only as producer: his moment of public glory as actor came, remarkably enough, with an episode of *Danger* scripted by Walter Bernstein, in which Ritt as a small-scale hood is also a dreamer who ends up on death row. Critics gushed that he was perhaps the best television actor working. Meanwhile, Bernstein slept on his couch.

27. Thanks to Nina Serrano, a student of Lumet's in the School for the Arts, for her recollections.

28. Quoted in Frank R. Cunningham, *Sidney Lumet: Film and Literary Vision* (Lexington: University Press of Kentucky, 1991), 18–19.

29. The first show, in February 1953, was "The Landing of the Hindenberg," written by Abraham Polonsky, directed by Lumet and highlighted by a narrative read by Cronkite with antifascist high notes and such unmistakable verbal sidebars for 1939 as "In Hollywood the motion picture producers again refused to agree to a closed shop and the [writers'] strike continues." On Polonsky's role in the series see Paul Buhle and Dave Wagner, *A Very Dangerous Citizen*, 174–79.

30. The "discovery" was by no means recent for figures like Lumet, Cronkite or even Eric Severeid (a former Left sympathizer who had turned sharply anti-communist), who apparently knew perfectly well that the episodes were written by hidden left-wingers.

31. See chapters 3, 4 and 6 for details on Aldrich's personal connections with the Left and his film projects with them.

32. The American Movie Channel documentary, "'Reel Radicals: 60's Revolution on Film," first aired April 2, 2002, also touched on television drama of the 1950s as background to changes in film of the 1960s, but only treated directors (including Lumet), not writers or actors. Norman Jewison is seen describing the film *Seven Days in May* as the first break with McCarthyism, the documentary (and Jewison himself) evidently overlooking the many subtle and not-so-subtle earlier treatments and the role of the blacklistees themselves in attacking the McCarthyite phenomenon. Among important noncommunist writers, J.P. Miller possessed a seriousness of purpose that placed him close to their artistic intent. An Emmy winner, Miller was dropped for his "depressing" dramas. See his obituary, Peter M. Nichols, "J.P. Miller, 81, Dies, Writer of Teleplays," *New York Times*, December 5, 2001.

33. Arthur Penn, in "The Crucible: An Oral History," 104.

34. See Judith E. Smith, *Visions of Belonging: Family Stories, Popular Culture and Postwar Democracy, 1940–1960* (New York: Columbia University Press, 2004).
35. It was said for years afterward that Chayefsky dreaded any official-looking letters addressed to "Sidney," fearing investigators had caught up with his youthful associations.
36. Actually, she got the part after first being turned down, then having Gene Kelly convince Dore Schary to vouch for her to the American Legion! A film part netted her an Oscar nomination and the award for best actress at the Cannes Festival—the last film offer she ever received. See Betsy Blair Reisz interview with Patrick McGilligan, in *Tender Comrades*, 554.
37. H. H. Aniah Gowda, *The Idiot Box: Early American Television Plays* (New York: Envoi Press, 1987), 22. One has the impression that this volume, actually printed in India, is composed of essays written decades earlier, close to the production era discussed.
38. The American Communist critical apparatus, a once-influential operation reduced to almost nothing (a small magazine named *Masses & Mainstream*, then just *Mainstream*) by the 1950s, struck some of its last sound blows at the limitations of *Marty* and Chayefsky in general. See John Howard Lawson, "Bold, Bawdy and Dull," *Mainstream*, 7 (July, 1958), especially 48–57, complaining mainly about the bad imitations of Chayefsky proliferating into what Lawson called "Mama-I-am-going-to-the-movies-with-Charles soap operas." Lawson, down on his own luck, insisted that Chayefsky could do better.
39. Ring Lardner, Jr., "TV's New Realism: Truth Sans Consequences," *The Nation*, 181 (Aug. 13, 1955), 132–34.
40. The harshest criticism was by "V.H.F.," likely a *nom de plume* for one of the black-listed screenwriters, in "TV: Electronic Bard," *Masses & Mainstream* 8 (August, 1955), 48–52; Milton Howard, "'Marty,'" 8 (January, 1955), 49–57, had been kinder.
41. Bernstein, interviewed by Paul Buhle, 1992.
42. Reginald Rose oral history excerpt, in Jeff Kisseloff, *The Box* (New York: Penguin, 1995), 239.
43. Ibid., 256.
44. The play is published in A. S. Burack, *Television Plays for Writers* (Boston: The Writer, Inc., 1957), 245–302.
45. "Author's Comment" to "Tragedy in a Temporary Town, " in ibid., 305.
46. The film co-starred most of the television cast, including friendly witness Lee J. Cobb, future *Defenders* star E. G. Marshall, and several well-known progressive actors of the 1950s–1970s, including Jack Klugman, Ed Begley, Jack Arden and Martin Balsam.
47. Gowda, *The Idiot Box*, 73. It's worth noting that the film adaptation of *Twelve Angry Men*, directed by Sidney Lumet, was edited by blacklistee Carl Lerner, whose career ended with a premature death. His final job was editing *Klute*.
48. William Boddy, *Fifties Television* (Urbana: University of Illinois, 1990), 198–200.
49. Robert Kass of the *Catholic World*, quoted in Kisseloff, *The Box*, 190.
50. William Boddy, *Fifties Television: The Industry and its Critics* (Urbana: University of Illinois Press, 1990), 200.
51. Ibid., 199–203.
52. Serling himself, of course, launched *Twilight Zone* that year. Ultimately, he wrote 92 of the show's 156 episodes, if not a record then an extraordinary accomplishment; as on-camera narrator, he was the most formidable presence of the avant-garde within the mainstream.

53. Max Wilk, *The Golden Age of Television* (Mt. Kisko: Moyer-Bell, 1989), 41–42.

54. Felix Jackson to his boss at CBS, Harry Ommerele, April 11, 1955, in correspondence folder, Box 5, Felix Jackson Papers, American Heritage Center, University of Wyoming in Laramie.

55. Harry Ommerle to Felix Jackson, December 15, 1953, ibid.

56. J. P. Miller wrote similar stories, *The Days of Wine and Roses* (about alcoholism) and *The People Next Door* (about a drug-addicted teen and her family), before being dropped.

57. Prindle, in *The Politics of Glamour*, 80–81, does not think so, but critical researchers on Reagan's past, such as Dan Moldea, would surely disagree. See in particular his *Dark Victory: Ronald Regan, MCA, and the Mob* (New York: Penguin Books, 1987).

58. Prindle, *The Politics of Glamour*, 86–87. The SAG's conservatives repeatedly beat back efforts at merger, aiming especially at the later attempted encompassing of the Screen Extras Guild, those barely working and scarcely paid actors at the bottom of the heap. Charlton Heston added fuel to the fire by campaigning for so-called "right to work" laws banning union shops in several states. In the view of SAG conservatives, the organization had no cause to consider itself part of the labor movement.

59. My *Sister Eileen*, starring Elaine Stritch, actually became a short-lived television series (1960–1961); so did *Margie* (1961–1962), based on a film (at its 1940s production, condemned by FBI agents) that had been based on other *New Yorker* short stories by McKenney. The author's sister Eileen was married to writer Nathanael West and died with him in a famous car crash in 1940.

60. See Max Wilk, *The Golden Age of Television*, 127. Susskind's sometime partner, Fred Coe, produced the *Philco-Goodyear Playhouse*, later *Playwrights '56*, and many specials; he went back to Broadway where he produced Chayefsky's *The Tenth Man* and Herb Gardner's *A Thousand Clowns*. For him, the end of live television was an especially great disappointment.

61. Thanks again to Alfred Brenner for these insights. Susskind personally took the mike for the syndicated late-night talk show *Open End* (1958–62), a vastly more liberal and whimsical version of the *Nightline* type.

62. The *New York Times* reviewed it mostly unsympathetically, claiming that it was both too close to *On The Waterfront* and too television-like in its pat solutions. Bosley Crowther, "Screen: On Brotherhood," *New York Times*, January 30, 1957. These charges seem unfair twice over; an attempt to credit Elia Kazan, still very much in favor, and to treat television as a lower form of art.

63. David Boroff, "Television and the Problem Play," in Patrick D. Hazard, ed., *TV as Art: Some Essays in Criticism* (Champaign: National Council of Teachers of English, 1966), 98–99.

64. As a fledgling actress in 1930s British cinema, she made her film debut directed by Bernard Vorhaus. After the Second World War, Lupino set out to make herself a director, and utilized Paul Jarrico as co-writer and (he claimed) uncredited co-director for *Not Wanted* (1949), a fascinating low-budget story of an immigrant mother giving birth to an illegitimate baby.

CHAPTER TWO

1. David F. Prindle, *The Politics of Glamour: Ideology and Democracy in the Screen Actors Guild* (Madison: University of Wisconsin Press, 1988), 76.

2. See the actors' revealing oral history in Jeff Kisseloff, *The Box: an Oral History of Television, 1920–1961* (New York: Penguin, 1995), 339–47.

3. See Nina C. Liebman, *Living Room Lectures: The Fifties Family in Film and Television* (Austin: University of Texas, 1995), 52–61.

4. See interview with Alfred Lewis Levitt by Larry Ceplair, in Patrick McGilligan and Paul Buhle, *Tender Comrades: A Backstory of the Hollywood Blacklist* (New York: St. Martins, 1997), 445–46. The couple worked four years, or about 30 episodes, on *Donna Reed* with knowledge of their status by Reed's real husband, Tony Owen. Alfred Levitt was offered the position of producer on the show but turned it down for fear of exposure.

5. Liebman, *Living Room Lectures*, 260–61.

6. This film also marked Marsha Hunt's return from the blacklist; although she was never a communist, Hunt had refused to testify against colleagues and friends. Thanks go to Hunt for comments made to Paul Buhle (and the audience) at a symposium on the blacklist in South Pasadena in 1997, sponsored by the Southern California Library.

7. David Marc, *Comic Visions: Television Comedy and American Culture* (Boston: Unwin Hyman, 1989), 181–82, 191–92.

8. David Puttnam (with Neil Watson), *Movies and Money* (New York: Knopf, 1998), 188–89.

9. See David Marc and Robert J. Thompson, *Prime Time, Prime Movers: From I Love* *Lucy to L.A. Law—America's Greatest TV Shows and the People Who Created Them* (Syracuse: Syracuse University Press, 1995), 141–52 for an acute overview of Huggins' career.

10. These personal observations and others are drawn from an interview by Prof. Robert Hethmon with Roy Huggins in June, 2000. Many thanks to Hethmon for his hard questions, and for making this tape available to us. Huggins died April 3, 2002.

11. Of the obituaries that appeared at his death, the most insightful on the subject of his western television shows was Anthony Hayward in the British *Independent* ("Obituary: Roy Huggins," April 8, 2002), from which these quotations are taken.

12. Probably it was no accident that some of the best of the parody westerns in pre-blacklist films owed heavily to left-wing writers: *Destry Rides Again* (1939), with its milk-drinking sheriff who refuses to wear a gun; *The Wistful Widow of Wagon Gap* (1948), an Abbott and Costello western that pins a badge to Lou's chest and pokes fun at the showdown with a small army of women carrying rolling pins; and *Traveling Saleswoman* (1950), a farce with gender-roles reversed and suitor Andy Devine chasing his bride, while comedienne Joan Davis ends the Indian/white range war with no bloodshed. No stranger to the Old Left in film and television, Mel Brooks created *Blazing Saddles* (1974), the best stop on this train, but returning blacklistees and friendly witnesses wrote or directed several others in the genre that the *New York Times* called "Mock Twain." *Texas Across the River* (1966), a Dean Martin vehicle directed by friendly witness Michael Gordon, is arguably the best of these.

13. Marc and Thompson, *Prime Time, Prime Movers*, 147.

14. Special thanks to Joan Scott for describing her episodes of *Surfside Six*. The script itself is in the Adrian and Joan Scott Papers, American Heritage Research Center, Laramie, Wyoming.

15. That the real story behind the series had political overtones was apparent to many viewers, including the writers for *Saturday Night Live*, who a generation later parodied the film in a sketch called "Run, Liberal, Run!"

16. Moreno, an avid supporter of civil rights causes, was one of the celebrity personalities to support Puerto Rican independence at the height of that movement during the 1970s.

17. A further irony: credited with executive status on many *Rockford Files* episodes was Meta Rosenberg, a prominent friendly witness—formerly married to left-leaning producer-director Irving Reis—who was Garner's agent and a compulsory part of any major deal with the star. Leaving the series, Huggins took retirement, although he returned in the middle 1980s for several mini-series. None of the rest of his work was particularly distinguished or politically interesting, although it included a miniseries of Arthur Hailey's *Wheels* (1978).

18. Duff, married to Ida Lupino, was graylisted after starring for five years in the popular radio series, *The Adventures of Sam Spade* (1946–1951) based on Dashiell Hammett's characters. Duff was guilty of the usual membership in various war-era committees, was named in *Red Channels* and couldn't find work in films or television for a half-dozen years. See an interview done shortly before his death by Mark Dawidziak, "Howard Duff and the Adventures of Sam Spade," in Ed Gorman, Lee Server and Martin H. Greenberg, eds., *The Big Book of Noir* (New York: Caroll & Graf, 1998), 353–62.

19. Protagonist Diamond, played by David Janssen in his first big role, was of marginal interest, but the show had a unique gendered angle. Diamond's very life depended on his telephone service and the intuitive reach of a woman who remained in the shadows except for her shapely legs. For most of the series, this happened to be Mary Tyler Moore, formerly the disembodied legs of a refrigerator commercial. Albert Ruben, interviewed by David Marc, March 9, 1998, archives in the Steven H. Scheuer Television History Collection, Syracuse University Center for the Study of Popular Television.

20. Ruben also wrote for *The People's Choice* (1955–1958), a vehicle for former child star Jackie Cooper, who played an ornithologist elected by a write-in vote to a city council seat of "New City, California," and who then faces the persistent objections of the mayor, his father-in-law. The series is best remembered for the running commentary of Cooper's dog, Cleo.

21. Star Trek's *Enterprise* was originally to have been captained by a woman, according to Roddenberry's first outline, a detail which prompts unanswered questions about the former L.A. cop's cultural politics and his feelings about the liberal left milieu around him.

22. *Naked City* was produced by none other than Charles Russell, who had also produced *You Are There* before being fired. In the new show, Russell continued his practice of hiring the most talented blacklistees he could find.

23. "New York Stories," an oral history by Peter Biskind. Special issue of *Premiere* (1994), 110.

24. Ibid.

25. Jack Klugman, interviewed by David Marc, 1996, Steven H. Scheuer Television History Collection, 65, 19, 31.

26. See Jeff Kisseloff, *The Box*, 482–98.

27. Albert Ruben, Al Brenner and Waldo Salt wrote episodes for *The Nurses*, and Brenner and Howard Dimsdale wrote for *Ben Casey*. Dimsdale also contributed episodes to *Mannix*, *Gunsmoke* and *The Bold Ones* under the pseudonym "Arthur Dales." Leo Penn, a graylistee, had worked on Huggins' shows, directed and sometimes co-starred in *Ben Casey* episodes.

28. The exceptions were, of course, *Beulah* and *Amos 'n Andy*, with predictable stereo-types reinforced. *The Nat King Cole Show*, in 1956, stirred a major controversy and could not attract sponsors. Hazel Scott, who played Beulah, was named in *Red Channels* and dropped. See Mel Watkins, *On the Real Side: Laughing, Lying, and Sig-nifying—the Underground Tradition of African-American Humor that Transformed American Culture, From Slavery to Richard Pryor* (New York: Simon & Schuster, 1994), 299–309.

29. Acknowledgment is happily given for a conversation with Howard Fast in 1996 about the complex relations between the original author and screenwriter with Kirk Douglas, who both made the film possible and greatly diluted the book's (and film script's) radical content. See Chapter 6.

30. As Sidney Hook and others announced enthusiasm for a new prospective wave of investigations into the entertainment world, Schlesinger insisted that as far as he was concerned, the ACCF had gone too far rightward in its public stands. Letter to "Jim," March 16, 1955, Box 7, American Committee for Cultural Freedom Collec-tion, Tamiment Library, New York University. Thanks to Daniel Bell for permission to examine these papers.

31. The parent Congress for Cultural Freedom remained very much in business with grants, conferences and publications like *Encounter*. Its successor, the International Association for Cultural Freedom, continued in operation with the same or similar "pass through" intelligence agency funding sources until 1979. Isaiah Berlin was perhaps its biggest name in later years, along with Arthur Schlesinger, Jr. and Arthur Koestler. See Frances Stonor Saunders, *The Cultural Cold War* (New York: The New Press, 2000), 417–27.

32. See Waldo Salt Papers, Art Special Collection, UCLA, for several *Nurses* scripts. Special thanks to Jennifer Salt for permission to use these papers.

33. Several episodes of *East Side/West Side* were rebroadcast on the Trio cable network during December, 2002, described in advance publicity as among the brilliant and challenging but commercially unsuccessful television series.

34. Stephen W. Bowie's brilliant essay, "East Side/West Side," in *Television Chronicles*, 9 (1999), 17–32, offers many details neglected here.

35. See Jack Berry interview in *Tender Comrades*, 55–89.

36. Arnold Perl, *The World of Sholom Aleichem: Acting Edition* (New York: Dramatists Play Service, Inc., 1953), 45–46, 51.

37. Mostel was, however, replaced in the film version with Chaim Topol.

38. Thanks to Adler for describing his role in the series in a telephone interview, Au-gust, 2001, and to Steven W. Bowie, who kindly provided us a copy of his 1996 in-terview with Adler. Adler's novel *Notes From a Dark Street* (1962) had received warm coverage in the press.

39. One of the most interesting, unique for its co-writing credit for Ossie Davis (with Perl), was "I Before E Except After C," about Puerto Rican teenagers whose ram-page is reinterpreted as the result of a troubled school system and society. Howard da Silva plays the kindly teacher who struggles to help them.

40. We are especially grateful to television scholar Stephen Bowie for sharing this insight.

41. Arnold Perl, "Who Do You Kill?" in Richard Averson and David Manning White, eds., *Electronic Drama; Television Plays of the Sixties* (Boston: Beacon Press, 1971), 50–91.

42. See Millard Lampell interview by Paul Buhle, in McGilligan and Buhle, *Tender Comrades*, 391–405. His reprinted speech appeared in the *New York Times* on

August 3, 1966, and was seen at the time as an indirect urging for a return of the blacklistees. *Eagle In a Cage* soon went into production as a theatrical film, earning praise, if not a renewed screenwriting career for Lampell.

43. See J. Fred McDonald, *Blacks and White TV: Afro-Americans in Television Since 1948* (Chicago: Nelson-Hall Publishers, 1983), 72; and Steven W. Bowie, "East Side/West Side," 23–24.

44. Perl, ill with heart problems that eventually killed him, left the show after disagreements with Scott and a long quarrel with Susskind. Thanks go to Eddie Adler for these insights.

45. As McDonald put it simply, "This was not the stuff of which successful weekly series were made. *East Side/West Side* was cancelled in April 1964 after twenty-six episodes." Fred McDonald, *Blacks and White TV*, 106. Bowie offers a more nuanced conclusion in "East Side/West Side," 28–29.

46. Ernest Kinoy, "Blacklist," in Averson and White, eds., *Electronic Drama*, 103, in the full script, 92–135.

47. Ibid., 134.

48. David Boroff, "Television and the Problem Play," in Patrick D. Hazard, ed., *TV As Art: Some Essays in Criticism* (Champaign, Ill.), 97–115. Boroff calls the "Blacklist" episode of *The Defenders*, discussed below, "television at the very edge of social maturity."

49. Thanks to Ruben for an email response, October 1, 2001.

50. Robert J. Thompson, *Television's Second Golden Age: from Hill Street Blues to ER* (New York: Continuum, 1986), 27.

51. Ruben's subsequent credits included the films *The Seven Ups*, *Visit to a Chief's Son*, *Foster and Laurie* and *Journey through Rosebud*; his television credits include *Reunion at Fairborough*; *The Belarus File*; *Incident at Dark River*; and *The Education of John Chapman*. Letter from Albert Ruben, December 6, 1999.

52. See David Marc, interview with Jack Klugman, Scheuer Television History Collection, Syracuse University.

53. The fifth of the Sunday Mystery Movie series was *Amy Prentiss*, starring Jessica Walter as a widow of the chief of detectives in San Francisco, who found her husband's old colleagues unable to grasp her intelligence. Al Brenner and Joan Scott wrote episodes of *McMillan* and *McCloud*, whose star, Dennis Weaver, had a strong liberal reputation.

54. The later impact of left-wing film noir and television writers' best crime-related dramas upon a uniquely artistic telenoir like *Crime Story* (1984–1986), co-produced by former antiwar demonstrator Michael Mann, could not be more obvious; nor the influence of *Naked City* on *Homicide* (1993–1999), producer Barry Levinson's tribute to the hand-held camera and the grittiness of Baltimore.

55. See Bernard Weinraub, "The Moods They Are A 'Changing in Films: Terrorism is making Government Look Good," *New York Times*, October 16, 2001. Scholar-critics making these observations cited by the journalist were Roy Simon, curator of television at the Museum of Television and Radio, and Thomas Schatz, Chair of the Department of Radio, Television and Film at the University of Texas, Austin.

56. Thanks to Al Brenner for this commentary on the views of himself and his friends, writers of serious television drama.

57. Fred Allen, one of the funniest and most critical radio voices, later described his obliging testimony in front of HUAC, naming former friends and colleagues, as the most disgraceful activity of his life. Thanks go to the late Leonardo Bercovici (whose wife committed suicide during the hearings) for recollections about kidding

of the rich snobs on his 1930s hit radio show, *Billy and Betty*. See interview with Bercovici by Paul Buhle, *Tender Comrades*, 32.

58. Powell also scripted one of the longest-lasting radio detectives, with a bit of noir, *Johnny Dollar*, who survived into the late 1950s.

59. See Paul Buhle, interview with Dick Powell, in Buhle, *From the Knights of Labor to the New World Order* (New York: Garland, 1997), 239–48, on the TWA's rise and fall.

60. In real life, Thomas' daughter, Marlo Thomas, has been one of the leading progressives of her generation of actors as well as the star of the first single-woman's show, *That Girl* (1966–1971).

61. Interview with Frank Tarloff by Paul Buhle, in *Tender Comrades*, 650.

62. Carl Reiner, *Paul Robeson Saved My Life* (New York: Cliff Street Books, 1998), a gag title but with real underlying meaning.

63. Ibid., 33–40 and 161.

64. David Marc, *Comic Visions: Television Comedy and American Culture* (Boston: Unwin, Hyman, 1989), 98.

65. Ibid., 98–118.

66. Ibid., 87.

67. Actually Al Levitt had headed such an old-style support committee in New Rochelle in the later 1930s, before leaving for Hollywood; it had been a neighborhood-based Popular Front movement advancing an Italian-American, antifascist working-class candidate for local office. See interview with Al Levitt in *Tender Comrades*, 445.

68. Powell, a student activist of the late 1930s and a longtime radio writer, played a quiet role in the Hollywood Left. He served as managing editor for the L.A. area newsletter of his wife's favorite organization, the Women's International League for Peace and Freedom, which served usefully to rally the middle class against the Vietnam War and subsequent imperial adventures.

69. See Bert Spector, "Clash of Cultures: The Smothers Brothers vs. CBS Television," in John E. O'Connor, ed., *American History/American Television* (New York: Ungar, 1983), 159–83. Revived and toned down for the 1970 ABC season, *The Smothers Brothers* crashed.

70. Thanks go to Wilma Shore Solomon, who in a 1996 interview discussed her late husband's role in this program. He had been a screenwriter in 1940s Hollywood and a writer, under assumed names, for assorted television comedy-variety specials during the 1950s–1960s.

71. Huggins recalled being bemused by Altman, who had hardly a single political impulse but adapted himself to the times. Always more interested in form than content, he was the first to introduce purposeful "mumbling" into films as the existential quality of normal life, in which people merely pretend they hear most of the words. Huggins, interview with Robert Hethmon.

72. This observation comes from several conversations of Paul Buhle with Lardner during the middle 1990s.

73. Larry Gelbart, *Laughing Matters: On Writing M*A*S*H, Tootsie, Oh, God! And a Few Other Funny Things* (New York: Random House, 1998), 10–17.

74. See Larry Gelbart, *Laughing Matters*, 205–15.

75. Their films included *Come Blow Your Horn* (1963), *Divorce American Style* (1967) and *The Night They Raided Minsky's* (1968).

76. Among the most notable *All in the Family* cast members was Betty Garrett, left-winger of the late 1940s and wife of Larry Parks, a friendly witness who never regained his career after stardom in the 1940s.

77. It was a comparison that Lear himself never acknowledged. But one of his executive assistants, speaking to Paul Buhle informally after an academic session of the Popular Culture Association in 1973 on the Left and popular culture, conceded that other Lear staffers had indeed and perhaps inevitably discussed it.

78. Tarloff, a perfectionist of his own kind, added that if scripts for Lear shows were more daring and politically closer to what the producer had in mind, they were not necessarily better *as scripts* than his work on earlier series. See interview of Tarloff by Paul Buhle, in *Tender Comrades*, 655.

79. Tarloff insisted that *The Jeffersons* "always had a black character [that] you could identify with—his wife, for instance"—and the validated presence of mixed marriages, then still practically taboo on television. See Tarloff interview, *Tender Comrades*, 656.

CHAPTER THREE

1. It might be noted that left-wingers Robert Lees and Fred Rinaldo had used the sight gags creatively in the early section of *The Invisible Woman* (1940), in which a shopgirl gets even with her bosses, and in *Abbott and Costello Meet the Invisible Man* (1951), one of the last of the duo's interesting films. The writing of Dick Powell in particular for television's *Topper* was apparently due to purely personal connections. But Gene Reynolds, of television's M*A*S*H, produced *The Ghost and Mrs. Muir*, which offered a natural site for "Tom August" and "Helen August," who were actually Alfred Levitt and Helen Slote Levitt.

2. See David Marc, *Comic Visions: Television Culture and American Comedy* (Boston: Unwin Hyman, 1989), 81.

3. Williams, son of an automobile executive, grew up in the Bay Area Jewish enclave of Tiburon, California, where he claims to have learned to mock authority. He went to New York and studied under Orson Welles' former producer and unrepentant radical John Houseman before returning to the Bay Area, where he became a notably anti-establishment stand-up comic. His personal attachments with young radical Hollywoodites are well-known; he provided the key voice for *Ferngully—The Last Rainforest* (1992), an earnest effort to teach kids about ecology and its enemies, the ruthless developers.

4. See the testimony of Maurice Rapf in his memoir, *Back Lot: Growing Up in the Movies* (Lanham, Md.: Scarecrow Press, 1999), 134–35. Gratitude is expressed for Rapf's kindly approval of our efforts.

5. The *New York Times* reviewer admired the idea of adapting a film from a story by Ray Bradbury, but considered the outcome altogether predictable, if notable for its innovative cinematography. See "Look Out! The Space Boys Are Loose Again," *New York Times*, June 18, 1953.

6. At the world premiere of *It Came from Outer Space* in the Pantages Theater in Hollywood on an evening in late October 1953, during the early scene in which boulders the size of refrigerators bounce in 3-D down the sides of the crater, director Jack Arnold gave a prearranged cue, and a series of catapults set up on either side of the screen pitched Styrofoam rocks into the audience. "You should have heard them scream," Arnold later recalled to an interviewer. Dana M. Reemes, *Directed by Jack Arnold* (Jefferson, N.C.: McFarland & Company, 1988), 33. Near the end of his career, Arnold directed *The Mouse That Roared* (1959).

7. For a discussion of the reception of *Dirty Harry* and its politics, see Patrick McGilligan, *Clint: The Life and Legend* (New York: St. Martin's Press, 2002), 201–12.

8. Thanks to Joan Scott for a phone conversation in September, 2001, about Daniel Mainwaring.

9. See Paul Buhle and Dave Wagner, *Radical Hollywood* (New York: New Press, 2002), 396–98, on Losey and *Lawless*.

10. Bruce Rux, *Hollywood vs. the Aliens* (Berkeley, Ca.: Frog, Ltd., 1997), 217, suggests that *Body Snatchers'* real innovation was the invasion of the bedroom, snatching the dreamer—a common UFO "abduction" scenario destined to become more common in future decades.

11. Siegel's autobiography was less than candid on such issues, and the possibility that he had played a larger if quiet role of getting blacklistees work. See Don Siegel, *A Siegel Film* (London: Faber and Faber, 1993), especially 178–79. The remake of *Invasion of the Body Snatchers* (1978) with Donald Sutherland and Jeff Goldblum, with Siegel himself in a cameo role, was heavy on the paranoia about the repressive powers of the state-as-alien, but lacked the verve of the black-and-white original. For the left-wing origins of the Dirty Harry saga in Polonsky's screenplay for *Madigan*, see Buhle and Wagner, *A Very Dangerous Citizen: Abraham Lincoln Polonsky and the Hollywood Left* (Berkeley: University of California Press, 2001), 199–203,

12. He rationalized that he had named only those previously named. Our gratitude to the late William Alland for a candid interview with Paul Buhle in Los Angeles in 1995 and to the friend who made that interview possible: a former son-in-law and continuing warm friend of Alland, Paul Richards.

13. One would not know from the film that for the most exciting part of the 1930s, the ILGWU's leading unit, New York Local 22 (which supplied most of the amateur actors for the theatrical spectacular, "Pins and Needles"), had seen a love match between social democratic leadership and Communist rank-and-file. After 1939 but especially after 1945, ILGWU President David Dubinsky, lionized in the film, had spearheaded the anticommunist globalism of the AFL, including its conspiratorial wing. See Paul Buhle, *Taking Care of Business: Samuel Gompers, George Meany, Lane Kirkland and the Tragedy of American Labor* (New York: Monthly Review Press, 1999), 138–45. Our thanks to the late president of Local 22, Charles "Sasha" Zimmerman, for an interview in 1981 on these and other issues.

14. Alland's first production, *The Black Castle* (1952), co-starred Boris Karloff and Lon Chaney, Jr., but was mostly a gothic would-be thriller—starring Richard Greene, a few years later the star of television's *Adventures of Robin Hood*. By 1960, he had produced almost a dozen pictures, nearly all of them in the space and horror genre.

15. Coming of age in the Midwest, Bradbury had an extended circle of literary friends that included Wisconsinite August Derleth, left-leaning Sauk City publisher of the late H. P. Lovecraft's work; Bradbury's stories first reached book edition in Sauk City. *Fahrenheit 451* was made into a lavish Truffaut film in 1966 starring Julie Christie, the director's first film made in English. *The Martian Chronicles*, a made-for-TV mini-series based on Bradbury's bestseller, was an oddly nostalgic bit of science fiction, uncertain but hardly optimistic. It was scheduled to be remade by the director of *The Majestic*, Frank Darabont, in 2003.

16. According to Dick Powell, president of the short-lived Television Writers of America, Bradbury was to be the main speaker at an event defending the blacklistees and the TWA, but mysteriously failed to appear. For his time, the writer must nevertheless be regarded as a civil libertarian.

17. Bruce Rux points out that assorted military intelligence veterans and CIA consultants also occasionally served as sci-fi film and television advisors. Rux, *Hollywood*

vs. the Aliens, 66–67. A sounder scholarly source is David Jacobs, *The UFO Controversy in America* (Bloomington: University of Indiana Press, 1975). See also the essays in James R. Lewis, ed., *The Gods Have Landed: New Religions from Other Worlds* (Albany: State University of New York Press, 1995).

18. A rocket scientist convinces an industrial consortium that it is vital for the United States to become the first nation to reach the moon, and that atomic energy is the answer. Refusing to be put off by a negative public clamor (possibly "subversive" propaganda), the scientist and crew go through various trials to reach their goal. The film was praised for its realism. George Pal is another interesting figure with many left-wing ties, perhaps merely incidental to his career. He won five Oscars but also collaborated with left-wing writers' and directors' projects in *The Great Rupert* (1950) and *The Naked Jungle* (1954). Robert Wise oversaw a retrospective of his work, *The Fantasy Film World of George Pal* (1986).

19. The future Superman film series was packed with Hollywood progressives including Christopher Reeve, Margot Kidder, Marlon Brando and Richard Pryor, and sometimes plots to match. The story of the noble (in several senses) Kryptonite on an unintended mission of earthly salvation has proved itself repeatedly (even uniquely among superheroes) open to leftish interpretation.

20. Among his later films: the corporate criticism, *Executive Suite*; *Odds Against Tomorrow*, *The Sand Pebbles* (which he insisted was an antiwar allegory) and giant hits, *The Sound of Music*, *West Side Story* and *Star Trek—the Film*.

21. See the interview with Wise in George Hickenlooper, *Reel Conversations: Candid Conversations with Film's Foremost Directors and Critics* (New York: Citadel Books, 1991), 166–80.

22. See, for example, John Fousek, *To Lead the Free World: American Nationalism and the Cultural Roots of the Cold War* (Chapel Hill: University of North Carolina Press, 2000).

23. This was the strangest of several projects written and directed by Albert Lewin, a former Marxist with close friends in the Hollywood Left but with his own artistic aims. Lewin was named for Albert Parsons, the eloquent anarchist martyr of the Haymarket affair in Chicago in 1886, and grew up in an anarchist colony. See Paul Buhle and Dave Wagner, *Radical Hollywood*, 407–08.

24. Alland interview with Buhle.

25. Reemes, *Directed by Jack Arnold*, 24.

26. However, a *Times* reviewer called it so "superlatively bizarre and beautiful that some serious shortcomings can be excused if not overlooked." "'This Island Earth' Explored from Space," *New York Times*, June 11, 1955.

27. Rux, *Hollywood vs. the Aliens*, 67.

28. *Variety*, in a rousing review, admired the film's "exploitation possibilities," especially those of Julie Adams, who "appears mostly in brief shorts or swim suits, and the males will like what she displays." "Creature from the Black Lagoon," *Variety*, February 10, 1954.

29. Alland, interview with Paul Buhle.

30. Alllison Graham, "Journey to the Center of the Fifties: The Cult of Banality," in J.P. Telotte, ed., *The Cult Film Experience: Beyond All Reason* (Austin: University of Texas Press, 1991), 109.

31. James had written several films before the blacklist, notably the U.S. adaptation of *Three Russian Girls* (1944), which won an Oscar, but for its camera work. A Los Angeles social worker during his post-blacklist career, he is best remembered for a

novel that he wrote as "Danny Santiago," *Famous All Over Town*, regarded as a Chicano literary classic until, at James' death, the true authorship was revealed.

32. Arkoff's death revived memories of the drive-in film schlock king. See Alan Harmetz, "Samuel Z. Arkoff, Maker of Drive-In Thrillers, Dies at 83," *The New York Times*, September 19, 2001.

33. *The Man from Planet X* (1951) was a more-or-less straight invasion story with unfriendly aliens, and *The Amazing Transparent Man* (1960) not much better. *L'Atlantide* (1961), during which Ulmer replaced Frank Borzage, was a color film about the use of Africa as testing ground for nuclear weapons and the discovery of a hidden race of immortals. Ulmer's *Naked Venus* (1958), putting European nudist camp footage into a film plot about a gentle French nudist whose American husband's family tries to take away her child, was another typically libertarian, Ulmerian feature. It remains, lamentably, a classic in soft-core porn little known even to Ulmer devotees; he had kept his name off the credits.

34. Bernard Gordon, *Hollywood Exile, or How I Learned to Love the Blacklist* (Austin: University of Texas, 1999), 64–65. Among other turkeys in this vein: *Psychomania* (1971), written by Gordon's boyhood pal and sometime screen collaborator Julian Zimet, has a surly bunch of British motorcyclists-turned-monsters halted by a New Age goddess-hag; and *Mysterious Island* (1961), adapted from Jules Verne's sequel to *20,000 Leagues Under the Sea* for director Cy Endfield, memorable if at all for Ray Harryhausen's special effects.

35. Political refugee and noiriste Curt Siodmak provided the story basis, and Gordon undertook a near-total rewrite of a first script attempt. Gordon was paid $1,500.

36. Gordon related to us his equal surprise that the strong suggestion of oral sex between newlyweds in a moving car seemed to have gone unnoticed and uncensored.

37. Gerald Mast, *A Short History of the Movies* (Indianapolis: Pegasus, 1995), 256.

38. Karl Marx, *Capital*, vol. 1 (New York: International Publishers, 1967), 233.

39. Bernard Gordon, interview with Paul Buhle, Los Angeles, 1994.

40. Endore had written or contributed dialogue to some of the best horror films of the early sound years, including *The Raven*, *Mad Love*, *Mark of the Vampire* (all 1935) and *The Devil-Doll* (1936). See Buhle and Wagner, *Radical Hollywood*, 116–18 for some details and a perspective on the Left's initial contribution to film horror. *Captain Sindbad* (1963), a final film appearing with his credit still under a pseudonym, was a merry and fantastic romp, easily the best of the Sinbad films, in color, with television actor Guy Williams in the starring role.

41. Actually, Gordon had one other science-fiction contribution of note, albeit sans credit, for *Day of the Triffids* (1962), a conventional retelling of John Wyndham's famous novel about plants that land on Earth and, until sprayed with salt water, bid fair to wipe out human habitation. Yordan hogged the screenplay credit.

42. Marx, *Capital*, Vol. 1, 234.

43. Eric Hobsbawm, *Primitive Rebels: Studies in Archaic Forms of Social Movement in the 19th and 20th Centuries* (New York: Norton Library Edition, 1965).

44. There were other films about Mexican rebels, but the most intriguing Left connection may be the obscure and still unrecovered series of films about the Cisco Kid ("Robin Hood of the Pecos") written in the 1940s by future blacklistee Louise Rousseau. She may possibly have continued, behind a front, with the 1950s Cisco Kid television series, syndicator Ziv's most lucrative performer on hundreds of local stations.

45. See *American Film Institute Catalog of Feature Films, 1941–1950, A-L* (Berkeley: University of California Press), 2000, 769, and materials on Salt below, chapters 6

and 7. The follow-up film for Salt was supposed to be *The Crimson Pirate* (1952), with largely the same plot. After Salt was fired, it was rewritten by producer Hecht himself along with friendly witness Roland Kibbee (or at least credited to them). *Crimson Pirate* was at any rate very close to the same film, this time with the exiled noble a seafarer and Eva Bartok playing the dame. Hecht, a former Communist, turned friendly witness and fired Salt. He later eased several blacklistees including Salt back into the industry. See "Statement" of Waldo Salt, Salt Papers, UCLA.

46. Our gratitude goes to Paula Weinstein, a film producer who is one of Hannah Weinstein's daughters presently active in Hollywood. Interview by Paul Buhle, Studio City, 1994.

47. *Captain Scarlett* was credited to Howard Dimsdale, another writer on the way to the blacklist and television work.

48. Interviews with Albert Ruben by Paul Buhle, 1994 and David Marc, 2000; and with Ring Lardner, Jr., by Paul Buhle, 1992. Ruben recalled, to Marc, that showing visiting ad agency executives around the set while evading all their questions about meeting the writers had a quality of extreme farce, a bit like a real-life version of *The Front*, with British accents.

49. Robin has more than a little in common with the lead in *Destry Rides Again*, avoiding use of his almost magical dexterity (bow-and-arrow, the original of the gunslinger's talent) and is full of good humor and satire. See Buhle and Wagner, *Radical Hollywood*, 138–41. Among other writers, Oscar-winning cinematic humorists Ring Lardner, Jr. and Robert Lees worked on the series, also Ian McClellan Hunter. See chapter 9 on the HBO/British film *Fellow Traveler*, in part about the making of *The Adventures of Robin Hood*.

50. Marguerite Roberts had performed a similar miracle a few years earlier with her uncredited script for *Ivanhoe* (1952): Elizabeth Taylor is the Jewess, the sexual and symbolic representation of an oppressed race and gender.

51. Perhaps the series' most notable accomplishment was the introduction of young actor Patrick McGoohan, destined to be the character of name in the cult series, *The Prisoner*, backed financially by the future Sir Lew Grade, whose financial support had made the earlier adventures of both Robin Hood and Sir Lancelot possible.

52. Among the blacklist details that elude research, 1940s film comedy writer Howard Dimsdale was said (in correspondence from Adrian Scott to Hannah Weinstein, recommending Dimsdale as a perfect writer for *The Adventures of Robin Hood*) to be highly successful in writing for television (as of 1955) under various pen names, and having essentially designed as well as written heavily for an unnamed children's show. What was that show? We may never find out.

53. See Buhle and Wagner, *Radical Hollywood*, especially 408–12.

54. As we'll see in chapter 4, the original option on that future Brando vehicle, *The Wild One*, had been bought by left-wingers, and the original script written by Ben Maddow. Thanks are also extended to Joan Scott for a phone conversation on September 1, 2001, about this episode. See *Radical Hollywood*, 181–87, for a description of the 1940s Left-written family films.

55. Lees, interviewed by Paul Buhle and Dave Wagner, in *Tender Comrades*, 439. Many thanks to Robert Lees for his discussion of the issues.

56. *Fiesta* (1947), co-written by Lester Cole, had Esther Williams as an American-educated member of the Mexican upper classes, so full of spunk that she wears her brother's clothes to fight a bull (before going off to marry).

57. *The Brave Bulls* (19501, written by John Bright, broke precedent with a documentary-style narrative of bullfighting. In the two decades to follow, a number of significant films were written by blacklist exiles and made in Mexico. One dealt seriously with children's themes. Hugo Butler, working under a pseudonym, wrote and produced in 1958 a prize-winning documentary *Los pequenos gigantes/How Tall Is a Giant*, about a Mexican Little League team that won an unprecedented victory at the U.S.-based Little League World Series.

58. See the interview with Faith Hubley in *Tender Comrades*, 279–304, discussing her late husband's and her own lives and work, and the further discussion of the puppet-toon *Alice* in *Radical Hollywood*, 410–11.

59. Back at Disney, screenwriter and blacklistee Maurice Rapf could claim that it was his script, written before he left the studio in 1947, that made *Cinderella* (1950) a story of rebellion and proto-feminism. As the blacklist settled in, the studio took away his credit. Rapf, who had scripted parts of *Song of the South* (1946) before it was drastically altered by Disney himself, also worked in the early 1950s on UPA projects, commercial and educational. Interview with Rapf by Patrick McGilligan, *Tender Comrades*, 524–37.

60. Hugh Kenner, *Chuck Jones: a Flurry of Drawings* (Berkeley: University of California Press, 1994), 13–68.

61. Norman M. Klein, *Seven Minutes: The Life and Death of the American Cartoon* (London: Verso, 1993), 230.

62. John Hubley and Zachary Schwartz, "Animation Learns a New Language," *Hollywood Quarterly*, 1 (July, 1946), 355.

63. Quoted by Stefan Kanfer, *Serious Business: The Art and Commerce of Animation in America, from Betty Boop to Toy Story* (New York: Scribners, 1997), 174.

64. Rick Lyman, "William Hurtz, 'Actor with a Pencil' Who Changed Face of Animation, Dead at 81," *New York Times*, Oct.29, 2000, manages not to mention Hurtz's striking Disney, or the political causes of UPA's decline and demise. In later years, Hurtz was a supervisor and director on *The Adventures of Rocky and His Friends*, and still later formed a company that made animation shorts about African American history. He ended up with the *Rugrats*.

65. Klein, *Seven Minutes*, 232–33.

66. Ibid., 235–37.

67. Harvey Kurtzman drifted onward to scripting the "Little Annie Fanny" strip in *Playboy*: an ignominious if income-sustaining fate. At his death, he was hailed by *Maus* author Art Spiegelman among others as the genius who had inspired a generation of postmodern comic strip artists. The authors acknowledge an interview conducted by Paul Buhle with Kurtzman at New York University in 1982, in which he described drawing backgrounds for a comic strip in the *Daily Worker* that urged racial integration, attacked McCarthyism, and encouraged a doomed cartoonists' union. Interview excerpted in *Shmate* 13 (1982).

68. Harold Meyerson and Ernie Harburg, *Who Put the Rainbow in the Wizard of Oz? Yip Harburg, Lyricist* (Ann Arbor: University of Michigan, 1995), 269.

69. Ibid., 292.

70. The whole animation adventure with *Finian's Rainbow* is recorded carefully, with many of Hubley's drawings reprinted, in John Canemaker, "Lost Rainbow," *Print* 47 (March-April, 1993), 62–65 and 121–23. The drawings were released for archiving in the early 1990s.

71. Norman M. Klein, *Seven Minutes*, 241.

72. "Kim Deitch Interview" conducted by Monte Beauchamp, *Comics Journal* 123 (July, 1988), 62.
73. Kanfer, *Serious Business*, 181.
74. Scott later claimed that unlike his fellow UPA-ers, he was never an ardent left-winger; but the show's satires on commercialism and the Cold War (even "Boris and Natasha," the funny Russian spy couple) rather belie the dissociation. See Kanfer, *Serious Business*, 184–85.
75. Faith Hubley was an antiwar activist in high school. After a divorce and a move to Los Angeles, she got assistance from her friend, Gerda Lerner; she worked at Columbia as a messenger and then as a script clerk on the Blondie films and Three Stooges shorts; worked on a sex education film with actor Eddie Albert as producer; and returned to New York and edited *Go, Man, Go*, the remake of the left-written fiction film about the Harlem Globetrotters. Patrick McGilligan interview with Faith Hubley, *Tender Comrades*, 288–90.
76. Aljean Harmetz, "Faith Hubley, Oscar Winner In Animation, Is Dead at 77," *New York Times*, December 10, 2001.
77. Faith Hubley interview, *Tender Comrades*, 300. Faith Hubley had not wanted to take part in *Watership Down*. Kanfer, *Serious Business*, 211, tells the story rather more optimistically for the outcome; reviewers liked it nearly as well as any non-Disney feature length animation ever, which is not perhaps saying much.

CHAPTER FOUR

1. Quoted in Peter Brunette, *Roberto Rossellini* (Berkeley: University of California Press, 1987), 109.
2. Quoted in ibid., 113.
3. Cedric Belfrage, "Orson Welles' *Citizen Kane*," *The Clipper* 1 (May, 1941, 12–14.
4. Quoted in Patrizio Rossi, "Roberto Rossellini," in John Wakefield, ed., *World Film Directors, 1: 1890–1945* (New York: The H.W. Wilson Company, 1987), 966.
5. The Cardinal's effort at censorship succeeded at first, but a resulting lawsuit, *Burstyn v. Wilson*, established for the first time First Amendment protection for films, at least when obscenity was not at issue. See Jon Lewis, *Hollywood vs. Hard Core* (New York: New York University Press, 2000) 97–99.
6. Gertrude Himmelfarb, "Remembering Robert Warshow," *Commentary* 56 (April, 2002), 45–51, occasioned by the reprinting of Warshow's *The Immediate Experience* (1962).
7. Rossi, "Roberto Rossellini," 966.
8. David Caute, *Joseph Losey: A Revenge Against Life* (New York: Oxford University Press, 1994), 106.
9. See the interview with the producer, John Weber, a former Hollywood unionist and agent, who gathered cash and fellow exiles for the effort, his last: John Weber interviewed by Paul Buhle, in Patrick McGilligan and Paul Buhle, *Tender Comrades: a Backstory of the Hollywood Blacklist* (New York: St. Martins, 1997), 694–97.
10. Foster Hirsch, *Joseph Losey* (Boston: Twayne, 1980), 55.
11. Ugo Pirro, *5 Branded Women*, translated by Stanley Hochman (New York: Pocketbooks, 1960).
12. Gabriel Miller, *The Films of Martin Ritt: Fanfare for the Common Man* (University Press of Mississippi, 2000), 37–40.
13. Ibid., 179.

14. Michael Sragrow, "A Noir Classic Makes It Back From the Blacklist," *New York Times,* July 16, 2000. Crowther had called *Rififi* "perhaps the keenest crime film that ever came from France." We note below, in chapter 6, the bitter attacks upon it by several others American critics, notably Pauline Kael.

15. Interview with Jules Dassin by Pat McGilligan in McGilligan and Buhle, *Tender Comrades,* 219.

16. François Truffaut, *The Films in My Life* (New York: Simon and Schuster, 1995), 210.

17. Jacques Doniol-Valcroze, "Une Vie de Chien," *Cahiers du Cinema,* April, 1955, 43.

18. Ibid., 44.

19. Truffaut, *Films in My Life,* 210.

20. On the other hand, *The Asphalt Jungle* had been co-scripted by fellow blacklistee Ben Maddow (with crime writer W. R. Burnett) and it is reasonable to conclude that the same artistic gestures were being passed around. See Paul Buhle and Dave Wagner, *Radical Hollywood* (New York: New Press, 2002), 344.

21. Truffaut, *Films in My Life,* 209.

22. Jean-Pierre Coursodon, *American Directors* (New York: McGraw Hill, 1983), 85.

23. Georges Sadoul, *Dictionnaire des films* (Paris: Microcosme/Editions du Seuil, 1965), 41.

24. Truffaut, *Films in My Life,* 211–12.

25. Two of the more recent borrowings were in Brian De Palma's *Mission Impossible* (1996) and Frank Oz's *The Score* (2001).

26. François Truffaut and Claude Chabrol, "Entretien avec Jules Dassin II," *Cahiers du cinema* 7 (May, 1955), 12.

27. Ibid.

28. Also called *Utopia,* the Laurel and Hardy vehicle is among the boys' most political films but lacks the familiar rocking-horse tempo of their classic collaborations. Here they inherit a newly formed island in the Pacific and while sailing toward it are beached and marooned on an atoll that has suddenly emerged from the ocean. When uranium is discovered on the atoll, the world's major powers start fighting over it in an ungainly allegory of the Cold War marked by the pair's physical decline, rather like the last films of The Three Stooges.

29. A tradition the English critic Raymond Durgnat once referred to as "respectable eccentricity taking murder lightly." Raymond Durgnat, "Paint It Black: The Family Tree of the Film Noir," in Lee Server et al., eds. *The Big Book of Noir* (New York: Carroll & Graf, 1998), 9.

30. Etienne Borgers, "Série noire" in Server, et al., *The Big Book of Noir,* 237–44.

31. See chapter 5 for discussion of *Ça va Barder* and Berry's other films before *Tamango.*

32. Among other connections going back to the 1940s, Dandrige co-starred in *The Harlem Globetrotters* (1951), a family film written by Alfred Palca and produced by Sidney Buchman; both of them were blacklisted immediately afterward. (The film was remade in 1954 as *Go Man Go,* with a front getting the credit for Palca's screenplay, the source of much confusion.)

33. See David A. Cook, *Lost Illusions: American Cinema in the Shadow of Watergate and Vietnam* (Berkeley: University of California Press, 2002), 260–66. Today, for the first time, blaxploitation has become a popular academic subject.

34. See the remarks by Berry on the film in the interview with Berry by Patrick McGilligan in McGilligan and Buhle, *Tender Comrades,* 81–82.

35. Maddow himself was evasive on the topic of his testimony, and his friend Walter Bernstein probably saw the personal issues most clearly. See Paul Buhle's interview with Walter Bernstein in *Tender Comrades,* 52–53.

36. Jean-Paul Sartre, *Saint Genet: Actor and Martyr* (New York: George Brazillier, 1963).

37. Lee Grant, phone conversation with Paul Buhle, November, 2001.

38. For Wexley's story, see Wexley interviewed by Pat McGilligan in *Tender Comrades*, 698–721. The other contemporary example of American neorealism, *Odds Against Tomorrow* (1959), is discussed in chapter 5, as part of what may be called the case of Harry Belafonte.

39. Richard Slotkin, *Gunfighter Nation: The Myth of the Frontier in Twentieth-Century America* (New York: Harper Perennial, 1993), 347–48.

40. Edward Countryman and Evonne von Heussen-Countryman, *Shane* (London: British Film Institute, 1999), 32.

41. Jack Schaefer, *Shane: The Critical Edition*, ed. James C. Work (Lincoln: Univ. of Nebraska Press, 1984).

42. Countryman, *Shane*, 12. Wilson's step outline is part of the collection of his papers in the Arts Special Collection at UCLA. Wilson was also deprived, by his status, of what might have been the best western of all: a script about the Industrial Workers of the World, those heroes of logging camps, agribusinesses and the open sea. The plan for a script is referred to in the Wilson Papers, UCLA. We gratefully acknowledge permission given to use the Wilson Papers by Becca Wilson.

43. Raymond Durgnat, "Paint it Black: The Family Tree of the Film Noir," 6. Durgnat cited three noir westerns, with *High Noon* the most on point. Sam Fuller's *Run of the Arrow* (1957) and Budd Boetticher's *Ride Lonesome* (1959) were the other two.

44. Robert Hethmon interview with Roy Huggins in April and May, 2000.

45. Maxim Gorky, *Selected Tales* (New York: Octagon Books, 1973), 56.

46. See McGilligan's interview with Zimet in McGilligan and Buhle, *Tender Comrades*, 734.

47. Antoine de Baecque and Serge Toubiana, *Truffaut: A Biography* (New York: Knopf/Borzoi, 1999), 104. The immediate source for *Jules et Jim* was Henri-Pierre Roche's novel of the same name.

48. Trumbo wrote *Cowboy* for producer Sam Spiegel in the early 1950s, fronted by Hugo Butler; by the time of its production, Delmer Daves had taken over, Butler was also blacklisted, and sole screenwriting credit was given to Edmund North, who had done some rewriting. See Bruce Cook, *Dalton Trumbo* (New York: Charles Scribner's Sons, 1957), 206.

49. Christopher Frayling. *Spaghetti Westerns: Cowboys and Europeans from Karl May to Sergio Leone* (London: Routledge & Kegan Paul, 1981), 153. Frayling's work has guided us in large ways on the spaghetti western.

50. Douglas quoted in David Zinman, *Fifty Great Movies of the 1960s and 1970s* (New York: Crown Publishers, 1986), 50–51.

51. For several years until near the end of his blacklisting, Trumbo worked closely with independent producer Eugene Frenke, who made the banned screenwriter an employee of Springfield Productions and then resold the projects. One of the best scripts, "Montezuma" (an Aztec adventure with Cortez), was sold to Kirk Douglas' Bryna Productions and served as a bridge to Trumbo's relations there. Like "Will Adams" (the tale of an English sailor who was the first of his countrymen to enter Japan), optioned repeatedly, "Montezuma" was never produced. Trumbo considered these two of his best. See Cook, *Dalton Trumbo*, 269–70.

52. Edwin T. Arnold and Eugene L. Miller *The Films and Career of Robert Aldrich* (Knoxville: The University of Tennessee Press, 1986), 214. The authors provide a good summary of Aldrich's political views here.

53. For a detailed account of the making of *Sodom and Gomorrah*, now known largely for its opening line, "Beware of Sodomite patrols!" see Christopher Frayling, *Sergio Leone: Something to Do With Death* (London: Faber and Faber, 2000), and see comments by screenwriter Hugo Butler's widow, Jean Butler, in her interview with Paul Buhle and Dave Wagner in McGilligan and Wagner, *Tender Comrades*, 174. Hugo Butler was in failing health as the film was being made, and his usual clever touches are largely missing.

54. Arnold and Miller, *The Films and Career of Robert Aldrich*, 31–32.

55. Much later, in *Ulzana's Raid* (1972), surely one of the finest westerns ever made, Aldrich would create a method of dealing with Indian (specifically Apache) culture that replaced liberal sentimentality with cold, hard, martial respect.

56. Cited in Frayling, *Sergio Leone*, 111.

57. We have been guided in this incident and in the political issues raised by the Eurowestern by the groundbreaking work of Frayling's *Spaghetti Westerns*, particularly 223–25.

58. Edgcumb Pinchon, *Zapata the Unconquerable* (New York: Doubleday, Doran & Co., 1941).

59. Cited in Frayling, *Spaghetti Westerns*, 224.

60. Ibid.

61. Ibid.

62. Abraham Polonsky, "Odd Man Out and Monsieur Verdoux," *Hollywood Quarterly* 2 (April, 1947), 406.

63. Often overlooked in discussions of this sort are the contributions to neorealism by the Mexican film industry. One great example must suffice: *Rebellion of the Hanged* (1954), written in part (although uncredited) by blacklistee John Bright, based on a story by B. Traven and with Traven himself (under an assumed name) on the set. See John Bright, *Worms in the Winecup: a Memoir* (Latham, P.A.: The Scarecrow Press, 2002), 211–24.

64. For a discussion of this point, see Paul Skenazy, *The New Wild West: The Urban Mysteries of Dashiell Hammett and Raymond Chandler* (Boise: Boise State University Press, 1982), 10.

65. This same quality was given a Yiddish twist in 1939 in *Destry Rides Again*, in crucial ways a Eurowestern made in the United States by German exiles in which the sheriff played by Jimmy Stewart was a kind of *shtetl filosof* armed with an understanding of the nature of social conflict, and who drew parables instead of pistols even though he was a dead shot. *Destry* was written in large part by left-wingers Gertrude Purcell and Henry Myers and produced by the king of Popular Front kitsch, Joe Pasternak. See Buhle and Wagner, *Radical Hollywood*, 138–41.

66. Andre Bazin, *What is Cinema?*, II, selected and translated by Hugh Gray (Berkeley: University of California, 1971), 141

67. The others are *For a Few Dollars More* (1965), *The Good, The Bad and the Ugly* (1966), and *Once Upon a Time in the West* (1969).

68. A reliable and informed list can be found in Thomas Weisser, *Spaghetti Westerns—the Good, the Bad and the Violent: A Comprehensive, Illustrated Filmography of 558 Eurowesterns and their Personnel, 1961–1977* (Jefferson, N.C.: McFarland & Co., 1992).

69. These directors were Damiano Damiami, Sergio Corbucci, Sergio Sollima and Giulio Petroni.

70. See chapter eight for a more thorough exploration of the issue.

71. Cenk Kiral interview with British film scholar Christopher Frayling, on Kiral's fan website, http://film.tierranet.com/directors/s.leone/sergioleone.html.

72. Dashiell Hammett, *Red Harvest*, in *Dashiell Hammett: Five Complete Novels* (New York: Wings Books, 1980), 107.

73. According to legend, Villa had the last laugh because he was able to remain virtually invisible to U.S. forces by maneuvering to make sure he was always between them and the blinding Mexican sun.

74. This character is played by Gian Maria Volonté, already famous from the villain's role in *Fistful of Dollars*. Volonté was perhaps the most politically committed of the Eurowestern actors. Another actor made famous in the Third World for his work in this subgenre is Tomas Milian, who was born in Cuba in 1937 and made his way to the United States in the 1950s, where he studied at the Actors Studio before finding his success as the cinematic fulfillment of the image of Che Guevara, complete with black beret and bandillero, in Sergio Corbucci's *Companeros* (1970), among many other films.

75. Brooks had worked around the Left since he scripted *Brute Force* (1947, directed by Jules Dassin) and his first novel became the basis for *Crossfire* (1947).

76. A near-miss collaboration of note was Ring Lardner, Jr., hired to write *The Cincinnati Kid* (1965), and Peckinpah to direct it. The director was fired after a week and replaced by Norman Jewison; Lardner's script suffered an almost identical fate, changed so much by Terry Southern (at Jewison's request) that little remained of the screenwriting genius' work. See Kenneth Geist, "The Films of Ring Lardner, Jr.," *Film Comment* 6 (Winter 1970–71), 48. We wish to acknowledge several conversations with Lardner, during the middle and later 1990s, about his later film work.

77. For a detailed discussion of *Willie Boy*, see Buhle and Wagner, *A Very Dangerous Citizen: Abraham Lincoln Polonsky and the Hollywood Left* (Berkeley: University of California Press, 2000), 209–13.

78. A brief account of the Peckinpah project may be found in John J. Michalczyk, *Costa-Gavras: The Political Fiction Film* (Philadelphia: Art Alliance Press, 1984), 146. The more detailed account of the Losey project is in David Caute, ibid., 454–455. Costa-Gavras' connections with Ben Barzman and the latter's critical role in framing the film Z are discussed in chapter 5.

79. Christopher Frayling, *Spaghetti Westerns*, 255.

CHAPTER FIVE

1. "15,000 See Debut of CinemaScope, New Film Process, in 'The Robe,'" *New York Times*, November 17, 1953.

2. "London Critics Hail CinemaScope," *New York Times*, November 22, 1953.

3. Bosley Crowther, "Now CinemaScope!" *New York Times*, September 27. 1953.

4. Its failure was all the more surprising because Christian Socialist Pichel's earlier biblical drama, *The Great Commandment* (1941), had considerable success with church rather than theater audiences, and his counterpart film, *Luther* (1953), was funded and distributed by the Lutheran Church (and made in Germany). Pichel was one of the Hollywood 19 who was not named in the hearings of the early 1950s, perhaps because he had moved his base abroad, out of harm's way, just before his death in 1954.

5. This holdover was heir to a curious tradition. The American Writers Congress, a major Popular Front institution of the 1930s, had ended in 1941 but retained its last

branches in Hollywood, and as such, served as co-sponsor of a local leftish academy and of the Hollywood Writers Mobilization conference of 1943.

6. Oral history of Helen Sloat Levitt by Larry Ceplair, UCLA, 1988.

7. Thanks are extended for conversations with Sylvia Jarrico between the middle 1990s and the present. Soon to be the ex-wife of Paul Jarrico, she remained a stalwart in the shrinking circle of blacklistees in Los Angeles and eventually married African American actor William Marshall.

8. "Reminiscences of Jerry Wald," interview by Robert and Joan Franklin, 1959, Columbia University Oral History Project, transcript at Columbia University archives.

9. The first issue featured an African American actor's own complaint and plea, "In the Film World a Negro Actor Looks for Work," by Irwin Moseley, January, 1953. The Levitts took it upon themselves to conduct private workshops for minority writers, a large boost to some of the earliest successful black screenwriters, but one that could not be readily acknowledged in Cold War America.

10. Sylvia Jarrico, "Evil Heroines of 1953," *Hollywood Review*, June-July, 1953.

11. John Howard Lawson, "Hollywood on the Waterfront: Union Leaders are Gangsters, Workers Are Helpless," *Hollywood Review*, November-December, 1954.

12. Keenly observed by Sylvia Jarrico, "The Big Screen & the Small One," *Hollywood Review*, n.d. [April], 1955.

13. See Lary May, *The Big Tomorrow: Hollywood and the Politics of the American Way* (Chicago: University of Chicago Press, 2000), 250, and more broadly, 215–56.

14. Jean Rouverol Butler later joked that she had "almost an orgasm" reading the story in print. Only at the beginning of her scriptwriting days, she had, with husband Butler, been looking for scriptable properties for years. Interview with Paul Buhle, 1994.

15. In the theme of mental disturbance, Frank Perry, who later worked with Abraham Polonsky, among other left-wingers, thus guided *David and Lisa* (1962), which brought actor Howard da Silva out of the blacklist; Robert Rossen's last film was *Lilith* (1964), a vehicle for Jean Seberg, Warren Beatty and Peter Fonda.

16. Michael Wilson, "Hollywood on the Brink of Peace: New Trends Visible—If You Squint," *Hollywood Review*, June-July, 1956. Wilson also cited *Giant*, *Tea House of the August Moon*, *The Pajama Game*, *Friendly Persuasion* and *The Solid Gold Cadillac* as hopeful signs. He did not add that he had written *Friendly Persuasion* himself (without credit) or that *The Solid Gold Cadillac* was written by friendly witness Abe Burrows, starring left-winger Judy Holiday.

17. See Joseph McBride, "A Very Good American," in *Written By* 6 (February, 2002), 26–33. *Written By* is the organ of the Writer's Guild, West.

18. Special thanks to Larry Ceplair for this insight into the collapse of the *Hollywood Review*.

19. Ring Lardner, Jr., *The Lardners: My Family Remembered* (New York: Harper-Colophon, 1976), 354.

20. In any case, the role of water in miner militancy in the southwestern deserts is an ancient and important one, as screenwriter Michael Wilson, a student of southwestern history since his early days working in an agricultural co-op in Baja, California, must have known. See Ramón Eduardo Ruiz, *The People of Sonora and Yankee Capitalists* (Tucson: University of Arizona Press, 1988), 70.

21. Norma Barzman, *The Red and the Blacklist* (New York: Thunders Mouth Books/Nation Books, 2003); we wish to thank Norma Barzman for her help, including an advance copy of the manuscript of her memoir.

22. Berry's *Je suis un sentimental* (in the U.S. the TV title was *Headlines of Destruction*, 1955), written by Lee Gold, had Constantine playing a journalist ordered by his boss to accuse a man of murder but who discovers that the man is innocent. *A tout casser* (*Breaking it Up*, 1967), has Constantine come to the rescue of a bar owner when he is threatened by a gang of bikers. The latter was re-edited without his consent and Berry went to court to keep his name off the credits.

23. See interview with Patrick McGilligan in McGilligan and Paul Buhle, *Tender Comrades: A Backstory of the Hollywood Blacklist* (New York: St. Martins Press, 1997), 81.

24. During the last months of his life in 1989, Barzman was honored with the Order of Arts and Letters, from the French Ministry of Culture. See Interview with Norma Barzman by Larry Ceplair, in McGilligan and Buhle, *Tender Comrades*, 15–22. The later films are taken up in Chapter 6.

25. The assassinated reformer (played by Barzman's friend Yves Montand) preceded an American-backed military coup of the Greek style.

26. See Chapters 6 and 7 for elaboration.

27. Bercovici worked on at least a half-dozen films produced in Europe in the fifties, notably the award-winning *Maddelena* (1954), but received credit on none. See Paul Buhle's interview with Bercovici in *Tender Comrades*, 28–42.

28. Scripted from a borderline anti-Semitic novel, *I Can Get It For You Wholesale* bore little resemblance to the original. Later upbeat theatrical versions (and still later revivals), notably starred young Barbra Streisand and her then-husband, Elliot Gould. Polonsky's script had a considerably tougher heroine than the produced film version, but in the film she was still quite hard. See Buhle and Wagner, *A Very Dangerous Citizen*, for a detailed discussion of the film, 145–55. The script original is in the Abraham Polonsky Collection, State Historical Society of Wisconsin.

29. There is at least one more important, utterly forgotten and to this date unavailable example: blacklistee Norma Barzman wrote and Bernard Vorhaus directed *Fanciulle di lusso / Luxury Girls* (1952), produced in Italy by a collection of blacklistees, about an expensive boarding school where a pregnant girl seeks an abortion. Well-received in Europe, it was as much as banned from the U.S. market and has never reappeared.

30. Credit for the screenplay went to her front, Jack Jevne, and also to Lewis Meltzer and Robert Lees. See the interview with Jean Rouverol Butler in *Tender Comrades*, 170.

31. Among other failed family projects: Hugo Butler and Luis Buñuel wrote a deliciously satirical script from Evelyn Waugh's black-humor novel, *The Loved One*, and George Pepper acquired the rights in 1957. It was too early for a satire this edgy. Jean Rouveral, *Refugees from Hollywood* (University of New Mexico Press, 1999), 211.

32. Regrettably, Bernstein's *Time Out: A Memoir of the Blacklist* (New York: Knopf, 1996) ends where his screen career resumes and he has hardly commented on the content of the film.

33. *Heller in Pink Tights* got Bernstein off the blacklist because of the prestige of the credits. See Walter Bernstein interview with Patrick McGilligan, in McGilligan, ed., *Backstory 3* (Berkeley: University of California, 1997), 97–101; and Bosley Crowther, "Screen: Loren Out West," *New York Times*, March 17, 1960.

34. Like so many left-linked productions, the second *My Sister Eileen* had multiple connections: this was Betty Garrett's last important role in films; like a handful of others, she managed a new career in television, notably in the Norman Lear atelier.

35. Another possibility is that Chodorov paid off the inquisitors. In any case, *Happy Anniversary* (1959) may have solidified the notion slowly gaining ground in middle America that "living together" (or having sex) before marriage, in the modern European fashion, was a natural precursor to the "companionate marriage" of approximate equals. *Happy Anniversary* was followed, a decade later, by Michael Gordon's direction of *The Impossible Years* (1968), this time with Niven and Lois Albright, with the anxieties of old marrieds—Niven as a university prof facing rebellious Berkeleyite children—realizing the need to adjust their own sensibilities.

36. "Happy Anniversary," *Variety*, October 27, 1958. At this late date, the absence of a Production Code Seal was considered a possible problem for neighborhood theaters with active Catholic pressure groups. Niven would prove a perfect foil for friendly witness Michael Gordon's rehabilitation, mostly in light comedies in which sitcomish family generational quarrels are updated to include campus rebelliousness and the emerging youth culture.

37. Frank Tarloff suggested that *Guide for the Married Man* was the life-story of an unnamed fellow American exile living in London; in any case, with Walter Matthau as star, the film carried the light tone throughout, and the "Hollywood endng" suggested a common observation of the 1970s that a little adultery would prove bracing to a marriage. Left ally Gene Kelly directed *Guide*.

38. Bosley Crowther, "The Screen: 'Cleopatra' Has Premiere at Rivoli," *New York Times*, June 13, 1963.

39. Eugene Archer, "'Cleopatra' Lures 10,000 to Broadway," *New York Times*, June 13, 1963. The producers had shrugged off an earlier problem, Walter Wanger's lawsuit seeking to prevent the release of the picture without his approval, as the first producer on the job. He attended the premiere anyway. "Wanger Files 2.6 Million Suit Against Fox over 'Cleopatra,' " *Variety*, June 6, 1963.

40. See interview of Marguerite Roberts and John Sanford by Tina Daniell, in *Tender Comrades*, 583–84.

41. Her non-westerns were similarly disappointing. *Diamond Head*, about a plantation family in Hawaii and the son who marries over the line, among the natives, was a soap opera. See "'Diamond Head' Emerges in Spite of Storms," *New York Times*, April 29, 1962.

42. British critics were the first to attack it as full of clichés, although Princess Margaret herself attended the London premiere, presumably to give honor to a liberal treatment of interracialism in the colonies. "Zanuck Film Scored in London," *New York Times*, July 27, 1957.

43. See the pre-release interview by Stephen Watts, "Hove to On 'Island In the Sun,' " *New York Times*, January 20, 1957; the initial review by Bosley Crowther, "The Screen: Race Problems and Scenic Beauty," *New York Times*, June 13, 1957; and the subsequent re-evaluation by the same reviewer, "Color or Class: Are Issues Evaded in 'Island in the Sun'?" *New York Times*, June 23, 1957.

44. Quoted in John Schultheiss, ed., *Odds Against Tomorrow: The Critical Edition* (Northridge, Cal.: Center for Telecommunications, California State University, Northridge, 1999), 238. More details about the production will be found in this volume and in Paul Buhle and Dave Wagner, *A Very Dangerous Citizen*, 180–86.

45. A third HarBel project, scripted by Polonsky, would have had Belafonte in a surrealistic musical about nuclear weapons and an intergalactic visitor with Danny Kaye and Zero Mostel. The unproduced scripts are in the Abraham Polonsky Collection

at the State Historical Society of Wisconsin. See Buhle and Wagner, *A Very Dangerous Citizen*, 185–86, 193–95. Thanks go to Belafonte for a brief conversation with Paul Buhle about Polonsky at a reshowing of *Odds Against Tomorrow* at Lincoln Center in 2000.

46. A more artful commercial failure a decade earlier had been *The Adventures of Robinson Crusoe* (1954), co-scripted by Butler and Buñuel, with Dan O'Herlihy as Crusoe and Jaime Fernandez as his Latino sidekick. O'Herlihy got an Oscar nomination but the film was not much seen in the United States. It has been unavailable ever since.

47. Kaminska, on stage since 1904, had rarely been seen in films, but was nominated for an Oscar for her role in *The Shop On Main Street* (1965). Sturdy progressives Eli Wallach and Anne Jackson had minor supporting roles in the film, but Gloria Foster as Belafonte's disillusioned ex-lover was exceptional, her most empathetic role in films. *The Angel Levine* was directed by Jan Kadar, who had directed *A Shop On Main Street*. For him, the film was a career disappointment that seems to have cost him possible assignments; he did most of his subsequent work on television.

48. Of their successors, Danny Glover and Avery Brooks seemed most keenly aware of what price left-wing African Americans had paid for a small measure of progress. Meanwhile, Donald Ogden Stewart's late career included script credits for two important films, Robert Rossellini's *Europa '51* (1951) and Philip Leacock's *Escapade* (1955), but his actual contributions have never been clarified. The latter, about the hopes of post–World War II youth for a Europe free of war and fascism, especially deserves rediscovery and revival.

49. Our gratitude for conversations with Gerda Lerner and film scholar Judith Smith about *Black Like Me*.

50. Thanks to Marshall for interviews in 1992. In mid-life, he married Sylvia Jarrico and remained a prominent figure in the diminishing Hollywood Left circles, teaching at Northridge, California State University until his retirement.

51. Thanks to the late Carleton Moss for an interview in Los Angeles in 1991. A few more relevant details about *Pinky* are in Buhle and Wagner, *Radical Hollywood: The Untold Story Behind America's Favorite Movies* (New York: The New Press, 2002), 395. See also Robert McG. Thomas, Jr., "Carlton Moss, 88, Who Filmed the Black Experience, Dies," *New York Times*, August 15, 1997.

CHAPTER SIX

1. Kerry Segrave, *Drive-In Theaters: A History from Their Inception in 1933* (Jefferson, N.C.: McFarland & Co., 1992), 54.
2. Ibid., 71.
3. Ibid., 37.
4. Barbara Wilinsky, *Sure-Seaters: The Emergence of Art House Cinema* (Minneapolis: University of Minnesota Press, 2001), 2.
5. Ibid., 125.
6. Ibid.
7. Many thanks to Richard Flacks (at Ann Arbor in those days and soon to be a founding intellectual of the Students for a Democratic Society) for these insights.
8. Janet Weiner, *How to Organize and Run a Film Society* (New York: Macmillan, 1973).
9. See Willinsky, *Sure Seaters*, 132–33.
10. *The Night They Raided Minsky's* (1968), produced by Norman Lear and Bud Yorkin shortly before their *All In the Family* days, is an apt example. A romp into the

vaudeville past, with historical snapshots of 1910s Manhattan flashed intermittently, it featured a fairly realistic view of burlesque (including the Top Banana routines, primitive costumes and crude gestures at art or entertainment) but a thin plot. It ended with star Britt Eckland inadvertently exposing her breasts and "inventing" the striptease. *Minsky's* was "daring" and, at least at some points, artful. Bert Lahr, who died during the shooting, gave a touching performance.

11. The film deal that had set the pattern for stars taking percentages of film grosses had been James Stewart's lucrative contract for *Winchester 73* (1950), its screenplay written in part by a future blacklistee. See David Puttnam, *Movies and Money* (New York: Knopf, 1998), 177.

12. Peter Biskind, *Easy Riders, Raging Bulls: How The Sex-Drugs-and-Rock'-and-Roll Generation Saved Hollywood* (New York: Simon & Schuster), 20–21.

13. The documentary *Darkness at High Noon* (2002), clearly meant to pillory Kramer by the ruse of defending Foreman, makes the producer as bad as or worse than his counterparts; on the contrary, Kramer had an exceptionally weak moment from which he soon recovered.

14. See Sidney Poitier, *The Measure of a Man: A Spiritual Autobiography* (San Francisco: HarperSanFranciso, 2000), 123–24.

15. "Critics Vote Prize to 'Defiant Ones,' *New York Times*, December 31, 1958

16. Bosley Crowther, "Screen: A Forceful Social Drama," *New York Times*, September 25, 1958.

17. Paxton (1911–1985), an especially close associate of Adrian Scott in the 1940s, had scripted *Murder My Sweet* (directed by Edward Dmytryk), *Crack-Up, Cornered* and *Crossfire* (both produced by Scott), *So Well Remembered* and *The Wild One*. His last film was *Kotch* (1971), directed by Jack Lemon and starring Walter Matthau—bold solid personal friends of many left-wingers. *Guess Who's Coming to Dinner* was Hepburn's last crusading liberal film and her last with Spencer Tracy, both playing perplexed parents who have to deal with the prospect of an African American son-in-law (in one of Sidney Poitier's best non-action roles). Hepburn got an Oscar for it.

18. Script in Mac Benoff Papers, American Heritage Center, Laramie, Wyoming. Mainly a radio writer, Benoff had worked for Danny Thomas, writing with Abe Burrows and a very young Larry Gelbart. After a dishonorable appearance before HUAC in which he sought to make as light as possible his past involvement, Benoff specialized in television work, including *Make Room for Daddy*, sharing staff space if not assignments with blacklistee Frank Tarloff. *Bless the Beasts*, about juvenile campers who save a herd of buffalo scheduled for slaughter, was his only notable film. Despite his antipolitical protestations and his reputation as a careerist lightweight, he ended his career still working on a play about Clarence Darrow, the great legal hero of the Left.

19. Kramer had also produced *Death of a Salesman* (1951) in an adaptation written by friendly witness Stanley Roberts; and directed *The Secret of Santa Vittoria* (1969), written by Ben Maddow and William Rose.

20. Vincent LoBrutto, *Stanley Kubrick: a Biography* (New York: Donald I. Fine Books/Penguin, 1997), 73.

21. The story is told rather differently, from Trumbo's point of view, in Bruce Cook, *Dalton Trumbo* (New York: Charles Scribner's Sons, 1977), 270–71.

22. See a recent judgment by Tony Pipolo, "The Modernist & the Misanthrope: The Cinema of Stanley Kubrick," *Cineaste*, 27 (Spring, 2002), 4–25, 49.

23. *Eyes Wide Shut* (1999), released after Kubrick's death, was based on Arthur Schnitzler's *Traumnovelle* (1926), a story that warns the modern sophisticate (like the M.D. played by Tom Cruise) not to succumb in early middle age to the alluring but disruptive memories of youth's lost sexual opportunities. Comparisons between feudalism and the unconscious are imaginative but ultimately forced and awkward in the U.S. context.

24. *Wild in the Streets* has Shelley Winters as mom of a rock star who wants a voting age of 14 and threatens incarceration of everyone over 30. *Angel* was a cult film about an overweight teenager with a rock-and-roll lover; amazingly enough, the teenager was played by future lesbian left-wing folksinger Holly Near!

25. Puttnam, *Movies and Money*, 210–11.

26. It's worth adding that Altman, basking in the success of the film, backed off from his initial, effusive thanks to Lardner, suggesting that he himself had rewritten the script from start to finish. As Biskind notes, the director had improvised from what Lardner had given him. Lardner himself was cheerfully cynical about the changes: Hollywood had changed without, in some respects, changing at all. See Biskind, *Easy Riders*, 97–98; the insight from a discussion with Ring Lardner, Jr., in Manhattan in 1998.

27. *Shampoo*, written by Robert Towne and Warren Beatty, was a social allegory and no less a Hollywood comic sex romp, with Beatty the bed-hopping film colony hairdresser and cuckolded capitalist Jack Warden watching a televised version of the war in Vietnam. It won blacklist returnee Lee Grant an Oscar for best supporting actress. From Ashby's standpoint it made possible both *Bound for Glory*, the bravura treatment of Woody Guthrie's life, and *Coming Home*. The photography of the last two was directed by Hollywood leading radical cinematographer, Haskell Wexler, who won an Oscar with *Bound for Glory*.

28. Apart from Spielberg's on-hand tribute to Polonsky in public ceremonies near the end of the old man's life, the producer-director's choice for screenwriter of his moral epic, *Schindler's List,* offered an inside Hollywood story: the son-in-law of a former Communist Party branch leader in Los Angeles, later in life a leading figure in the Southern California Library, and the main surviving entity of the Popular Front milieu. The same savant, Marvin Goldsmith, also served until his death as guide to this book's authors as they conducted initial interviews with Hollywood old-timers; Goldsmith had known virtually all of them in the 1940s.

29. Waldo Salt might be seen as the rare exception. But the influence of left-wing screenwriters and directors in teaching film, largely at the University of Southern California but also in many other places (California State-Northridge, New York University, Dartmouth and others) connected them with many would-be filmmakers. *Creative Differences: Profiles of Hollywood Dissidents* (Boston: South End Press, 1978), edited by David Talbot and Barbara Zheutlin, contains interviews with still others who consider themselves to be successors. One of the most important, Mark Rosenberg (a former Madison SDS member with Paul Buhle), died of a heart attack near the beginning of what appeared to be an extremely promising career. His widow, Paula Weinstein (daughter of Hannah Weinstein) has been an important figure in the Hollywood Left, on the screen and off.

30. See Biskind, *Easy Riders*, 197–254. Jennifer Salt, a friend of Scorsese's in these days, told us in a June, 2002, interview in West Hollywood, that the affinity was natural; they both made "that kind of movie."

31. "South Africa Bans 'Finian," *New York Times*, October 28, 1968.

32. The meanness of the first reviews still impresses. See Renata Adler, "Screen: 'Finian's Rainbow' back from Missitucky," *New York Times*, October 10, 1968. Adler claimed to be defending the legacy of the original stage version from misappropriation, but as so often, she protested too much. Although rather too Disneyesque and miscast, the film had some fine moments.

33. Actually Nichols, son of impoverished immigrant Jews who had barely escaped with him from Berlin in 1931, started out as an actor, studied with Lee Strasberg, and formed a small improv group with left-wing folksinger Alan Arkin (of the Tarryers), Barbara Harris, Paul Sills and Nichols' longtime collaborator, Elaine May. The social satire of Nichols and May was a staple of the late 1950s sophistication, but he broke up the act, returned to acting, then directing. His later films were not especially notable, with the exception of *Silkwood* (which he also co-produced, in 1983), one of the most hard-hitting of political films and most working class feminist films ever.

34. A more thorough discussion of *Midnight Cowboy* follows in Chapter 7.

35. Huggins, interview with Robert Hethmon, June, 2000. See Chapter 3 on Huggins.

36. Andrew Sarris, "Midnight Cowboy," in *Confessions of a Cultist: On the Cinema, 1955–1969* (New York: Simon and Schuster, 1970), 441–45.

37. *Going Away* was, uniquely, based upon interviews with Vietnam vets. Did they recollect their Vietnam experience or were they actually reflecting established media images? This question is posed in Jerry Lembke, "From Oral History to Movie Script: The Vietnam Veteran Interviews from Coming Home," *Oral History Review* 22 (Summer-Fall, 1999), 65–86. Lembke examined the transcripts made for Salt in preparation for a never-made "making of Coming Home," proposed by Jane Fonda.

38. Foreman actually returned in 1955 to testify in closed session but apparently spoke only of himself, giving no names. He allowed his name to be used on a major film only in 1961, and returned to the United States finally only in 1975.

39. Most of the attention, even before the film had been finished, naturally went to producer Sam Spiegel and director David Lean. See, for example, Howard Thompson, "Lean Views from a New 'Bridge,'" *New York Times*, December 15, 1957. Foreman is mentioned in passing, Wilson not at all.

40. See David Puttnam, *Movies and Money*, 210–16.

41. Andrew Sinclair, *Spiegel: The Man Behind the Pictures* (Boston: Little, Brown, 1987), 1–19.

42. Ibid., 74–85.

43. Ibid., 7.

44. Ibid., 107–15. He had wanted to rewrite Pinter in *Accident*, and had a series of other failures before closing out.

45. Melina Mercouri, *I Was Born Greek* (Garden City: Doubleday, 1971), 1–66, 89.

46. *Stella*'s director, Michael Cacoyannis, was destined for fame with *Zorba the Greek*— taking a job refused by Dassin over a disagreement in the casting of Anthony Quinn as the happy-go-lucky protagonist. We owe much of the larger interpretation here to Dan Georgakas, a prominent Greek-American scholar and a long-time editorial associate of *Cineaste*.

47. Mercouri, *I Was Born Greek*, 124–25, 129–31.

48. Ibid., 136–49.

49. See Bosley Crowther, "The Screen: Recruiting Jewel Thieves," *New York Times*, September 18, 1964, in which Crowther suggested *Rififi* had been remade—but in the style of *Never On Sunday*. The reviewer found Istanbul dazzling, and Dassin's

first use of color "like a child with a new paint box . . . absolutely wild." All in all, it was "diverting entertainment."

50. Mercouri recalled that a soccer crowd chanted "Zyl, Zyl," for him. Mercouri, *Born Greek*, 163.

51. Like most Dassin films shot in Europe, *Up Tight* remains unavailable.

52. See the Dassin interview with Patrick McGilligan in *Tender Comrades*, 222–24.

53. For a recent observation, see F. X. Feeney, "Odd Man In: The Legacy of Dalton Trumbo," *Written By* 6 (February, 2002), 34–41.

54. See especially Bosley Crowther's acid comments in "Sensational Sob Stores On Screen," *New York Times*, July 25, 1965.

55. Actually, *Hawaii* has a few good scenes as Max Von Sydow's character, a missionary, depicts the collapse of the Calvinist personality when confronted with what the *New York Times* critic noted was "the spectacle of beautiful native maidens (for the first time in a Code-approved Hollywood spectacle) who do not wear bras." Vincent Canby, "Screen: 'Hawaii,' Big Long Film, Has Its Premiere," *New York Times*, October 11, 1966.

56. Abraham Polonsky, remarkably enough, was the screenwriter working on the adaptation—remarkable because Koestler was a darling of cold warriors, with absolutely no sympathy for blacklist victims. Unfortunately, the script has been lost.

57. Fast's candor in a conversation on *Spartacus* between Howard Fast and Paul Buhle in 1996, in an academic conference at the University of Pennsylvania honoring Fast, is gratefully acknowledged here.

58. See LoBrutto, *Stanley Kubrick*, 167–93.

59. Bosley Crowther, "Exodus," *New York Times*, December 16, 1960.

60. Meanwhile, Lester Cole, as "Lewis Copley," delivered the screenplay for the small-budget *Operation Eichmann* (1961), a good little film, with Holocaust survivors tracing the war criminal to Argentina and beyond, then kidnapping him for return to Israel, where his crime seems too monumental for any known punishment. See Howard Thompson, "Screen: Stalking a Nazi," *New York Times*, May 4, 1961 for an intelligent commentary.

61. FTA (1972), as noted above, was a barely scripted film version of Jane Fonda's overseas road show designed to win over GIs to antiwar sentiment, a sort of Bob Hope tour in reverse. It disappeared without notice but had documented the moment and demonstrated once more Trumbo's sincerity. Roger Greenspun, "Jane Fonda's 'F.T.A.' Show Now a Film," *New York Times*, July 22, 1972.

62. In retelling this story and Grant's own role in production, the *Times* omitted Tarloff entirely. Murray Schumach, "Hollywood 'Father Goose' Saga," *New York Times*, May 17, 1964.

63. Tarloff's final credit was *Once You Kiss a Stranger* (1969), a badly made action film.

64. Pauline Kael, "Propaganda—Salt of the Earth," reprinted in *I Lost It At the Movies* (Boston: Little-Brown, 1965), 332.

65. Ibid., 340.

66. Ibid., 342.

67. Ibid., 345. Kael's response to *Sight and Sound* is on 343–46.

68. In particular, their coalescence around the film they loved to hate, *Dr. Strangelove*. See Andrew Sarris, "The Fire Within," in *Confessions of a Cultist: On the Cinema, 1955–1969* (New York: Simon and Schuster, 1979), 119–21.

69. See Kael, "The Mark," in *I Lost It At the Movies*, 155–59. While "commendable," the film, she charged, manipulated the viewer by making the accused protagonist

(earlier jailed for sex with a male minor) innocent of seducing and killing another. It was "made with intelligence rather than with art—but perhaps not with too high an order of intelligence" (156). She does not mention Sidney Buchman, the screenwriter, but the point is clear enough.

70. Pauline Kael, "The Making of 'The Group,'" in *Kiss Kiss Bang Bang* (Boston: Atlantic Monthly Press, 1968), 83, an essay originally published in 1966.
71. Ibid., 88.
72. Ibid., 71.
73. Ibid., 75, 79.
74. Ibid., 84.
75. Ibid., 96.
76. Ibid., 136.
77. Ibid.
78. Ibid., 138–39.
79. Ibid., 161.
80. Ibid., 238.
81. Ibid., 245.
82. Ibid., 248.
83. Ibid., 248.
84. Ibid., 276.
85. Ibid., 281.
86. Ibid., 331
87. Ibid., 182.
88. Ibid.
89. Ibid., 339. Unpredictably, but far less often than her admirers would admit, Kael is favorable towards *Intruder in the Dust* (perhaps she knew that screenwriter Maddow had given secret testimony in 1960?), *The Sweet Smell of Success*, and *National Velvet*; in the last she was probably not aware that crucial scenes, probably Anne Revere's moral address to young Liz Taylor, had been written by the uncredited and soon-to-be-blacklisted Howard Dimsdale. Revere would also soon be proscribed.
90. Andrew Sarris, *Confessions of a Cultist*, 122, 200, 441–43. Sarris also had kind words to say about a single film written by Abraham Polonsky (and one of his least distinguished), *Madigan*, very likely because of Don Siegel's usual deft direction (352).
91. Ibid., 41. The critic admired director Jean Renoir, a central figure in the French Popular Front cinema of the 1930s.
92. Ibid., 131.
93. See the careful description of the film and its value in Frank Cunningham, *Sidney Lumet: Film and Literary Vision* (Lexington: University Press of Kentucky, 1991), 257–85.

CHAPTER SEVEN

1. Thematic connections can be revealing: Redgrave's great starring role was in *Isadora*, the biopic of radical dancer Isadora Duncan; when Al Pacino's cop character in *Serpico* begins dating an actress-dancer, he is seen coming to the precinct with a book under his arm: *My Life*, by Isadora Duncan, one of the totemic volumes of American radicalism.
2. SAG's internal politics offered a counterpart: in 1971, when right-winger Charlton Heston stepped down as president, a battle royal found progressives like

Donald Sutherland and ex-blacklistee John Randolph, with Dennis Weaver at the top of the slate, running against Heston's heirs. Sutherland campaigned vigorously, blending progressive politics with actors' self-interest. Rival John Gavin responded with much red-baiting, and in the end the conservatives won again, but progressives had made real inroads. In 1973, Weaver got 70 percent of the vote for president. In 1974, SAG's board repealed the Loyalty bylaw, a decisive moment in entertainment union history. David F. Prindle, *The Politics of Glamour* (Madison: University of Wisconsin, 1988) 100–112. Ed Asner, veteran of the same caucus, won in 1981, although conservatives managed to demonize and ultimately defeat him.

3. By that time, he had also produced *Sons and Lovers* and Odets' last screenwriting credit, the Elvis Presley vehicle *Wild In the Country*.

4. "Reminiscences of Joanne Woodward," interview by Robert and Joan Franklin, Columbia University Oral History Project, 1959, transcript at Columbia University Archives.

5. Ravetch, a rabbi's son, had been in MGM's heavily left-wing Junior Writers Department during the 1930s, worked his way up and got his first real credit in 1947, with story and co-script for *Living In a Big Way*. His connection with Wald, in the middle 1950s, proved decisive, doubly so: he had considered himself a comedy writer. See Pat McGilligan interview with Ravetch and Frank, Jr., in *Backstory 3* (Berkeley: University of California Press, 1997), 283–86.

6. It may be noted that a snappish John Howard Lawson, his own career over, could not forgive the limitations of Ritt's films, lashing out at *The Long, Hot Summer* and *No Down Payment* as utterly incomplete—as if Lawson's own Hollywood efforts had not been undercut by compromises. See John Howard Lawson, "Bold, Bawdy and Dull," *Masses and Mainstream* 7 (July, 1958), 30–31.

7. In fact, barn burning had been associated with rural radicalism since at least the 1820s and in peasant life centuries earlier. It was practically the peasant or tenant's only direct action that, unlike rioting, might not earn corporal punishment.

8. Some critics observed that Welles bore a striking resemblance to the Big Daddy played by Ives himself in *Cat on a Hot Tin Roof* (1958), in which he also played opposite Newman. It was, as they used to say in the comic book trade, a "swipe," in this case a good one.

9. Gabriel Miller, *The Films of Martin Ritt: Fanfare for the Common Man* (Jackson: University of Mississippi Press, 2000), 35.

10. See Walter Metz, "'Signifying Nothing?' Martin Ritt's *The Sound and the Fury* (1959) as Deconstructive Adaptation," *Literature/Film Quarterly* 27 (1999), 21–31.

11. Miller, *The Films of Martin Ritt*, 81.

12. Sally Field, "Foreword," in ibid., xv-xvi.

13. Pauline Kael, *For Keeps* (New York: Dutton, 1994), 10. This comes in the attack on *Hud*. Sarris, whose parents had sided against the Communists in post–World War II Greece, declined to join liberals in the United States and Europe opposing the return of the military to power in 1979. Thanks go to Dan Georgakas for this information.

14. Kael, ibid., 13.

15. See Miller, *The Films of Martin Ritt*, 60–61.

16. Guy Trosper (1911–1963) was author of a half-dozen first-rate screenplays. A westerner (born in Wyoming), he was described by FBI informers as "CPL," that is, "Communist Party Liner."

17. Kael admired *Broken Arrow* and proposed it for children's viewing. Probably she did not know of the script's authorship. She had no good words for any other film written by Maltz, in any case.

18. Pauline Kael, *Kiss Kiss Bang Bang* (Boston: Little, Brown, 1968), 50.

19. Andrew Sarris, *Confessions of a Cultist on the Cinema, 1955–1969*, (New York, Simon and Schuster, 1970), 225.

20. Cited in Miller, *The Films of Martin Ritt*, 121.

21. So important was the story of the Mollies to Ritt and screenwriter (and producer) Walter Bernstein that they began discussing the project while working in TV nearly 20 years before they made the film. See Miller, *The Films of Martin Ritt*, 108.

22. Kael charged, preposterously, that the film was virtual propaganda for the Black Panther Party, unfairly portraying whites as conspiring against Johnson and playing upon the guilt of white audiences in a downright Brechtian technique. See Kael, "Clobber-Movie," in *Deeper Into Movies*, 158–61.

23. Surprisingly, Kael actually praised *Sounder*: Ritt had been tamed, perhaps Americanized. She changed her mind again later, of course.

24. Stanley Kauffman, *Before My Eyes: Film Criticism and Comment* (New York, Harper & Row, 1980), 242–43.

25. Ibid., 244.

26. Eric Lax, one of Allen's biographers, says that after Allen introduced himself to Burrows and gave him some jokes to read, the older writer wrote letters recommending him to Sid Caesar, Phil Silvers and Peter Lind Hayes but urged him to stay out of television and screenwriting in favor of the dignity of Broadway. Eric Lax, *Woody Allen: A Biography* (New York: Knopf, 1991), 87–88.

27. That the former *Time* magazine film reviewer Richard Schickel, a ferocious opponent of the blacklistees, would write the latest of documentaries about Allen's work, was another of those Hollywood curiosities.

28. Our thanks to the southern organizing director and later UNITE president Bruce Raynor, for discussions of these issues. His succession to leadership in the merged union UNITE in 2001, after a considerable succession of over-paid and severely bureaucratic cold warriors in the needles trade at what was one of the happy moments in a discouraging period for organized labor.

29. Gabriel Miller, *The Films of Martin Ritt*, 170.

30. Adele Ritt, interviewed by Paul Buhle, Los Angeles, 1994.

31. Gabriel Miler, *The Films of Martin Ritt*, 192.

32. See the review by Janet Maslin, "Film: Streisand in 'Nuts,' " *New York Times*, November 20, 1987, which compliments Streisand and co-star Richard Dreyfuss while complaining bitterly, as expected, about the script and direction.

33. Pauline Kael, *For Keeps*, 3–14.

34. Bernard F. Dick, *Hellman in Hollywood* (Rutherford, N.J.: Farleigh Dickinson University Press, 1982), 124. Stanley Kauffman, as cited in ibid.

35. Actually, *Seize the Day* (1986), starring Robin Williams and based on Bellow's novel, was an altogether creditable film, but the avant-gardist, antiwar and egalitarian Williams was miscast as the politically conservative, Israel-obsessed novelist. Clement Greenberg appeared as a repellent, overbearing creature in *Pollack* (2000), a film that mourned one of the greats of abstract expressionism.

36. On Kael's characteristic attacks upon homosexuality both male and female, see Ed Sikov, "Circles, Squares and Pink Triangles: Confessions of a Gay Cultist," in

Emanuel Levy, ed., *Citizen Sarris, American Film Critic, Essays in Honor of Andrew Sarris* (Lanham, P.A.: Scarecrow Press, 2001), 255–65, quoted on 258.

37. See the hostile comments by Renata Adler, "The Apes, the Fox and Charlie Bubbles," *New York Times*, February 25, 1968.
38. Dick, *Hellman in Hollywood*, 120–24.
39. Bosley Crowther, "Toys in the Attic," *New York Times*, August 1, 1963.
40. Bosley Crowther, "The Screen: 'The Case,' " *New York Times*, February 19, 1966.
41. Dick, *Hellman in Hollywood*, 135.
42. "Questioning Miss Hellman on Movies," *New York Times*, February 27, 1966.
43. Indeed, the film's appearance was marked with a celebrity event benefiting the Committee for Public Justice, a constitutional rights group that Hellman herself founded several years earlier. Among the prominent figures on hand: Woody Allen, Leonard Bernstein, Mike Nichols and Claudette Colbert. Jennifer Dunning, "'Valentino,' and 'Julia' bring Stars Out in the Rain,' *New York Times*, October 3, 1977.
44. Perhaps the most astounding element was for the *New York Times* to hail the film, (see note 45).
45. Janet Maslin, "Critic's Notebook: Movies Try to Get a Handle on Our Times," *New York Times*, December 20, 1977.
46. See Judy Klemsrud, "Vanessa Redgrave—'The Only Person Who Could Play Julia,'" *New York Times*, October 2, 1977. The title is a phrase from director Zinnemann, shrugging off the interviewer's question of a lesbian connection between the two characters and suggesting the real relation between the two was teacher and student.
47. Maslin, "Critic's Notebook." Redgrave had the additional odd status of being a prominent British Trotskyist, mirroring the past identity of some of the prominent New York intellectuals, but with her sympathy for the Palestinian plight guilty of a cosmopolitanism that they had long since renounced.
48. Pauline Kael, "A Woman for All Seasons," reprinted from the *New Yorker* in Mark W. Estrin, ed., *Critical Essays on Lillian Hellman*, 257.
49. Jean Rouverol (Butler) offers a slightly different version: Salt had no pride in his television work. His youngest daughter, when visiting him, reportedly observed, "We wouldn't worry so much about you, Daddy, if we thought you loved what you were doing." Rouveral, *Refugees from Hollywood* (Albuquerque: University of New Mexico, 2000), 205.
50. Many thanks to screenwriter (and former actress) Jennifer Salt, Waldo Salt's daughter, for granting us an interview (Paul Buhle in Los Angeles, May, 2002), and to historian Gerda Lerner, an acquaintance of Salt and a close friend of his second wife, Eve Merriam, for crucial insights.
51. Norma Barzman has pointed out that it was Salt who in this film (*The Shopworn Angel*, 1938) created the persona of the loveable hayseed that millions came to love as Jimmy Stewart.
52. Abraham Polonsky, "Une expérience utopique," *Présence du cinema* no. 14 (June 1962), 5–7. Reprinted in full in Paul Buhle and Dave Wagner, *A Very Dangerous Citizen: Abraham Lincoln Polonsky and the Hollywood Left* (Berkeley: University of California Press, 2000), 196–197.
53. Waldo Salt papers, Special Arts Collection, UCLA.
54. Robert Hillman and Eugene Corr, *Waldo Salt: American Screenwriter*, a documentary film in the American Masters Series, produced by WNET-TV (New York), 1990 and narrated by Henry Fonda.

55. *Midnight Cowboy* was met with notable bitterness by traditional liberal critics like Andrew Sarris. See chapters 6 and 8 on the cold warriors' response to the return of the blacklistees.
56. See Michel Fabre and Pierre Rissient, "Entrétien avec Joseph Losey," *Cahiers du Cinema* (September 1960), 3.
57. Vincent Canby, "A Marvelously Foolhardy 'Day of the Locust,'" *New York Times*, May 10, 1975.
58. Andrew Sarris, "Midnight Cowboy," in *Confessions of a Cultist*, 441–45.
59. Kauffman, *Before My Eyes*, 152–53.
60. Our thanks to Jennifer Salt for a discussion of her father. See also Peter Biskin, *Easy Riders, Raging Bulls: How the Sex-and-Drugs-and Rock 'n' Roll Generation Saved Hollywood* (New York: Simon and Schuster, 1998), 230–33.
61. Actors' unionism revolved around the bread-and-butter issues of the underemployed majority quite as much as the politics of the leaders. If SAG leader Ronald Reagan had as much as given away payments from residual showings, Dennis Weaver's regime restored them in substantial measure. Through the 1970s, the union remained militantly supportive of organized labor, in keeping with a perceived need for wider solidarity—an especially sore point for conservatives. The ascension of Reagan to a bigger presidency in 1980 incited further years of internecine warfare. Sometimes the Left won later, but never managed a much-desired merger with AFTRA.

CHAPTER EIGHT

1. Quoted in David Caute, *Joseph Losey: A Revenge on Life* (New York: Oxford University Press, 1994), 44.
2. Brooks Atkinson, "Theater," *New York Times*, November 6, 1934.
3. "Theater," *New York Times*, July 26, 1936.
4. Caute, *Joseph Losey*, 171–77.
5. Gladwin Hill, "Theater," *New York Times*, August 1, 1947.
6. For a helpful discussion of the use of Method in acting specifically for film, see Patrick McGilligan, *Clint: The Life and Legend* (New York: St. Martin's Press, 2002), 75.
7. Raymond Durgnat, "Losey," in *Film and Filming*, May, 1966, 28.
8. Caute, *Joseph Losey*, 284.
9. Eagerly hoping to return to Hollywood, he offered Columbia a statement apologizing for his communist past while remaining adamantly unwilling to name anyone else. This half-gesture did him no good.
10. Katherine Bliss Eaton, *The Theater of Meyerhold and Brecht* (Westport: Greenwood, 1985), 62.
11. James Leahy, *The Cinema of Joseph Losey* (London: A. Zwemmer Ltd., 1967), 29.
12. For a discussion of the films Losey made in Hollywood before the blacklist, see the authors' *Radical Hollywood* (New York: The New Press, 2002), 338–41.
13. Losey to Scott, July 6, 1960, in Scott Papers, American Heritage Center, Laramie, Wyoming.
14. Did Losey himself have a special insight into what was then considered "deviant" sexual behavior? His first wife, avant-garde fashion designer Elizabeth Hawes, thought so when she came home find him in bed with another man. See Bettina Burch, *Radical By Design: The Life and Style of Elizabeth Hawes* (New York: Dutton, 1998), 77.

15. In fact, Carey played more or less the same role as in *The Lawless*, where as a former Popular Front journalist he intervenes to protect a victimized Chicano youth (and capture the heart of the strongest woman of the community). In *The Damned*, he is an outsider of the same left-liberal quality, a scientist struggling to find the right and moral thing to do. One could suggest that Carey himself, who shifted from film to television, was at his best in these roles, too rarely offered to him.

16. Edward Murray, *Nine American Film Critics* (New York: Ungar, 1955), 118.

17. Anthony Storey, *Stanley Baker: Portrait of an Actor* (London: W.H. Allen, 1977), 103.

18. Quoted in David Caute, *Joseph Losey*, 163. Tynan, writing a few years earlier for *Mainstream*, a Popular Front journal seeking (unsuccessfully) to move away from the rigors of the American Communist Party, would have been intimately familiar with the sentiment of former Communists in the United States and the United Kingdom still on the Left.

19. These popular performances were the bad conscience of bourgeois realism in the two decades before World War I. See Mel Gordon, *The Grand Guignol: Theatre of Fear and Terror* (New York: DaCapo, 1997).

20. Jean-Pierre Coursodon (with Pierre Sauvage), *American Directors*, II (New York: McGraw Hill, 1983), 205.

21. This is an old theme in English literature, beginning with Mary Shelley's *Franken-stein*, which metaphorically depicts the working class as an artificial creation, assembled from the limbs of the displaced peasantry by a middle class that then abandoned it. Similar themes, at least through Forster, are sounded in the great middle-class novels. Losey dispenses with the uplift.

22. James Palmer and Michael Riley, *The Films of Joseph Losey* (Cambridge: Cambridge University Press, 1994), 40.

23. Michael Billington, *The Life and Work of Harold Pinter* (London: Faber and Faber, 1996), 57.

24. Ibid., 52, 91.

25. Caute, *Joseph Losey*, 186.

26. Billington, *Life and Work*, 151.

27. David Thomson, "Pinter's Films Intimidate With Words and Silence," *New York Times*, July 15, 2001

28. Caute, *Joseph Losey*, 182.

29. Nicholas Mosley, *Accident* (New York: Coward-McCann, 1966).

30. Nicholas Mosley, *Efforts at Truth: An Autobiography* (Normal, Ill: Dalkey Archive Press, 1995), 170.

31. Caute, *Joseph Losey*, 255.

32. Among victims of the blacklist, a taste for Marcel Proust was unusual but not unknown. Abraham Polonsky regarded Proust as the greatest aesthetic influence of his own young intellectual days. See Buhle and Wagner, *Abraham Lincoln Polonsky: A Very Dangerous Citizen* (Berkeley: University of California Press, 2001) 30–31.

33. Walter Benjamin, "On the Image of Proust," in Benjamin, *Selected Writings*, II (Cambridge: Harvard University Press, 1999), 243.

34. Harold Pinter, *The Proust Screenplay* (New York: Grove Press, 1977), 3–6.

35. Caute, *Joseph Losey*, 289.

36. Quoted in ibid., 290.

37. Trotsky has been unlucky in his screen representations; see, most recently, the performance of Geoffrey Rush as Trotsky in *Frida* (2002). Co-credit for the script went

to Clancy Sigal, a late member of the Hollywood Left just before the blacklist, and best remembered for his 1961 novel *Going Away* bearing partly on that experience.

38. Some of this reputation no doubt derived from his association with Brecht, who became vulnerable to the charge after he decided to settle in East Berlin upon his return to Europe, even though Brecht's primary motivation was that he had a better chance of creating a theater of his own there than in the western sectors. The truth is that Brecht's avant-garde theater was not truly welcome anywhere.

39. Caute, *Joseph Losey*, 298–99.

40. Fred Lawrence Guiles, *Jane Fonda: The Actress in Her Time* (New York: Pinnacle, 1981), 257.

41. Mercer was an English dramatist who wrote primarily for TV. Among the other lines he had deleted before Fonda's intervention was Nora's excited discovery that earning pay for work was "almost like being a man." Quoted in Caute, *Joseph Losey*, 299.

42. Quoted in ibid., 300.

43. Losey had offered the part to Shirley MacLaine, a forceful personality and a noted Hollywood liberal—saddled, however, with the gamin role that she rarely escaped. Would the film have been better or worse for her presence? We know only that it would surely have been different. Caute, *Joseph Losey*, 298.

44. Quoted by Bruce Cook, *Brecht in Exile* (New York: Holt, Reinhart, 1982), 178–79.

45. Caute, *Joseph Losey*, 180.

46. Noted in John Schultheiss, ed., *To Illuminate Our Time: The Blacklisted Teleplays of Abraham Polonsky* (Los Angeles: Sadanlauer Publications, 1993), 86. To deepen the irony further: the screenwriter of *Martin Luther* was reluctant friendly witness Allan Sloane, who would make a major contribution to television drama, especially with blacklistee fellow writers on *East Side/West Side*.

47. Ibid., 87.

48. "Oh, you're a poet? How nice."

49. Caute, *Joseph Losey*, 375.

50. Ibid., 449–50.

51. Frederic Jameson, *The Geopolitical Aesthetic: Cinema and Space in the World System* (London: BFI, 1992), 9.

52. Vincent Canby, "Monsieur Klein," *New York Times*, November 6, 1979.

53. Caute, *Joseph Losey*, 428.

54. Vincent Canby, "Philander Bar None," *New York Times*, November 11, 1979.

55. Ibid.

56. Dan Georgakas and Gary Crowdus, "Interview with Vincent Canby," *Cineaste* X (Winter, 1979–80), 3.

57. Caute, *Joseph Losey*, 428.

58. Vincent Canby, "Films," *New York Times*, August 29, 1986.

59. Quoted in his obituary: Todd McCarthy, "Helmer Joseph Losey Dies at 75, Worked in Europe after Blacklist," *Variety*, June 27, 1984.

CHAPTER NINE

1. *Miss Evers' Boys* (1997), the HBO Emmy winner directed by another old friend of the blacklistees, Joseph Sargent, dramatized the Tuskeegee Study of African American men whose infections with syphilis during the 1930s were intentionally kept secret from the patients and left without treatment for decades, supposedly for the sake

of medical study. *Fail Safe* (2000), a telefilm remake produced by George Clooney, remained close to the original. Among Bernstein's most neglected films is *The House on Carroll Street* (1989), a tale of McCarthyism in the early 1950s as a left-winger learns about a Nazi official secretly brought to the United States and as much as protected by the FBI, much like the real-life Operation Paperclip. Critics didn't like it much, but Mandy Patinkin is especially interesting as a legal heavy in the Roy Cohn mold. Among other notable later features were several of John Berry's works discussed above, and a 1990 film that he directed and coscripted with Lee Gold, *A Captive In the Land*, about a pair of Russian and American scientists trapped together in the Arctic, discovering each other as human beings; and *Tell Me a Riddle* (1980), Lee Gold's masterful adaptation of Tillie Olson's work.

2. Thanks to John Randolph for a conversation with Paul Buhle in Los Angeles in 1992. Randolph was especially enthused about his role in *Prizzi's Honor* (1985), a Polonsky-like allegory of capitalism as organized crime.

3. An episode of *The Education of Max Bickford*, aired March 31, 2002, actually focused on the right of an extreme conservative to speak on a liberal campus—and how to expose his real agenda. Dreyfuss, as Bickford, assists students in understanding the innocence of the Hollywood victims who, as one student suggests, claimed their First Amendment rights not knowing that they would go to jail for their insistence. Even with a gentle drift toward the political center, *Max Bickford* did not survive the 2001–2002 season.

4. Bosley Crowther, "Screen: A Forceful Drama," *New York Times*, September 25, 1958.

5. Alvah Bessie, "'Take Care,'" in *Film Culture* 50/51 (1970), 16–21.

6. Interview with Bernard Vorhaus by John Baxter, in Patrick McGilligan and Paul Buhle, *Tender Comrades: a Backstory of the Hollywood Blacklist* (New York: St. Martins, 1997), 680.

7. Jules Dassin, interviewed by Patrick McGilligan in *Tender Comrades*, 223.

8. Interview with Anne Froelick by Paul Buhle in *Tender Comrades*, 259. Trumbo's legendary drinking was recounted to us by Joan Scott; Ring Lardner, Jr., recalled to us anecdotes about his own drinking and Michael Wilson's was related by various friends, including Jean Butler.

9. Walter Bernstein recalled Rossen, then a friend, discussing the basic idea for the film back in the later 1940s as a story drawn from the pool halls and street life of Rossen's Lower East Side origins. See the interview with Walter Bernstein in *Tender Comrades*, 47–48; a portion of this interview that did not appear in the volume, but was conducted by Paul Buhle with Bernstein in 1996, covered more of his recollections of Rossen.

10. Thanks to Antonia Dosik, Atlas' daughter, for providing information on her father to us.

11. See Schlesinger's unrepentant red-baiting, "Hollywood Hypocrisy," *New York Times*, February 28, 1999.

12. "An Oscar Protest," *New York Times*, February 24, 1999.

13. Flier in Albert Maltz Papers, State Historical Society of Wisconsin.

14. Thanks for this recollection from Sarah Cooper, staffer of the Southern California Library for Research and Social Change.

15. Kirk Douglas, "Never Lose Your Sense of Humor," *Parade Magazine*, January 6, 2002.

16. Following a gala and much-discussed reception in January, a large exhibition at the academy and a smaller one in the UCLA library, a screening (*Tender Com-*

rade, starring Ginger Rogers and Robert Ryan) and yet another panel. The reception featured many current stars and other notables; the scholars' and blacklist victims' forum in March, 2002, included former Abbott and Costello screenwriter Robert Lees, sometime screenwriter and blacklistee widow Norma Barzman, along with blacklist scholars Larry Ceplair, Robert Hethmon and Paul Buhle. The Writers Guild magazine, *Written By*, also devoted a special issue (in February 2002) to the blacklistees, with a photo of Norma Barzman on the cover and an extensive essay by Joseph McBride on Michael Wilson's career. The academy's Blacklist Exhibit was reassembled for a conference on *Salt of the Earth* in Santa Fe, February-March, 2003.

17. See Suart Klawans, "The Hollywood Three," *Nation*, February.4, 2002, 36–37. This review is the more interesting because the same critic, only weeks earlier, had condemned *The Majestic*, mainly on grounds of a misuse of Jim Carrey's comic talents.

18. Thanks go to the late Conrad Lynn for some details here; he spoke on a Schomberg Library panel with Paul Buhle in memory of C. L. R. James a few months after the Caribbean-born revolutionary's death in 1989. See also Paul Buhle, *C. L. R. James: The Artist as Revolutionary* (London: Verso, 1989), the "authorized biography."

19. In his autobiography, Conrad Lynn (who had also been hauled before HUAC in the 1950s), wrote that in one of his last conversations with him, Malcolm said he was "grateful" that the SWP newspaper, the *Militant*, "was printing his speeches in full because his message was at least being circulated." Conrad Lynn, *There is a Fountain: The Autobiography of a Civil Rights Lawyer* (Westport, Conn.: Lawrence Hill & Company, 1979), 187–88.

20. David Leeming, *James Baldwin: A Biography* (New York: Alfred A. Knopf, 1994), 158, 231.

21. Ibid., 297, 299.

22. Ibid., 299

23. Another C. L. R. James devotee and a close friend of one of the authors, the late Stan Weir, who was memorialized as a character in several Harvey Swados novels but especially in *Standing Fast*, had known Baldwin since the 1950s and, after his friend's death, wrote a memorable memorial essay about him. See Stan Weir, "Meetings with James Baldwin," in *Against the Current* 18, New Series (January-February, 1989). Baldwin once wrote that as a teenager he had been "a convinced fellow traveler. I marched in one May Day parade, carrying banners. By the time I was nineteen, I was a Trotskyite. . . ." James Baldwin, *No Name in the Street* (New York: The Dial Press, 1972), 31.

24. See Des Martin, 'The Big Story' *Episode Guide* at The Classic TV archive, www.geocities.com/TelevisionCity/Stage/2950.

25. Leeming, *James Baldwin*, 301.

26. Spike Lee (with Ralph Wiley), *By Any Means Necessary: The Trials and Tribulations of the Making of 'Malcom X'* (New York: Hyperion, 1992), 8–10.

27. Phil Patton, "Who Owns 'X'," *New York Times*, November 8, 1992.

28. Isabel Wilkerson, "Young Believe Malcolm X Is Still Speaking to Them," *New York Times*, November 18, 1992.

29. "Just Whose Malcolm Is It Anyway?" *New York Times*, May 31, 1992.

30. James Baldwin, *One Day, When I Was Lost: A Scenario Based on "The Autobiography of Malcolm X"* (London: Michael Joseph, 1997).

31. Telephone interviews by Paul Buhle with Rebecca Perl and Walter Bernstein, respectively, in 1992.

32. Hilton Kramer, "The Blacklist and the Cold War, " *New York Times*, October 3, 1976.
33. Ibid.
34. Even the most comprehending future attacks on the blacklistees sounded, then, terribly familiar. See, e.g., Terry Teachout, "They Admit It!" *National Review*, July 7, 2002, 46–47. This is a review of *Radical Hollywood*.
35. Actually, "male chauvinism" had been discussed at length in the later 1940s, as the Congress of American Women positioned itself to become the most influential Popular Front institution. Then the end came. Gerda Lerner had been a leader of the CAW in Los Angeles.
36. Nonetheless, Laurents considered the outcome badly censored and sought to restate his viewpoint in the theatrical drama, "Jolson Sings Again," in 1999. See his interview with Frank Rich in "Decades Later, Naming Names Still Matters," *New York Times*, March 14, 1999.
37. See Buhle and Wagner, *A Very Dangerous Citizen: Abraham Lincoln Polonsky and the Hollywood Left* (Berkeley: University of California Press, 2001), 146–54.
38. Enid Nemy, "Tents are Pitched in Times Square for Benefit," *New York Times*, September 19, 1968; Judy Klemesrud, "'Funny Girl' Takes Whirl Into Fashion," *New York Times*, June 8, 1968.
39. Vincent Canby, "Stark Is Basking in 'Funny Girl' Sun," *New York Times*, September 19, 1968.
40. He also freely adapted life to fiction: the real Viertel became an anticommunist, although not a friendly witness; Jiggy gave friendly testimony, became an alcoholic and died in a car accident.
41. Arthur Laurents, *Original Story By* (New York: Knopf, 2000), 278, 298.
42. Decades later, in 1995, Streisand made a Harvard speech defending the right of Hollywood celebrities to speak out on politics (albeit as a defense of Bill Clinton). See Maureen Dowd, "Barbra, the Speech, Plays to a Packed Crowd," *New York Times*, February 4, 1995.
43. Arthur Laurents interviewed by Patrick McGilligan, in *Backstory 2*, 155–56.
44. Victor Navasky, "Did *Guilty By Suspicion* Miss the Point?" *New York Times*, March 31, 1999.
45. David Marc, in an observation that apparently never reached print.
46. A short list: *The Asphalt Jungle* (1950); *Planet of the Apes* and *Madigan* (1968); and *Nuts* (1987).
47. Michael Sloane, "Fact Into Fiction: Writing 'The Majestic,'" Scriptmag.com, January-February, 2002, 34. Sloane insisted that the blacklist was essentially a framing device for the narrative and closed on the note that his own fear of buckling under similar pressure "helped me write the scene" in which Carrey confronts the committee: "I forgot the facts and wrote into the far. It's a great feeling to be able to do something like that" (37). Sloane, a gay screenwriter who shared an Oscar for short-subjects, went to Hollywood High with director Darabount.

INDEX